Offensive Football Strategies

American Football Coaches Assocation

Human Kinetics

Library of Congress Cataloging-in-Publication Data

Offensive football strategies / American Football Coaches Association.
   p. cm.
  A collection of articles previously published in the AFCA's proceedings from its annual meetings and its annual summer manual.
  ISBN 0-7360-0139-5
  1. Football--Offense--Congresses. 2. Football--Coaching--Congresses. I. American Football Coaches Association.

GV951.8.O34 2000
796.332'2--dc21

                                                          99-047997

ISBN: 0-7360-0139-5

Managing Editor: Cynthia McEntire; **Assistant Editor:** John Wentworth; **Copyeditor:** Marc Jennings; **Proofreader:** Sarah Wiseman; **Graphic Artist:** Francine Hamerski; **Photo Editor:** Clark Brooks; **Cover Designer:** Jack W. Davis; **Photographer (cover):** © Joe Robbins; **Photographers (interior):** page 1 Jim Witmer; page 49 Tom Roberts; pages 153 and 277 © 1997 G. Newman Lawrance Sports Photography; **Mac Illustrators:** Tom Roberts, Mic Greenberg, Kristin King, Denise Lowry, Kim Maxey, Sharon Smith, Tara Welsch, and Brian McElwain; **Printer:** United Graphics

Human Kinetics books are available at special discounts for bulk purchase. Special editions or book excerpts can also be created to specification. For details, contact the Special Sales Manager at Human Kinetics.

On the cover: Joe Hamilton, former All-American quarterback at Georgia Tech, calls an audible after reading the defensive keys, typical of the strategic maneuvers used by successful offensive teams.

Printed in the United States of America   10 9 8 7 6 5 4 3 2 1

Human Kinetics
Web site: http://www.humankinetics.com/

United States: Human Kinetics
P.O. Box 5076
Champaign, IL 61825-5076
1-800-747-4457
e-mail: humank@hkusa.com

Canada: Human Kinetics
475 Devonshire Road Unit 100
Windsor, ON N8Y 2:L5
1-800-465-7301 (in Canada only)
e-mail: humank@hkcanada.com

Europe: Human Kinetics, P.O. Box IW14
Leeds LS16 6TR, United Kingdom
+44 (0) 113-278 1708
e-mail: humank@hkeurope.com

Australia: Human Kinetics
57A Price Avenue
Lower Mitcham, South Australia 5062
(08) 82771555
e-mail: humank@hkaustralia.com

New Zealand: Human Kinetics
P.O. Box 105-231, Auckland Central
09-523-3462
e-mail: humank@hknewz.com

Contents

Part IV Down-and-Distance Decisions **277**

Gaining Key Yardage

Dominating the Red Zone

Introduction

Selecting articles for this book was almost as difficult as choosing plays to run on a key fourth quarter drive. Unlike a run or pass play, however, the measures of success for our decision-making are much less objective than the number of yards gained, first downs attained, or points scored. And yet, as the clock ticked down toward publication time, the tough calls had to be made. No audibles, either!

The selection task was daunting given the choice of hundreds of worthy articles from AFCA Summer Manuals and Proceedings spanning 40 years, from 1960 through 1999. The simple approach would have been to select the works of the most high-profile coaches. And certainly we have big names, such as Paul "Bear" Bryant, Tom Osborne, Marv Levy, Joe Paterno, LaVell Edwards, and Steve Spurrier. But their entries are mixed among those of many less well-known assistant and non-Division I coaches, as our primary objective in selecting articles for the book was to assemble a complete and complementary collection of works that represents all four of the last decades, prevailing offensive trends during that period, a variety of formations and play options, and coaches from different levels, conferences, and schools of thought.

The result is *Offensive Football Strategies*. With 73 articles by many of the best offensive tacticians in modern football, the book is an extensive educational reference for any serious student of the game. And the material is accompanied by more than 700 diagrams to help you take the material from the book to the chalkboard.

Part I provides a look at the total picture, from developing an offensive philosophy to communicating the chosen attack. John McKay provides excellent ideas for fitting your system to your personnel, and Hayden Fry and Bill Snyder share some wily ways to get an edge each play before the snap.

Parts II and III are the meat-and-potatoes of the book, with in-depth sections on the running and passing games, respectively. The Running Game is organized according to formation; bet you can guess which sections Tubby Raymond and Emory Bellard belong in. The last section presents a handful of option packages, perhaps highlighted by the Freeze Option that Dick McPherson's Syracuse teams ran so successfully. The Passing Game consists of 28 articles covering a wide range of topics, from Mike White's Flare Flood scheme, to Joe Tiller's H Back attack, to Merv Johnson's pass protection techniques.

Part IV wraps up the book with a number of winning insights for managing down, distance, and clock situations. The ten articles provided will prepare you for success on third down, in the red zone, and as time is winding down.

Whether you prefer the run or pass, opt for power, speed, or deception, or favor one specific system over a multidimensional approach, this book offers a wealth of information to apply to your team's offensive attack. If you fail to find dozens of things to add to next season's playbook, read closer. *Offensive Football Strategies* will help you move the chains and score more than ever before.

Key to Diagrams

⊕   Center

◯   Offensive player

●   Ball carrier; intended receiver; TB position variations (Sheridan)

◌   For pre-snap shifts, original position before motion

╫   Handoff

◐   Potential ball carrier on option play

→   Running direction, motion route (Fry)

- - ┥ | - - ➤   Motion route (Restic); optional route (Molde); defensive route (Baker)

E | S   Original position of defensive player before motion

↑ | T   Blocking route

⚹↑ | ⚹↑ | ↑⚹   Shows continuing motion after block

─ ─ ─   Pass or pitch

●───●   Run to here and stop

| | Hash marks on field

⌇➤   Indicates running motion

| ➤   Two step motion (Chaump)

▮▮   Feet (Chaump)

▽ | ◇ | V   Defensive player; may also use position abbreviation

Position Abbreviations

QB	Quarterback		PST	Playside tackle
T	Tackle		OG	Onside guard
C	Center (offensive), corner (defensive)		IB	I Back
LB	Linebacker		FS	Free safety
G	Guard or Goal line		SS	Strong safety
ST	Strong tackle		TB	Tail back
SG	Strong guard		WR	Wide receiver
QT	Quick tackle		LT	Left tackle
QG	Quick guard		RT	Right tackle
TE	Tight end		LG	Left guard
FB	Full back, flanker back		RG	Right guard
N	Nose tackle		DE	Defensive end
BSG	Backside guard		E	End
BST	Backside tackle		SE	Split end
PSG	Playside guard		LOS	Line of scrimmage

PART I

The Game Plan

Part I—The Game Plan

Creating an Offensive Philosophy

Joe Paterno

We have an offensive concept, an overall season plan, and strong beliefs about techniques and strategy. But we also copy what others have done successfully and adjust our plan from week to week. If we see something that looks good, something we have trouble defending, we probably will incorporate this into our attack.

What follows may stimulate a new approach to your overall program. Or maybe it will force you to reevaluate your own offensive concepts. There are lots of ways to skin a cat, and I believe the minute we think we have the absolute best way to do something and close our minds to anything else, we are on our way down.

Offensive Emphasis

Your whole coaching approach to offense must be different from your defensive strategy. Defensively, you lose games by your mistakes. You wait and react, you stymie the unexpected, you rely on static environs such as the width of the field and hash marks. Yes, defense does have some ability to force the issue and certainly must be combative, but in essence, defense is a "watch and ward" type of action. Defense is the art of preparing for any eventuality.

Conversely, offense is all about attack, assault, and surprise—striking the first blow. Offense must have the ability to force the defense into mistakes and then exploit these errors. You should and at times must take chances if you are to surprise the defense. With this general definition in mind, let's get into more specific thoughts about effective offensive football.

Speed

Mobility with adaptability is almost unstoppable. It follows from this that speed (which includes quickness) is the single most important aspect of football. In evaluating our personnel and our offensive designs, speed is the first consideration.

Adaptability

To be mobile and adaptable, your formations and tactics must be flexible. For this reason we believe in a broad-based operational scheme. We want an offensive system that will get us in and out of as many formations as we could possibly want—broad but simple. Likewise, we want a numbering system that allows us to add plays without confusion. We want a plan to put the ball in play that will help us keep the defense off balance and allow us to exploit defensive weaknesses on the LOS.

Opportunity

"Opportunity in war is more often to be depended upon than courage" is an old military saying. How true this is in football. Striking when the opponent is confused or demoralized is one of the truly classical offensive tactics. That's why we have what we call "Bingo" plays—low-consistency plays that give the offense the ability to exploit opportunity when it's presented.

We divide our offense into *low-consistency* and *high-consistency* plays. Unless our play selection is dictated by a specific situation, the only important facet of our offense we have to have organized is what we can count on from each offensive play. You can't want too many low-consistency plays or you'll be spending too much time on junk. On the other hand, your high-consistency plays won't stay that way very long if you don't keep the defense respectful of what can happen to them if they overplay these "bread and butter" plays.

Element of Surprise

You have to have a flair for attack based upon surprise and speed. Surprise, the unexpected, helps you tactically and psychologically. Under two-platoon football, defenses are too knowledgeable and too well trained to be beaten with the same methods every week. We like to change the game early in the contest and we believe especially in surprise in key situations.

Team Strengths

An old military stratagem is "Try to select the terrain on which you want to do battle." Don't play their game, make them play yours. Don't be defeated because you are weak where they are strong. (I suppose this comes under being adaptable.) This is why comparative scores are so misleading. Exploit your strength against their weakness. Again, the nature of good offense is initiative. The offense has the initiative; use it to make the other team play your game.

Balance

Offense means mobility with adaptability, it means to shatter with surprise, and it means being able to take advantage of key opportunities. It then must necessarily demand balance—balance between run and pass, power and finesse, inside and outside plays. Without that balance, it becomes relatively easy for the defense to cut off areas where you may strike, and also the means by which you strike. Without offensive balance, the defense can concentrate on fewer than all the aspects of offense and consequently reduce its projected mistake potentials.

To move the football today, you must be able to pass well. Even successful running teams know when and why to pass, and intelligently use passing to supplement their strong running games. More and more, the passing game

is the determining factor. I don't believe you can consistently move the ball (even with overpowering personnel) without a superior passing game.

Practicing Third and Fourth Down Plays

The best way to teach offense is to practice game situations. We can isolate percentages and defensive weaknesses easiest by simulating situations. We practice what we will do in certain situations: the third and eight, our goal line offense, our coming out offense, the four down area, the three down area, long yardage plays, quick switch plays, waste down plays, two-point plays. This is the easiest way to identify mistake-prone areas where defensive emotion rather than discipline emerges. We do very little with first and second down calls except in certain areas of the field because in almost every instance we can never sufficiently reduce the defense probability.

Execution and Morale

High morale is chiefly a result of good practice and eventual execution. If you can't execute, I doubt you can have good morale. If you don't have real morale, then you can't instill the necessary confidence in your offense to surprise, seize opportunity, be mobile, and adapt. Regardless of your offensive philosophy, scheme, and ingenuity, your team must have confidence that they can execute. All of your thinking eventually has to be tempered by the realistic appraisal of what your people are capable of doing well. This, then, has got to be the first tenet of any offensive philosophy: do what your people can do well.

Offensive Formations

We have a broad-based, flexible numbering system for our plays, and a simple but viable means of naming our offensive sets. We flip-flop completely. We like the flip-flop because we can teach more offense with this system. By having a strong side and quick side, we have more plays that our people can execute because they don't have to be complete football players. We can get by with a small, quick man at quick tackle, a slower, stronger man at strong tackle, and so on. Our East formation (figure 1) we number from strong side across to our split end. The opposite is West (figure 2).

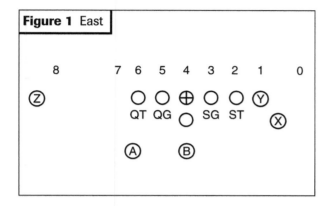

Figure 1 East

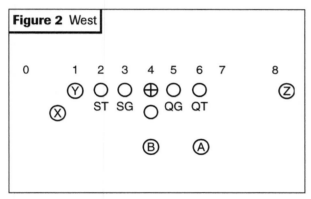

Figure 2 West

We number from the strong side across regardless of where the strong side is positioned. When a play number ends in two, everybody knows it is going over our strong tackle, regardless of whether he is right or left.

We set our formations either with East and West or with Right and Left. Now, if we want to get our wing back wide, we say Easterly (figure 3). The opposite is Westerly. We also have Eastern (figure 4).

If we want our TB (or as we call him, our "A" back) to line up behind the strong side, we say East T (figure 5), Easterly T (figure 6), or Eastern T (figure 7). If we want a split backfield, we merely say East Split (figure 8). If we want a double wing, we call East Slot (figure 9).

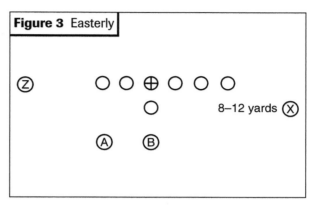

Figure 3 Easterly

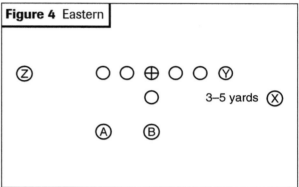

Figure 4 Eastern

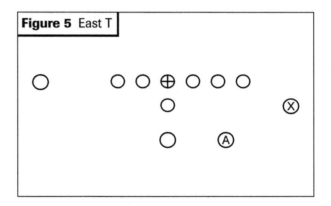

Figure 5 East T

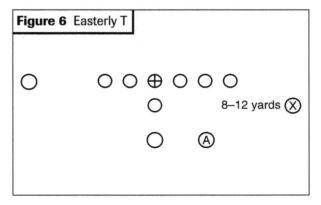

Figure 6 Easterly T

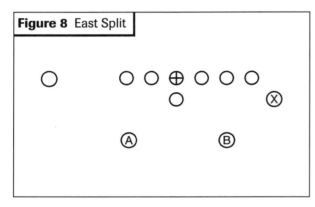

Figure 7 Eastern T

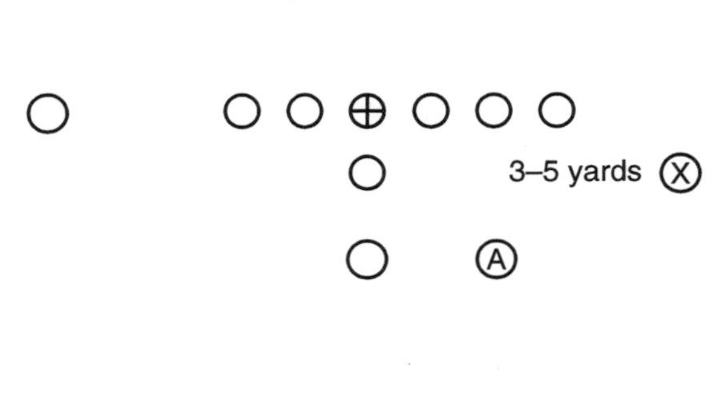

3–5 yards

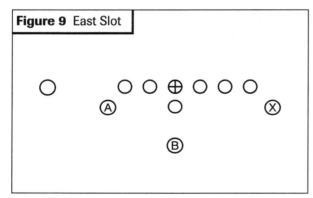

Figure 8 East Split

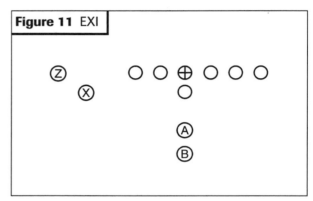

Figure 9 East Slot

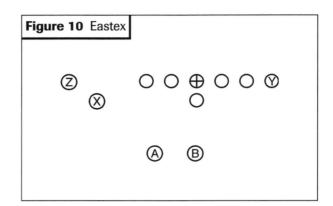

Figure 10 Eastex

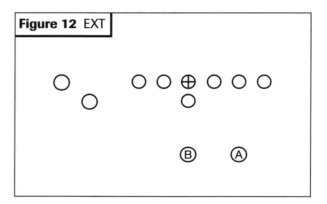

Figure 11 EXI

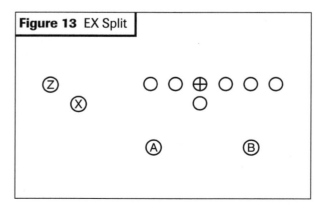

Figure 12 EXT

Now if we want to get our X back on the same side as our split end, we call Eastex (figure 10). The X indicates a cross, so Eastex means the X back crosses over. From this arrangement, we will have EXI (figure 11), EXT (figure 12), and EX Split (figure 13).

In order to give ourselves more flexibility we have a Right formation (figure 14). Its opposite formation is Left. If we want to get into the Pro I, we are Right I (figure 15). We can also very easily go into Right Split (figure 16), Right T (figure 17), and so forth.

Figure 13 EX Split

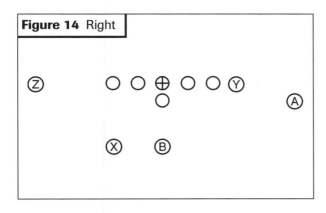

Figure 14 Right

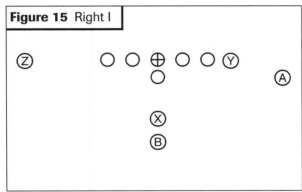

Figure 15 Right I

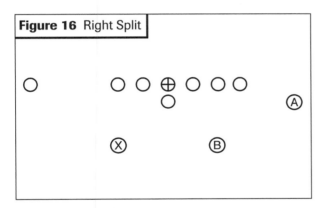

Figure 16 Right Split

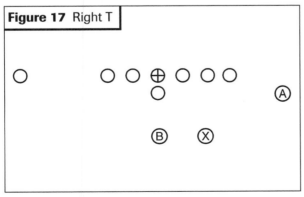

Figure 17 Right T

Since we are discussing formations, let me tell you that we try to standardize our splits. We have never done a good job of having our linemen intelligently split, so we go one foot by the guards, 18 inches by the tackles, and a minimum of two feet by our TE. He is the only player we coach on splits because at times we like him to vary from two feet to three yards.

We line up as far off the ball as we legally can. There are two reasons for this. First, it helps our pass protection. By being further away from defensive people, we have more chance to adjust to blitzes and stunts. And on one-on-one pass protection, we can keep away from the rushers longer. Second, we are a "fire out" football team, and we believe that by being back off the ball, we can still fire out and yet recover enough to adjust to stunts.

Snap Count

We try to achieve three things with our snap count. First we want to fire out together and reduce illegal procedure penalties. I don't care if we fire out ahead of the defense; I'm chiefly concerned that we come off precisely together. For this reason, we use an arrhythmic count.

Second we want enough variation to keep the defense off balance. For years we came out, got down, and took off on the QB's first word, but a couple of seasons ago we noticed that the defense was starting to get in a groove and could time stunts and blitzes extremely well because we had gotten into a set tempo. Now we go from an up position, which we merely call "quick up"; or we come out up and go down, which we call "hike up"; or we come out down and go quickly which we call "quick"; or we come out down, then come up and go back down, and we merely call this "hike."

Third we want the ability to change a play on the LOS or, to say it another way, we want to "automatic" plays on the LOS. We don't like to use a lot of audibles, but we will audible for certain reasons. We audible to eliminate the poor call against certain defenses. If we run across the Split 6 or Split 4 defense, we don't intend to change all our blocking rules to be able to run all our offense against it. We merely tell our QB that certain plays can't go against this defense and if, when he calls the play, he finds them in the Split 6, he should change the play on the LOS.

Another reason we audible is if we have a preference for the way we want to run a play (especially sweeps), perhaps either to or away from a monster, rotation, or an overshift. To effect this, we call the formation and the word "automatic" in the huddle. Then the QB calls the play on the LOS. This way, we don't have to worry about linemen or backs not picking up the change on the LOS.

Finally, we use an "if" situation. We put the word "if" in front of a running play in the huddle and when we come up to the LOS, the QB determines whether he can execute the play successfully. "If" he can't, he uses a code word that changes the run to the pass off the run we called. We usually have a play-action pass off every key running series in our offense.

Options

You cannot possibly hope to have any consistency in your offense without options. We have just mentioned the option of changing or calling the play on the LOS. In addition, we feel we must have optional blocking for certain plays. We use tackle and center calls.

We teach optional running to our backs. "The hole is where you find it" is a basic part of our ability to execute options within our offense. Our linemen are taught to block through people and take them in any direction they can or that they may want to go. It is imperative then that our backs execute the proper cut "to daylight." We have optional pass routes on several of our basic pass lanes; our QBs attempt to read coverage and have the option to go to an alternate receiver; we have the option pass or

run and, finally, we have the traditional option play—pitch or keep.

Our running game is still a four-on-three or three-on-two power game. If you play us straight, we use our back to double-team, or we double-team with two linemen and use our back to block an end or LB. If you offset, gap, or loop, we hope to seal off linemen, isolate a LB or end, and block him with a back. We complement this type of power running game with the quick pitch, the fake and pitch, the counter, and the trap, and most important, with our passing game.

Passing Game Principles

We pass to keep our running game good; we have to pass on any down and must have play-action passes. If we are to consistently ask our halfbacks to block ends and LBs, then we have to fake the power run at these people and either go outside with pass or run possibilities or throw into the area for which the LB is responsible. Consequently, we are great believers in the play-action pass, and we will have a pass which comes off the fake we have in our offense.

We have to pass to keep the ball. We need possession-type passes. Our theory is to spread the defense by opening up and to get into a formation with which we can develop four of the possible six short zones. When developing four zones, we will work on three on one side. The way people throw the ball today, the traditional four short zones concept of two flats and two hooks is outmoded. So we develop plays that will put people in the flat zone. For this reason, we have evolved into the split backfield and our Eastex formation. If we won't develop three zones on one side, then we have a one-on-one situation on our wide receiver, and we will throw to him.

Finally, we pass to score. This sounds kind of ridiculous, but we sometimes lose sight of it and fail to take advantage of superior receivers and passers.

1968 Proceedings. Joe Paterno is head coach at Penn State University.

Adapting Offense to Personnel

John McKay

Personnel not only affects your offense, it is your entire program. Constant evaluation, manipulation, counseling, etc., of your personnel over the entire year is probably the single most important factor in a winning program.

Discussing personnel abstractly is much the same as drawing plays on a blackboard. There is theory and there is the actuality. It is difficult to discuss personnel in generalities since personnel is different for each coaching staff and is very specific. Therefore, I will cover how our personnel affected our program and hope to provide enough general information to be of help.

One of the things taught in educational psychology is to allow for individual difference. Many times coaches overlook this. Some coaches know and prefer a ball control offense; others prefer a wide open passing game. We all have our likes and our dislikes, but we sometimes overlook the people available to do what we like. If you want to win, you should learn to like what your people can do. This will change every year and can change more than once in a single season.

This year we had a very large offensive line, our largest ever, and it was important that we use the size advantage. Therefore, we told our larger linemen to stay on their feet to take advantage of their natural strength and size rather than use the scramble-type block that is successful for smaller, quicker people. If we were bullheaded and demanded that our large people learn the scramble block, they would not have been as effective.

Likewise in play design, we consider the abilities of our personnel. Our guards were large, not particularly mobile, and much better at drive blocking than they were at pulling and leading. Their abilities and lack of specific abili-

ties certainly affected our attack. The pass patterns that you run should be the pass patterns that your people can run. If your end or flanker can run an excellent up pattern, then you should run up patterns, assuming that the QB can throw the ball. If your ends run excellent out patterns or hook patterns, use them because what your people can do is what's going to work. It is impossible to successfully run a sprint-out pass offense with a non-running QB. It would be difficult to run a good belly and belly keep series with an inadequate fullback. Each of us knows these things to be true. However, we have all coached against people who have used the same plays, blocked the same way, game after game, year after year, because it's what the coach knows or what succeeded in the past. Strategy and tactics will and must change from game to game and certainly from season to season with the players available. As my old college professor used to say, "Nothing is more constant than change."

After the season, I sit down with my staff to discuss each player's past performance: how he graded on last year's films, his personal characteristics, what we feel he can do best, his weaknesses. We grade our people as to who is the best and who is the worst. Like everyone else, we want the best people in the game. I know that no athlete on our offensive line or defensive line is good enough to play in the offensive or defensive backfield, so we don't expect a player like Ron Yary to be a halfback for us, and we certainly wouldn't expect a player like Earl McCullough to be an offensive guard. We naturally have to allow for certain physical characteristics, but we all want our winners to play. Since this affects our formations, I want our coaches to think about this, make recommendations, and decide who we are going to play.

We have four major objectives for spring practice: determine who will play; determine where he will play; teach physical technique; and learn what formations work best with our personnel.

We scrimmage almost every day in spring practice to find out who is competitive, who will hit, and who will play when he is tired. After determining who will play, we decide where they are going to play. We experiment. For instance, we like our tackles to be guards and our guards to be tackles. We even like our TEs to be tackles. We like all our flankers to play tailback, and we like our split ends to play tight end. We want our running backs to be wingbacks at some time. We make sure our QBs, regardless of their running abilities, run the football and that our halfbacks and fullbacks pass some. If you don't see your people do most everything that they can possibly do in their position, it is difficult to give a true evaluation of where they should play.

Once we decide where our people are going to play, we teach physical technique. We do not believe in teaching toughness because we would rather recruit competitive people who are tough by nature, although they will certainly become tougher once they are exposed to a good, organized program. We want to see how many times a player can execute his techniques. I do not demand that a player execute exactly the way everyone else does as long as he gets the job done, but I want my coaches to be demanding in the way they teach technique.

We scrimmage a lot in spring practice to find out what offense, what formations, what series we run best with the people we have. Therefore, we will run many plays in spring practice and will try just about anything that we want to see our people do.

We evaluate our personnel in comparison to the people we are going to play. Unfortunately, in spring practice you can compare yourself only to yourself. Many of us have been fooled by comparing our best to our second best rather than our best to our opponent's best. You can be both too easy and too critical on your people when you compare them to one another.

In deciding where people are going to play, compare your feelings about your own personnel to the defenses you are going to face. Look at your schedule to see if you will face one predominant defense or if you're going to see two or three defenses throughout the season. When you place your people, when you decide on the formations that you are going to use, do it with these defenses in mind. The defense that we see most is the defense that Notre Dame uses. If this is the defense that we are going to see the most, it is certainly the defense we practice against the most. It's the one we evaluate our people against. It is too easy to practice offense against your own defense, which may be completely different from the defense you are going to play against.

We all have traditional rivals, some of us more than one. It is important for keeping our jobs and keeping our alumna happy that we defeat our traditional rivals as often as possible. We would be foolish not to spend a great deal of time practicing against the defense used by our traditional rivals. Fortunately for us this year, UCLA and Notre Dame, two traditional rivals, both used the same defense as did four or five other teams we faced.

Whoever coaches your junior varsity people should be a good, demanding teacher. Make sure that he gives you the picture you want to see. It is virtually impossible to train a QB adequately unless he gets a true picture of your opponent's pass coverage in practice. If you are not as demanding with your junior varsity squad as you are with the people who are going to play, then you are not doing as good a job of preparation as you should. In film evaluation, in the traveling your coaches do between seasons, in the clinics you go to, and the people you discuss football with, find out everything you can about the defenses you are going to face. Make sure you get these points across to the people who are helping you get ready for the game.

In eight years at USC, we have used several offenses. In 1960 we were using a two TE wing T offense (figure 1). We had a large powerful line with people like Marlin McKeever, Ron Mix, Mike Bundra, Dan Ficca, and many others. We did not have a great deal of size in the backfield nor a great deal of speed, but we had a talented QB named Willy Wood so we used the option series, a lot of belly and belly keep, and were pretty much a ball-control offensive team. During the 1960 season the rover defense was very popular, and we had trouble moving the ball against the rover back to the wide side of the field, especially on the hash marks.

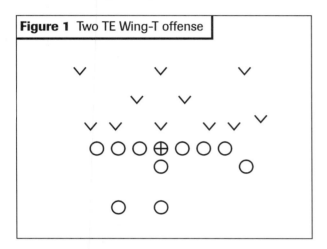

Figure 1 Two TE Wing-T offense

In 1961 we decided to go to the shifting I formation (figure 2). With the shifting I, we tried to line up in an I formation, find out where rover was, and shift away from him. We did no running as such from the I formation. We found a definite advantage to this in that we did get away from rover. Our passing game was a little better in getting receivers open but we didn't put a great deal of pressure on the defensive line to get ready.

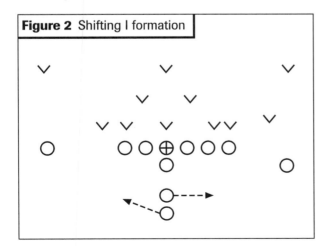

Figure 2 Shifting I formation

In 1962 we went to sprint out and direct action from the I formation (figure 3). We also wanted to run as soon as we lined up on the ball so that the defense would have to commit. We wanted to stop them from calling stunts after the shift, as they did in 1961, and make them find a basic pattern of defense, making our blocking more simple. We won the National Championship in 1962. We had an excellent flanker named Willy Brown, an excellent split end named Hal Bedsole, QBs Pete Beathard and Bill Nelson, fullback Ben Wilson, and an average college tailback named Ken Delcoate. Now that is excellent personnel. Everyone else was pretty average for our competition, so we wanted to use the plays these people could do best. We ran very little inside game in 1962, even though the threat was there. But we won with what Pete Beathard and Bill Nelson could do best: sprint out and run or pass the ball to excellent receivers.

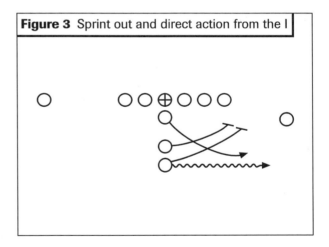

Figure 3 Sprint out and direct action from the I

In 1963 we had pretty much the same personnel, but people were beginning to figure out the proper way of stopping the sprint out QB. So in 1963 we went to a play-action pass game and, because we had an excellent tailback named Mike Garrett, we also ran a great deal of the inside game. Our attack was based on running the ball between tackles until forced to do something else. If you do bring people in to stop us from running between tackles, we fake our best play and run a pass play in the areas where these people are left.

In 1964 Pete Beathard was gone and we went with Craig Fertig, who was an excellent passer but could run the hundred-yard dash in about eleven minutes flat. We went to the dropback pass, and he was very successful for us. One of the great moments in Trojan football history was the final game of the 1964 season when we defeated Notre Dame 20-17, with a great deal of the victory going to Craig Fertig and his passing.

The 1967 season brought us O.J. Simpson, a great runner and a fine all-round football player. He was certainly the biggest single factor in our winning the National Championship, personnel-wise. The major coaching points for our QBs that year were, regardless of what play is called, give the ball to O.J. 30 to 40 times a game. If you have a good runner, give him the ball as many times as he can carry it. Don't let the defense force you out of giving the ball to your best back. Find the formation, find the play, do something to make sure that the best back carries the ball.

The 1967 season was very exciting and rewarding for us. We did several good things. The adjustments we made for and during the 1967 season helped us win. We anticipated facing the Notre Dame defense and felt that one of the fine ways to attack this defense theory-wise was to use a wingback and two TEs with a flanker (figure 4).

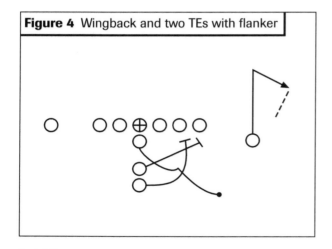

Figure 4 Wingback and two TEs with flanker

This formation works against the Notre Dame defense because after the snap this defense becomes a form of gap 8. Therefore, we want to try to force it to have 9 gaps to cover on the running game. On the passing game, we want maximum protection both back side and front side and in many instances use a single receiver. This defense is adjustable much the same as the wide tackle 6. With a split end or with field position on a hash, it is easy to overshift slightly, giving you an unbalanced defense into your strength. This formation helps eliminate overshift and helps eliminate some stunts with a split end or without a wingback.

Injuries certainly affect how personnel dictates your offense. We had our share of injuries this season. By the time we reached the Rose Bowl, we had lost our flanker, our fullback, a defensive tackle, and an offensive guard. Though we still had our QB and Simpson as tailback, these injuries forced us to change formations more than tactic and strategy. I want to credit Coach Paul Bryant of Alabama for what I want to say next: have a plan for everything that can happen. This is more possible than you think. Put some thinking into it. Plan what you will do if there are coaching changes at your opponent's school, if there are coaching changes on your staff, if you lose your best player, best receiver, or QB for a quarter or the entire game.

It is possible to waste free time by not sitting down and thinking about football and situations that are difficult to practice. I have talked with my staff about sideline procedure, half-time procedure, after-game procedure because these things involve a great deal of emotion not present during practice. Sit down and discuss these things with your staff and team; it will help.

In closing, personnel is the biggest factor in winning. The coaching staff who knows how to handle people, who has a plan to handle people, and who works at it doesn't take the easy way out by saying we didn't have the horses this year. These are the people who have the best record over a period of years.

1968 Proceedings. John McKay was the head coach at the University of Southern California.

Implementing the Multi-Flex System

Joe Restic

A Multi-Flex System is capable of many variations. The term "Multi-Flex" denotes multiplicity and flexibility in the truest sense. For a system to be totally multiple, it must have the built-in capacity to use a number of sets in a manner that places maximum pressure on the defense regardless of field position. Being totally multiple is not enough; the system must have complete flexibility. This will allow you to work the most advantageous part of your offense.

If *multiplicity* and *flexibility* are the goals, then the *system* is the key to achieving these goals. The system must be simple. This puts your knowledge and experience as a coach to the test. How can I arrive at a totally multiple and completely flexible system that is simple? This may sound dichotomous, but it is in the realm of possibility, and therein lies the challenge.

The initial step and logical place to start is with the offensive sets. One must incorporate a combination of Zero-, One-, Two-, and Three-Back sets into the basic system.

Zero-Back Sets

A departure from basic thinking must take place in order to properly defend Zero-Back sets. These sets present a five-off-the-line receiver problem the defense must effectively handle. In the Trips set (figure 1a), four receivers out the same side force a change in linebacker and deep back drop, as well as positioning adjustment. This set can be most effective versus five-under coverage. The Spread set (figure 1b), a combination of two out one side and three out the other, pressures the defense to play relatively balanced because of receiver deployment.

If man-blitz is being used, a linebacker-receiver mismatch could result. A lack of proper coverage on one of the receivers could be another possibility because of failure to identify the set. This capability in your offensive system has value because it presents the defense with time commitment and adjustment problems in a radically different way. In some cases, it forces the defense to come up with an automatic call when the Zero-Back sets show. This is advantageous to the offense if it has the built-in flexibility to capitalize on these defensive moves.

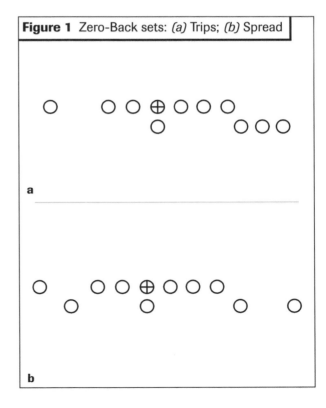

Figure 1 Zero-Back sets: *(a)* Trips; *(b)* Spread

One-Back Sets

One-Back sets (figure 2) put a running back in one of three backfield positions. Stress the full-back position or put your top running back to maximum use as a primary ball carrier.

These looks also force opponents out of eight-man front—blitz—man-to-man thinking. In the passing game, they present a four-off-the-line receiver problem for the defense. These sets are convertible to the Zero-Back sets by simply controlling the remaining back in a flare sense. The Deuces formation (figure 2b) also gives the defense the wingback problem combined with the wideout pass threat to either side.

Two-Back Sets

The immediate advantage of the Two-Back set (figure 3) is a two-back run offense with the threat of the wideouts in the passing game. These sets give you the flexibility of placing the wingback in a position to pressure the contain portion of the defense and at the same time allow you to use him as a third running back. A system of flare and check flare action must be incorporated to control the underneath coverage if you expect to fully capitalize on the pass. The remaining backs can also provide maximum protection when not being used as shown.

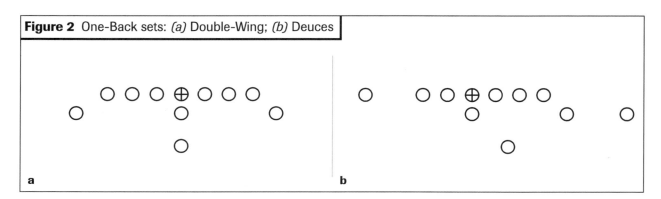

Figure 2 One-Back sets: *(a)* Double-Wing; *(b)* Deuces

a

b

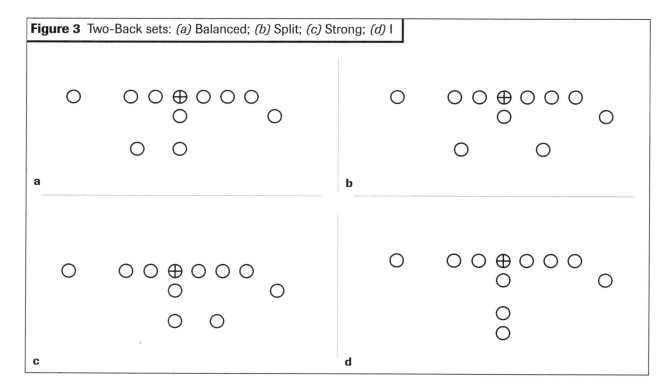

Figure 3 Two-Back sets: *(a)* Balanced; *(b)* Split; *(c)* Strong; *(d)* I

a

b

c

d

Three-Back Sets

With Three-Back sets (figure 4) you can quickly attack either side of the ball with all your backs. The defense is forced to play a balanced front with LBs committed to the run. The LBs must be strong enough to handle two lead blockers versus the isolation game. You can develop an effective play pass and counter-type action to take advantage of the defensive commitment to these run-oriented formations. All the backs are in a position to fake, fill, block, or carry in a variety of offensive maneuvers.

The set possibilities have been presented. The key lies in selection. You must incorporate a minimum of one formation from each example into your system based on the capabilities of your personnel.

Using Motion

The second step in the development of the Multi-Flex System involves the use of motion. How much and what type of motion do you need? These questions can only be answered after an assessment is made of the value of motion in an offensive system. What are the values to be derived from the use of motion?

1. Motion can be used to change the nature and look of the offensive sets.
2. Motion can be used to get from one formation to another, thereby forcing a quick decision and adjustment on the part of the defense.
3. Motion can be used to confuse and to negate the ability of good football players by lessening read and reaction time.

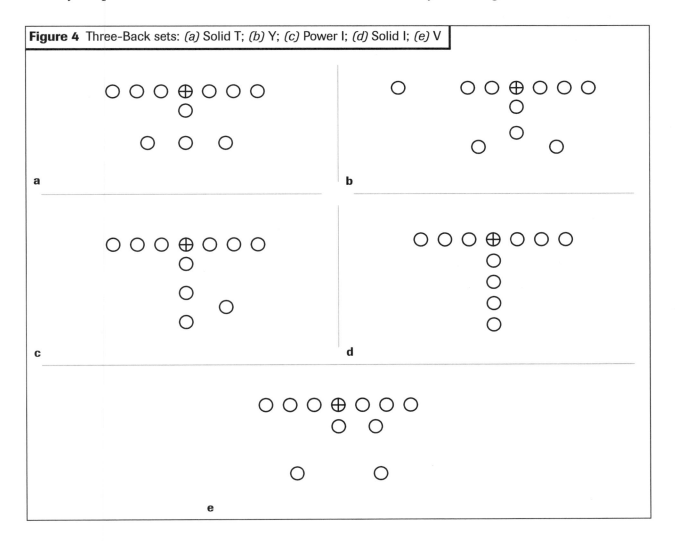

Figure 4 Three-Back sets: *(a)* Solid T; *(b)* Y; *(c)* Power I; *(d)* Solid I; *(e)* V

4. Motion can be used to put offensive people in a better position to get the job done that they are assigned to do.

5. Motion should be used to improve execution in the ballcarrying, blocking, and receiving areas of the game. It should not be used as a frill.

For example, the set in figure 5 initially presents a wing and wideout problem to the defense.

1. Motion across the formation creates a Wide Twin set with a back in a position to establish a flood threat to that side.

2. Fly motion through the backfield places the back in a position to become a ballcarrier, faking back, or lead blocker to the other side of the formation.

3. Motion out from the formation presents the wideout problem to either side of the formation.

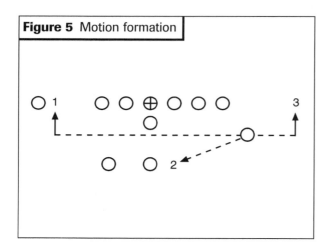

Figure 5 Motion formation

In figure 4, the defense had to prepare for the Wing, Pro, Solid T, and Wide Twin sets, which were created by the use of single back motion. The example in figure 6 projects another look at single back motion from the same basic Wing T set.

1. A Double-Wing set is created with the Wide Twin problems to the motion side.

2. Fly motion aids the back in execution of his assignment.

3. Deuces formation is the result of motion through the formation.

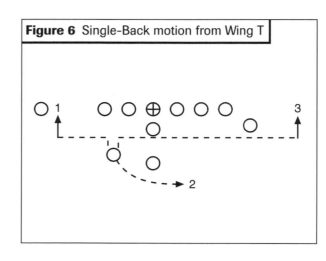

Figure 6 Single-Back motion from Wing T

This formation presents the defense with a wing and wideout problem to the same side. The pass defense must also handle three receivers off the LOS to that side.

In figure 5, the defense had to get ready for the Wing T, Double-Wing, and Deuce formations. The example in figure 7 pictures a Double Wing-Slot formation.

1. The Deuces formations are created by set back motion either direction.

2. In the single-back sets, remaining back motion results in the spread-type looks.

The Zero-, One-, Two-, and Three-Back sets combined with single-back motion give you the variations necessary to develop a totally multiple and completely flexible system. This system will put maximum pressure on the defense by allowing you to jump an offensive cycle every week during the season.

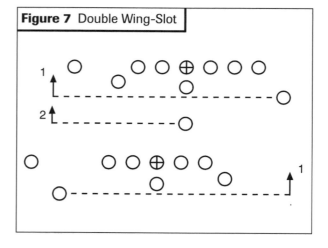

Figure 7 Double Wing-Slot

1975 Summer Manual. Joe Restic was head coach at Harvard University.

Using the Spread Offense

Bob Devaney

The Spread formation is one of our two basic formations. We also use the I formation, which we copied from Johnny McKay as closely as we could. We don't run it as well as they do, but we try. This is the formation we use in most short-yardage situations and a lot of times on first down. We use the I formation right and left. We use it with a Tight Slot (figure 1a) and also with a split man out there, so we have two split receivers wide on one side (figure 1b).

We scouted ourselves during the season, and we found that when we lined up on first down in the I formation, we were running the ball 90 percent of the time. So, in our game plan against LSU, we came out the first half and threw the ball every first down out of an action pass. It did help us some. We try to throw action passes out of this I formation and use it on running downs.

When we get in a situation where we have to throw, we like to get four or five receivers out.

The Spread is a good throwing formation, and it also cuts down on the number of defenses you're going to face. You can get several defensive secondary calls, but they're basically going to need to have four men spread out around the secondary. It is difficult for them to lay you successfully in a three-call. Many teams that use a monster defense are at a loss to try to lay anything but a three-call. This helps us in that respect and, of course, a team can use a four-deep cloud or they a four-deep man-to-man, but we feel we can have a pretty good chance of moving the ball.

Our Spread formation is used right and left (figure 2). Our Spread Left or Right is the way the split end goes. This past season, we were blessed with a FB who was a fine blocker, a good pass receiver, and a tough, though not a quick, runner. If you had a quick runner at FB who was an adequate blocker, this formation would be even more effective. We number wide from

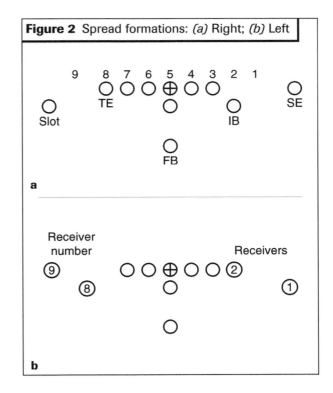

Figure 1 I formations

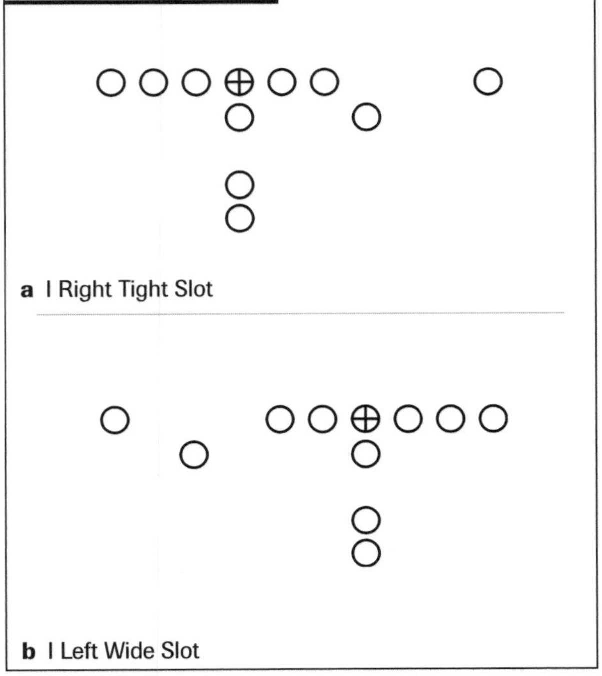

a I Right Tight Slot

b I Left Wide Slot

Figure 2 Spread formations: *(a)* Right; *(b)* Left

a

b

right to left. We also number our receivers. Our wide receiver to the right is number one; our wide receiver to the left is number nine. Our number two receiver is the slot back in Spread Right or a TE in Spread Left. The number eight receiver is second receiver in on left. We use the term "swing sharp" or the term "flare" to refer to the FB, the fifth receiver, who isn't numbered.

We call running plays by using the number of the hole and the number of the backs. Our backs are numbered QB, number one; slotback, number two; FB, number three; and I back, number four. Our holes are numbered from right to left, one to nine. A play over our four hole with the I back carrying the ball would be called 44. We then add a description to the play such as 44 Iso or 44 Counter, etc. If the slot back were to carry the ball, the play over the three hole would be a 23 play over the right tackle or a 27 play over the left tackle.

In calling our plays, first we give formation, i.e., Spread Right or Spread Left, then the play number and the starting count. In our starting count, we go on the first sound or we go on one or two. We call two numbers prior to the first HUT so that we may check off a play at the LOS if advisable. Our cadence is arrhythmic. When our players come out of the huddle, they get down on the ball in a three-point stance. In our Spread formation, we use few running plays.

Our wide running play to the right is a sprint option called 31 sprint (figure 3). Our play over the tackle hole is 33 draw (figure 4). Our four hole play is 44 trap (figure 5). We have the same plays to the left, i.e., 39 sprint, 37 draw, 36 trap. These are plays that can be called either in the huddle or at the LOS.

In addition to these basic running plays, we use a 23 or 27 counter (figure 6); 11 or 19 draw, a QB draw right or left (figure 7); and an 11 or 19 fullback take, a fullback play to the right and left (figure 8). I will diagram these plays with the blocking against a 4-3 defense, which is the most common defense we face at the present time.

We can change our play at the LOS by simply repeating the play called in the huddle such as 31. The next number called is the play that we had changed to; that is, "39 one" would be changing from a sprint right to a sprint left. We also may change from a run to a pass or a pass to a run. We have two automatic passes to the right

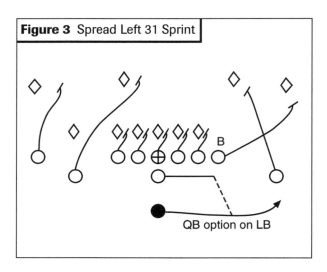

Figure 3 Spread Left 31 Sprint

QB option on LB

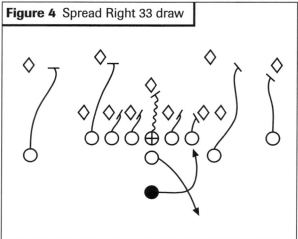

Figure 4 Spread Right 33 draw

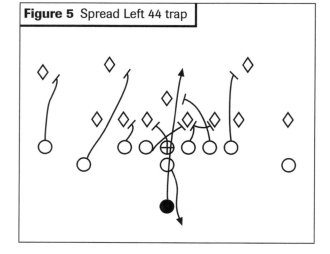

Figure 5 Spread Left 44 trap

and two to the left, along with the three automatic running plays each way. Keeping automatics to a minimum and practicing them regularly can be a great advantage; however, there is a definite danger in trying to automatic too

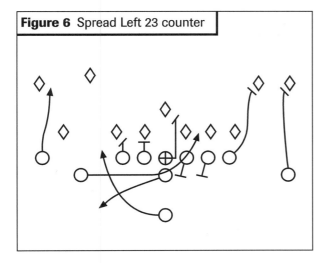

Figure 6 Spread Left 23 counter

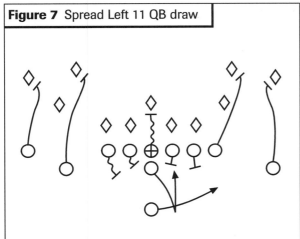

Figure 7 Spread Left 11 QB draw

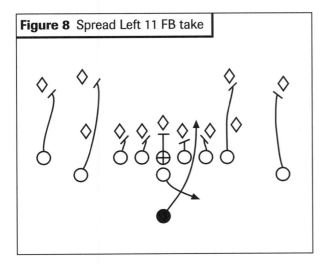

Figure 8 Spread Left 11 FB take

throwing in the direction he is moving or of using the run option. The semi-dropback pass that we use is a 70 series pass where the QB will sprint to a position behind the tackle on the side of the play to a depth of seven yards. In our 70 series, the QB is given three seconds to release the ball and must read the defense before setting up so that he knows which side to throw to. In reading defenses, our QB keys the LBs on delay patterns and keys the defensive safety when throwing a deep pattern. The line blocking on our 50 series is aggressive, much like a running play. The pass protection on our 70 series is semiaggressive on the onside and a swinging gate-type block on the offside. Our 50 series is used on running downs and our 70 series generally on long-yardage or definite passing downs. However, we will throw the 70 series pass in other than long-yardage situations.

Our 50 series action passes and our 70 series dropback passes are shown in figures 9-14. Our action pass to the right would be 51 (figure 9); our action to the left would be 59 (figure 10). Our semi-dropback pass to the right is 71 and to the left is 79. In calling our pass plays, we designate the type of pass, such as 51, and then the route of the number-one receiver, such as "51 one out." We do the same in our 70 series, that is, "71 two under" (figure 11), and "79 eight out" (figure 12). Our FB will block the end on the side where the play is called unless he is involved in the pattern. If we involve our FB in the pattern, our QB will roll in one direction, such as 71, and throw back the opposite way, such as "71 nine hook," in which case we could call flare (figure 13) or swing sharp (figure 14), which would send the FB in the pass route.

Our passing game this past year had a high percentage of completions (63 percent). Part of this was due to the ability of the offensive blocking, the receivers, and a fine job by our two QBs. However, we also attribute this fine passing percentage to the fact that we spent a great deal of time with our QBs on reading defenses and throwing the percentage-type pass. We do not often try to go deep on long-yardage downs but will throw under patterns and delay patterns in front of retreating LBs. On the normal or short-yardage downs, we

many plays, and also there is a danger if you don't use automatics in practice during the week.

Our pass offense is relatively simple in that we have two types of passes. The 50 series pass is an action type where the QB has the choice of

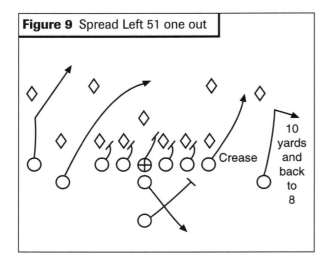

Figure 9 Spread Left 51 one out

Crease

10 yards and back to 8

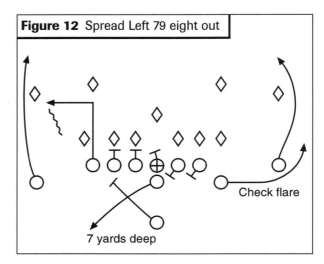

Figure 12 Spread Left 79 eight out

Check flare

7 yards deep

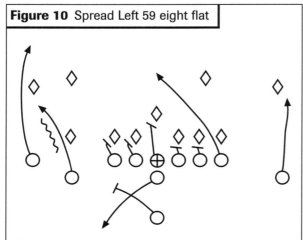

Figure 10 Spread Left 59 eight flat

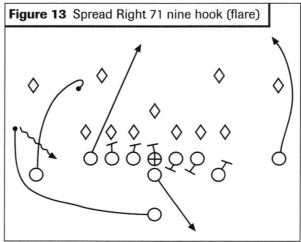

Figure 13 Spread Right 71 nine hook (flare)

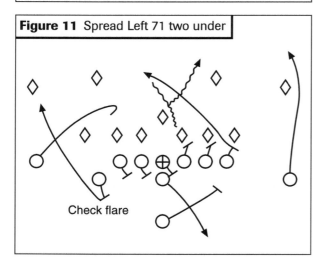

Figure 11 Spread Left 71 two under

Check flare

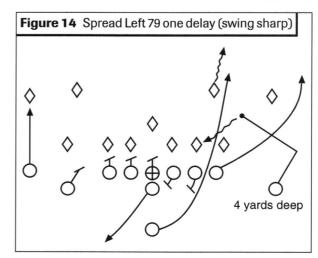

Figure 14 Spread Left 79 one delay (swing sharp)

4 yards deep

mix our short action pass with the deep pattern, usually thrown out of a running action. We also make liberal use of screens and draws to make our passing game more effective.

The use of the check off or audible has kept us away from the bad play in most instances, and this has been very beneficial to both our running and passing games.

1971 Proceedings. Bob Devaney was the head coach at the University of Nebraska.

Communicating the Plan

Jack Bicknell and Sam Timer

So that we may develop our system of play calling as well as our general means of communicating game day, it is essential that we give some background on what we at Boston College do offensively. We must also discuss our philosophical approach to offensive football.

Number one, we are going to throw the football. Number two, we are going to use as many formations as we can. Number three, not only are we are going to force our opponents to defend our formations, we are going to make them defend the field horizontally as well as vertically in regard to our throwing the ball, and in regard to where we throw it from. Obviously, to accomplish what we do offensively requires a number of things, among them the total concentration and effort of all our people. This is our system.

Starting on Sunday and concluding Tuesday, we put together our offensive game plan. This procedure, I am sure, is the same as everyone else's. It requires a great deal of film work, an analysis of our upcoming opponents' personnel and what they are attempting to do defensively, and an evaluation of the problems that we can create versus their scheme. We attempt to break down our attack conceptually so that what we do on each hash mark is different from what we do in the middle of the field. We may at times attempt to do the same things in the middle of the field as we do in the boundary, but we try to disguise this by using a different formation or formations.

Once our concepts have been established, we break them down into categories: the vertical (down and distance) and the horizontal (left hash, middle of field, right hash). When we are dealing with the down and distance aspect of our game plan, we have four pass and four run options in each category (i.e., first and 10, second and normal, etc.). Within this concept, we want to allow ourselves four calls that will give us,

when we pass, the option to either get us up the field or the ability to attack any zone widthwise.

When running the ball, we want to be able to strike anywhere with either some type of option run or what we consider to be a standard running play. We want to have at least one gadget in each category, whether it be a run gadget or pass gadget. We hope with this format, and the ability to use multiple formations, we do not allow any predictability to get into our play selection.

With this approach to the game, we now carry these concepts into what we consider the second phase of our game plan. That is, we take what we think are good plays versus our opponent, run as well as pass, and categorize them into 14 areas we have allocated in our game plan. (Remember, we have at least four options in any of these categories!)

1. First and 10 (off each hash mark and middle of field)
2. First and X (11+ yards) (off each hash mark and middle of field)
3. Second and short (1 to 3 yards) (off each hash mark and middle of field)
4. Second and normal (4 to 7 yards) (off each hash mark and middle of field)
5. Second and long (8 to 10 yards) (off each hash mark and middle of field)
6. Second and X (11+ yards) (off each hash mark and middle of field)
7. Third and short (1 to 2 yards) (off each hash mark and middle of field)
8. Third and normal (3 to 5 yards) (off each hash mark and middle of field)
9. Third and long (6 to 10 yards) (off each hash mark and middle of field)
10. Third and X (11+ yards) (off each hash mark and middle of field)

To this point, we have 10 categories. Our 11th is what we do versus their prevent defense. The 12th category is what our concepts will be when we are in our "hurry up" (or two-minute) offense, and our 13th is what we call zone F (the plus 15-yard line). The last category is our goal line offense, and where and what we want to do executionwise here.

In each of these categories, we list the number of times we have seen our opponent in this situation: the fronts, the coverage, and the blitz percentage. The play call is made from this input, as well as what we have philosophically developed as an offensive staff and felt was the optimal way to attack, keeping in mind what we want to do.

Once our game plan is set, we go into the implementation of the game plan, incorporating our entire offensive staff, our head coach, and a graduate assistant so that we may verbalize throughout the game. Our hookups are as follows. Our QB coach (in the press box) is tied by phone to the head coach (sideline) and the receiver coach (sideline). Another system, independent of the system to which the head coach, QB coach, and receiver coach are linked, links our tackle coach (press box) with our offensive line coach (sideline). Our running back coach is not tied electronically to anyone, but works closely with our receiver coach on the sideline, to identify our offensive backs' pass protection schemes and how they are matching up with our opponents.

Play selection is made by a coach in the press box and sent to the field to both head coach and receiver coach. As the head coach signals the formation to the QB on the field, the receiver coach sends in the play. The receiver coach also sends in the proper people tied to the formation called. This facet requires a great deal of concentration from our players because of the number of formations we use (averaging 28 per game) and the number of players we use.

The tackle coach simply records the fronts we are seeing and gets verification of them to our line coach so that he may communicate with our linemen on the field. Our graduate assistant charts the coverages and confirms or rejects the notions as to what, historically, our opponent has done up to this point.

The key to proper communication is to have a plan and believe in it. We decide during the week what our plan is. The key to proper execution is not to "chicken out," but to follow it. "Paralysis by analysis" is a common problem of many offensive staffs.

1985 Summer Manual. Jack Bicknell is the head coach at Boston College. Sam Timer is the quarterback coach at Boston College.

Running the No-Huddle

Chan Gailey

Probably the question we are asked most often is, "How does the no-huddle work?" This article will cover three basic areas of the no-huddle: why we use the no-huddle; how we communicate it; and how and why our option game fits in with this concept.

Why the No-Huddle

First, let me say that we do not use the no-huddle to affect the defense nearly as much as we use it to help ourselves. Also, some of the things mentioned were not thought of before we put in the no-huddle but were found to be true and valid after we had used it for a while.

Initially, we had five reasons for considering the no-huddle.

■ How it affects linemen. If linemen move seven and one-half yards from the ball to the huddle and jog that same distance back to the LOS, by the end of each play they have traveled fifteen yards. Multiply that by a minimum 60 plays and you can see we save our linemen approximately 900 yards per game. Therefore, they should be fresher in the fourth quarter.

■ How it affects practice time. By not using a huddle, we can run approximately one-third more plays in practice. (For example, we used to run 20-22 plays in a 15-minute period. Now we run 28-30 plays in a 15-minute period).

■ How it affects our QB. By being at the LOS, our QB gains an extra three or four seconds to scan the defense. This gives us a better chance to make the proper checks.

■ How it affects the tempo of the game. Tempo is one of the most unexplored offensive advantages. The two things that the offense knows is "where" and "when". We all seem to spend our time on the where and never give much time or effort to when. By lining up at the LOS, we push the defense into a tempo they are not accustomed to. We relate this idea to gears in a car. First gear is the gear most everyone uses. Both teams huddle then go to the LOS and execute their plays. In second gear, the offense does not huddle; therefore, the defense cannot huddle either. This changes the tempo. Third gear is hurry-hurry offense; with the no-huddle, you can get into this tempo at any time. Now we have the ability to speed up the game or slow it down according to our wants and needs. This keeps the defense off balance.

■ How it affects the defense. The defense needs to prepare differently for a no-huddle offense. They must shift into second gear. If we can cause them to spend 10 minutes of practice time a day on developing a different form of communication, that translates into 40 minutes of preparation time spent on something other than defending the actual plays (10 minutes per practice day times 4 days of practice). Also, defense elicits a great deal of emotion—slapping each other, pumping up each other, etc. This is almost eliminated since there is no time to regroup.

We have found several other ideas to be true as we used our no-huddle offense. First, as coaches we teach what is important. Since the huddle has nothing to do with winning or losing the game, we end up spending more time on fundamentals and the actual plays we use.

Second, the no-huddle allows coaches to make corrections visually. Often in a huddle, we try to explain how we want something done—a blocking scheme, back's cut, etc. For us, all corrections are done at the LOS, and the players see exactly what we want. The defense is right in front of them.

Third, since we can run more plays in practice, a lot more conditioning occurs during the entire practice. Therefore, we are able to cut back on the amount of sprint work as the season continues. During the game, since more plays are being run and we are at the LOS for every play, our concentration has improved, especially when we are tired.

Finally, we have found that communication and execution of our minute-man or two-minute offense is much easier. Our players are accustomed to hearing the play called from the LOS and are better able to handle the hurry-up situation. Also, speeding up play at times in our regular offense gives them a better concept of the faster pace we want in the minute-man situation.

Communication

We signal formation and play at the same time. An advantage we have in our Wishbone offense is that we do not flip-flop a lot of people. Only our TE and SE change. We use a red wristband to show the right halfback his alignment and where to go if motion is necessary. We use no wristband on the left wrist but use the same signals for the left halfback. The SE always goes to the wide side of the field and the TE goes into the boundary. We use one signal to switch them or to get them on the same side to create an unbalanced situation.

To call the play at the LOS, we use a combination of live and dead words combined with live numbers. For example, our QB might say, "Ready! Over 33, Over 33" or on the next down he might say, "Bingo 33, Bingo 33." Now the defense does not know whether we are running Over, Bingo, or 33. The number is live only if the word is dead. It sounds complicated but it is really very simple and easy for the players to learn.

But will defenses be able to figure it out? First of all, I don't believe they can. It is a little too complicated for the untrained ear. Second, I sure hope they try. Every minute they spend trying to decipher our calls and signals is another minute they are not working to defeat our plays.

We've been asked how we communicate the snap count to our players without the other team knowing it. We have a few ways to do this but for obvious reasons I cannot relate exactly how we do it. However, I can give you the different ideas we looked at. One way is to determine your snap count by the down marker (for example, in Play 33 the snap count is 3, in Play 61 the snap count is 1). If you use this method, you must devise some way to derive the snap count for plays in the 0, 5, 6, 7, 8, and 9 holes. Another way would be to let all plays to the left be on 1, all plays to the right on 2, and all passes on 3. You will be surprised to see how quickly the players can learn this method. This also would be valuable when used in a huddle. We all are looking for ways to cut our words, whether in the huddle or not.

Communication at the LOS is easier than ever in the no-huddle. Our linemen are accustomed to being informed at the line and pay close attention to every word the QB says. We also have tried to make our audible system easier by pairing our plays. This gives the QB the option to say only the word "opposite", and we can attack the other side of the defense with the same play.

The Option With the No-Huddle

We feel strongly about the following ideas in our Wishbone option offense. I think you will see how the following ideas fit in with the no-huddle concept:

- We base our entire offense on the triple option play.
- We want to take a few other complementary plays and learn to execute them very well.
- The majority of our passing time is play-action off the triple option look.
- The defense calls the plays for us.
- We want to isolate defenders and control pursuit.
- We want to be able to attack the entire field with the run and the pass.
- When in doubt, call the triple option.

1985 Proceedings. Chan Gailey was head coach at Troy State University. He currently is head coach of the Dallas Cowboys.

Gaining a Pre-Snap Advantage

Hayden Fry and Bill Snyder

We have always been impressed and enthused by the diversification of an offense like that of the Dallas Cowboys, primarily in its ability to create so many offensive looks by using motion and shifting, yet still maintain a relatively basic attack.

Having to prepare defensively for such an attack has certainly given us a great deal of re-

spect for its advantages. One of the more convincing examples was several years back in the summer all-star game between a John McKay-coached group of pro-bound collegians and a sound representative team from the NFL. With the college all-stars in possession at the goal line, Coach McKay lined up his offense in a slot formation and sent the slot back in motion across the backfield to create a Pro alignment (a basic maneuver by today's standards). To adjust to that simple motion, the professionals moved seven defensive people. From that point on, we have been convinced that any time you can disrupt the continuity of a defense that much with offensive movement (motion or shifting) before the snap, you can create a distinct advantage.

After weighing the advantages and disadvantages, we committed ourselves to an offensive philosophy that stresses multiple sets, extensive shifting, and motion. This offensive approach has met perfectly the needs of our personnel and program. Notable disadvantages are

1. it can disrupt offensive timing and thus lead to poor execution,
2. it may cause defensive adjustments you are not prepared to block or throw into, and
3. the threat of delay-of-game penalties always exists because of the time required for shifting and motion.

There are certainly other problems that can occur, but these three are the ones we have to deal with most frequently. We might add here that very basic to our attack is the concept that there must be a very definite purpose for each motion and each shifting pattern. We won't create movement without a purpose, one that should create an offensive advantage.

Advantages of Presetting and Multiple Sets

We have found the following to be definite offensive advantages for us in the extensive use of *presetting* (shifting and motion) if our preparation is sound both on and off the field.

Neutralize the Defense

We can neutralize the defense to base alignments and secondary calls, limiting stunts and forcing a more controlled, balanced defense. The trend in defensing multiple sets, shifting, and motion has been to eliminate as many

adjustments as possible and be as sound and simple as you can. Too much is involved in having a different adjustment from every defensive alignment depending upon weak motion, strong motion, trips, sets, etc.

Most people also prefer to make all adjustments with only the secondary and not disrupt the continuity of the front seven. This further dictates the need to be simple and minimize the number of adjustments, as we all know the cost of one mental mistake in a defensive secondary. We can virtually eliminate the overload secondaries that have become so popular in the past few years through the use of simple motion as indicated in figure 1. Motion to a balanced Spread set forces the defense to disband overload coverage.

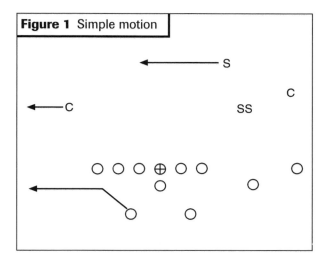

Figure 1 Simple motion

We also have found that with a variety of offensive sets and presetting, we often eliminate defensive pressure from LBs (stunts) because they may be involved in making an adjustment. We often align in or shift to a "No-Back" offensive alignment (figure 2), which forces alignment adjustments by both the secondary and LBs. Perhaps as important is the ability to preset in that same No-Back set and shift back into a basic Pro or Slot set with I or split backs (figure 3).

The value in this comes from the desire of the defense to keep its adjustments simple and basic, therefore taking its adjustment alignment first and then shifting back to the base alignment minus stunts when the offense shifts to a basic set.

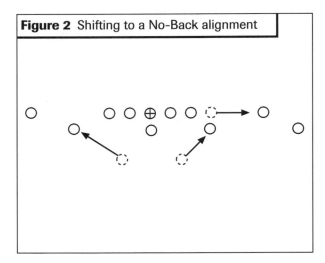

Figure 2 Shifting to a No-Back alignment

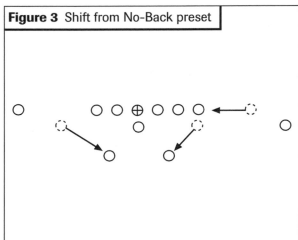

Figure 3 Shift from No-Back preset

Create Mismatches

We can create personnel mismatches by changing the strength of the offensive formation, eliminating the flip-flopping of defensive personnel. The obvious situation is the slot motion, which forces the secondary to roll the free safety up as a strong safety (figure 4) or run the strong safety across the backfield (figure 5), slowing and changing the angle of his support.

Against defenses that use strong and weak ends and/or LBs (and in some cases tackles), the presetting of the TE should force the defense into misalignments (strong end and LB on weak side, and weak end and LB on TE side). This can easily be created by shifting the

TE from the true I alignment (figure 6), as the Kansas City Chiefs made popular several years back, or aligning him on one side and shifting to the other (figure 7).

In order to prevent the defense from determining the strength of the offense by placement of your flanker on a Pro set, he and the split end can always align on the LOS (one always on the right, the other always on the left). Whichever one will become the flanker can back off when the TE shifts (figures 6 and 7). When shifting from one side to the other (figure 7), the TE should not touch a hand to the ground until he has shifted to his final position. This would create an illegal procedure penalty if your wide receiver is on the LOS.

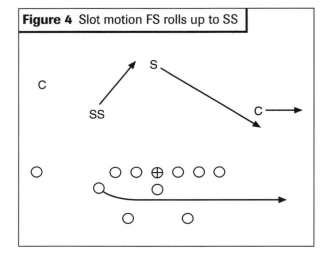

Figure 4 Slot motion FS rolls up to SS

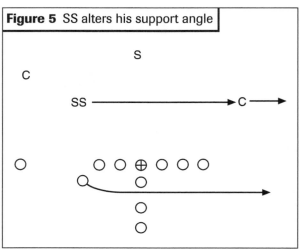

Figure 5 SS alters his support angle

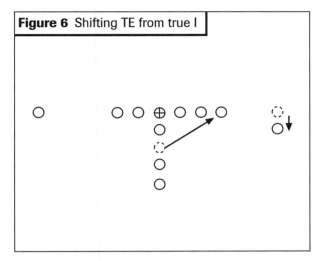

Figure 6 Shifting TE from true I

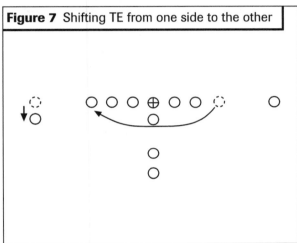

Figure 7 Shifting TE from one side to the other

Disrupt the Defense

We can disrupt defensive concentration and protect against defensive recognition of offensive set tendencies. If offensive alignment is important to all eleven defensive players, then the change of that alignment must create a change in the defenders' alignment, and/or responsibility, and technique.

Against a non-presetting offense with no motion or shifting or, at best, predictable movement, the defender has considerable time to concentrate on alignment, responsibility, technique, and set tendencies. On the other hand, consider the uncertainty of a defender who has thought all of this through, has the play diagnosed, is ready to execute his assignment perfectly, then a sudden offensive shift takes place,

changing his responsibility, technique, alignment, and even the tendency of what the offense might run. Being a well-drilled player, he quickly fixes the new set of data in his mind, and an offensive player now starts in motion. He must again assemble all the necessary information required for him to execute properly. We believe that establishes grounds for defensive confusion and little time to recognize offensive set tendencies.

Control Secondary Coverage

We give ourselves the opportunity to control the defensive secondary coverage. With most defensive adjustments to motion and shifting coming from the secondary, it is necessary to limit its coverages to a minimum and not vary in the types of adjustments it makes to motion and shifting into Spread and Trip sets.

We have all seen or even been part of a secondary that has a different coverage or responsibility for every single type of motion. The opportunities for confusion are obvious, which is why most defensive people now prefer to get back into the safest and most protective coverage they have against multiple set and presetting offenses. By presenting that threat, we feel that we can force the coverage back to the base call. This allows us to devote more practice time working against base defensive alignments and less time preparing for all the variations that we feel we will not have to line up against.

Control the Defense's Time

We can force the defense to spend more preparation time on alignments and adjustments, and less time on execution and repetition. Basic to any sound defense is to be certain that you do not get beaten on alignment. That philosophy takes a great deal of preparation and practice to make and coach alignment adjustments in preparing for a multiple set team that utilizes extensive shifting and motion. This takes away practice time from defensive execution against each offensive play or series. The defense must prepare for your entire attack from all sets and possible motion, yet you may prepare only those "short list" plays best suited for that defense.

Eliminate Double Coverage

We can eliminate the ability of the defense to double cover or bump and run with our wide people. Motion and shifting both have prevented double coverage by a walked-off defensive end or LB or by a rolled-up corner or safety. For example, a balanced Spread set (figure 8) should seldom draw any type of double coverage because of the threat of the inside receivers.

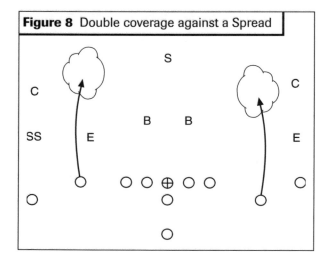

Figure 8 Double coverage against a Spread

If that holds true, you may eliminate double coverage by either executing your offense from a Spread or presetting in a Spread set and motion or shift to the alignments you prefer. We find the same to be true with No-Back sets. They normally force the defense out of any double coverage. Slot motion normally eliminates double coverage on your flankerback (figure 9), although it may create timing difficulties for your QB.

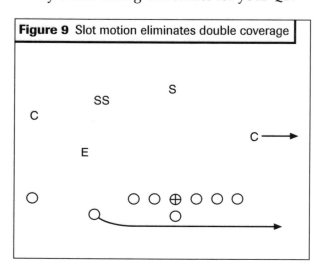

Figure 9 Slot motion eliminates double coverage

Shifting your TE as shown in figures 6 and 7 also allows you to eliminate or at least control the double coverage on the split end because the defense cannot distinguish which side is weak and which is strong until it is too late. If, for instance, the weak side defensive end chooses to double the split end and declares which side he is going to (as the offense comes out of the huddle) by following the split end, a shift by the TE may leave him doubling the flanker and force him to check back to a normal alignment (figures 10 and 11), or allow the ball to be snapped without a strong side defensive end.

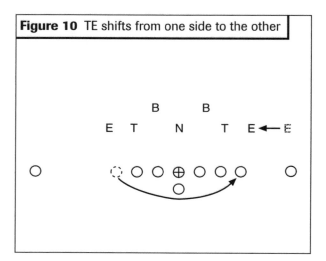

Figure 10 TE shifts from one side to the other

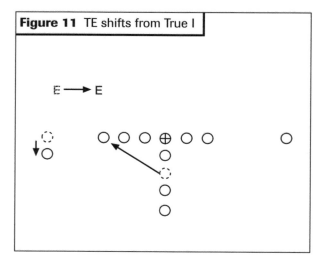

Figure 11 TE shifts from True I

Create Excitement

We can present an exciting style of play for both the fans and the players. We may not do anything different from anyone else after the ball is snapped, but the movement prior to that creates what our fans consider an exciting style of play. This is extremely important in a metroplex area such as Dallas-Fort Worth, where three other major schools and a professional team all compete for the same entertainment dollar.

Players also are motivated by this style of play and find it exciting, challenging, and fun. When executed properly, this offense adds

points on the scoreboard in a hurry. These examples are only a few of the things we do to execute our philosophy of extensive motion, shifting, and multiple sets. In competing for the entertainment dollar, we have adopted the philosophy "Win or lose, look good doing it!" As each situation is different, this style of offense may or may not be best for your program, but it has certainly benefited ours at North Texas State University.

1978 Summer Manual. Hayden Fry was head coach and Bill Snyder was an assistant coach at North Texas State. Snyder is head coach at Kansas State University.

Creating the Pass-Run Bind

George DeLeone

The success of the 1987 Syracuse University football team was based on many factors. Our defensive football team played exceptionally well throughout the season, which certainly helped our offensive players and coaches maintain an aggressive, attacking temperament. However, our 1987 players' unselfishness, practice work ethic, belief in the mental phase, and determination to succeed on game day made the real difference in our program. With those factors as a backdrop, our offense had a legitimate chance to contribute its share to team success.

As our offensive staff set goals prior to the season, three general objectives stood out. To be successful, we had to present a balanced run-pass threat to the defense, give the defense a diversity of offense to defend, and respect the football. Here's a closer look at these objectives.

1. *Present a balanced run-pass threat to the defense.* We did not feel we were strong enough to *just* run or *just* pass, but we knew we could be highly efficient in both areas when the defense could not gang up on one area or the other in each down and distance situation. Our staff also was committed in our practice organization to get both the run and pass game re-

hearsed effectively. Our final rushing and passing statistics for the 1987 season indicated that we had exceeded our goal for balance. In 11 games, we had 2,325 total yards rushing (211 rushing yards per game) and 2,518 total yards passing (229 passing yards per game).

2. *Give the defense a diversity of offense to defend.* Each week in our offensive plan we will have plays selected from each one of these components: option football; play-action passes off the option looks; fullback game off option looks; power game; play-action passes off the power game; dropback passes; and screens and draws. We tried to not allow the defense to tune in to one area without leaving themselves vulnerable to one of our other components.

3. *Respect the football.* This was accomplished with a tremendous emphasis on the practice field and in our offensive meetings by our coaches to the extent that it became a great point of pride among our players. Our 1987 statistics showed this emphasis to be well worth the effort. In 11 games, we were intercepted 11 times in 250 passes attempted. We lost nine fumbles, and of those nine fumbles, only four were lost by running backs. Our season turnover ratio was +11.

Let us now take one segment of our offense and try to illustrate with a specific example how we try to put the defense in a pass-run bind with our option game and pass off our option action.

The freeze option has been the starting point of our option package for the past three years, and in 1987 our three-wideout formation gave us the opportunity to spread the defense and make it defend the entire field. Figure 1 shows the freeze option run to the two-receiver side.

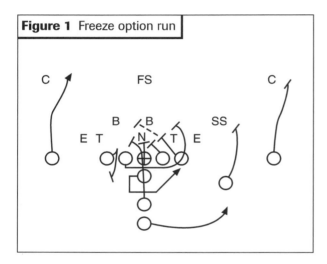

Figure 1 Freeze option run

The first defensive adjustment will be to play a tough brand of SS play. As the SS creeps tighter to attack the stalk block of the inside receiver, we throw the dump pass to place him in a pass-run bind. This play-action pass gives our perimeter blockers a chance to make very difficult stalk blocks because of the pass threat when the QB comes down the line on our option action.

Figure 2 shows our option pass to the two-receiver side (see figure 2). Coaching points:

Z: Run an eight-yard hook over your position.

Y: Get width and run an arc course to the outside number of the SS. Allow the SS to slip inside you, stay wide, and throttle down once you clear the SS. Width is more important than depth. Ball should be caught on the move.

X: Run a 16-yard in route.

Tailback: Freeze on snap until QB's second step hits the ground, then sprint into pitch phase. Be ready to block SS blitz if it comes.

Fullback: Hand at five yards. Run the midline with your pads down and come over the football. Be ready for frontside LB run through.

QB: Step off midline, reach the ball back to FB and ride to your front hip. Come down the line and sell the option. Read the SS. If SS bites on option, throw to TE. If SS hangs on TE, throw to Z on hook. Stay on the LOS.

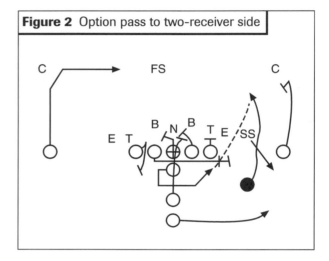

Figure 2 Option pass to two-receiver side

The next way that we will try to attack to make the defense defend the entire width of our three-wide formation is to run the freeze option to the one-receiver side. Note that our single receiver will block the corner whether it is three deep or two deep (see figure 3).

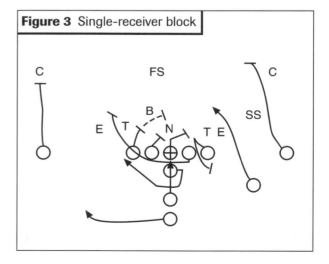

Figure 3 Single-receiver block

The man that we now will try to place in a pass-run bind is the boundary corner. If he is a thorn in our side as a run defender, we must take advantage of his aggressiveness by hitting the play-action pass in behind him to our single receiver (see figure 4). Coaching points:

X: Versus hard corner, run to outside number of corner. Fake a block and slip outside to sideline. Width is much more important than depth. Versus a three-deep cover, run an eight-yard hook over your position.

Y: Eight-yard hook.

Z: Eight-yard hook.

QB: Versus two-deep cover, stay on line and sell option. Make the corner bite with your action; stay with X as long as you can.

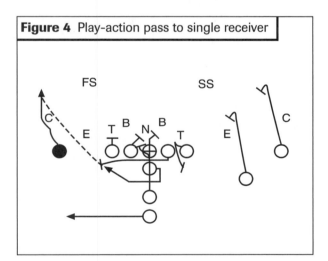

Figure 4 Play-action pass to single receiver

Another option that has been extremely successful for us has been the load option from the I formation. This play has allowed us to option the SS who usually has pitch, which has allowed for some great running opportunities for our QB (see figure 5).

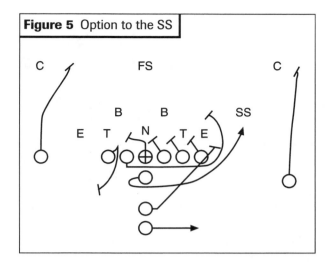

Figure 5 Option to the SS

The defensive adjustment is to realize that another run defender is needed to the load side. This defender often comes from the FS position. We now will try to place the FS in the run-pass bind by running a Z post in behind him off the same load option look (see figure 6).

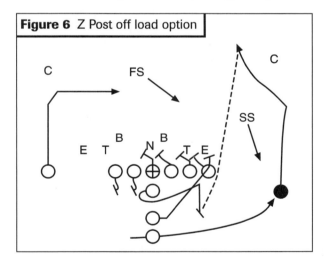

Figure 6 Z Post off load option

Although our offensive staff attempted to put our players in the best possible position to win each and every week, X's and O's were only a small part of our success. The motivation, drive, and performance under fire by our players were our real keys to victory.

1988 Summer Manual. George DeLeone is the offensive coordinator at Syracuse University.

Scoring Through the Double Eagle

Homer Smith

With the stunning success the Chicago Bears had with Buddy Ryan's Double Eagle defense, offensive coaches everywhere will be wise to have game plans ready for it. Chances of the Double Eagle being used to surprise opponents in 1986 are pretty good.

This article came out of a preliminary effort to integrate downhill blocking and receiving assignments into the alignment shown in figure 1. The letters are from our UCLA system in which each kind of defender is given his own letter identification. In the K position, the Bears played a strong safety-type athlete.

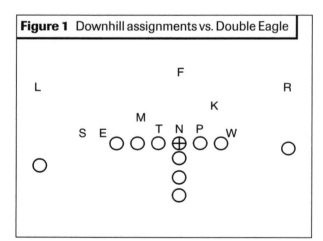

Figure 1 Downhill assignments vs. Double Eagle

The defense has three prominent features:

1. When both backs in a two-back offense start to one side, it is difficult for the back side tackle to block the back side LB. It is almost as difficult for the back side guard and back side tackle to execute a scoop block on the defenders playing over them.

2. In protecting a passer, it is difficult for the offensive guards not to take the man over them and for the center not to be left to block a nose guard by himself. Furthermore, it is extremely difficult for a center to block a noseguard who can rush on either side of him. A pass-protection block is made relatively easy when a blocker can deny a defender a route to the inside, invite him to the outside, and then ride him to the outside knowing that the QB can step forward. A center cannot deny a noseguard one route in the same way, and a dropback passer cannot step forward to help the center when the defender does get past him. In other words, there is no outside rush route to invite a rusher into if you are a center and your passer is dropping back.

3. The W, K, M, E, and S are all linebacker-type athletes. Working together, the M, E, and S can make it difficult for pass blockers because most of the time just one rushes. However, it is difficult to assign one blocker to the one who rushes when any one of the three may be that one.

It is also difficult to double-read when three rushers are working together. A double-read by an offensive lineman and a back on a defensive lineman and a LB normally tells both attackers to watch the LB so the lineman can block the defensive lineman when the LB drops into the pass defense. Obviously, this is difficult when three defenders take turns being rushers and droppers.

Running

Plays that have both backs going to the same side usually encounter an unblocked back side LB. Figure 2 shows the scoop blocks that would be required to get full-flow plays started.

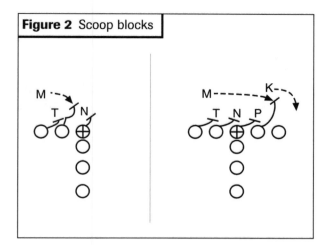

Figure 2 Scoop blocks

Scoops are gettable when defenders are playing into gaps. They are difficult when a defensive lineman hits directly into an offensive lineman. This defense seems to feature a technique that makes it difficult for a back side offensive tackle and guard to scoop the back side defensive tackle and LB.

By presenting a constant naked-bootleg threat, it might be possible to pull the outside split end-side defender upfield with a naked fake and get a cut-back play outside of the back side tackle and guard. Figure 3 shows the blocking for both FB and TB plays. Good technique and discipline in the bootleg faking is the key to these plays.

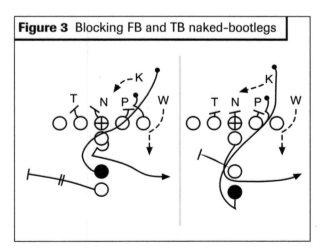

Figure 3 Blocking FB and TB naked-bootlegs

The sprint draw play works well when the fullback can block to the side of the initial fake and the tailback can run all the way back to the other side on a backward scoop block. Figure 4

shows the back side tackle and guard attempting to entice defenders upfield to the outside, while the center and onside guard and tackle execute the backward scoop block to get the tailback a running lane over the center.

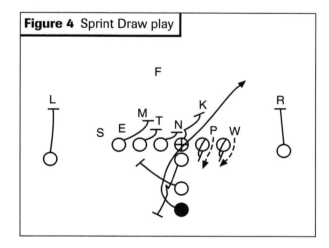

Figure 4 Sprint Draw play

This is uphill football, but there does not seem to be another good way to execute a sprint draw against the defense. The standard counter sweep, with a guard and tackle leading a tailback away from the direction of an initial fake, is not a good play because it is difficult to block the back side LB. Figure 5 shows the fullback attempting to get through on the LB.

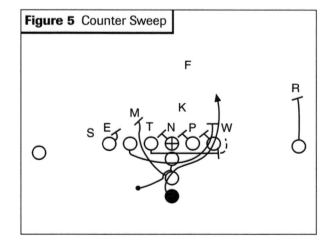

Figure 5 Counter Sweep

The play that would get everyone blocked would be an off-tackle-type play run with counter action. Figure 6 shows the tailback and fullback starting to one side, then curling back to the other side. The idea is that the initial action of the play would make it possible for the back side offensive tackle to block the back side LB. This is an unconventional play, but it should nail the defense. Getting enough counter action to give the back side tackle a downhill block on the back side linebacker is everything in running against the Double Eagle.

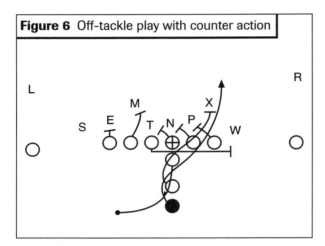

Figure 6 Off-tackle play with counter action

Veer option coaches would say that the counter dive and counter option (figure 7) should work well. The idea is that the counter action should give the back side tackle a chance to get the LB. The problem is in running the basic veer option to set up the counter option. The presence of the SS on the LOS makes the basic option very difficult.

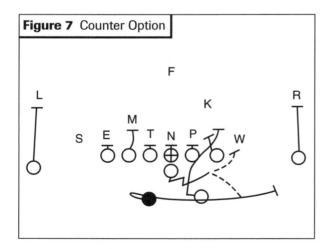

Figure 7 Counter Option

The Bears run a straight dive play in their offense. One wonders if they do it in an effort to defeat their own defense. A quick dive makes it difficult for the back side LB to get to the point of attack in time. A play we call the SMU option seems to have a chance. Figure 8 shows the tackle bouncing up to get the back side LB, while the back side tackle attempts to get the middle safety. Blocks by the split end and fullback are gettable, and the end man on the line should be optionable. If F is assigned to tackle on the LOS against an option, the split end can push the cornerback back and then block F.

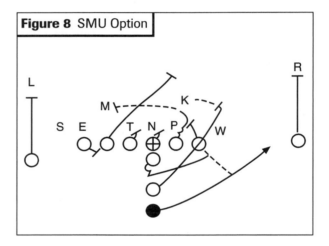

Figure 8 SMU Option

Conventional trap plays have the trapper moving in the direction of the fake. Figure 9a shows this conventional blocking with the onside LB unblocked. If the onside LB takes the fake of a trap option, the play could work. The problem is that the trap option is not practical because of the presence of the SS on the LOS. A backward trap play is a possibility, however. Imagine the outside lineman on the split end side going unblocked with a trap play away from the fake by the QB and tailback. With the design shown in figure 9b, it should be possible for the back side tackle to get the back side LB, who has two backs faking in his direction. The problem, though, is to get a viable option play to go with the fullback trap.

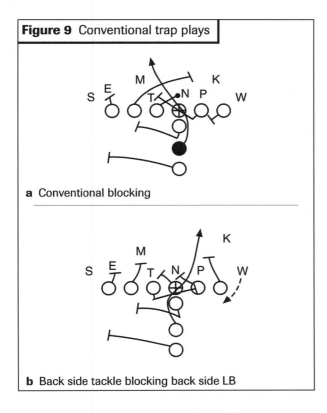

Figure 9 Conventional trap plays

a Conventional blocking

b Back side tackle blocking back side LB

Protecting the Pass

Five defenders rush a dropback passer. The problem is that it is difficult to get the five linemen on the five rushers. If the center is going to have help on the middle guard, one of the tackles has to be assigned to a LB or to the inside. This means that one of the receivers must be assigned to one of the outside rushers, leaving six pass defenders against four receivers.

This pass defender/receiver ratio is highly important. If there are six pass defenders against four receivers, the pass defense has a 33 percent advantage over a pass pattern. If there are seven against five, it has only a 28 percent advantage. The defense would like to tie up two receivers and be able to play five against three, where it would have a 40 percent advantage.

One of the ways to protect a dropback passer is to assign one tackle to a LB and tell him to help to the inside if the LB does not come. This gets four linemen on three most of the time.

A back is left on the two outside defenders on the tight end side, and the ball must be thrown "hot" if both of them rush. Again, one of the features of the defense is that any one or two of the three tight end-side LBs can rush. There can never be great forward passing with the protection. The pass defender/receiver ratio is not good, and the tight end, who must be the "hot" receiver, can be covered by the remaining LB.

If possible, employ double-reading. The problem is to do it with two pass blockers against three defenders. If the TE splits so one defender has to go with him, a double-read can be executed.

Though not easy, the tackle can block the LB if he rushes and the outside defender if he does not. By double-reading, the offense makes it difficult for the defense to tie up one of the receivers with just one of two LBs (e.g., K or W). Figure 10 shows K rushing, W dropping, and the backfield receiver releasing. If K had dropped and W had rushed, the tackle would have blocked W. At best, however, dropback passing has proved to be very difficult against this defense.

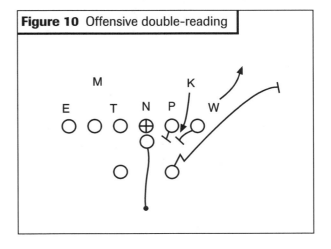

Figure 10 Offensive double-reading

When the passer moves to one side, the center, onside guard, and onside tackle can block down on the three interior defenders. They can deny the rushers any onside escape. If the passer moves to the outside in the same way that he steps forward after dropping back, the blocks are "downhill." The problem is to apply the other blockers so these angle advantages can be enjoyed.

Figure 11 shows a strong formation in which both backs can participate in a double-read on the three potential rushers (M, E, and S) even though the passer moves. The FB can block M but adjust to block E if M does not rush. The TB can block E but adjust to S if M does not rush. Either can proceed into the pattern if his secondary target does not rush. Although this protection does nothing to get five receivers into a pattern, it does get blocking angles on T, N, and P.

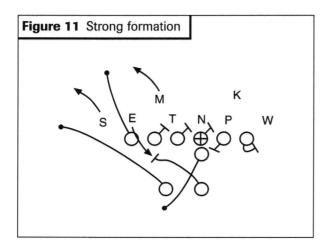

Figure 11 Strong formation

The principle in this protection can be used with play-action passes. In figure 12, all eight of the potential rushers are accounted for. The TE releases if either E or S drops. The FB is assigned to the end and the TB to the LB. One of the backs almost always has to take a rusher.

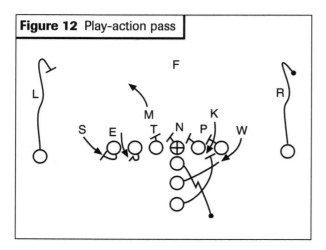

Figure 12 Play-action pass

The only way to get five receivers against this defense is to throw an onside screen pass to the back, who must always block one of the five rushers. Making the screen receiver a viable threat puts five receivers against six defensive backs, making the advantage of pass defenders over receivers just 17 percent. Figure 13 shows a dropback pass from a formation with a TE split. If the TB is in a double-read on the right side and the FB is a viable screen threat on the left, the defense must defend against five receivers.

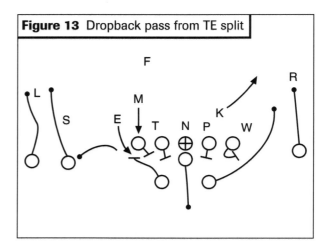

Figure 13 Dropback pass from TE split

Mouse Davis, the leading advocate of the run-and-shoot, has perfected a way to get a blocker on any defender covering a screen receiver man-for-man. The screen is very important in getting the ratio of pass defenders to receivers back to where it favors the offense.

Varying Formations

Next, can formation variations put the defense in awkward positions? The defense was pioneered over pro hash marks, which leave a six-yard swatch in the middle in which to start plays. Is the defense a different threat in high school and college?

If it were not for the defender outside the TE, the defense could not hold up against a conventional off-tackle play. Figure 14 shows a formation with a flankerback into a sideline against a Double Eagle with no man outside the TE. The off-tackle play would split the defenders and hit a void.

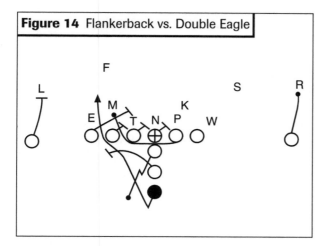

Figure 14 Flankerback vs. Double Eagle

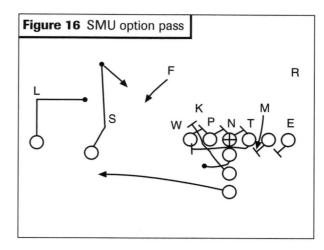

Figure 16 SMU option pass

With the same formation against the Double Eagle played with S outside the TE, there is a vulnerability to the wide side against the option shown in figure 8 (page 34) and the pass in figure 12. Bringing the receiver on the single-receiver side into a tight position does nothing to the defense. While there is not a defender on the LOS outside the TE, there is a defender five or six yards off the line and watching the TE (figure 15).

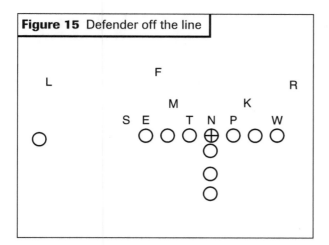

Figure 15 Defender off the line

Spreading two receivers to the wide side of the field simplifies the pass protection and opens the way for an SMU option. In a dropback pass play, a double-read can be executed on the strong side because S is removed. Figure 16 shows an SMU option pass. The assumption is that F can be kept off the LOS by the threat of the slot back slipping by S and going deep.

A formation with three speed receivers, no TE, and two running backs simplifies only the pass protection. The LBs can still cross the centerline on flow, and the threat of the noseguard rushing can still force one of the pass receivers to block one of the five rushers. A formation with two spread and two tight receivers leaves all seven of the linemen covered and an unblocked tackler behind them (figure 17). If the cornerbacks can hold up in single coverage, it is almost impossible to run the ball with eight tacklers playing over seven blockers. M and K do not have to cross the centerline to tackle. S is unblocked.

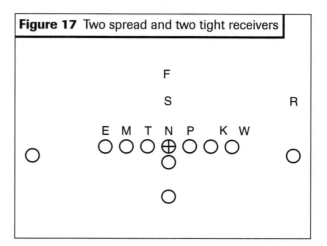

Figure 17 Two spread and two tight receivers

Walking a TE from one side to the other only invites the defense to walk one of its men. Motion by a flankerback that changes formation strength might make it difficult for the defense to coordinate assignments among the three LBs who play on the two-receiver side, but it does nothing to affect the threats of the LBs crossing the centerline and the noseguard giving the center an "uphill" pass-protection assignment. Figure 18 shows change-of-strength motion.

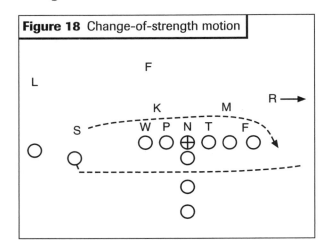

Figure 18 Change-of-strength motion

Conclusion

A bigger problem than finding plays for the basic form of this Double Eagle defense is finding them for the variations of it. The defensive planner uses that basic alignment as a "base" from which to launch all kinds of forays into other designs. The total problem is horrendous.

Through football history, defensive coaches have tried to position their players so that blocking is more difficult than shedding blockers. Offensive coaches have always caught up with them and kept the ball moving to new yardage records. At the moment, however, if only in the NFL, this defense has shut down offenses that had comparable talent and plenty of time to practice. Most offensive coaches can defeat defenses as long as they have the chalk, but this defense seems to hold its own on the chalkboard without a defensive coach in the room.

1986 Summer Manual. Homer Smith was the offensive coordinator at UCLA. Smith is offensive coordinator at the University of Arizona.

Passing to Set Up the Run

Al Molde and Marty Higgins

Experience is a great teacher and unquestionably has helped me shape my coaching philosophy. A philosophy is very important to recruiting, handling players, coaches, and the public, and your football system. All philosophies must blend together into a coaching philosophy.

Our football system philosophy has three priorities, and they are certainly not unique to us! However, we believe strongly in their order, and they provide the structure and guidelines necessary for the development of our program.

1. *Play solid, aggressive defense.* This is our highest priority. It sets up our program. With few exceptions, we try to recruit players who can play defense first. Unquestionably, you win championships by playing great defense.

2. *Have excellent special teams.* Special teams provide opportunities to make game-breaking plays. We assign importance to their function in several ways. First, we have a coordinator for special teams. Second, we assign practice time daily to achieve excellent play. Last, we aren't afraid to use our top players on these teams.

3. *Use a "ball control" pass offense.* We want an offense that can generate first downs, control the clock, produce points, and provide big play capabilities.

As in any philosophy, changes have occurred from time to time, but for many years now, the basic principle of "pass to run" has remained unchanged. We go into every game attacking the defense with a variety of passing schemes and look for run opportunities as the game progresses.

Most of our running success results from QB checks at the LOS. We use the pass to set up the run. It doesn't matter too much how you get up and down the field; the bottom line is always whether you do or not. Experience, though, has taught me that it is very important to have an offense that can generate first downs, thereby controlling the clock. Throwing the ball to move in a hurry to score points is great, but I've come to learn that it isn't enough.

To use an analogy, first downs are just like putting money in a savings account. Consider that every time you generate a first down, two things happen: you gain another piece of the game clock by keeping the ball, and it puts you closer to a potential score. If you generate (i.e., "save") enough first downs, you'll usually win, which in turn will provide job and financial security! Therefore, it's very important to have an offense that can generate first downs, not just points. Unfortunately, many coaches still believe that there is only *one* way to have an offense that can generate first downs consistently: run the ball first. Throw only when forced, because as the old adage says, "Three things can happen and two of them are bad."

Times have changed and the game has changed, too. It has been my experience, and it is my belief, that a ball-control offense can be set up with the pass just as effectively as with the run. In support of my position, consider the following statistics for 1988 attributable to our pass offense:

- 22 first downs/game average
- 76 plays/game average
- Four-minute possession time advantage/ game
- 410 total yards/game average (260 pass/ 150 run)
- 30 points/game average

These statistics are for a team that, more than once, has been referred to as "pass happy." In reality, we threw the ball 48 percent of the time and ran it 52 percent. These statistics easily could be those of a traditional run-oriented team. It's important to note, also, that they are not unique to this year's team, but instead follow a pattern that we have developed over the past several years. Correctly stated, we are a ball-control passing team.

The basic philosophical principles behind the operation of this offense follow:

- Use the dropback pass as the base of the offense (3-, 5-, 7-step).
- Use the screen and draw to counter defensive rush.
- Limit the number and sophistication of run plays.
- Follow basic rules to cover alignments and formation strengths according to field position.
- Use personnel and formation changes situationally.
- Use a signal play-calling system.
- Use possession pass schemes, one-on-one isolations as the most common strategy; deep throws taken when defensive alignment most vulnerable.
- Look for run balance during games, often via checks.

Advantages and Disadvantages

The following are significant advantages of this type of offensive system:

1. Recruiting. You can utilize the skills of more player types. Also, offense attracts speed (receivers, backs, etc.) and it's easier for linemen to play in this offense.

2. Practice. Depth problems are minimized. Offense allows practice with intensity for longer time periods with less risk of injury.

3. Offense creates defensive problems: formation spread forces defense to cover whole field; isolates defenders in one-on-one situations via four quick receivers; horizontal stretch makes "reading" coverages easier.

4. Offense blends with well "two-minute" philosophy.

5. Offense has spectator appeal.

Some possible disadvantages are that it is more difficult to maintain pass/run balance and it is not a good goal line/short-yardage offense.

Formations and Alignments

Over the past few years, we have probably seen all conceivable fronts, coverages, and blitz packages that have been devised to throw off protections and pass routes. With this in mind, we feel we have developed a very sound approach to the one-back offense.

We feel that whatever coverage the defense shows, we are able to adjust our routes. We have a high-percentage route into any given coverage. The routes shown in the following figures are drawn up versus cover two and cover three. I have done this to give you some examples of the route adjustments we make against different coverages.

Middle-of-Field Alignment

Figures 1 and 2 show our middle-of-field alignment versus cover two and cover three.

Hash Alignment

Figures 3 and 4 show our hash alignments against cover two and cover three.

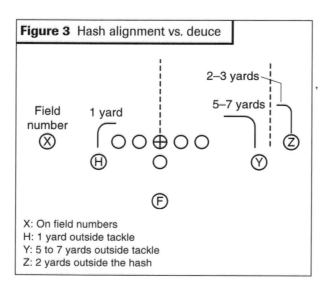

Figure 1 Middle-of-field alignment vs. deuce

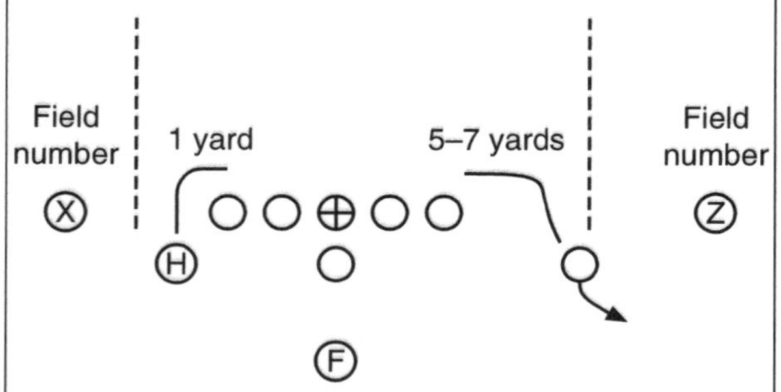

WR: On field numbers
H: 1 yard outside tackle
Y: 5 to 7 yards from tackle

Figure 2 Middle-of-field alignment vs. ace

WR: On field numbers
H: 1 yard outside tackle
Y: 5 to 7 yards outside tackle

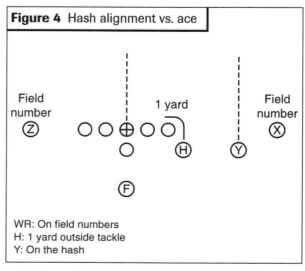

Figure 3 Hash alignment vs. deuce

X: On field numbers
H: 1 yard outside tackle
Y: 5 to 7 yards outside tackle
Z: 2 yards outside the hash

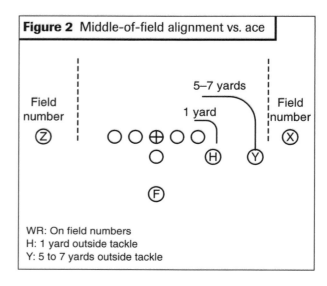

Figure 4 Hash alignment vs. ace

WR: On field numbers
H: 1 yard outside tackle
Y: On the hash

Three-Step Drop

When we use our quick game, we expect a completion. We want a first down or very short yardage on the next down. Usually on a quick out, we gain seven yards; on the post or fade, about 10-12 yards. While the post and fade are not as high a percentage as the out, they are most likely to produce a big gain. Figures 5, 6, and 7 show three-step drop plays against the deuce.

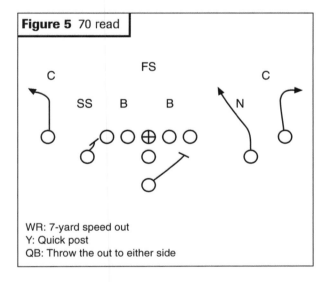

Figure 5 70 read

WR: 7-yard speed out
Y: Quick post
QB: Throw the out to either side

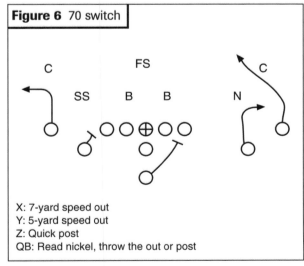

Figure 6 70 switch

X: 7-yard speed out
Y: 5-yard speed out
Z: Quick post
QB: Read nickel, throw the out or post

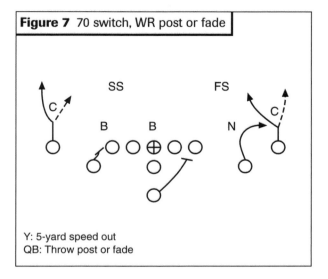

Figure 7 70 switch, WR post or fade

Y: 5-yard speed out
QB: Throw post or fade

Five-Step Drop

In zone situations, we have five receivers out on pass patterns. This allows us to stretch the coverage, maximize seams, and adjust our routes downfield to take advantage of the coverage.

In blitz situations, we may have as few as three receivers in the pass route. In man coverage, the receivers must get open fast; they need to change directions quickly and run precise patterns to shake the defender. Figures 8-12 show five-step drop plays against ace and deuce formations.

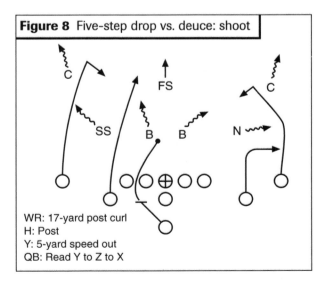

Figure 8 Five-step drop vs. deuce: shoot

WR: 17-yard post curl
H: Post
Y: 5-yard speed out
QB: Read Y to Z to X

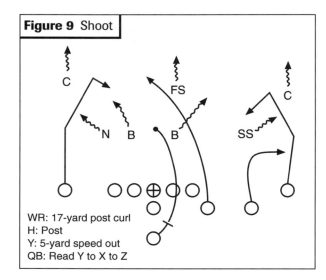

Figure 9 Shoot

WR: 17-yard post curl
H: Post
Y: 5-yard speed out
QB: Read Y to X to Z

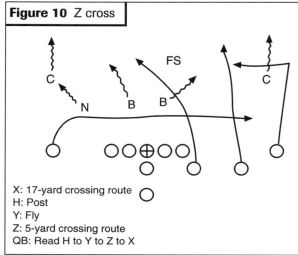

Figure 10 Z cross

X: 17-yard crossing route
H: Post
Y: Fly
Z: 5-yard crossing route
QB: Read H to Y to Z to X

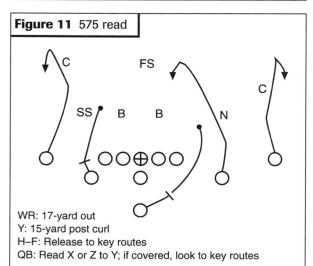

Figure 11 575 read

WR: 17-yard out
Y: 15-yard post curl
H–F: Release to key routes
QB: Read X or Z to Y; if covered, look to key routes

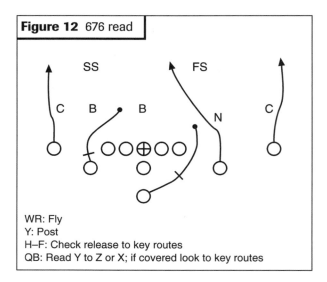

Figure 12 676 read

WR: Fly
Y: Post
H–F: Check release to key routes
QB: Read Y to Z or X; if covered look to key routes

Run

We limit our running game to basic plays incorporated into our audible system, allowing the QB to take advantage of weaknesses resulting from the defense's concern in defending the pass. The plays we have the most success with are the draw (figure 13), pitch (figure 14), and counter sweep (figure 15).

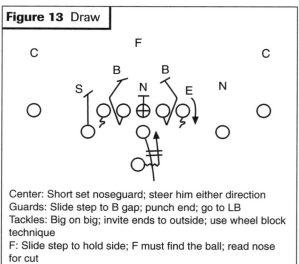

Figure 13 Draw

Center: Short set noseguard; steer him either direction
Guards: Slide step to B gap; punch end; go to LB
Tackles: Big on big; invite ends to outside; use wheel block technique
F: Slide step to hold side; F must find the ball; read nose for cut
QB: Use normal drop technique; don't raise up ball; hand off ball on third step

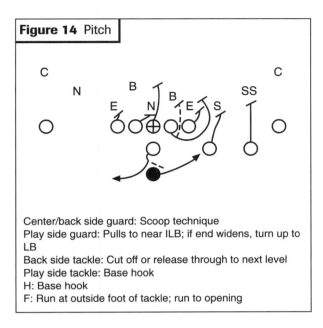

Figure 14 Pitch

Center/back side guard: Scoop technique
Play side guard: Pulls to near ILB; if end widens, turn up to LB
Back side tackle: Cut off or release through to next level
Play side tackle: Base hook
H: Base hook
F: Run at outside foot of tackle; run to opening

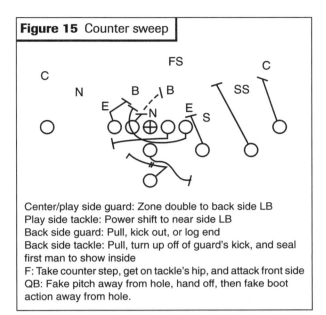

Figure 15 Counter sweep

Center/play side guard: Zone double to back side LB
Play side tackle: Power shift to near side LB
Back side guard: Pull, kick out, or log end
Back side tackle: Pull, turn up off of guard's kick, and seal first man to show inside
F: Take counter step, get on tackle's hip, and attack front side
QB: Fake pitch away from hole, hand off, then fake boot action away from hole.

1989 Proceedings. Al Molde was head coach and Marty Higgins was an assistant coach at Western Michigan University.

Running to Pass

Ted Tollner

We decided two years ago when putting together our present staff that we wanted to continue throwing the football at San Diego State. The question was what to do for a running attack and how to best combine it with an efficient and productive passing attack.

Many people feel that trying to run an option attack with play action and dropback pass is too much. We felt this would be true only if we tried to make all the reads that pure veer option teams make. We have eliminated most of the reads and have cut down the number of running plays in our attack so that we have enough time to work on developing the passing game.

The basic part of our running attack is simple but is enough to simplify and control the secondary coverages we see. This is probably the biggest reason we are using the option offense. It makes the passing game more efficient because of less variety in coverages that we must work on. We are a pass-oriented team and therefore feel that we must have a simple, unsophisticated option running attack if we are going to execute with any efficiency. We are presently running the dive, cutback dive, dive option, counter, and counter option as our "optionlook" attack (figure 1).

We must be able to execute these running plays well enough to make our opponents defend with a sound structure. We hope, by doing this, to limit the variety of coverages and make it easier for the quarterback to recognize the coverage. Last year, we played against predominantly a 50 front with five basic secondary

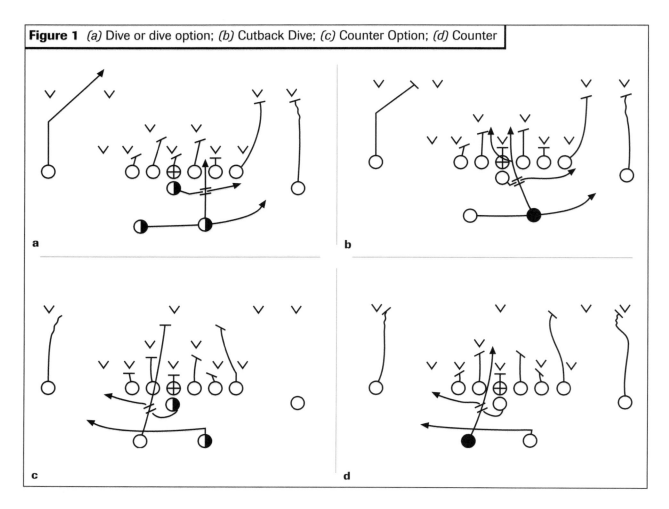

Figure 1 *(a)* Dive or dive option; *(b)* Cutback Dive; *(c)* Counter Option; *(d)* Counter

coverages: strong zone with corner force; strong zone with safety force—QB or pitch; man with free safety; two-deep zone; and two-deep man (figure 2).

Assuming we have controlled secondary coverages to some degree, we will now discuss the play-action passes we use and how we determine specific routes. A certain amount of guesswork is involved, but we do follow a sequence based on what the defense is doing and has done in prior games. We use the basic fake dive-dump pass to the TE as a starting point (figure 3).

We have a good percentage receiver against most coverages. We adjust when we determine what the defense is doing. We make every attempt to get the ball to the TE (figure 4), the initial primary receiver. The TE takes an out-

side release and looks for the ball as he turns upfield. The TE should not bend inside toward the inside LB but should maintain width while attempting to get inside the SS. If by eight yards the ball is not thrown, he turns outside to the sideline at a 45-degree angle. We flex the TE as an adjustment if the defense is pinching the tackle and scraping the inside backer to help in TE dump. This flex also creates a greater distance for the FS to cover.

The flanker should cut down his split to encourage corner force. He runs a takeoff or streak pattern with an outside release off the line to stretch the field as wide as possible. The split end runs a post pattern to set up the throwback pass. We have a variety of individual patterns to the split end that will have predetermined calls.

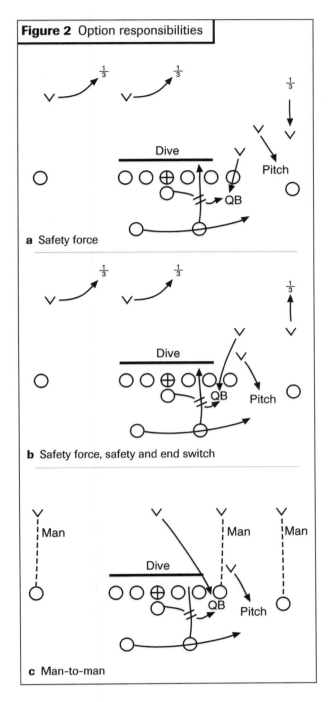

Figure 2 Option responsibilities

a Safety force

b Safety force, safety and end switch

c Man-to-man

The quarterback has a four-phase technique on the play:

1. He opens out to FB at a slight angle backward for two steps. He makes a good ride fake to FB to hold the LB.

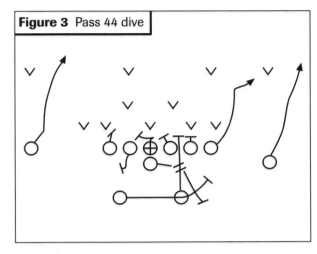

Figure 3 Pass 44 dive

2. He resets his right foot and hits the TE, if open.

3. If the TE's not open, he resets three steps and throws a streak pass to the flanker.

4. If the flanker is not open, he throws to the TE turning out to the sideline or out of bounds if the TE is not open.

Another strong side combination we like off the same play fake is good when the strong safety has run support but hangs and commits late (figure 5). He can take the dump pass away by hanging. The corner is loose playing the deep third.

We throw off the SS. Usually, he is too late to help on the out pattern by the flanker. If the safety runs hard to the out after hanging on the dump, we throw behind the seam to the TE. The linebackers are not a factor because of their initial commitment to the run. The QB will fake to the FB and hit a quick dump to the TE. If the TE is not open, the QB resets three steps and keys the strong safety.

We have one other strong side combination (figure 6).

We look for two secondary adjustments to make this pass successful. Many teams run the FS on a hard flat angle to the TE, attempting to take away the dump pass. The TE bursts hard upfield to the post. Some teams with SS support run the safety hard in the out pattern,

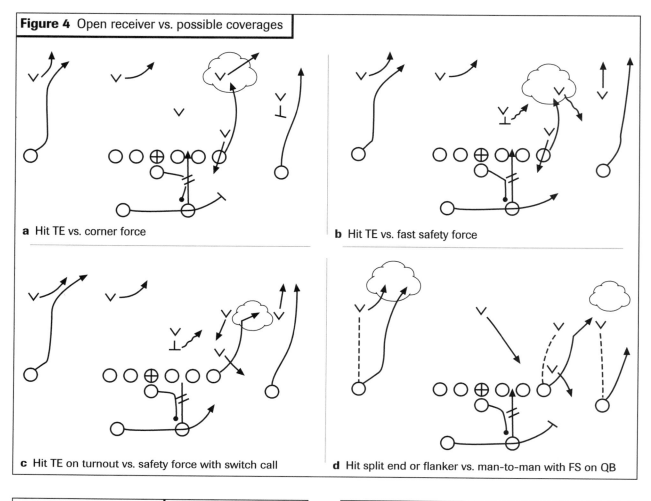

Figure 4 Open receiver vs. possible coverages

a Hit TE vs. corner force

b Hit TE vs. fast safety force

c Hit TE on turnout vs. safety force with switch call

d Hit split end or flanker vs. man-to-man with FS on QB

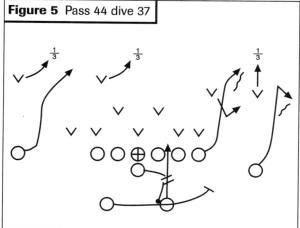

Figure 5 Pass 44 dive 37

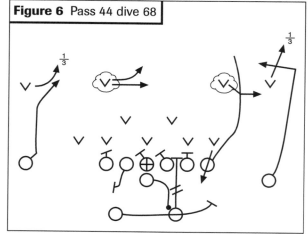

Figure 6 Pass 44 dive 68

recognizing the play fake. We then change the flanker's pattern to a 15-yard curl behind the safety.

The QB's continuity is (1) a good fake to the FB, (2) a look to the TE as on the dump pass reset and a throw to the TE on post if the FS has taken a poor angle, and (3) if the FS covers the TE, a throw to the flanker on a deep curl behind the SS. Again, LBs are not a key factor if you run the ball well enough for them to respect play action.

The next step in this sequence is using the split end on a variety of individual throwback patterns. Defenses involve the FS in strong side run and pass responsibilities if we execute some of the previously mentioned plays. This gives us a one-on-one situation with the corner and split end. The pattern we use depends on the technique and position of the weak side corner. Sometimes the weak side end is also a factor in pattern selection. We usually throw the quick post first if the corner does not come inside to take it away. From the quick post, we adjust to the other patterns.

We also have a crossing or drag pattern to the TE that is most effective against some teams (figure 7). If a defense elects to rush the back side end, there is a big hole for the TE to work into once he clears the weak inside linebacker. We have the TE release inside and get depth beyond the inside backers before crossing the field. The ball is normally about 15 yards deep. The QB will make a good dive fake to the FB and reset five steps. He looks to the split end running a post seam pattern first. If he's not open, the QB hits the TE on his drag route.

Figure 8 Quick screen to SE off dive option fake

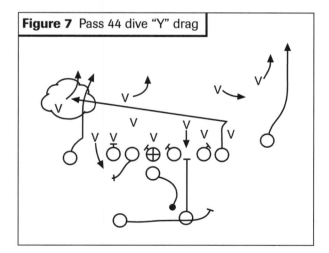

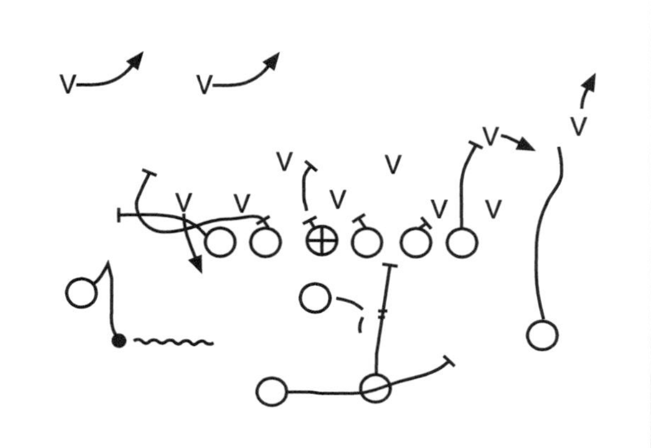

The quick screen to the split end also integrates very nicely into the same action (figure 8). Many people play the weak corner loose, knowing that he is one-on-one with our split end on play action strong. The QB makes a quick fake to FB, sets, and throws. The split end takes two fast steps upfield, pivots, and comes back toward the QB. The tackle releases on the corner, and the guard blocks the first color inside the corner.

This basically is how we try to integrate the strong side dive-dive option run with a series of play-action passes. We do the same basic things from the counter-counter option look. We also found that the same action is excellent from a variety of other formations.

Figure 7 Pass 44 dive "Y" drag

1975 Summer Manual. Ted Tollner was an assistant coach at San Jose State University. Tollner is head coach at San Diego State University.

PART II

The Running Game

Part II—The Running Game

Drilling for Error-Free Execution

Homer Rice

The ultimate objective of an offensive drive is to score. This can be accomplished only by eliminating individual mistakes. Eliminating individual mistakes is the surest way to keep the offensive drive moving and eventually score. We stop ourselves in various ways: bad call by the QB, missed assignment, missed block, fumble, penalty, interception. One mistake will break a drive and often result in poor field position. It is almost impossible to win the tough game without maintaining adequate field position.

We spend many hours training QBs to select intelligently the best play for the situation. QBs have many training aids available—the down and distance charts, the vertical and horizontal zones, press box advice, and other situation tendencies. Even if he has made the best selection possible, the defense may not be what he expected when he arrives at the LOS. To prevent a bad play, he must be able to check and take advantage of the defensive alignment.

Even when the QB makes the best call, the play must have simplicity to avoid missed assignments. If a player knows who to block, he can then learn how to block. The unforgivable interception and the lost fumble not only stop a drive but also turn the ball over to the opponent.

Drills to Develop Skill and Discipline

We must have simplicity, consistency, and ball control to develop an adequate offense. We obtain these by repeating execution, adhering to assignments, and giving the individual the tools to excel. Therefore, it is imperative to drill the individual to precision. By repetition, we are striving for the day when the player will react involuntarily to all situations. By doing things habitually or naturally, he can start concentrating on his ultimate assignment.

The offensive back is an intriguing figure in any attack. He must have speed, quickness, and toughness and always be in shape to sprint. He is called on to block, carry the ball, tackle, receive and throw passes, and sometimes to make the big play. Even if this play was not blocked very well, he always tries to slash through at the point of attack as a ballcarrier, rip over a LB, twist away from an upcoming secondary defender, and outrace the defensive pursuit for six points.

The big play may not occur many times in one season, but I firmly believe that we must practice it anyhow. We must give our offensive backs the tools of the trade. They must believe that every time they line up and are called upon to carry the ball, they are potential scorers.

Although we are running to score, we must face reality. The minimum distance a back should gain is four yards. Our backs must be sold on this four-yard theory. It is the "bread and butter" of our offense. Consistency of this rule will move the ball and keep the offense in gear.

Gaining maximum performance from our backs and adhering to the four yards or more perspective is vital in our preparation. A daily ritual is necessary to check points, statistics, and accomplishments, and gain an attitude of improvement. A player should report to daily practice striving to be better when he leaves. With this attitude, he has a chance to achieve greatness.

Working under Charlie Bradshaw at the University of Kentucky, I set up the offensive backfield drills we believed vital to our ultimate goal. I called them our "bread-and-butter drills." Each drill begins with alignment and stance progressing beyond a scoring line. I studied many films to find out what happens to a ballcarrier en route to the goal line. Through intensive study of films and the methods of other coaches, we develop our drill program.

Each drill begins with alignment and stance. Without linemen properly spaced, it is sometimes difficult to line up perspectivewise. Without correct alignment, it is impossible to work on timing. To ensure correct line up, we have devised our own LOS: a fire hose with numbers painted at correct intervals to designate each offensive lineman. The fire hose is easy to handle and can be rolled up and put away after the drill. It is also convenient to move from spot to spot. Another must for alignment is to line off the field with five-yard markings for at least twenty yards. This is important so that the deep backs can judge their depth.

The stance is always given a quick glance, which is important for many reasons. First of all, the back must have a good stance to move quickly straight ahead, left, and right. He must do this without raising up. A stance that permits a back to raise up slows him down, preventing a good takeoff, and causes him to block too high and prevent the quick burst of speed necessary to explode through the point of attack. These are the check points of a good stance:

- Feet: toe-instep alignment pointing straight downfield wide as shoulders; back cleats of up foot touch the ground
- Ankles: good bend, flexible
- Knees bent forward over the toes and slightly inside of the feet
- Hips closed to insure balance
- Back level
- Head up only 45 degrees with neck relaxed
- Eyes forward

- Down hand vertical and slightly inside of the back foot with fingers bridged
- Up arm cupped around front of knee in ready position

To move forward properly, the weight rolls forward over the up foot, preventing the long step of the back foot. The weight precedes the feet; the feet follow. To move left or right, the player snaps his eyes in that direction, mentally shifting the weight to the opposite foot. Almost simultaneously the weight is released in the direction of the desired path. The eyes can and will control the body actions.

When a back cannot control his stance and begins to lean or tip in the direction he is going, a type of four-point stance can be used. We extend the up arm down into a sprinter's technique (thumb inward, fingers out) with the elbow pressing inside the kneecap. This position will lock the stance and prevent leaning, helping the back make a good takeoff in any direction.

Another necessity for each drill is to have a center for your QB exchange. It is senseless to expect timing to develop unless each play starts with a snap. When the varsity center reports, I always put someone on his nose, in a gap, or retreated as a LB, so the center also may gain aptitude.

Figure 1 shows the area necessary to incorporate the bread-and-butter drills. The area distance is 20 yards in both length and width, two-thirds the width of the football field. We measure by one boundary line and two hash

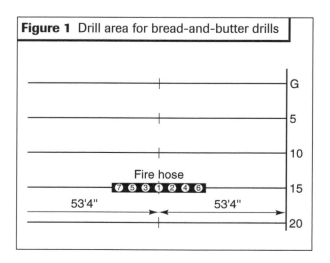

Figure 1 Drill area for bread-and-butter drills

marks. The hose (LOS) is always placed 15 yards from the goal line. In each play, our ballcarrier or faking ballcarrier must sprint the required 15 yards to the goal.

Gauntlet Drill

The first drill is the gauntlet (figure 2). Each drill begins with this setup. The coach calls the formation and play. A manager slides the fire hose with the point-of-attack number in line with the gauntlet lane. The center and backs break the huddle and report to the line.

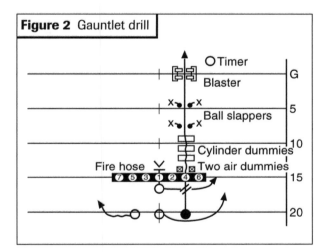

Figure 2 Gauntlet drill

For simplicity in explanation, let us assume the play is a straight handoff to the right halfback and that number four is the point of attack. We place two players at this spot; normally, I alternate my QBs. They set in a football position, shoulder to shoulder with two air dummies straddling the four lane directly on the hose. Three yards away, toward the goal line, three large cylinder dummies are placed horizontally and spaced one yard apart. Next, four players serve as the gauntlet. At the end of the 15 yards from the LOS is a blaster machine.

The play begins with the center-to-quarterback exchange. This is the first checkpoint. Emphasize a smooth snap and proper cadence and takeoff. The center blocks as the QB moves away. We stress that QBs turn their heads in the direction they are going, pocket the ball, and step. Look-pocket-step is a progressive method, eventually smoothing out all three segments simultaneously.

On the snap, the backfield starts with real emphasis on the ballcarrier. Check the stance, the start, the pocket the ballcarrier makes for the ball, and that his eyes are looking in the direction in which he is supposed to run. A correct start will give him a quick burst of speed. He must not raise up, adhering to the short-first-step principle.

The pocket is made by raising the inside elbow with the thumb down, palm out. This prevents the elbow sagging in the line of the handoff. The outside hand is placed in the crease of the outside hip, fingers spread. The ballcarrier's eyes must stare toward the point of attack and not at the ball.

At the handoff spot, we emphatically tell our QBs to "look" the ball into the pocket. The ball starts in with two hands and finishes with one hand as the hands are brought back to the pocket. The ballcarrier takes the handoff with the top hand covering one end of the ball and the bottom hand sliding underneath, covering the other end. Both hands remain on the ball.

After the handoff, the back is ready to break through the two dummies. If his shoulders are higher than the dummy holders, they will close up and not let him through. Soon he understands that he must run with weight forward, body leaning, and shoulders lower than the two tacklers. His forehead spears through the crack as his shoulders spread the lane. His legs pump like pistons to accomplish a smooth break. When a ballcarrier does not break through smoothly, we say, "You're standing at attention." This is our way of saying, "Go back and repeat."

After the breakthrough, a mental test takes place. If the carrier is only thinking of the LOS breakthrough, he will fall down as he crosses the point of attack. This is exactly what happens to a back in live combat. Many times he is not tackled, just bumped; yet he assumes he is being tackled and falls down. If he is mentally thinking of scoring and going all the way through the gauntlet, he will do all the requirements necessary to score.

To remind our backs of this necessity, we place the three cylinder dummies next in line. To get over them, he must pick up his feet. His head must come up, or after the breakthrough he will look silly tripping and falling on the ground in front of his teammates. Another important item at the point-of-attack breakthrough is teaching the ballcarrier that he must hit the small crack with his shoulders square. This will not only assure him of ample force to split the two defenders but position him for cutbacks later on.

After the back clears the three cylinder dummies, four teammates begin slapping the ball. The first two strike from underneath while the next two swing their fists downward. The back must have two hands on the ball or he will fumble. In fact, we expect him to keep both hands on the ball throughout the entire drill. Only when he breaks into the open, do we allow him to use one hand and then the ball must be cradled in the outside arm.

Carrying the football correctly is characteristic of a great back. We teach the cross-arm method. The ball is carried across the body, scraping the rib cage. The elbow is clapped tightly over one end, and the fingers completely cover the front end. As the back runs, the ball scrapes across the body as opposed to the point pushing forward. The point pushing forward will cause a fumble when a tackler strikes the side and pins the elbow to the side. The cross-arm action allows the back to run with weight well forward and keep the other hand in access to the ball ready to clamp back down. We do not teach the stiff-arm. We prefer that the runner keep both hands on the ball and depend upon his shoulders and leg drive.

Once the back clears the gauntlet area, he approaches the last obstacle, the blaster. The blaster is a machine with powerful force of resistance. This simulates the goal line and completes the course the back must travel from the center snap until he crosses the goal.

Backs are clocked as they complete this course. If the back is lined up four yards deep for a straight handoff, he actually travels about 20 yards. He has to work for the yardage and do it the football way. This is as close to the nearest evaluation of time we can establish for a running back. It is amazing, but the 9.8 speedster is not always the fastest football runner.

Many 10.5 sprinters can equal or better the track star. A good back times consistently around 3.2 seconds. In a five-minute period, 9 to 10 backs will get six or seven attempts. We post the times on the squad bulletin board each day so each player will be encouraged to move higher on the list.

The gauntlet drill can be adjusted to run any play by sliding the fire hose until the running lane aligns with the gauntlet lane. The gauntlet setup stays in one place for the entire period.

Burma Road Drill

The Burma Road drill starts exactly as the gauntlet does. Any play or action may be used. To arrange for the point of attack to be in line with the setup, slide the fire hose until the number reaches the two air dummy holders.

The Burma Road drill (figure 3) directs the back off course after he steps over the cylinder dummies. Place another air dummy holder two yards from the third cylinder dummy. This holder takes one step forward as the back clears the last cylinder, forcing the back to bump into the air dummy and veer right. Awaiting the ballcarrier is a large bell-bottom dummy. He must drive into the bell bottom with his right shoulder, pivot around, attack another bell bottom with his left shoulder, pivot around again and turn upfield, scoring through the blaster. We do not change the ball to the opposite arm as we pivot. Both hands are

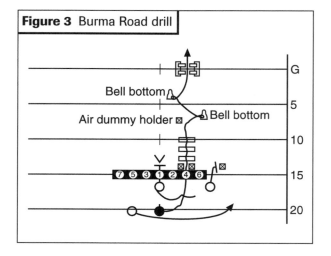

Figure 3 Burma Road drill

on the ball as it is received from the QB. If the QB misses a handoff, he runs whatever course the ballcarrier was assigned.

Another "must" in all drills concerns the fumble. We expect everyone in the drill, including the dummy holders, to "dogfight" for the ball.

The Burma Road drill teaches the ballcarrier that when turned, he can spin, pump his knees high, stay on his feet, and score. Many times the only recourse of a back caught in a congested area is to spin out. Quickness, balance, and proper mental attitude are attributes of a great back.

Circle Crab Drill

The circle crab drill (figure 4) starts the same way as the gauntlet. As in the Burma Road drill, an air dummy holder bumps the back as he clears the third cylinder. This collision forces the back to his right. A shirt (scrimmage vest) is placed on the ground a few yards away as a marker. The ballcarrier puts his left hand down, spins to his left, and, working around a complete circle, scrambles to his feet. He sprints to the next marker, puts his hand down, and, completing another circle, comes up running through the blaster. The circle crab drill helps the ballcarrier realize that when falling, he can put his hand down and push back to normal running form. The push-up is another tool a back can use to stay on his feet.

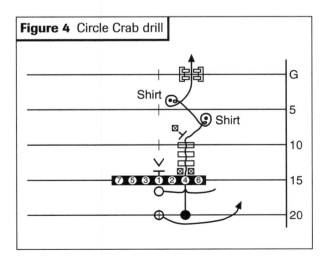

Figure 4 Circle Crab drill

Stay-in-Bounds Drill

How many times in studying films have you seen a back running down the sideline permit himself to be pushed out of bounds without offering any resistance? For some reason, the ballcarrier feels this is what he is supposed to do. This is fine when the situation requires stopping the clock, but under normal circumstances, we expect the good back to resist going out of bounds and gain as much yardage as possible.

The stay-in-bounds drill (figure 5) develops the technique of running down the sidelines. The fire hose is set on a hash mark. The play called is directed into the boundary, creating a situation whereby the ballcarrier runs out of room and must turn upfield. As he makes the turn, three defenders with air dummies spaced three yards apart await him. Each holder greets the ballcarrier with force, attempting to push him out of bounds. The dummy holder meets the ballcarrier in a football position two yards from the sideline.

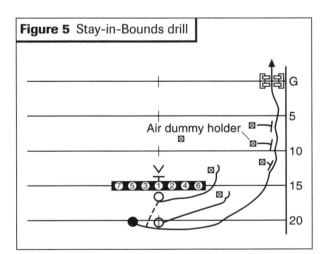

Figure 5 Stay-in-Bounds drill

At this stage, the carrier must learn two important points. First, he squares his shoulders so that they point upfield. Second, he attacks the defender. He does not wait to be pushed, blocked, or tackled. He drives his inside shoulder under the shoulders of the defender, turns upfield, and completes the drill by scoring through the blaster.

The Read-and-Polish Drill

In the read-and-polish drill (figure 6), we set up two cylinder dummies vertically at the point of attack. Between the two cylinders we place a "read" man. He will take a cylinder dummy and move it left or right. This keeps the ballcarrier concentrating. He must be ready to break the opposite way. This is identical to his lineman's block. If the back will methodically run at the lineman's block with shoulders square, he will be able to make the cutback or hit the lane at full steam should it open at the point. This is the "read" for the ballcarrier.

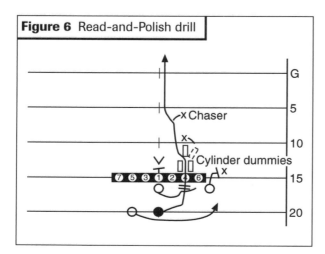

Figure 6 Read-and-Polish drill

After the back makes the break or cuts back, we again insist he get upfield. Eight yards from the "read" dummy we align a "chaser." The "chaser" grabs the hips of the ballcarrier, and we expect the carrier to give him some move and score.

Although we block during all the drills, the polish-and-read drill emphasizes more blocking. We employ the climb block, which is a running shoulder block, and the roll block technique.

Organization of Drills

Not enough can be said in regard to the time and place for the execution of the described backfield drills. During the spring sessions, it is important to use these drills daily. Spring is a time to concentrate on fundamentals. The drills are designed to develop the individual soundly in fundamentals. In the fall, more concentration can be focused on the tactical situations. In the fall, we like more variety in the drill periods. It is important to keep the players interested and at the same time keep them attuned to their individual responsibilities.

The daily practice schedule naturally dictates the time available each day for drill periods. Regardless of the schedule, I believe in the following daily organization. Most of the backs will have some part in the specialty period, which precedes a scheduled practice. It is imperative they report to the field a few minutes early. Our centers and QBs are the first people to report. They must get things rolling with "on-the-line" operation, the snap exchange-cadence session. Each offensive play begins with a snap; therefore, it is essential to begin each day in this manner. After the center-quarterback on-the-line, the centers warm up for the spread punt snap. The QBs start pumping the passes to be thoroughly warmed up for specialty period and the entire practice.

While the centers and QBs work, the other backs jog to a running area. They work on form running, knees pumping like pistons, arms pushing forward. Gradually the tempo picks up and they begin to stride. After a few times back and forth in a 30-yard area, a coach calls the backs to the ropes. Here they complete their running techniques. They will make three trips through the 20 yards in ropes: on the first trip, they step in every square; on the second trip, they cross every other square; and on the final trip, they step in every other one with real speed. As they finish their final trip through the ropes, they report to their respective specialty areas.

Sometimes we substitute a handoff drill for the ropes, especially during two-a-day preseason practice. The backs gain a sense of belonging to the ball and also fake taking handoffs. The fake is performed by slapping the bottom hand on the elbow of the up arm.

After specialty period and formal practice begins, the backs should sprint. It is stimulating to observe a real back working in every drill through individual, group, and team periods.

Every day, one of the main drills should be used to gain an attitude for practice. Drills can be alternated or used as a need presents itself. This drill should be timed and recorded.

At least two periods of read-and-polish should follow to time the plays for that week, then one period of passing with the offensive ends before going into team periods and the kicking game.

Game or scrimmage film should be used to prove to the back the value and importance of drill work. Point out to him in the film those plays where one of the "tools" enabled him to score, gain more than four yards, or make a first down. Keep score on these points and you will be amazed at the intensive progress made toward the ultimate goal.

1966 Summer Manual. Homer Rice coached at the high school, college, and professional levels and is former head coach and athletic director at Georgia Tech.

Perfecting Quarterback Fakes

George Chaump

Five factors make up the deceptive phase of offensive football. First, the QB's natural ability must be recognized and developed. Second, the QB must adhere to basic faking and ball handling principles. Third, the QB must be flawless in all techniques and specific maneuvers. Fourth, the offense must display deception in the development of each play. Fifth, all backs must be disciplined to carry out their fakes.

QB Traits That Aid in Faking

Speed is best improved one way: by running. At every practice session, as part of our warm-ups, we do a series of form runs, and at the close of practice we sprint. A running program is also included in the players' winter workout program. Quickness in operating is best improved through practice and by repeating basic maneuvers. As the QB gains experience, a natural outgrowth is confidence, which he must possess if quickness is to improve.

A QB gifted with large hands has a distinct advantage when it comes to faking and ball handling. A major part of ball handling and

faking is the ability to completely control the football. Large hands enable the QB to do this with relative ease and a high degree of confidence. Our excellent QB, Rex Kern, a great ball handler, has hands that measure 8 1/2 inches from the extremity of his middle finger to the start of his wrist. His hand span from the extremity of his thumb to the extremity of his index finger measures 9 1/2 inches. One can readily understand how he is able to handle the ball so adroitly!

We attempt to improve our QB's hand quickness by using three ball-handling drills borrowed from Coach Chuck Purvis. The first is a wrist roll. The QB takes the ball in one hand and quickly turns it to the outside by rotating his wrist inward as he fully extends his arm outward. The ball is returned as quickly as possible, and the drill is repeated on the other hand. This football is moved from hand to hand as many times as possible in a one-minute time period.

Next we have the QB move the ball around his body, passing it from hand to hand behind his back. Direction is changed every few seconds. This drill is also done for a one-minute duration.

Our next maneuver is a figure eight, done by moving the football between the legs in this desired pattern. Direction is changed every few seconds, and we ask our QB to move the ball as rapidly as possible for one minute.

Foot quickness is developed by skipping rope. A good number per minute to shoot for is 180. Rex Kern, whose feet are extraordinarily quick, can do as many as 200 per minute.

A movie study will bear out that the best faking quarterbacks have a high degree of flexibility in their hips and knees. Hip and knee flexibility can best be improved by skipping rope, running, and engaging in various agility drills.

Basic Principles of Ball Handling and Faking

To fully develop the skills to be a good faker and ball handler, a QB must diligently adhere to certain fundamentals. These must be repeated until they become a habit.

1. After the snap, immediately place the ball in your third hand, the stomach.
2. Eliminate all false steps.
3. Operate with your back as close to an upright position as possible.
4. Operate with the ball as though it's on a horizontal plane, with the back point positioned belt-buckle high.
5. Keep your elbows close to your body.
6. You should not have to stretch for a handoff or fake.
7. Handoffs and fakes are made with the QB and other backs hitting as closely as possible without bumping pads. Shoulder pads should be worn while practicing handoffs.
8. Always look the ball or fake into the intended ballcarrier's pocket.
9. Always head- and eye-follow a fake, never a handoff.
10. After a handoff, accelerate to your ensuing fake.

11. Reduce the relative speed between yourself and the handoff back. We do this by giving with the back as the handoff is made. This technique is called feathering the ball.
12. Adjust to different pocket levels by flexing the hips and knees.
13. The most important factor in faking is quickness. Never be satisfied; always work toward improving it.

The QB Stance

A good stance is important, as it is the point where ball handling and faking start. We like our QB to be comfortable in his stance. We do not want him to slump over the center, but prefer him to stand with his back upright and his knees and hips slightly flexed. His arms are slightly bent as he buries his hands to his wrist plus an inch. This dictates the distance he will be back from the center. We like his feet about armpit width, with his toes even and feet aligned in a parallel position. His head should be upright and his eyes looking straight ahead.

QB Techniques

QBs should master three basic techniques: the kick-out step, the open step, and the reverse pivot.

The Kick-Out Step

Immediately before giving the snap command, the QB will cheat a step by pushing off his far foot and stepping at an angle in the opposite direction. Our original reason for adopting this maneuver was to gain that ever-important fractional-second time advantage. This is beneficial; however, we soon realized a very helpful indirect result—the elimination of the false step on other QB maneuvers. Through practicing and using this technique, the QB fully understands weight distribution and redistribution. The kick-out step is a built-in drill against false stepping.

We kick out only on certain cycles. One caution: as the QB kicks out, he must be certain to exert upward pressure against the center's buttocks. It is easy for him to move his hands back as he steps back. This must be coached against.

Open Step

The QB distributes his weight to his far foot and pushes off this foot, stepping with the other in the opposite direction. We use a kick-out on some cycles; however, this depends on the specific play we call.

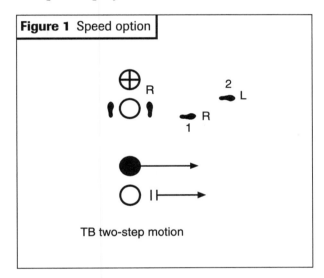

Figure 1 Speed option

TB two-step motion

The open step is used on the speed option, sprint-draw, sprint run or pass, smash, and pull-up pass. In the speed option (figure 1), the QB kick-out steps at zero degrees and moves rapidly to the option area.

In the sprint-draw (figure 2), the QB kicks out at 45 degrees and sprints to his handoff position. The TB fakes by bootlegging to the run-pass position.

In the sprint run or pass (figure 3), the QB kicks out at 45 degrees and fakes the handoff and bootleg to the run or pass position.

For the smash (figure 4), the QB does not kick-out step. Instead, he open steps at 90 degrees then steps back and deep in order to clear for the FB. The QB gives the FB enough time to see where to run. The QB pivots and gets a good hand fake to the TB, then bootlegs to that side.

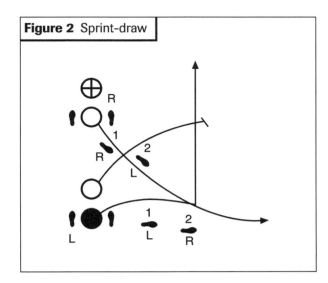

Figure 2 Sprint-draw

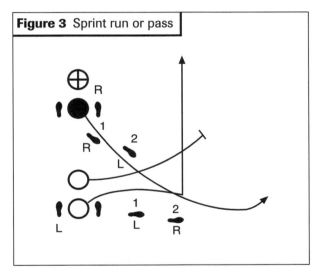

Figure 3 Sprint run or pass

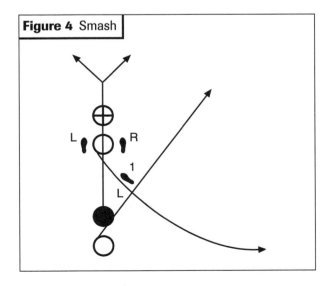

Figure 4 Smash

For the pull-up pass (figure 5), the QB kick-out steps at 60 degrees. He pulls up behind the inside foot of his tackle at a depth of seven yards.

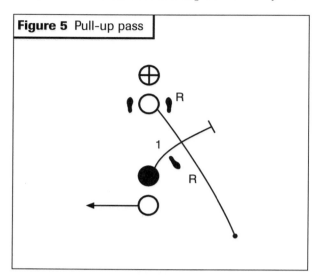

Figure 5 Pull-up pass

Reverse Pivot

For the reverse pivot, the QB distributes his weight to the ball of the opposite foot. At the snap, he pushes sharply off this foot, redistributes his weight to the ball of his near foot, and executes his desired pivot. As he pivots, he flexes his knees and hips in order to lower his center of gravity, giving him a smoother pivot. We use the reverse pivot on the FB belly, FB slant, and blast option. Whether we use a belly or slant is primarily dependent on the defense and the type of blocking we use. For the FB belly (figure 6), the QB reverse pivots at 135 degrees, synchronizes the handoff with the FB, and rides with him to a 180 degree pivot. After the handoff, the QB accelerates to his option fake.

For the FB slant, the QB reverse pivots at 180 degrees. The handoff takes place near the LOS. The FB takes a slant course, using a forward cross-out step. The QB uses a full pivot or else he may miss the handoff to the FB, who is hitting quickly because of his slant course (figure 7).

For the blast option (figure 8), the QB open steps at zero degrees, followed quickly by a reverse pivot at 135 degrees. He locates the TB and gives him a short ride fake. The QB continues to the end, gaining ground in route, and executes the option.

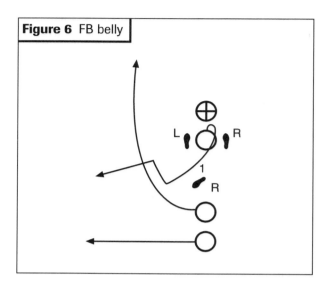

Figure 6 FB belly

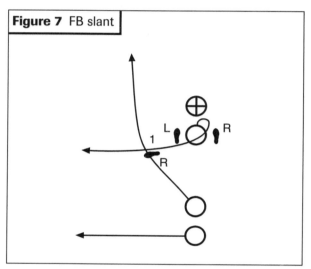

Figure 7 FB slant

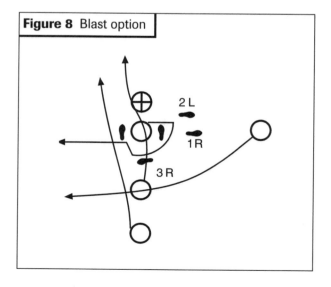

Figure 8 Blast option

It is easy for the QB to develop a false step when reverse pivoting. Some coaches allow this; some even teach it. We are against it, first because we believe it takes away valuable time, and second if you are a team that uses pulling guards, the false step by the QB places his feet in a position where he is apt to trip or slow the guard.

Overall Offensive Deception

Our development of the running offense from the I formation is different from most I teams. We do not use a strict power-type TB offense, using the FB as a glorified guard. Ohio State has been famous for its vaunted fullback offense. Herein lies the first difference: the FB remains in ballcarrying tactics. Our reason for this is twofold. First, aligned in the middle of the formation, he is in optimum position to strike up the middle or off-tackle either way. Second, he is in optimum position to hit the defense quicker than any other back.

As basic as FB handoffs are, we do display deception as these plays are executed. The TB is in ideal position to attract attention, and we use him so he will. The phenomenon of the FB and TB splitting as we run these plays is what we refer to as the "divergent effect" (figure 9).

The TB dashes outside to get in option phase. His course attracts the end, who respects him by loosening, and the defensive back, who

must be ready to play the option pitch. The course of the TB gives us the deceptive look known as the divergent effect.

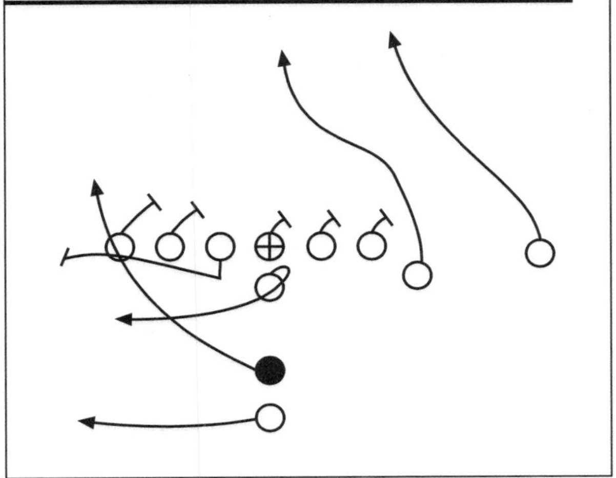

The other series in which this effect is predominant is the sprint-draw series (figure 10). The TB hits inside and may be the ballcarrier, while the FB diverges to the outside as a blocker. It is imperative that the QB sprint at top speed in order for the defense to react to the outside.

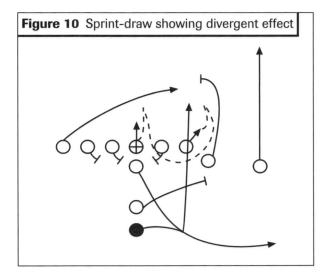

Figure 10 Sprint-draw showing divergent effect

The TB takes a cross-over followed by a regular step, getting his shoulders perpendicular to the LOS and giving the impression that he is running wide. The defense overreacts outside. He quickly plants on the second step and heads for the tackle, where he cuts accordingly.

The QB fake after the handoff should be quick and deliberate. He completes the act of trying to force outside movement on the defense, and his quickness getting outside will add to the deception of the play.

A good QB faking technique becomes very important. We teach our QB to keep both hands on the ball until the last second, at which time he withdraws the ball and places it on the inside groove of his far hip. With his forward hand, he gives an exaggerated follow through, simulating the "feathering" hand-off technique. He quickly bootlegs to his run-pass position.

The deceptiveness of this play has been very effective, especially on the defensive end, who is the main man to beat on the play. To influence him, we send our WB on an inside release. This, combined with a good inside fake by the TB,

Figure 9 FB slant showing the divergent effect

strongly influences the defensive end and encourages his initial reaction to the inside. He becomes a relatively easy block for the FB, who overthrows on him.

The other concept that makes our I attack unique is our respect for the "lighthouse effect." This is created when both backs, aligned in the center of the formation, hit the defense at the same point. Because of their alignment and movement, they attract the defense. For this reason, our attack does not emphasize the popular power and blast plays featured by most I teams.

We apply the "lighthouse effect" in our offensive approach so that we may deceive the defense. We attack from plays utilizing this principle. Our basic application is the blast option (figure 11).

> QB: See figure 8.
>
> FB: Blocks over the play side guard.
>
> TB: Follows with a good fake.
>
> FB and TB: The lighthouse effect.

The WB's technique is another maneuver that adds to the highly deceptive look of this play. He is not put in motion, but leaves on the snap command. Because of his alignment, he is hidden until he comes in phase to receive the option pitch. The heavy action on the blast faking also attracts defensive attention and traffic that tend to hide him until the final seconds of the play.

Figure 11 Blast option

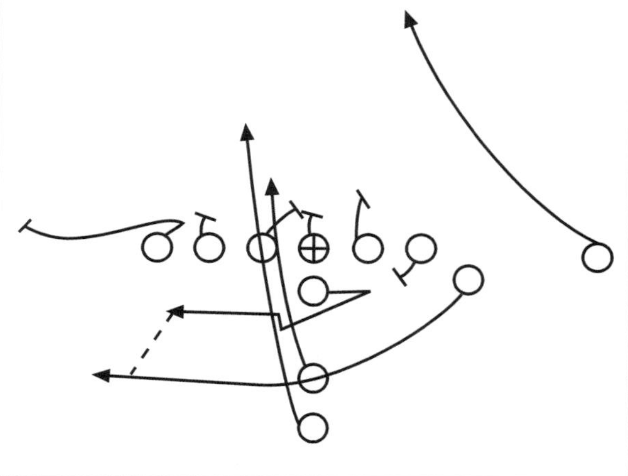

The final phase of deception deals with the backfield group in total. All backs must fully carry out their fakes on every play. If a back is not directly involved in the play, he has a tendency to save it for when he carries. This must be guarded against! All backs must be reminded about their faking in every practice session. Faking must become a habit! The true test of good faking is the number of times a back is tackled when he doesn't have the ball.

These are the basic principles, techniques, and thoughts we feel help achieve deception. It should be kept in mind that although faking starts with the QB's finesse, deception is the result of total team interaction.

1970 Summer Manual. George Chaump was an assistant coach at Ohio State University.

Integrating the Wing-T

Harold "Tubby" Raymond

It is with humility that I discuss our rushing game. Although we have adjusted to defensive trends, we still use offensive principles that originated at Delaware 20 years ago from a philosophy that was developed 40 years ago. This philosophy continues to serve us well.

We have stayed with the same philosophy not only because it has been successful for us, but also because the cycle of football trends has made our attack unique. Consistency of philosophy has helped reduce coaching error because we know what we can and cannot do.

Our players have benefited, too, because it takes time to learn the execution of a football play. Staying with the same philosophy has helped develop some athletes of modest ability into effective football players and has enabled us to maintain a high level of hitting intensity and quality of execution.

Formations don't win football games, players do; but formations largely determine what you can run successfully, and a system of offense helps determine offensive efficiency. The two-back Pro formations with two wideouts lend themselves to the passing game, while the three-back Texas Wishbone lends itself to the rushing game. The Delaware Wing-T in many ways combines these formations. We have a three-back offense, but unlike the Wishbone, ours has three eligible receivers near the LOS to discourage nine-man defensive fronts and force three-deep coverage.

As with the Pro formation, we have the advantage of spread receivers, with our ends keeping the three backs in position to block, fake, or carry the ball. The Wing-T formation (figure 1) lends itself to a balance between running and passing. Three backs make multiple running threats, while the distribution of receivers facilitates passing.

Most of the 50 or more formations we used this year fall into two general categories: those with the wing to the TE and those with the wing to the spread end. The line splits of our guards and tackles are two feet. The TE splits three feet to two yards with a man playing ahead on him. He splits until the man on him becomes aware

of the inside gap and moves inside to be outflanked by our TE. The wing is two yards off the ball, two to three yards outside the TE's normal position, in excellent position to prevent penetration by the DE and establish the flank.

Our fullback and deep back have their heels at four yards and are in a two-point stance, which enables them to move laterally, anticipate the opening, and read the offensive line blocking. We like the man in the dive spot on the outside leg of his tackle because he has an excellent blocking position both on linemen and LBs and can release easily to become the fourth receiver. The split end splits to four to six yards against a three-deep defense with two defensive men outside of his tackle (figure 2). He splits six to eight yards against a four-deep defense (figure 3). The split end applies the same split rules whether to the side

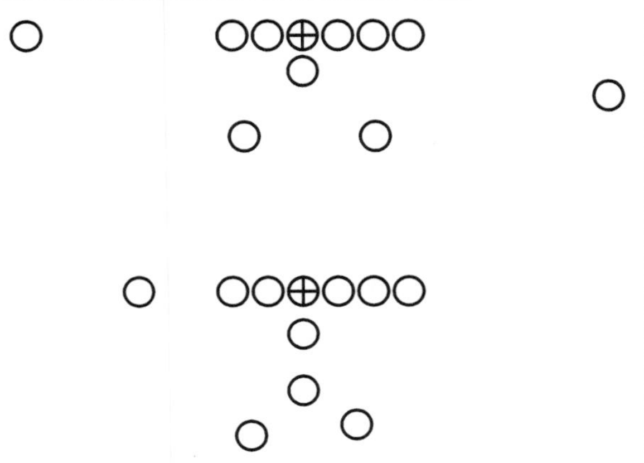

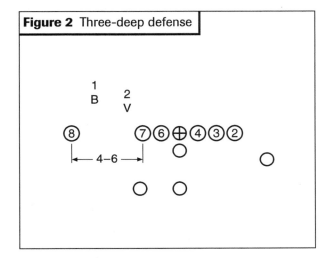

Figure 2 Three-deep defense

Figure 1 Pro and Wing-T formations

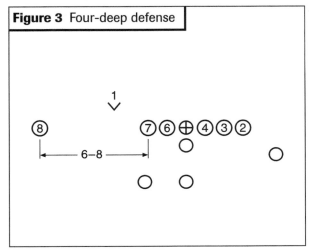

Figure 3 Four-deep defense

of the wing or away from the wing. We prefer that both of our ends be of the tight end type.

While the rush is the basis of our attack, we depend on a balance of passing from play-action passes. The QB fakes keeping the ball at the flank either to or away from the flow of backs at no more than six yards deep. This QB action tends to freeze the defense. The threat of the QB keep is our option play, as he may run or pass rather than pitch the ball backward. The Delaware Wing-T is designed to minimize error, and we have attempted to eliminate high-risk plays in an effort to avoid turnovers or long-yardage situations.

Each formation has its own theory of attack, and we attempt to create defensive assignment conflicts, stressing men with dual defensive assignments and determining what each defensive man can and cannot do. In this formation both the split end and wingback have flanking positions, yet a wide release by the end will prevent a three-deep secondary from leveling off, and a wide release by the wingback will force three-deep man coverage.

Man coverage of the wingback assures individual coverage of the spread end and affects the support of the weak flank. If we can force the defensive halfback to cover deep, we force one of the front four to cover the flat. This is the first assignment conflict. There aren't enough defensive men to assume all responsibilities away from the wing. If we can force number four to cover the flat, number three must contain the QB, and we have angles on one and two (figure 4).

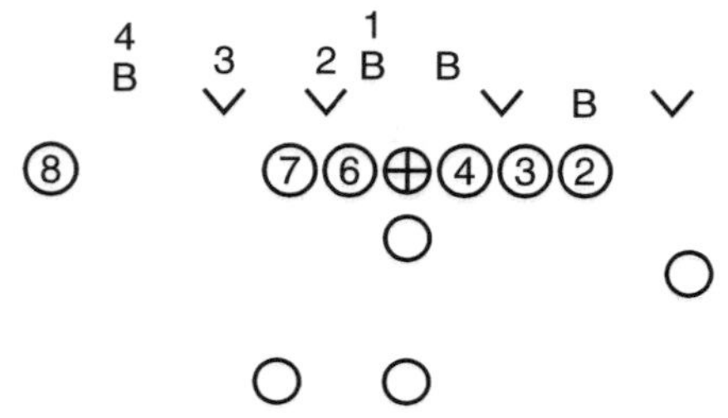

We prefer spread formations against four deep, since it almost assures us of being able to attack a seven-man front. Here, the end has the conflict of sealing the off-tackle play and containing the QB (see figure 5).

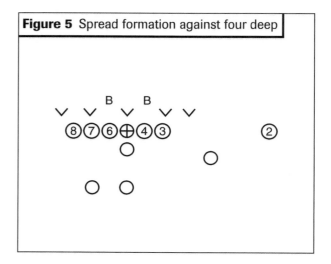

Figure 5 Spread formation against four deep

We shift formations about one-third of the time from one wing formation to its mirror, or from a three-back I with the TE behind the QB to an unbalanced end over formation or one of our two basic formations. Shifting tends to eliminate the flip-flop of defensive men and gives the defense only a second to make its final adjustment.

I would like to diagram four basic plays for you to further demonstrate the idea of multiple threats and defensive assignment conflicts. I will not attempt to show our blocking adjustments for all spacings, but for the most part will show our offensive philosophy against a Split Six.

Let's look at the flank away from the wing to a flexed end with flow in that direction. We like to establish the belly game first. Remember that the end should have some contain responsibility and the backer may have flat responsibility. With this spacing, we begin with the cross block. Our left tackle blocks the gap, and our left guard pulls and traps. The center and offside linemen reach, then fire on the first men in their area. The left half steps toward the defensive end, then blocks through the hole. The QB reverse pivots and completes the ride to the FB two yards from the line, giving the FB complete freedom to select the opening. The FB

Figure 4 Man coverage of the wingback

may wind back using the fire blocks of the center and right guard. The proximity between the left half and the FB is very much like the blast from the I formation. The right half leaves in motion through the FB's original spot and bends around the QB to block the end, completing the fake of the keep pass at that flank. The spread end fakes on a man in a walk-away position but releases outside and runs a sideline pattern if the backer plays on him (see figure 6).

The same play may be run to the wing with the TE blocking the backer (see figure 7).

If we successfully force the backer to cover the flat with the end containing the QB, we do not have to block the end and will use fold or gut blocking. This resembles the triple-option play to the FB. The line blocks as it would for the cross block, but the guard turns through the hole to block the backer. The left half runs at

the end, then releases into the flat while the split end runs a 15-yard sideline. Both the end and backer have assignment conflicts (figure 8).

If we can run this play to a spread end, we can also run it to a TE and release him (figure 9).

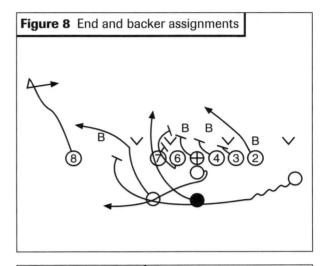

Figure 8 End and backer assignments

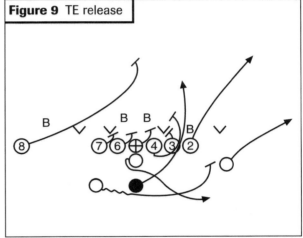

Figure 9 TE release

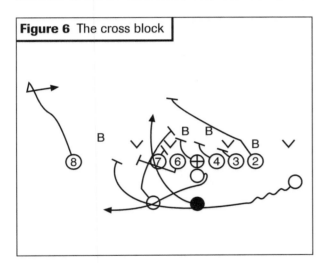

Figure 6 The cross block

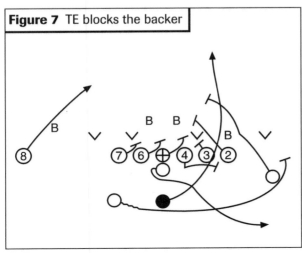

Figure 7 TE blocks the backer

When the backer, concerned with the threat of the FB, scrapes off, the counter from this action places the backer in conflict. He cannot stop the FB and still get part of the counter. The right half who leaves in motion blocks at the flank, and the FB drives for the inside leg of the tackle. The left half rocks his weight on his left foot, bends his path back toward the QB and turns straight upfield, reading the blocks on the backers. He will perpendicularly cross the LOS. The center blocks the backer alone. He is chasing the FB. The right guard and the right tackle post lead the backer, who is supposed to fill the middle. Both ends block at the cutoff. The QB continues to fake behind the right half's block (see figure 10). This play is effective to the wing in motion, and the left half may flare in either direction (figure 11).

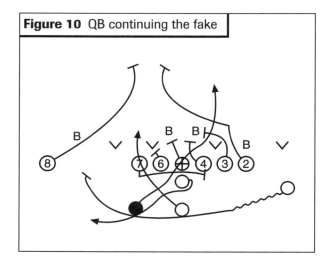

Figure 10 QB continuing the fake

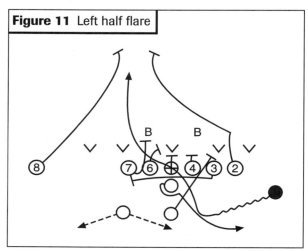

Figure 11 Left half flare

When the end becomes concerned inside, we run our sweep. The spread receiver widens as long as the backer plays ahead on him. If the backer goes into a walk-away, our end stops. If the backer plays head on, the end releases outside. If he goes to the walk-away, the end crackbacks on him. The left half runs one and a half yards outside the tackle and attacks the first free man inside. If the end floats, the left half turns inside and walls off. The onside guard pulls with depth and reads the left half. He blocks out on the first thing outside of the left half's block, while the back side guard pulls

and turns in. The center reaches to protect the attack-side gap as the FB fills the offside gap. The right tackle and end run at the cutoff and block out and back, respectively. The right half leaves in motion and receives the ball with controlled speed, threatening the flank. He reads the left half's block to determine his cut, and the left guard blocks out. The ballcarrier then cuts straight upfield, perpendicularly crossing the LOS.

I should point out that the right halfback is at his original spot when the ball is snapped, but his momentum really makes the formation unbalanced and again places the ballcarrier close to the primary blocker. The defender at the flank finds himself confronted with blockers and ballcarrier at the same time (figure 12). This play has been particularly effective to the wing (figure 13).

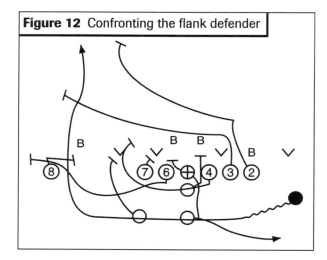

Figure 12 Confronting the flank defender

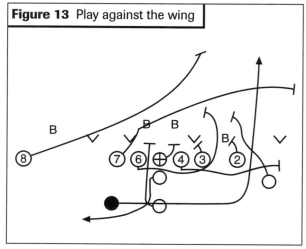

Figure 13 Play against the wing

The way to stop our sweep is to chase the pulling guard and scrape behind the blocking. When we recognize this situation, we give the ball to the FB. The left tackle fires out and picks the scraping backer up as he chases the guard. The center blocks right as the right guard pulls with a step of depth, then turns up to block through the hole. This step by the guard puts the FB close to the primary block and again resembles the I blast (see figure 14).

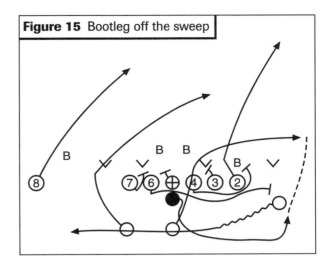

Figure 15 Bootleg off the sweep

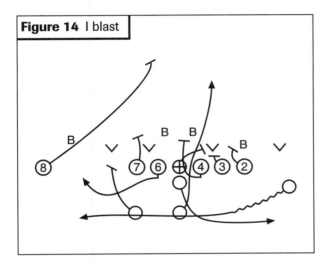

Figure 14 I blast

Finally, our option play, an outstanding phase of our offense, is our waggle or bootleg off the sweep (figure 15). The backs fake the sweep as the right half leaves in motion. The right tackle blocks on, the center blocks the first man on or left, and the left tackle blocks the second man. The first guard pulls and turns in to block the first man showing, which is set up by the TE's release as he flags inside. The back side guard pulls, allows the FB to fill in front of him, then reads the first guard's block. He blocks out on the first man outside of the right guard's block. The FB fills and blocks anything around, but then slides into the flat. The left half runs an across pattern after faking a block on the end. The split end posts. The QB fakes a sweep handoff, then flattens out and threatens the flank. He has a legitimately blocked running play in front of him, a cleaned out deep corner, and the FB to dump the ball to if he cannot turn the flank.

1972 Proceedings. Harold Raymond is head coach at the University of Delaware.

Face-Lifting the Wing-T

Harold Raymond and Ted Kempski

I'm not certain whether it's defensive trends or fear of embarrassment that is the greatest catalyst for offensive innovation. We at the University of Delaware have struggled to accommodate defensive trends and continually make an effort to maintain a low embarrassment profile. We are familiar with the imposition of humility as we have experienced our share, but we are extremely proud of our offense, the Delaware Wing-T.

Conducting a "face-lift" of any kind necessitates a brief look at what you have to work with. First, the Wing-T is an offensive system that employs many formations and, though a four-back, running-oriented attack, its formations lend themselves to a balance between the run and pass. This year, we were in the top five teams nationally in total offense but never appeared in the top five in either rushing or passing. We reached true balance in passing 30 percent of the time.

It remains series or sequence football. Each play of a series relates to others of the same series, and blocking patterns of one series often relate to those of another. It is package football, which forces defensive adjustments and creates new defensive conflicts. It is flow football that simultaneously threatens several points of attack with a continual threat of the QB keeping the ball either with or away from the flow of the play.

The Dive Back

Much has been said about the advantages of our wingback (figure 1) but far too little about the significant position of our dive back in the basic formation.

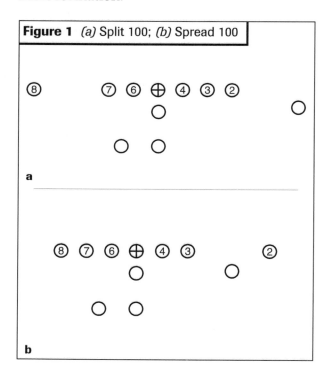

Figure 1 *(a)* Split 100; *(b)* Spread 100

The wingback presents the threat of a third immediate deep receiver, creates a blocking angle, and widens the defensive front, but the dive back position is equally important. He has excellent blocking angles at the flank, unlike Veer, I, or Wishbone halfbacks, and is in position to quickly become the fourth pass receiver. Figure 2 shows the dive man as a deep receiver.

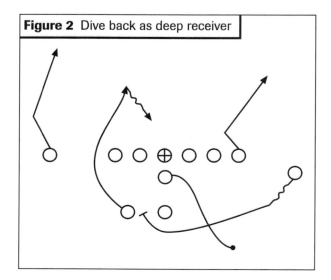

Figure 2 Dive back as deep receiver

The threat of the sweep at the flank forces the cornerback and safety to the flexed end to support while the cornerback and safety to the TE tend to remain at home to cover the TE and the FB. This frees the dive back deep through the middle.

Finally, we spread skill requirements over several positions so that we are not dependent upon one player of exceptional skill. Not that we won't use one if we have him, but sharing those responsibilities is often effective. This year, seven running backs ran 200 yards or more, with our three starters running 743, 742, and 598. Seventeen receivers shared 203 completions.

Sample Problem and Solution

We have selected a particular problem and will show you our solution. It is an excellent example of the direction of our offensive growth. Our basic misdirection or buck sweep was in many ways the basis of our attack, but against the Oklahoma defense, it became more effective to the TE than the flexed end because it often forced a halfback to block the tackle (figure 3).

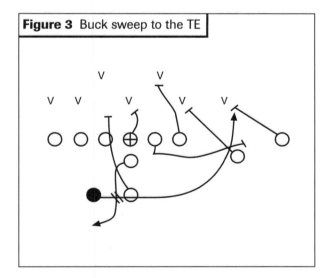

Figure 3 Buck sweep to the TE

The option is probably the greatest concept of offensive football since the development of the forward pass and became an excellent solution to a particular problem. It created strength from weakness and has helped immeasurably.

Using the Option

In order to discuss the use of the option, it is important to understand the evolution of the Delaware Wing-T. The development of the wingback, dive back, and flexed end has provided us with angles at multiple flanks (figure 4).

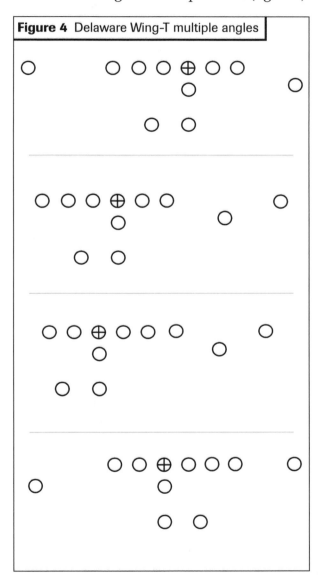

Figure 4 Delaware Wing-T multiple angles

In the past, we experienced success by attacking the most vulnerable of the eight flanks and creating the conflict of support or coverage through the play-action and misdirection passing. Recent defensive adjustments found our flexed-end attack wanting. Our attack has been and continues to be designed around three basic series: buck sweep, belly, and sprint out (figure 5).

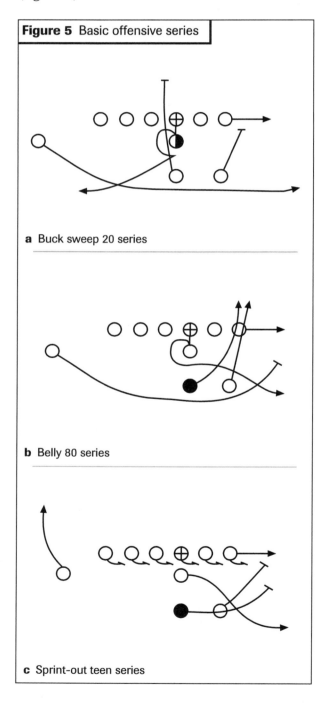

Figure 5 Basic offensive series

a Buck sweep 20 series

b Belly 80 series

c Sprint-out teen series

To maintain the integrity of our sequential approach to offense, we developed the option within each of these three basic series (figure 6).

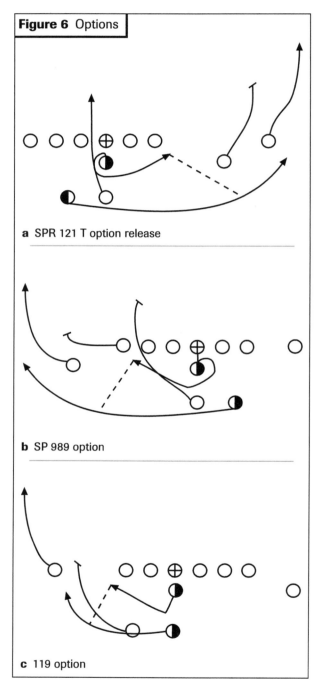

Figure 6 Options

a SPR 121 T option release

b SP 989 option

c 119 option

Although we have experimented with the trap option for several years, we do not intend to take credit for originating the concept. It totally fits in with our buck sweep series. SPR

121 trap option enables us to run this series to the flexed end with consistency (figure 7). The SPR 121 trap option pass naturally adds to the conflict of support or coverage (figure 8).

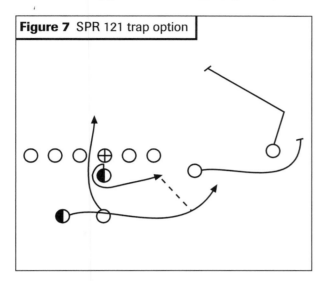

Figure 7 SPR 121 trap option

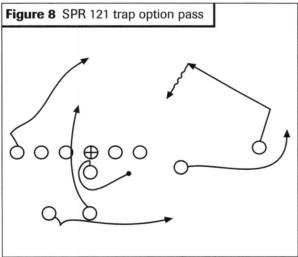

Figure 8 SPR 121 trap option pass

In addition to giving us a successful flank, the trap option augments one of our most dangerous plays, the waggle to the TE (figure 9). Note the similarity between the two.

We have also experienced success running the trap option to the weak side (figure 10a). The utilization of the wingback as the pitch man provides us with an additional blocker at the flank (figure 10b) and also augments the motion waggle.

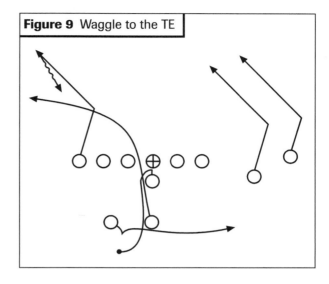

Figure 9 Waggle to the TE

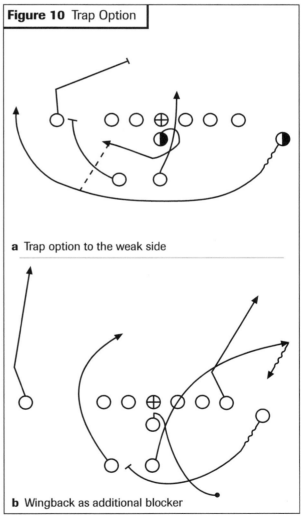

Figure 10 Trap Option

a Trap option to the weak side

b Wingback as additional blocker

We strive to develop deception not only with our backfield series but also with the sequential aspect of our line blocking schemes. The combination of the belly, belly keep pass, and belly option provides a good example of this (figure 11).

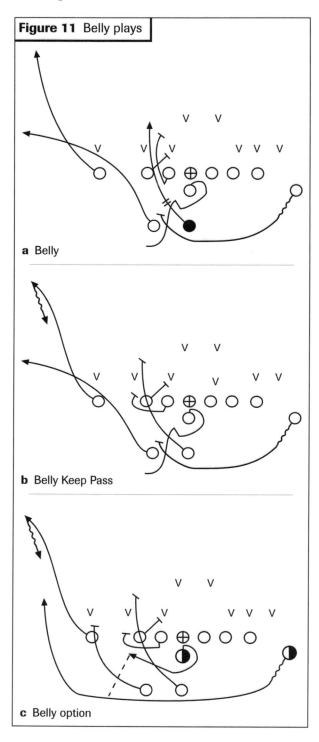

Figure 11 Belly plays

a Belly

b Belly Keep Pass

c Belly option

The sprint-out (figure 12) has long been an important aspect of our offense because it provided us an attack away from the wing without motion. The addition of the sprint option (figure 13) has given this series the sequential parity we were looking for.

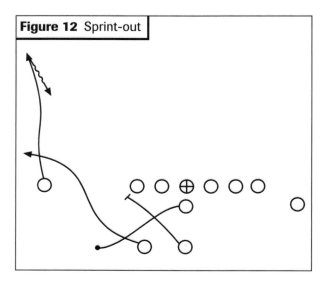

Figure 12 Sprint-out

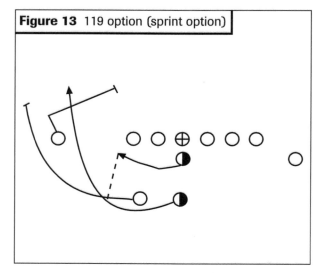

Figure 13 119 option (sprint option)

By using extended motion with the sprint series, we developed an additional flank by outnumbering the defense with the Cross Flanker concept (see figure 14).

In conclusion, we have added a new dimension to the Delaware Wing-T by forcing the defense to stop the power sweep at one flank and the option at the other with the waggle being antagonistic to both.

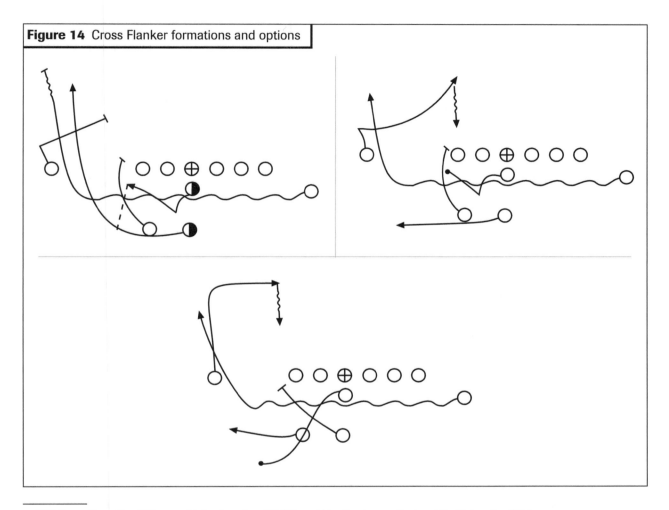

Figure 14 Cross Flanker formations and options

1979 Proceedings. Harold Raymond is head coach and Ted Kempski is offensive coordinator at the University of Delaware.

Featuring the Fullback in the I

Dick Sheridan

At North Carolina State, we are primarily an I formation team, but we vary the alignment of the tailback (figure 1). We have two wide receivers in the game most of the time, but we also substitute a second TE to give us the formations in figure 2.

We believe that we must be able to rush the ball successfully to be a consistent winner. Our goal is to have a hard-nosed, physical, "come right at you" running game as the starting point of our offense. Also we want to be able to attack defenses with an option package, and we don't think we can be a complete offensive team without an effective, efficient passing game.

Instead of discussing the more familiar I formation tailback plays (sweep, draw, isolation,

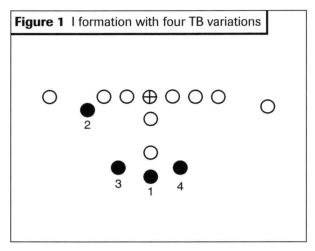

Figure 1 I formation with four TB variations

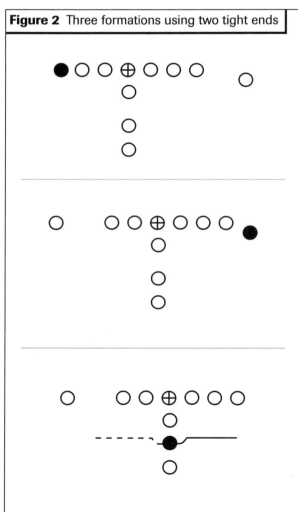

Figure 2 Three formations using two tight ends

1. A give to the fullback on an option
2. An inside dive with base or trap blocking
3. A give to the fullback off of sweep action with base or trap blocking
4. Replacing the tailback as ballcarrier without changing the play for the offensive line

In the triple-option, the QB reads the defense to determine whether to give the ball to the fullback or keep the ball to option the defensive end. In figure 3, the fullback can carry the ball on the basic veer scheme if the defensive tackle does not close. A variation of the veer is a "loop" call (figure 4) for the offensive tackle, who releases outside to seal the LB. The fullback receives the ball if the defensive tackle widens with the release of the offensive tackle.

It is important to establish our fullback inside to make all options and outside plays more effective. We use a variety of schemes to dive

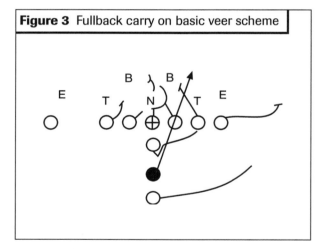

Figure 3 Fullback carry on basic veer scheme

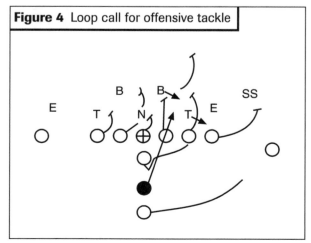

Figure 4 Loop call for offensive tackle

etc.), we will concentrate on the different ways in which the fullback carries the ball in our I offense. There are four general ways that our fullback gets the ball:

the fullback inside to attack the defense with a quick-hitting play. Figure 5 is a base play to the fullback where the reaction of the nose man determines the fullback's path. In figure 6, we trap a lineman; in figure 7, we trap a LB.

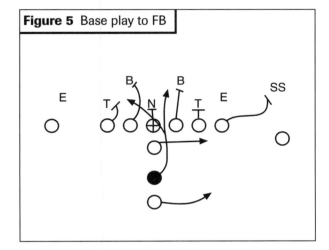

Figure 5 Base play to FB

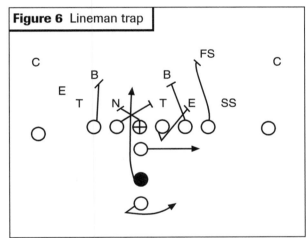

Figure 6 Lineman trap

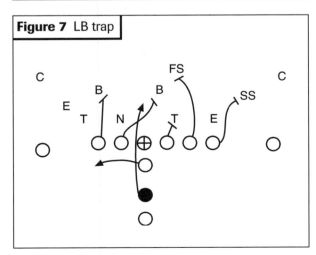

Figure 7 LB trap

The third general way in which we give the ball to the fullback is off of tailback sweep action. The QB fakes the pitch to the tailback and then hands the ball to the fullback. We use a variety of blocking schemes to attack different defensive alignments. In figure 8, the fullback runs off the tackle's block and can possibly bend the play behind the center's block. Against an even front, the fullback's arc is tighter and he reacts to the block of the offensive guard (figure 9). We also trap an even defense with a tackle (figure 10), using the same ball handling. The final play off of sweep action that we use is a guard trap against an odd front (figure 11).

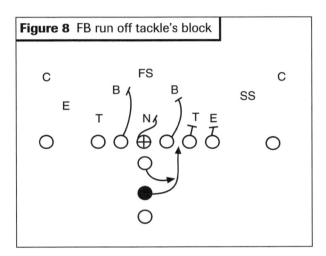

Figure 8 FB run off tackle's block

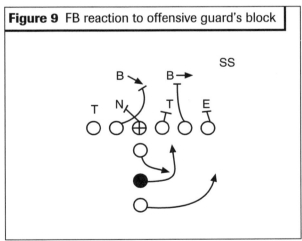

Figure 9 FB reaction to offensive guard's block

The final general way our fullback carries the ball is by replacing the tailback as ballcarrier on some of our basic tailback plays. Our offensive line does not change, but the the QB alters his ball handling. The tailback sweep is a primary

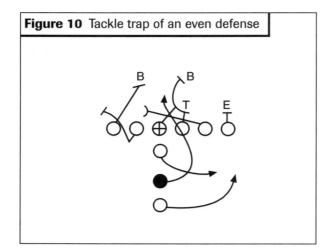

Figure 10 Tackle trap of an even defense

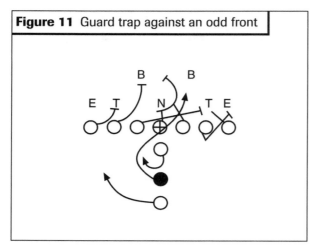

Figure 11 Guard trap against an odd front

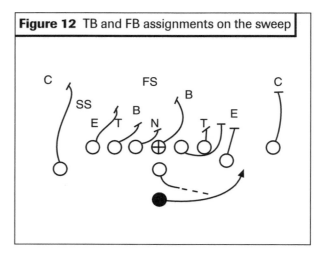

Figure 12 TB and FB assignments on the sweep

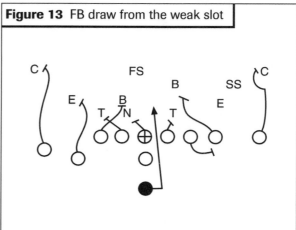

Figure 13 FB draw from the weak slot

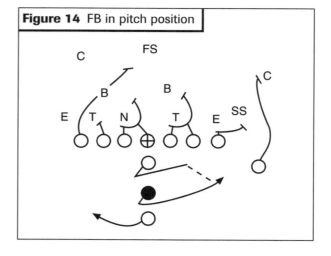

Figure 14 FB in pitch position

play in our offense. Without changing offensive line assignments, we can sweep with our fullback when we break the I alignment. In our dropback passing game, we align the tailback in a weak slot, and from this formation we switch the assignments of the tailback and fullback on the sweep (figure 12).

The tailback draw is a basic play that we can run with the fullback carrying the ball. In figure 13, the fullback draw from the weak slot formation changes only the block of the TE from the assignments of the tailback draw. The TE blocks the onside LB instead of the strong safety.

On our basic counter option play, our fullback dive is back side, and the tailback receives the pitch. A variation with changing blocks involves a sweep fake by the QB and tailback, and counter action by the fullback to put him in pitch position as shown (figure 14).

Most I formation teams use the tailback counter off draw or isolation action. We can use the same blocking scheme to give the ball to the fullback. We fake sweep action opposite, counter the fullback, and run off of the back side guard's trap on the defensive end behind the lead block of the back side tackle (figure 15).

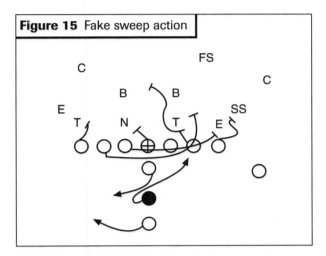

Figure 15 Fake sweep action

The final play that can involve our fullback as a ballcarrier is the lead option. Our tailback becomes the lead blocker and we option the weakside tackle. The onside tackle and guard are responsible for the LB and free safety (figure 16).

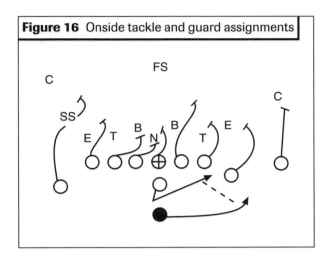

Figure 16 Onside tackle and guard assignments

Although we have the capability of a variety of schemes and actions for the fullback, we usually go into a game with only three or four fullback plays. Our entire attack will be more successful if we can effectively involve the fullback as a ballcarrier and not just a blocker.

1987 Proceedings. Dick Sheridan was head coach at North Carolina State University.

Shifting in the I

Tom Nugent

College, professional, and high school teams are using I formation variations with flankers, wings, and motion. Lately there is a trend toward a shift from the basic alignment.

The basic formation is, of course, the starting point. Everything begins with this set. We always move from the huddle to this formation, which has seven men on the LOS (figure 1). Everyone is in a preliminary stance (semiupright).

Figure 2 illustrates the movement of the backs. All moves or shifts are made on the command, "Ready—down." On this signal,

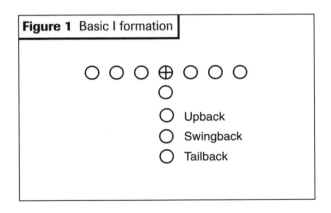

Figure 1 Basic I formation

Upback
Swingback
Tailback

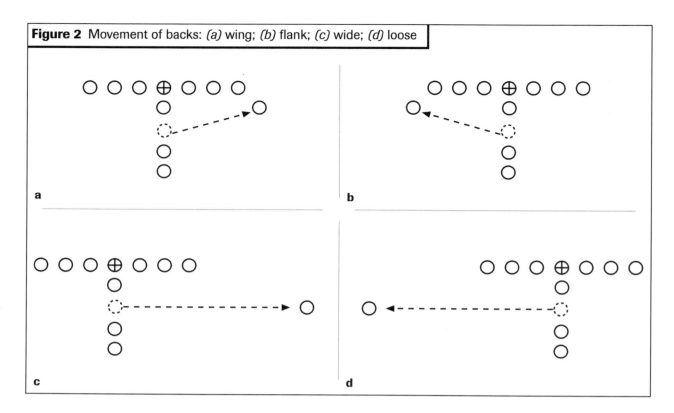

Figure 2 Movement of backs: *(a)* wing; *(b)* flank; *(c)* wide; *(d)* loose

players move to the formation called in the huddle. Often, we drop into the basic with no moves and run from that set.

Preliminary Stance

Linemen and backs assume the same stance. Bend from the waist, hands on thighs (just above the knees), heads up, and eyes looking downfield.

The Shift

On the word "down," linemen drop into position (moving right or left to get an angle if desired) in two counts. Backs do not have a cadence but move so that all are in a three-point stance at approximately the same time. When a back is moving to a wide or loose position, the remaining backs do not wait for him to reach his final position. When he moves to a wing or flank set, however, the full backfield drops into position at approximately the same time.

Movement of the Ends

Nearly all end moves are made directly from the huddle. West (figure 3) moves the left end while East (figure 4) applies to the right end. In figure 5, we combine a movement of an end with a back. The end goes directly from the huddle; the back moves on a shift. Figure 6 shows a back in a loose position with a split right end.

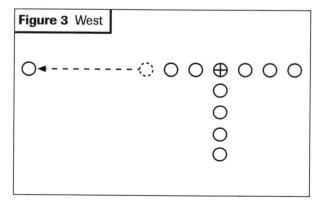

Figure 3 West

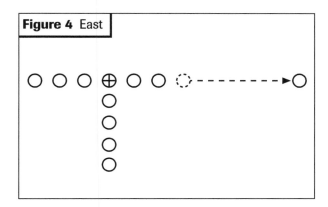

Figure 4 East

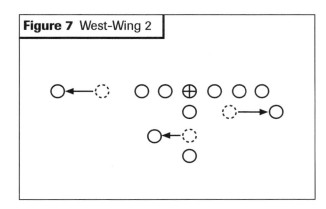

Figure 7 West-Wing 2

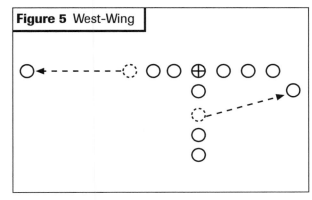

Figure 5 West-Wing

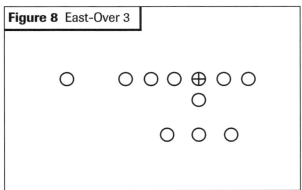

Figure 8 East-Over 3

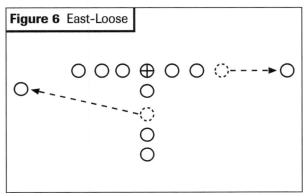

Figure 6 East-Loose

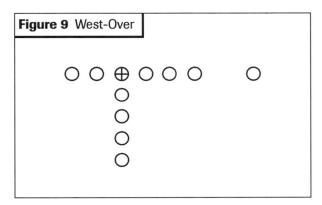

Figure 9 West-Over

We often use an end "over" (figures 7 and 8). We make this adjustment from the huddle and, as with most adjustments of the ends, it is not a part of the shift. The West-Wing 2 formation (figure 7) shifts the swingback into the LH position. The East-Over 3 formation (figure 8) has all backs at home. The left end is over on the right side of the formation (figure 9). The right end is over on the left side of the formation.

Here is the biggest development in our shift of the past year. When moving into the more standard or orthodox offensive sets, we use our "up" back, who is located directly behind the quarterback in the basic or starting formation. He shifts to the TE position. This is most effective with East and West. It allows one of the ends to step off the line into a backfield position, and an eligibility problem is solved. We call the entire adjustment North (to the right; figure 10) or South (to the left; figure 11). North tells both ends to go directly from the huddle to a split position. On the command, "ready—down," the end on the side to which the up back moves steps back off the line. Figures 12 and 13 show North and

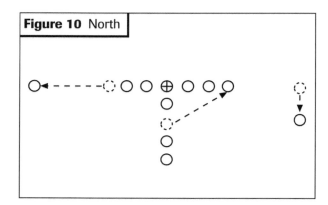

Figure 10 North

South with more orthodox formations. The swingback shifts into LH position. The tailback drops into FB slot. The swingback shifts into RH position while the tailback again drops into normal FB slot.

The use of a split end with a Wing or a Flank is called in the huddle (terms East and West; figures 14 and 15). Wing and Flank without end adjustments are seen in figures 16 and 17.

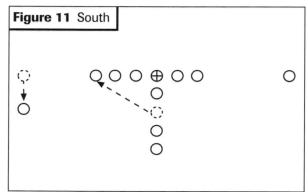

Figure 11 South

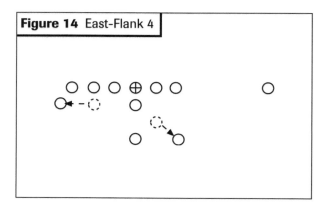

Figure 14 East-Flank 4

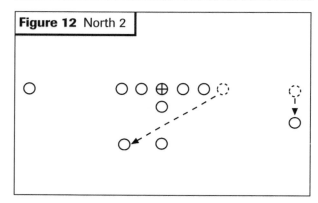

Figure 12 North 2

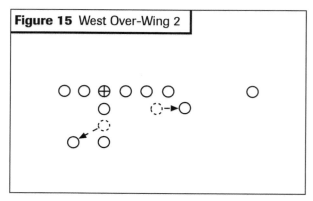

Figure 15 West Over-Wing 2

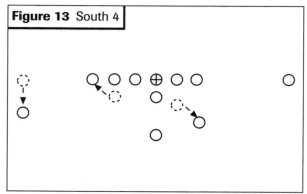

Figure 13 South 4

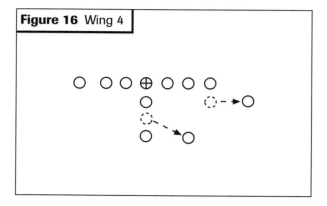

Figure 16 Wing 4

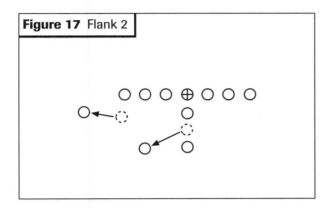

Figure 17 Flank 2

Motion With the Shift

For years we have used motion with the I formation but find that it is most effective when not used with the shift. The time element is a deterring factor.

The best man to put in motion is the tailback. If the deep man, or tailback, is not suited to this type of play, then one of the other men can be used. We have used the third man or swingback for our motion the past two years.

Variations With North and South

Our newest development with formations North and South has to do with the tightening of an end without breaking the consistency of our rules.

On any North or South call, both ends automatically take a split position from the huddle with the shift. The up back moves into the line as a TE and the split man moves back off the line, making both eligible for a forward pass (figures 8 and 9). To keep an end in his normal position in this formation, we use the terms A-SLOW and B-SLOW (figures 18 and 19).

This method is suggested only if specific personnel are desired for certain plays. Otherwise, the same formations can be selected with a simpler use of terminology (figures 20, 21, and 22).

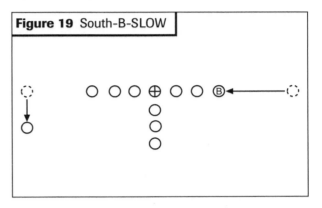

Figure 18 North-A-SLOW

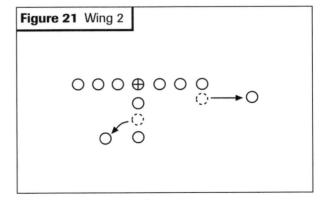

Figure 19 South-B-SLOW

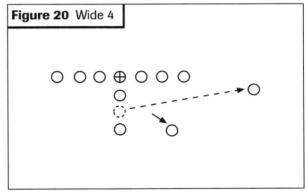

Figure 20 Wide 4

Figure 21 Wing 2

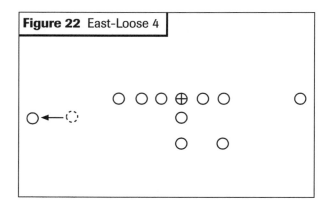

Figure 22 East-Loose 4

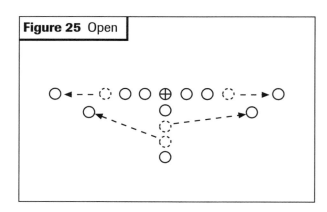

Figure 25 Open

The Split is another popular backfield set used frequently. This involves the movement of all backs with the shift (figures 23 and 24).

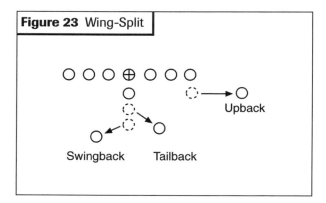

Figure 23 Wing-Split

Upback

Swingback   Tailback

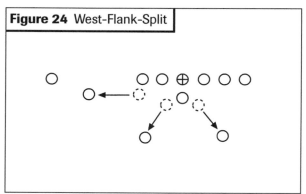

Figure 24 West-Flank-Split

Finally, in the Double-Wing or Double-Slot, the up back shifts to the right, the swingback to the left, and the tailback remains in his normal spot. Both ends move out five to six yards. We describe the entire maneuver with the word "open" (figure 25). The ends and backs move as part of the shift.

Conclusion

Shifting from one formation to another creates immediate problems for the defense. Why not test the opponent's defensive plan and preparation to the extreme? It is difficult enough to make proper adjustments to an offensive alignment when a team comes directly from the huddle to the setup from which they will run or throw. Showing one offensive set, then suddenly moving to another provides a problem to tax the teaching ability of any coaching staff.

Double-time defensive preparation is required and two objectives are realized: it forces your opponent to spend most of his time getting ready defensively, limiting and restricting his offensive work; and it diminishes aggressiveness and keeps opponents "on their heels." Uncertainty is demoralizing.

Here are some fundamental rules that should help.

1. From week to week, select the offensive sets best suited to upset the defensive adjustments of your opponent.

2. Stress those that work on individual weaknesses, putting your strength against their weakness.

3. Use a minimum of plays, but run them, if possible, from many formations and variations.

4. Devise a "formations" drill that will ensure compliance with the rules, eliminate errors, and show a thorough understanding of moves.

5. Work on the shift so that final stance becomes a comfortable position from which each player can move at top efficiency.

6. Develop an automatic system that stresses simplicity.

Automatic System

LOS calls are effective when used properly. We use them approximately 10 percent of the time but practice the system one-third of our offensive time. Our QB always calls the name of a play after the command "Ready—Down." Ninety percent of the play calls are false. When a true call is to be made, his team is alerted in the huddle. They are listening this time!

Here is the sequence of calls. In the huddle only the formation and the words, "line of scrimmage" are given. It instructs the team that they will be given the actual play on the LOS. The team breaks the huddle and lines up in the basic formation. On "Ready—Down," they shift to the formation call and listen for the play. The QB gives the play and, after the customary pause, gives the snap signal. We often run plays from our basic formation. Ninety percent of the play calls in the game are false; ten percent are true. Defensive guessing invites disaster.

Beat an individual according to his alignment. Do not attempt to beat a team defense with an automatic system. Is the end wide? Tight? Does the guard play the gap? Is he head-on? Where is the linebacker? These are the types of questions the QB asks himself before making the true call.

Springing the Upset

An upset is a combination of sound preparation, correct analysis, and good luck. Without a generous amount of each, a true upset is very unlikely.

Mental attitude is a vital factor and the psychological approach can be the key to success. Nothing is as effective as the proper psychological approach. Sound preparations, special plays or series, lucky bounces, and fumbles can play a vital part once the mental problem is handled.

Search out the motivating force. Concentrate on the key to why you should lose. The obvious strength of a heavily favored opponent quite often can be its Achilles' heel.

Conference records and current standings can often give you the incentive. Beat the champs, stop the bowl team, revise the standings, escape the cellar—one of them may be the key.

Pride, personal and group, is an important asset. It provides the missing ingredient. Someone, somewhere, somehow must ignite the spark that will set off the emotional explosion necessary for the true upset.

1963 Summer Manual. Tom Nugent was head coach at the University of Maryland.

Developing an I Series

Tom Osborne

Offensively, we try to develop a series of plays with a basic running play, a counter play off of the basic run, and a pass off either the basic running play or the counter play.

I would like to cover our counter sweep series. The basic running play in this series is the counter dive play. We block our counter dive as shown in figures 1, 2, 3, and 4.

The counter play off the counter dive is the counter sweep, blocked as shown in figure 5.

Against 5-2 spacing, the LG pulls and blocks the DE either in or out. The RG reads the block of the LG, breaking either inside or outside of the LG block on the DE. It is important that the LG blocks clearly, so the RG can read whether or not he has turned the DE in or blocked him

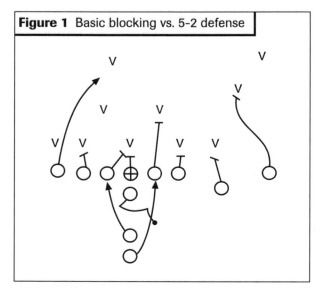

Figure 1 Basic blocking vs. 5-2 defense

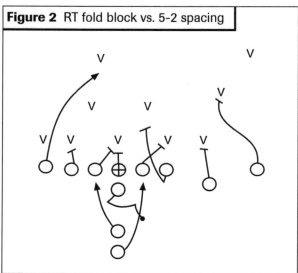

Figure 2 RT fold block vs. 5-2 spacing

Figure 3 Counter dive blocking vs. Pro 4-3

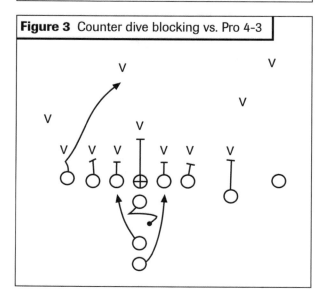

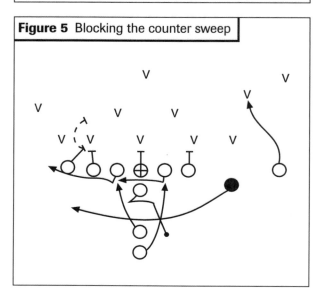

Figure 4 Counter dive blocking vs. Split 6

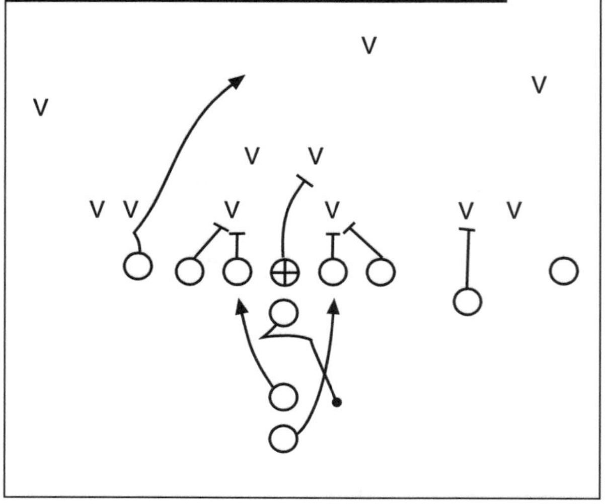

Figure 5 Blocking the counter sweep

out. The ballcarrier (WB) reads the block of the RG, then cuts inside or outside of the DE. The FB drives at the area vacated by the pulling LG. If a LB plugs the area, he immediately cuts him down; if nobody penetrates, the FB hunts the onside LB. At times, the FB breaks outside of the double-team of the TE and LT in order to get to the LB. The IB drives at the area of the pulling RG and blocks anyone penetrating. If no penetration, he picks up the offside LB. Figures 6 and 7 show blocking versus other defenses.

The pass that complements the counter dive and counter sweep is the counter sweep pass (figure 8). We normally make this a sequence pass, looking from the TE to the FB in that order.

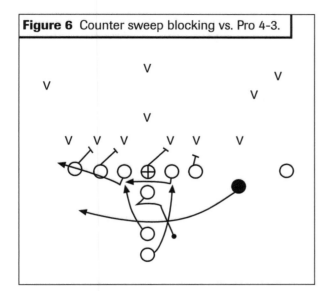

Figure 6 Counter sweep blocking vs. Pro 4-3.

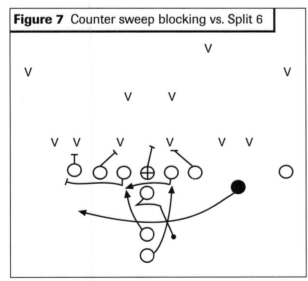

Figure 7 Counter sweep blocking vs. Split 6

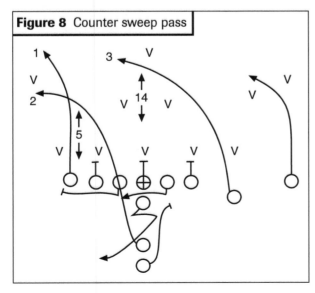

Figure 8 Counter sweep pass

Isolation Series

The second series that I would like to discuss is our isolation series. The isolation is our basic running play. Figures 9, 10, 11, and 12 show the different ways we block it.

The companion counter play to the isolation play that we run is what we call the isolation sweep. Figure 13 shows how we block the isolation sweep.

The iso sweep is blocked slightly differently from the counter sweep. Since the FB dives

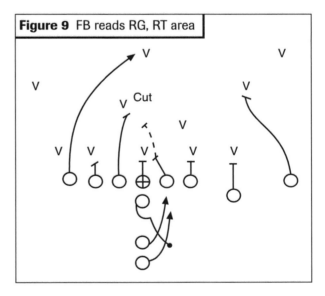

Figure 9 FB reads RG, RT area

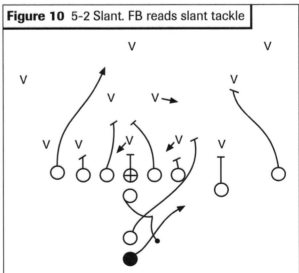

Figure 10 5-2 Slant. FB reads slant tackle

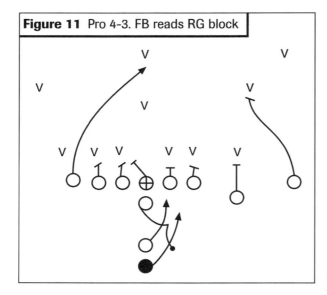

Figure 11 Pro 4-3. FB reads RG block

over the RG area, we need to protect the LB area against a plugging LB. We bring the LT inside on a slant path. He blocks a plugging LB, a MG slanting his way, or the offside LB. As a result, the TE has to block the onside tackle by himself instead of double-teaming with the LT.

The iso sweep has more misdirection than the counter sweep because both the IB and the FB dive opposite the play. (The FB dives to the onside in the counter sweep.) However, the iso sweep is not as strong a play since the TE always has a single block on the DT and the FB is lost as an onside blocker. Figures 14 and 15 show isolation sweep blocking against other defenses.

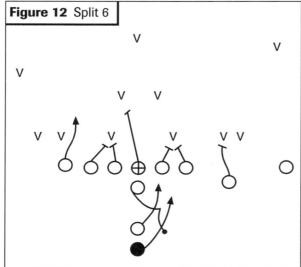

Figure 12 Split 6

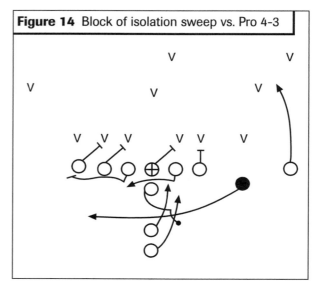

Figure 14 Block of isolation sweep vs. Pro 4-3

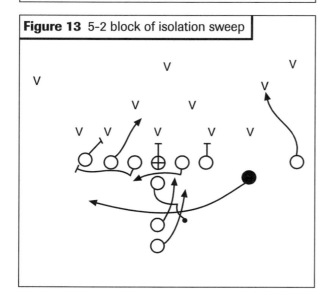

Figure 13 5-2 block of isolation sweep

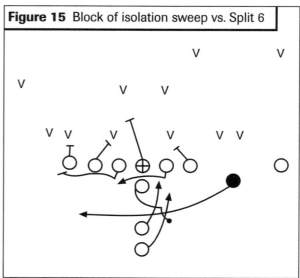

Figure 15 Block of isolation sweep vs. Split 6

Companion Pass Play

Figure 16 shows the pass we frequently use as companion to the isolation play. We drop the uncovered offside lineman (including the center) to pick up the offside defensive end. The onside linemen and the FB and IB run a true isolation action and emphasize the fake. The QB makes a good fake and then reads the safety (three deep). If the safety reacts up to play the run, the QB throws to the TE. If the safety hangs deep, the QB throws to the SE running an 18-yard square-in. The play fake should hold the LBs shallow enough to hit the SE behind them.

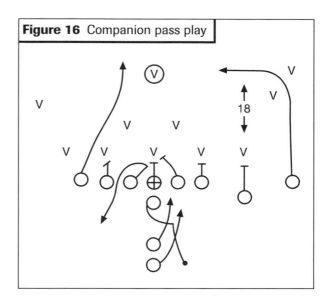

Figure 16 Companion pass play

1976 Proceedings. Tom Osborne was head coach at the University of Nebraska.

Running the Option From the I

Dave Triplett

We have been a traditional I formation team for eight years during which we fluctuated between pass and run. As our recruiting produced better and better players, we decided to focus on a solid, diversified running game. We felt that giving the ball to the I back 20 times a game was too one-dimensional an approach. We were interested in getting the FB and QB more involved in the running game. This necessitated more option-type football.

Our philosophy at the University of South Dakota stresses the team aspect of winning. We are interested in playing good, solid running defense. We stress technique and pursuit. We play three-deep. We don't want to give up the big plays. On offense, we are interested in generating first downs. First downs keep the clock on your side, and an opponent's offense off the field. First downs lead to field position and points. Our kicking game is our top priority. We feel it is the number one way to keep the offense and defense in good field position. If we can get our opponent to start from his 20-yard line, and we start from our 40, we are going to win.

Running the option out of the I fits nicely into our philosophy. As our offensive line has gotten better, we have been able to throw less and run more.

We use four option-type plays as the basis for our attack: the zone dive, zone option, triple option, and loaded option. We feel we need to be ready to run all four of these in any game. We also will run one good, solid tailback play and our play-action passes.

Success in option football depends on the following factors.

1. *Personnel.* We try to put our best players in the middle. Our center has to be the best offensive lineman. Our guards are the next two. Our QB obviously needs to be a great player. Our fullback and tailback both must be good backs. We don't want a castoff playing fullback. At times this year we put our tailback there. We want to have our best offensive football players inside so we can establish the inside run and get our best backs to either side of the formation.

2. *I formation versus split backs.* There are a number of advantages to being an I formation team. First, you basically can have one dive back all the time, and one pitch back. This helps execution. We are able to practice on one thing all the time. We can recruit smaller, quicker tailbacks because we know they most often will get the ball outside. Second, we can still run our traditional I formation runs and play-action passes.

3. *QB decision-making.* The QB must be a solid option technician and a good decision maker. There are some intangibles here, but you can coach this, too. He must be schooled to avoid the bad play and not force the big play. This is a team game. If he stays poised and cool, the team will win. The QB must realize he doesn't have to do it all himself.

4. *Ball handling.* We spend a lot of time on this. We feel it is essential to emphasize the mesh and the pitch. Most of this centers on the QB, but we make both parties responsible. Mistakes in ball handling are sometimes physical but can be the result of poor decisions.

5. *Dive track.* Our fullbacks must understand the importance of getting on the dive track and staying there. We block it for two to three yards. They must hit it square, low, and in the proper gap to make two more yards. We are interested in averaging three or four yards on this play. We spend 10 minutes a day on this aspect and tell our fullbacks they must be the toughest guys on the track. We work numerous drills with them in order to accomplish this (figure 1).

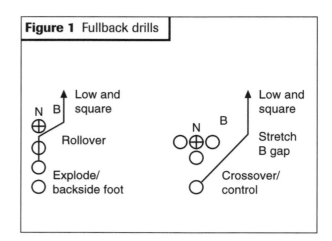

Figure 1 Fullback drills

6. *Read drill.* We spend one to two periods a day on this, trying to incorporate all the looks we are going to get. We spend most of the time on the triple option. We are trying to get a maximum number of repetitions with two backfields. We can incorporate a lot of the other aspects into this: decision making, dive track, mesh, pitch (figure 2).

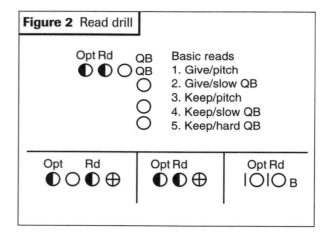

Figure 2 Read drill

7. *Perimeter blocking.* Our wide receivers must realize they have to be blockers first. They must understand the importance of their blocks on front side option plays, the dive play inside, and option plays away. We teach their blocking technique in a lot of ways, the same way we teach pass protection. We don't need big hits, but good position. This comes from perfecting the base technique (set-mirror-punch-recover) and tremendous hustle.

8. *Staff.* I have been fortunate to have a great staff here at USD. They have done a super job in helping us be successful.

The zone dive (figure 3) is a play we need to be able to run every week. We go into a game planning to run it 10 to 15 times. The key to this play is to check it properly and handle the noseguard. Most defenses react to the zone scheme in such a way as to give the fullback a seam in the B gap. If the B gap is plugged, we tell the fullback to be an instinctive runner. He has to be careful of cutting it back too quickly.

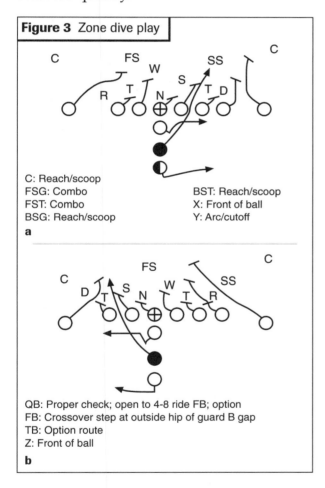

Figure 3 Zone dive play

C: Reach/scoop
FSG: Combo
FST: Combo
BSG: Reach/scoop

BST: Reach/scoop
X: Front of ball
Y: Arc/cutoff

a

QB: Proper check; open to 4-8 ride FB; option
FB: Crossover step at outside hip of guard B gap
TB: Option route
Z: Front of ball

b

The zone option (figure 4) is a two-way option designed to get the ball pitched. We run this play to take advantage of our speed, and if we get a lot of weak fronts. The key is pinning down the play side LB with either the tackle or the fullback. In a lot of ways, this play is similar to the I-back sweep. If the LB is running out, we have a companion play that works well. It is a designed QB follow play.

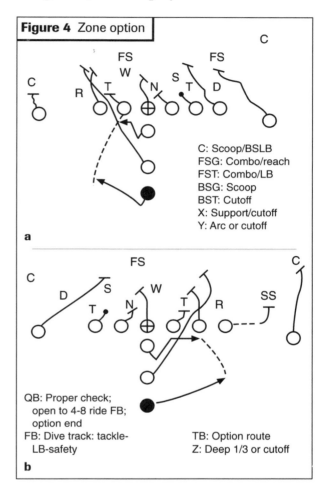

Figure 4 Zone option

C: Scoop/BSLB
FSG: Combo/reach
FST: Combo/LB
BSG: Scoop
BST: Cutoff
X: Support/cutoff
Y: Arc or cutoff

a

QB: Proper check; open to 4-8 ride FB; option end
FB: Dive track: tackle-LB-safety

TB: Option route
Z: Deep 1/3 or cutoff

b

The triple option (figure 5) is similar to the old Inside Veer or triple to the fullback in the Wishbone. The big difference is the FB's. This play is a good companion to the zone dive. It forces the noseguard to play the double-team and can wear him out. Also, it puts the fullback on a path the play side LB has to honor. It is hard for a five-technique to close all the way. With the long ride, the tight path, the LB is frozen, allowing the ball to get outside. We tell the QB, when in doubt he should give it. This was our best method of getting the ball outside this year. We tell the receivers to block like the ball will be pitched.

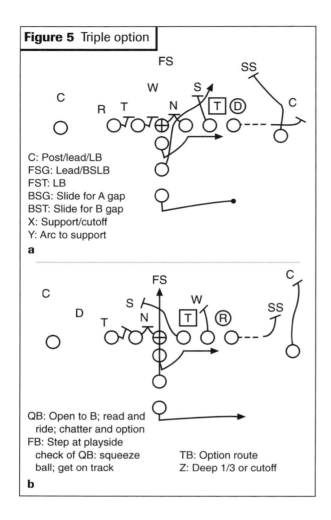

Figure 5 Triple option

C: Post/lead/LB
FSG: Lead/BSLB
FST: LB
BSG: Slide for A gap
BST: Slide for B gap
X: Support/cutoff
Y: Arc to support

a

QB: Open to B; read and ride; chatter and option
FB: Step at playside check of QB: squeeze ball; get on track
TB: Option route
Z: Deep 1/3 or cutoff

b

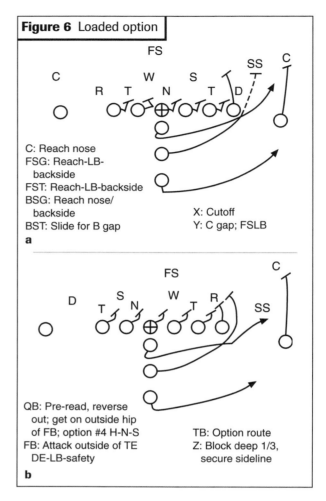

Figure 6 Loaded option

C: Reach nose
FSG: Reach-LB-backside
FST: Reach-LB-backside
BSG: Reach nose/backside
BST: Slide for B gap
X: Cutoff
Y: C gap; FSLB

a

QB: Pre-read, reverse out; get on outside hip of FB; option #4 H-N-S
FB: Attack outside of TE DE-LB-safety
TB: Option route
Z: Block deep 1/3, secure sideline

b

The loaded option (figure 6) has been one of our most successful plays over the last six years. It is especially effective against goal line defenses. It is a cross between the outside veer and the loaded out of the Wishbone. The key block is the TE. If we can seal the LB, we know we can make yards. We cannot allow inside penetration, but that is not hard. The fullback has to read the reaction of the defensive end. Also, the QB needs to be aware of down and distance. This play is a pure QB keeper.

We like to use different formations to run our base plays (figure 7). We use these on the hash, or in the middle if a team is overshifting. Primarily, we try to take care of the alley football player with our X. Second, if a team doesn't adjust properly, it gives us a man advantage to the wide side and a chance for a big play. Finally, if we get a team overshifting strong, we can come back weak. We will run three of our plays coordinated with the motion. When in doubt, we will run the plays strong. The key to the loaded and triple is where the back side corner lines up. The key to the zone dive is the same as we discussed earlier.

Most important, it is essential for a coach to understand and make proper use of his personnel. We have been blessed with good option people. If we had passing people, we would adjust. Either way, a team concept approach to winning is the only way to success.

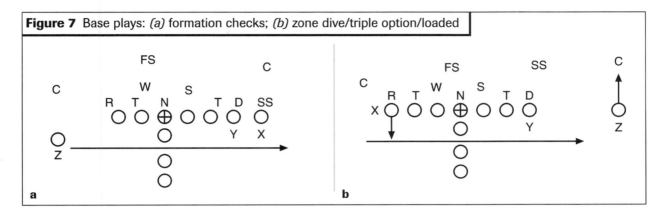

Figure 7 Base plays: *(a)* formation checks; *(b)* zone dive/triple option/loaded

1987 Proceedings. Dave Triplett was head coach at the University of South Dakota.

Winning With Basic Schemes

Pete Schmidt

In 1989, we at Albion College changed our offensive thinking, and the results have been outstanding for us. One of our thoughts was to commit our team to a consistent running game. This year we wanted to develop the following run concepts:

1. Rely on bread-and-butter plays and do not invent new plays each week. This gave our players confidence, allowed them to improve each week, and enabled them to play aggressively.

2. Be as simple as possible. This helped our players perform with confidence and enabled them to perform with a high degree of efficiency in pressure situations.

3. Carry no fat in the run game. Each play serves a specific purpose. We could not afford to practice plays that would not get called on game day. Many good plays were left out.

4. Run the ball versus defenses that loaded up against the run. We did not want the defense dictating when we would pass.

5. Do not change offense in goal line and short-yardage situations. We had a limited amount of practice time, and we wanted to use plays that created momentum to get us there.

6. Be as aware of how the defense is playing as of where they were playing.

7. Emphasize perimeter blocking. These were the blocks that enabled us to make some big plays.

8. Develop a system of blocking that would not change. This allowed our players to become proficient because techniques and skills did not change. We employed three basic blocking schemes: zone, draw, and gap.

The selection of formations was based on our talent. We determined the I formation with two wide receivers would be our basic look, and we implemented it 80 percent of the time. We supplemented our basic look with several one-back/three-receiver formations. Our offensive line splits varied based on the plays called, and the size and type of defense of our opponent.

Our slant play (figure 1), an off-tackle power play, has been our best running play for the past six years. Our zone techniques require lateral movement; therefore, our linemen maintain a balanced stance. We ask our linemen to make contact on their second step and maintain a base to sustain the block. Finishing the block is very important, yet the offensive lineman's body must move in a single direction. It is critical that we move defenders off the LOS at the point of attack. We also teach blockers to use depth steps to cover up defensive linemen aligned play side.

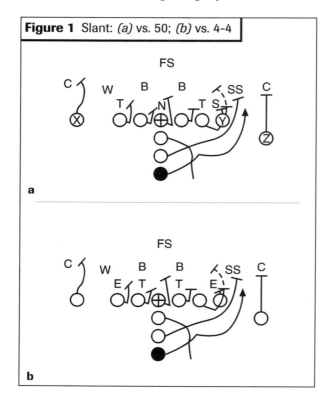

Figure 1 Slant: *(a)* vs. 50; *(b)* vs. 4-4

In figure 1a, we zone to the front side tackle versus a 50 defense. This play has been very successful versus a reading style of defense. We ask our QB to open at four o'clock, make the handoff on his second step, and fake a play-action pass or bootleg action.

We like to run this play to both our tight and split sides, based upon how the defense aligns its front. Our tailback uses a drop-open step and takes a course at the inside leg of our TE. He must maintain this course and read the TE's block.

This is critical as it allows our tailback to cut inside should a defensive lineman cross his face.

Our fullback takes the same course and strongly blocks the force or number four. Our TE executes a reach block. The front side tackle goes through the outside number of the defensive tackle to the LB. The front side guard gets depth and scoop blocks the defensive tackle. The center and back side guard execute the same zone techniques. The back side tackle uses a cutoff technique.

In figure 1b, we zone to the TE versus a 4-4 defense. The slant play can be run against a variety of defensive fronts from multiple formations. It enables our linemen to play a physical style of football. It allows our running back to use his natural instincts and run to daylight. We use a minimum number of adjustments, but this play requires a lot of repetition in practice.

Figure 2 shows our option play, blocked with our zone rules and techniques. We blocked this play the same as our slant play. Our QB makes an open pivot, fakes to the fullback, and executes an option technique against the number four defender. Our fullback attacks the B gap with a dive fake and slides outside to block. Our tailback runs an option course. We used this play versus some eight-man fronts, blitzing defenses, and as a change-up.

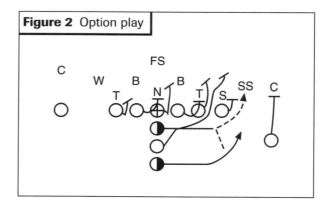

Figure 2 Option play

Our inside zone play (figure 3) was best versus 4-3 and reduction defenses. We ran our inside play from both two-back (figure 3a) and one-back (figure 3b) formations. We employed basic zone principles, but several defenses dictated that a man-blocking scheme be used. The tailback ran a belly course at the outside leg of the front side guard. Our fullback blocked the outside LB on the weak side. The QB executed an open pivot at five o'clock, made the exchange, and faked boot action away. Our front side blockers executed a power-go technique and tried to create good movement at the point of attack. Our blockers' shoulders stayed square when blocking this play as opposed to the slant play. This play also allowed for greater cutback possibilities for our tailback.

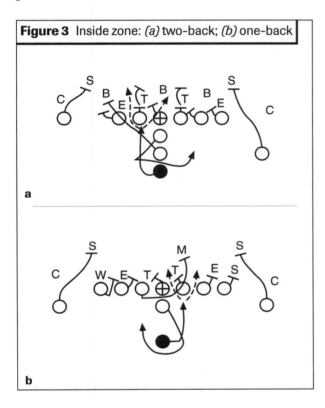

Figure 3 Inside zone: *(a)* two-back; *(b)* one-back

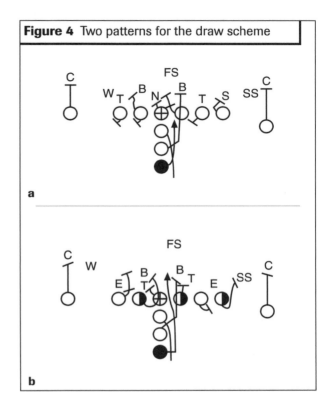

Figure 4 Two patterns for the draw scheme

Our lead draw play (figure 4) is designed to attack aggressive defenders by creating a vertical stretch between the LBs and defensive line. The defensive linemen are drawn upfield by the pass set of the offensive line. The LBs are frozen by the delayed action in the backfield. This is a sound play versus a variety of fronts and allows our tailback to run to daylight. We have also found this play to be very good versus blitzing defenses.

Our QB open pivots at five o'clock, hands the ball deep to our tailback, and fakes a play-action pass. The tailback takes a slide step, delays, and option runs the football, reading the defensive linemen. Our fullback lead steps, crosses over, and reads the B gap area.

He is responsible for the Mike LB. Our TE and front side tackle set for the defenders on or outside. The rest of the line executes our gap pass protection scheme away from the call.

Figure 5a shows our off-tackle power play with delayed back action. The back's counter steps allow the back side tackle to lead the ballcarrier through the hole behind the back side guard's kick-out block. The front side tackle and tight end double-team to the back side LB. The front side guard and center gap block to the back side. Our fullback takes a course at our back side tackle. Our tailback executes a counter slide-step and runs at the inside leg of the tackle. The QB opens away from the point of attack at six o'clock, executes the exchange, and fakes the boot. We used this play from a one-back set, and it was good versus 4-3 and 40 front teams.

Figure 5b shows off-tackle power with the fullback kicking the outside LB. The ball is run tight off the swipe combination and breaks off the lead block of the back side guard. The fullback must kick out with his head inside. If we get a spill technique, he cuts his outside leg. He must know the ball will go inside of

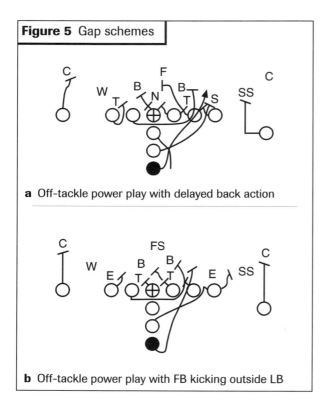

Figure 5 Gap schemes

a Off-tackle power play with delayed back action

b Off-tackle power play with FB kicking outside LB

guard leading through to the front side LB. We handle the strong safety with motion or formation adjustments. We do not like this play versus a tight-playing strong safety.

Our draw trap scheme (figure 6) is a trap play with center draw action. It counters aggressive wide rushing defenders. We run the trap from one-back and two-back formations.

Our running game is based on these five plays. They allow us to attack a variety of fronts with good consistency. We averaged 5.8 yards per carry, which enabled us to maintain a + 34 turnover ratio. We meshed them with a play-action pass system that led to a national title.

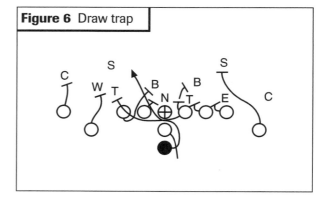

Figure 6 Draw trap

him every time. The tailback's course is at the tackle's inside leg. He runs tight to the swipe; he cannot bounce this out. Our blocking remains the same with the exception of our

1995 Proceedings. Pete Schmidt was head football coach at Albion College. Schmidt is assistant head coach and quarterback coach at Indiana University.

Incorporating the Sprint Draw

Don Christensen and Howard Ross

"Regardless of what you put in, every game boils down to doing the things you do best, and doing them over and over again." This well-known Lombardism governs a great deal of our thinking on how to move the ball. Several additional guidelines influence us as well:

1. Every well-designed play presupposes the ability to block and properly execute the play.
2. There is a limit to the number of plays, techniques, rules, and skills that can be mastered.

3. The offense you run and believe in must be tailored to the talents of the players available.

4. Offense is an eleven-man proposition. Every man is indispensable. We count on everyone to do his job.

The sprint draw to the slot side is one of the bases for our attack. Figure 1 shows the preliminary action of the play.

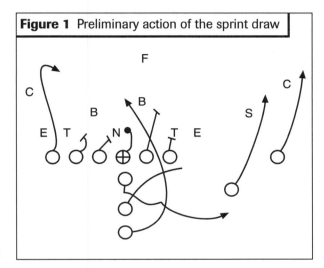

Figure 1 Preliminary action of the sprint draw

Quarterback

The QB steps away from the center for a three-step mesh point with the tailback, who is about four to five yards deep and approximately as wide as the inside of the offensive tackle's original alignment. His shoulder faces the sideline. He hands off the ball somewhat forward.

Fullback

The fullback lines up with his feet close to parallel, five yards from the ball, aimed at a point straight through the offensive tackle's stance. He blocks the first wrong-colored jersey to show outside the tackle's block and blocks the man through his outside thigh. It is important that the fullback's block is the same on all plays in the series, so we don't telegraph

the play with the angle of the fullback's approach.

Tailback

Starting with a lead step, the tailback goes to the hand-off spot, keying the movement of the first down lineman on defense. The tailback's shoulders should face the LOS so he can see the move to the running lane wherever it occurs from tackle to tackle. The complete footwork of the QB-TB exchange is shown in figure 2.

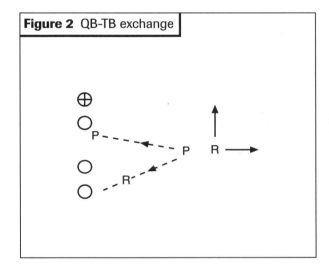

Figure 2 QB-TB exchange

Onside Guard and Tackle

The assignments of the guard and tackle are taught together, as each must be aware of and thoroughly understand what the other's responsibilities are. The guard and tackle must block number one and number two between them, with the tackle usually blocking the down lineman and the guard usually blocking the LB. If both are down, the tackle blocks inside unless either one calls switch. Blockers must get a side on the defender, not allowing themselves to be squared, as this makes the running lane for the tailback vague. Figure 3 indicates the application of this against some common defenses.

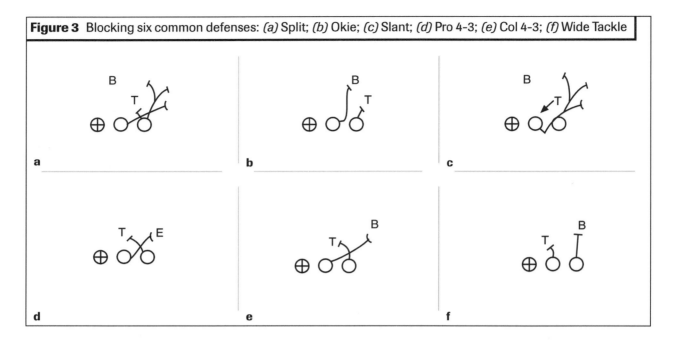

Figure 3 Blocking six common defenses: *(a)* Split; *(b)* Okie; *(c)* Slant; *(d)* Pro 4-3; *(e)* Col 4-3; *(f)* Wide Tackle

Center and Back Side Guard

The center and back side guard block zero and back side number one between them, using the appropriate technique to accomplish this (see figure 4).

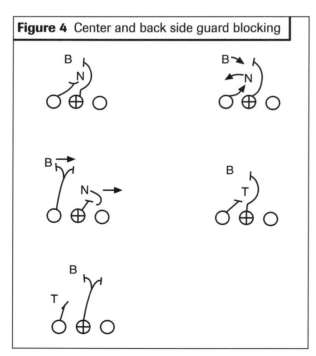

Figure 4 Center and back side guard blocking

Back Side Tackle

The back side tackle blocks back side number two and cuts off the back side pursuit. He steps to the inside and forces the lineman to go behind him. If the DT slants, the tackle must take him hard across in the direction of the slant, forcing him as deep and inside as possible. The back side tackle never has responsibility downfield, but focuses on cutting off the back side pursuit.

Receivers

Every play is a pass to the receivers. Receivers are not very sincere about faking a pass play when they know it's not going to happen, and secondary defenders become proficient at reading these intentions. To preserve the integrity of the play, the QB can keep the ball and run on the corner with the threat to run or pass. Because the receivers are not involved in blocking, the play can be run in either direction from any formation that leaves the I tandem intact. Assignments are taught in terms of wide receiver, inside receiver, and single receiver.

Receivers are asked to read the coverage on the move and run a route according to the coverage. Our contention, though it is an over-simplification, is that with full flow to one side, coverages can be classified into invert zone, corner roll, or man. Yes, there are many coverage possibilities, but based on what the receiver sees in his area, this classification is stable. It is important that the QB is a threat to run the corner and that we have confidence to run the play in any down-and-distance situation.

Wide Receiver

If the cornerback jumps on the wide receiver, trying to force him inside, it is an obvious corner roll. The receiver should stay outside and get to the "sweet spot," an area near the sideline, about 14-17 yards deep (figure 5). If the cornerback gives a cushion, he probably has deep one-third responsibility, so the receiver should run an out cut at about 12 yards. If he is playing tough and to the inside, it's man coverage, and the receiver runs the 12-yard out cut. So, in review, versus the corner roll, the receiver goes to the sweet spot; against anything else, he cuts out.

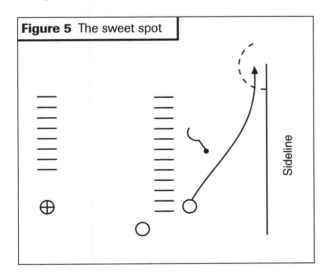

Figure 5 The sweet spot

Inside Receiver

If an invert zone shows, the inside receiver gets 10-12 yards deep, turns to the inside, and gradually fades to the outside with the flow of the play, facing the QB and trying to feel the open space. We call this a settle route. If the strong

safety goes to deep outside one-third or stays near the hash mark but gives plenty of cushion, we treat this as a rolled corner and the inside receiver settles. If the strong safety plays man (often, the inside-out position of the CB on the WR will tell you), the receiver runs a flag route, looking over his outside shoulder. Review: zone—settle; man—flag (see figure 6).

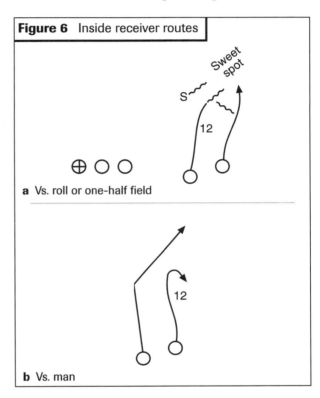

Figure 6 Inside receiver routes

a Vs. roll or one-half field

b Vs. man

The QB, as he clears the fake to the tailback, will look for the outside receiver, running either a 12-yard out (which takes some timing), or to the sweet spot (which demands that the QB throw the ball to the sweet spot and the receiver be under control enough to catch it). On this pattern, we coach the QB to throw an incomplete pass to the space, so that neither the strong safety nor the CB can make the interception. We coach the WR to get there under control and catch it. If the QB cannot throw to the wide receiver, he looks to the inside receiver. If an end is dropped off in front of the settle route, the QB must run. The best and earliest results come from a QB who is a good runner and who likes to run the ball.

Single Receiver

The single receiver runs a 12-yard curl route. As he turns, he finds the inside LB on his side and comes back to the QB in the open lane. If the QB is forced to pull up by the defensive end, he looks for the throwback or scramble ahead and gets what he can.

Here are some coaching points worth noting:

■ *Tailback key.* If the DT stays outside our OT, the TB looks to the noseguard for his slant. This is part of the reason for making sure your tailback faces the LOS when receiving the ball.

■ *Guard and fullback.* If the DT slants inside and the end comes hard and tight, the guard will not be able to get around his OT to block the LB. When the end is that tight, the guard will block him right there, usually trying to cut him. The fullback sees this in front of him, steps around the guard's block, and picks up the LB. This part of the play takes some repetitions.

■ *Quarterback options.* On the called running draw play, if the end comes hard, the QB can keep the ball and exercise the option to run or pass. The pass will be all right, as the OG is blocking the end at the LOS, and the back side tackle does not go downfield.

■ *Blocking alternatives.* When we know that the OT's block is going to be to the inside, we exchange assignments between the OG and the FB. The guard will kick out the end, and the fullback will turn up inside and block the LB. Figure 7 shows this scheme.

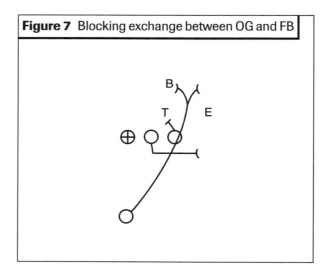

Figure 7 Blocking exchange between OG and FB

This series of plays includes a called TB draw that can end up as a QB run or QB pass; a called alternate blocking scheme that is an intended TB draw and can end up as a QB run or pass; and a called QB run or pass, which will be just that. On this play, we pass-block the back side in case the QB pulls up and must throw back. The tailback blocks the noseguard if the noseguard slants to the play side or gets off the center to the play side. We can also run a couple of alternate pass patterns when we are facing a steady diet of man coverage. These have a separate number and are not read.

1977 Summer Manual. Don Christensen and Howard Ross were assistant coaches at Montana State University.

Teaching the Triple Option

Emory Bellard

At Texas A & M, we were interested in developing a balanced, mirrored offense. We knew that to throw the ball with consistency, we must have at least one receiver deployed who was selected for his ability to run routes and catch the ball. In our study and from past experience, we knew that it was tough to establish a sound running game into a split end. This fact was uppermost in our study, and the only play we could see that could be sound against all the various defensive alignments was the triple option.

In studying teams that used the triple option, the major problem we saw them experience was blocking the corner when the pitch was made. We decided that we could handle this situation by using a "lead back" principle a la the Split-T.

Another problem was the insecurity of the exchange between the QB and the hand-off back on the inside option. We decided to handle this problem by positioning our hand-off man in the middle, which allowed us to train the one man and also allowed our QB to secure the ball in the pocket, then read the key, rather than reading the key, then securing the ball on the handoff. This has proven successful; fumbles on this exchange have been virtually nonexistent. With these things in mind, we decided that the triple option (figure 1) was to be our basic offensive play.

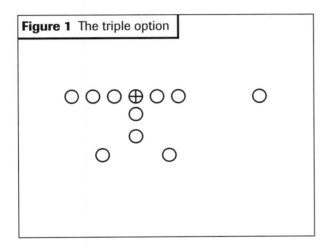

Figure 1 The triple option

We then positioned our backs in what we thought was the most advantageous alignment from which to run the triple option, the formation known as the Wishbone-T). We knew that with the triple option we could threaten six points along the LOS before the ball was snapped, which would give us balance (see figure 2). We studied defenses to determine how the various defensive structures would have to play us, at least from a theoretical standpoint.

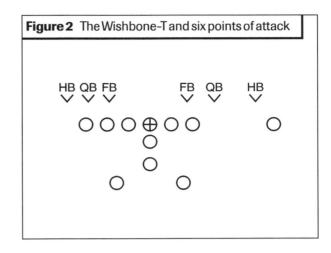

Figure 2 The Wishbone-T and six points of attack

We knew that we could drive one man deep with our releasing end because of the pass threat (figure 3). We knew that this man could not have a deep responsibility and be responsible for the pitch at the same time. Therefore, we would have a sound block on the man we would refer to as number one from the outside.

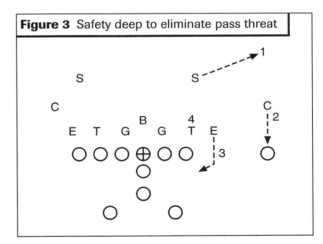

Figure 3 Safety deep to eliminate pass threat

We knew now that the next man in from the outside would have to be responsible for the pitch (figure 4). We termed this man number two from outside.

Obviously, now the number three man from the outside will be responsible for the QB. The position of the number four man from the outside dictates how they will play the fullback: inside out (figure 5) or outside in (figure 6).

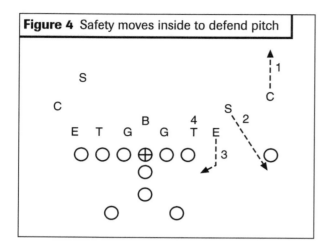

Figure 4 Safety moves inside to defend pitch

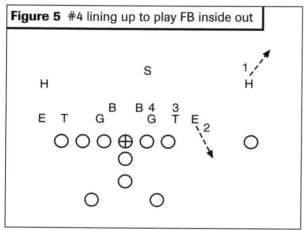

Figure 5 #4 lining up to play FB inside out

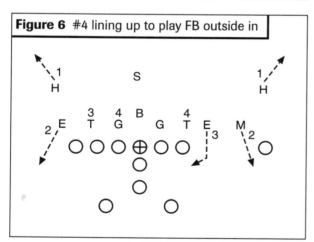

Figure 6 #4 lining up to play FB outside in

We took these principles and applied them to all the various defensive structures, and decided that all defenses would fall into one of three categories: umbrella, three-deep with a balanced eight-man front, and three-deep with an unbalanced eight-man front.

Because this one basic play forced defenses into individual isolated areas of responsibility, we were able to apply our offense. We knew what we wanted to do, and now we had to teach it. The basic concepts of teaching the triple option (figure 7) are contained in the following comments.

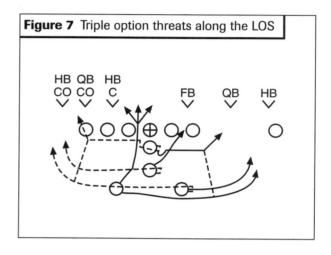

Figure 7 Triple option threats along the LOS

Prior to the snap, the triple option threatens six points along the LOS, but once the ball is snapped, the triple option is committed to one side. In order to maintain balance, the counter offense now threatens the remaining three points along the LOS (figure 8). With these three plays, we are able to establish and maintain balance. Due to the nature of the triple option, halfback counter, and counter option, we are running plays with a built-in, automatic system that should have us calling the best one for a high-consistency gainer.

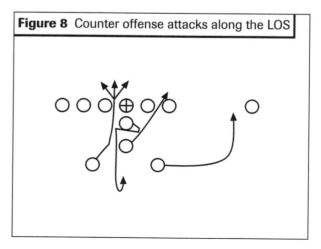

Figure 8 Counter offense attacks along the LOS

Halfback Counter

The following points cover keys to success with the halfback counter play (figure 9) for the right and left halfbacks, the fullback, and QB.

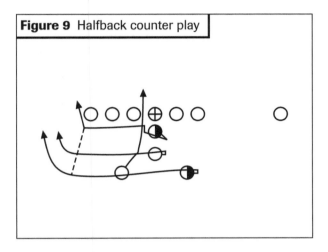

Figure 9 Halfback counter play

The right halfback fakes an arc block on number two from the outside, as on the 52 veer. The fake must threaten the man responsible for the pitch. He holds this defensive man from pursuit on the halfback counter and sets up the block for the veer. He should carry the fake to the LOS and stay involved in the play.

The fullback fakes on the path, as on the 52 veer, coordinating the handoff fake with the QB's jab fake. He sinks the fake and blocks the first defensive man to appear outside his faking path.

The left halfback's first step should be with his right foot on approximately a 40-degree angle toward the LOS. This should establish a path that will have his right foot on a line at the center's left foot. His shoulders should be square to the LOS. He should have his eyes up and be ready to cut off the block of the offensive left guard. He should run for daylight.

The QB's execution is actually in three parts: fake, handoff, and follow-through fake. For the fake, the QB open-steps with his right foot, as on the first step of the 52 veer. This step will be shortened slightly. The second step is with the left foot. It should come up in a coordinated movement with the ball as the QB makes a jab fake to the fullback. The step should end up slightly in advance of the right foot; he must not overstride. This step puts the QB in position to adjust (third step) to the ballcarrier. On the jab fake, he keeps the ball level and returns to the belt buckle for the handoff.

The QB should now be in position for the handoff. The QB steps to the ballcarrier with his right foot slightly toward the LOS and on such a path that it will not interfere with the running line of the ballcarrier. This is the adjustment step. He positively places the ball in the pocket of the left halfback. His weight should be on the right foot. For the follow-through fake, he drops straight back and sets up as if to pass at an approximate depth of seven yards.

Counter Option

The following points cover the keys to success for the counter option (figure 10) for the right and left halfbacks, the fullback, and the QB.

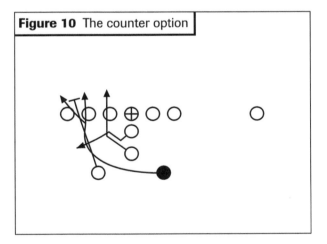

Figure 10 The counter option

The left halfback executes exactly the same as on the halfback counter play except that he does not deviate from his faking path. He should be faking through the center-guard gap. He does not alter the path. He tries to make five yards on the fake.

The fullback counter steps right (coordinating a head and shoulder fake with a short parallel step with the right foot) and then breaks on a parallel path to his left. He takes an aggressive angle for the outside leg. If run toward the TE, he becomes the first supporting back to the defensive end. If run toward the split end, he hits number 2 from the outside.

The right halfback counter steps right (coordinating a head and shoulder fake with a short parallel step with the right foot) and then breaks on a parallel path until he receives the pitch. He rides the outside hip of the lead blocker (the fullback), staying alert for the pitch after the counter step.

The QB's initial fake is exactly the same as on the halfback counter. The difference in execution comes as he takes the adjustment step (the third step). As he steps back to the faking left halfback, he turns so that his shoulders are square to the sidelines and his right foot is in front. As the halfback fakes by, he makes a short jab ride with him. His eyes should be up and alert for pressure from the defensive end. As the faking back clears, he explodes to the outside, freezes to force the defensive end, and pitches the football or takes an obvious keep.

Inside Belly

The following points are the keys to success in running the inside belly play for the right and left halfbacks, the fullback, and quarterback.

1972 Summer Manual. Emory Bellard was head coach at Texas A & M.

The fullback starts on a path exactly as if on a 53 veer but, as the ball is placed in his pocket for the ride, he turns straight upfield and sinks the fake. He does not alter from this path!

The left halfback leads the first man inside the defensive end. He takes the first step so as to establish a path on a direct line from his stance to the target. On his approach, he uses his speed and stays down to be in a hitting position from stance to contact. He puts his head in the middle and does not pick a side.

The right halfback's first step is a lead step with his left foot on a parallel path. From that point, he runs an arc tight on the outside hip of the lead blocker. He runs for daylight off the block.

The QB open steps with his left foot and places the ball in the pocket of the fullback, as on the veer. The second step is an adjustment step as he flows with the fullback. As the ball gets to a point even with his right hip, he disconnects sharply. The next step is with the left foot slightly off the LOS, and he now steps with the right foot to hand off to the ballcarrier. Steps are left-right-left-right, with the second and fourth steps as adjustment steps.

Adding to the Triple Option

Charlie Taaffe

We are a Wishbone team on offense, which means we primarily run the football, and approximately 60 to 65 percent of our rushing attack is based on the triple option. The triple option is where our offense begins, but we have also felt the need to develop a package that complements our base offense. It is imperative to not allow the defense to scheme methods to remove our fullback as a running threat in our offense.

In the Wishbone, the fullback *must* run with the ball. Over the years, we have had to devise

ways for our fullback to be a factor in the offense—the triple option is not enough! The trap/trap option series has given us a consistent method of keeping the fullback involved.

The Fullback Trap

The FB trap has given us a consistent play that can be executed against most defenses (figures 1, 2, and 3). Generally, we trap the first defensive lineman past the center and have

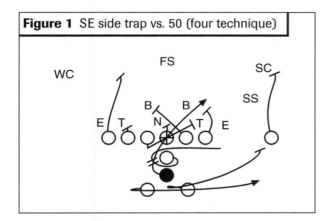

Figure 1 SE side trap vs. 50 (four technique)

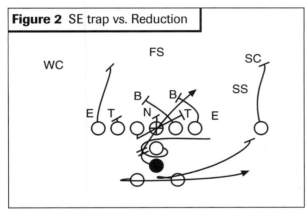

Figure 2 SE trap vs. Reduction

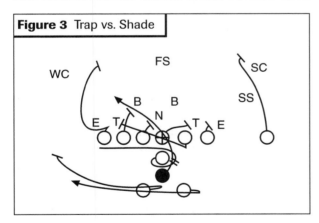

Figure 3 Trap vs. Shade

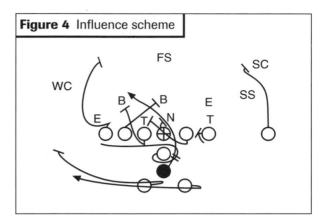

Figure 4 Influence scheme

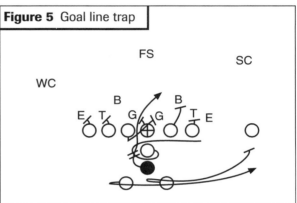

Figure 5 Goal line trap

the ability to change the direction of the play at the LOS based on the alignment of the defensive front (figure 4). We do not prefer to trap a four-defender side. If we elect to trap an "A" gap defender, we add the term "goal line" to our trap play (figure 5), which allows us to trap most goal line defenses and to assist the fullback in knowing where the trap will occur.

The fullback aligns with his heels five and one-half yards from the front tip of the ball. This could vary slightly, depending on the fullback's speed. The fullback should know prior to the snap where the trap will occur based on the defensive alignments. On the snap, the fullback runs an "S" course, putting the play side foot in front of the offside foot (crossover). It is important that the fullback does not step outside the offside foot. We would like the FB to stay tight to any down block, stay inside out of the trap block, and break off the block on the PSLB.

The QB executes a full turn (360 degrees), or "whirlybird" action, as has become the popular description of this move. We prefer this action because of the holding effect it has on the LBs and free safety. On the snap, the QB reverse pivots slightly past six o'clock. His second step (balance step) must insure that his shoulders will be perpendicular to the LOS. The third step is a ride-and-follow-the-fullback turn to the inside, sink the mesh, and carry out the option fake.

The Trap Option

Once the trap has been established and LBs begin to step up on play recognition, the defense makes itself vulnerable to the trap option (figures 6, 7, 8, and 9). The QB action and subsequent mesh with the FB has the potential to freeze the LB and free safety. When this occurs, it is time to run the option off the trap

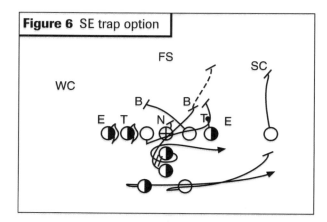

Figure 6 SE trap option

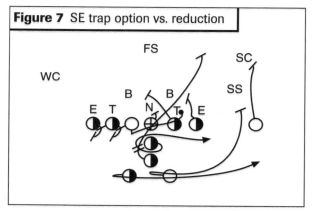

Figure 7 SE trap option vs. reduction

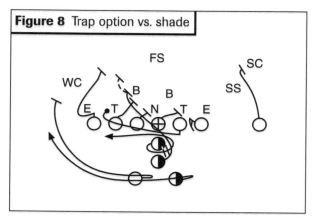

Figure 8 Trap option vs. shade

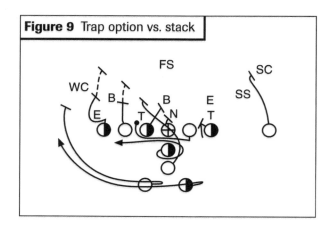

Figure 9 Trap option vs. stack

fake. The backfield action is identical to the trap; everything must look the same. A good coaching point for the QB is to "sneak a peak" at the pitch key on the first step. The whirlybird action allows the QB to accomplish this, since he does not have his back to the pitch key. This is particularly helpful to the open end side.

The pitch back can assist the QB by recognizing hard pressure and calling to the QB as the stunt is recognized. The line blocking is identical to the trap; on the trap option, we "log" the same defender who is trapped on the trap play. This has the potential to create conflict for the defensive lineman.

Versus a 5 technique who plays heavy (squeezes a veer release), we have the option to use a reverse body block by the PST.

The trap option gives us a misdirection type of option play that has an excellent freeze effect on the LB and free safety. Of course, it is imperative to establish the FB trap in order for the trap option to be successful.

The Trap Option Pass

The trap option pass is an excellent series because the pass look is identical to the trap/trap option. When we throw off the trap option series, we have specific ideas in mind. We want to control the pitch support to the TE and SE, control the FS support on the option, and take advantage of a fast-flow LB. Any number of routes can be used to accomplish these objectives (figures 10, 11, and 12).

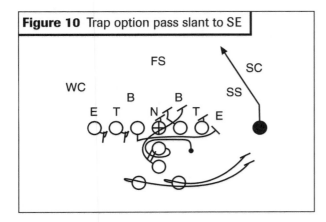

Figure 10 Trap option pass slant to SE

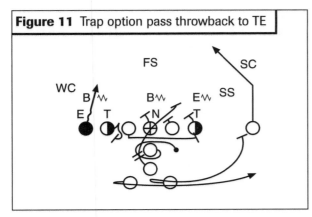

Figure 11 Trap option pass throwback to TE

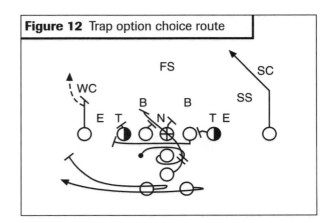

Figure 12 Trap option choice route

On the choice route (figure 12), the TE (Y) will have three options:

1. Versus a soft corner run, he stops the route at nine yards.
2. Versus a corner that squats, he runs the streak and sells the option!
3. Versus a hard corner, he runs a fade adjustment.

This series has been a supplement to our Wishbone triple option attack. The trap keeps our fullback a threat in the offense, the trap option provides a misdirection option with tremendous freeze potential on the LB and FS, and the trap option pass takes advantage of a secondary that aggressively supports against the option phases of the series.

1993 Summer Manual. Charlie Taaffe was head coach at The Citadel. He is the head coach of the Montreal Alouettes.

Training the Wishbone Quarterback

Pepper Rodgers

The Wishbone QB has one absolute requirement: he must be an aggressive runner. Without an athlete who looks for spaces between pursuing defenders and who is eager to keep the ball himself, the offense will not work. Speed and size help at the QB position just as they do at any position, but aggressiveness is the key and the only absolute requirement.

A Wishbone QB—with the reading of defensive linemen on the triple-option play in addition to the passing, ball handling, and optioning—has a bigger job than other T quarterbacks do, and the offense needs an athlete who will work hard to prepare himself, think positively, and concentrate totally in game action. However, again, aggressiveness is the element without which the offense will not work.

Execution of the Read

The first problem is to find the defender to read. Option theory holds that a single defender cannot take both the QB and the pitch man or both the pitch man and the downfield receiver. It takes three defenders to stop the outside dimensions of the play. If a fourth can be moved to the outside defense, there is no way to handle him. Assuming that one of the eleven defenders is over the center or at middle safety, just five defenders are on each side and two of them must play the inside. Just three men are available to play the QB, the pitch man, and the receiver.

In simplest terms, then, and counting from the outside in, the fourth man in must either be blocked or eliminated by the read. That suggests the rule for triple optioning—the fourth man in must be blocked or read. A later section deals exhaustively with counting problems. Basically, if the fourth man is a LB, he will be blocked. If the fourth man is a lineman inside of the tackle, he will be blocked by the tackle. But if he is a lineman on or outside of the tackle, he will be read.

The problem of dealing with the latter will be discussed first. It is on this type of man that the fundamentals must be learned. The all-important thought process will be explained first, followed by the geometry of fitting the athletes together for smooth ball handling.

The execution of the basic play begins in the mind of the QB. Which man does he read? What are that man's responsibilities? Is he number four or is he number three? Is there a cross stunt possibility? Where is the man who will take the QB if the ball is taken to the outside? The most difficult part of the execution takes place in the thought process before the ball is snapped. And it can be impossibly difficult unless the athlete understands something about mind/eye/muscle coordination time.

An analogy will make the point. A baseball hitter, in his mind, does not think of hitting the ball if it comes across the plate and not hitting it if it does not. He is going to hit every ball that is pitched. He makes a move to hit every ball. His only reaction is to check up and not swing. In other words, he does not give his mind/eye/ muscle coordination two reactions to make, just one.

This principle applies to the QB's decision to give the ball or disconnect it. For the easiest reads, he might not need to think this way, but for the toughest, for the fast ball, he will. He steps away from the center with the intention of giving the ball to the FB and leaves himself only the reaction of disconnecting on certain reads. Or he steps with the intention of disconnecting and gives only if he gets a certain signal. An athlete will not grasp this approach the first time or the first five or fifty times he tries to read; but he will in time, and it will help him.

Again, the most difficult part of execution takes place in the QB's mind before the ball is ever snapped. If only a few defense and tackle movements needed to be read, there would be no problem. But they get difficult to the point where the give and disconnect signals are equally strong.

Having an approach clearly in mind before stepping away from the center can be every bit as important as it is for a baseball hitter to move to hit the fastball before it ever comes off the pitcher's hand.

Working With the Fullback

Along with a clear and positive thought process, a QB needs a smooth and sure hookup with his FB. The exchange from the center has something to do with this, as does the position of the FB's bottom hand and extension of the QB's arms and a number of other details. First, the exact positioning and movements of the center, QB, and FB will be explained; next, the actual mechanics of handling the ball.

The QB's first movement with the ball is sharply away from the center, and the ball exchange technique must fit accordingly. On no other T formation play is the movement of the ball more sharply away from the center because the QB tries to get the ball hooked up with the FB as quickly as possible. The center should grip the ball just as he would if he were going to pass it. The QB fits his hands together with the anchor points to the center being the fingernail of the middle finger of the right hand (anchored to the middle seam of the center's pants) and the inside of the right thumb (touching the center's butt). If an imaginary line bisecting the angle formed by the QB's hands points at the rear tip of the ball as it lies flat, the position is good.

The QB's arms are slightly bent at the elbows, and the fingers are taut as though they are reaching for the ball. The ball is moved on a line so that it will wedge into the QB's hands. This means that the center must use only one hand to move the ball and that his elbow must bend during the motion. The middle finger of the QB's left hand is pointed out at 45 degrees, and the hand of the center rotated somewhat less than 90 degrees. This takes pressure off the hands of both athletes.

The purpose of the technique is to ensure the exchange for the extreme movement of the ball, which happens on 90 percent of the plays in the Wishbone offense. Having the center actually push the ball through the V formed by the QB's hands and having the ball wedge into rather than slap onto the hands gives the insurance. When a QB operates along the LOS or when he is not pressured to move the ball quickly, a less precise technique will suffice.

The QB's feet should have a sensation of gripping the ground through the cleats. The first step places a foot on a line 45 degrees from the other foot. The arm opposite the direction of the step is extended until it is completely straight. The ball is not pulled into the belly and then extended; neither is it swung around with straight arms. It is merely moved as efficiently as possible to the FB's pocket.

If the FB's heels are lined up 13 feet from the forward tip of the ball, and if a short lead step puts him on a course that will run the middle of his body over the outside foot of a guard who has split 24 inches, then the QB's extension of the ball should put it in the FB's pocket. The

QB's step actually cannot control how far his arms reach. The angle of the body along with the length of the step controls this. It is enough to tell the QB to form the 45 degree line between his feet and to ride the FB with straight arms.

Two more important fundamental moves are needed to get everything hooked up so that a read can take place and a give or a disconnect can be made. The ride movement of the arms must be started as soon as the one arm is extended on the 45-degree angle. For the QB to ride by feel as he might in a belly series attack would put too much ball pressure on the FB.

Ideally, the ball would be fitted into the pocket with the FB feeling it with his arms but with only the back of a wrist touching his belly six inches from the center of the pocket. While the ride takes place, the FB folds his arms and hands softly over the ball but he should not be aware of pressure on his stomach until the decision is made by the QB to give. This ideal position will be approached if the ride action is started as soon as the arm is extended.

The other important fundamental has to do with the positioning of the head. A defender is watched, but the head should allow for the peripheral vision to see as much of the ride as possible. The eyes go to the defender, but the head turns slightly farther away.

With thought processes in order and hookup geometry accurate, the giving and disconnecting mechanics are not difficult. To give, the back hand is pulled away, the front hand presses the ball, and the arm follows the FB slightly farther than it does on the disconnect. The hands are then brought together for the fake. To disconnect, the ball is snapped away with the back of a wrist, keeping the FB from feeling any ball pressure. The grip on the ball must be secure because it is often pulled through the hands of the FB.

The QB's movement off the FB's tail is an acceleration, whether he has the ball or not. In faking, acceleration is the single most important thing; in optioning at the perimeter, acceleration means inches gained on the defense. In order to accelerate, the QB's second step is not forward with the ride. Instead, it hangs in the air waiting to start the sprint. The ride is actually made on one foot, although it does not seem to help the QB kinesthetically to think of actually being on the one foot as the arm ride is made.

Confidence Is the Key

It is a mistake to try to read until there is confidence about everything that leads up to it. Confidence, not perfection, is the key, and with it the QB can proceed to make the simplest of all reads. A defensive lineman can be put outside of the offensive tackle and told to move straight ahead or down the line. The defensive movement shows even before the hookup, and deciding to give or disconnect is a simple matter. It was to deal with almost this clear a movement that the triple-option play was developed, but today it is seldom that simple. The next step is to have the defender not move at all part of the time, to get a dividing line between give and disconnect reads.

At first the QB will tend to stare at the defender, but after some days of work he will begin picking up more and more in his peripheral vision. And the encouraging thing about starting a QB in this technique is that he can be assured that he will not have to execute anything he is not confident about. Remember, always, that the option play from the Wishbone formation with no read at all is a very good football play.

1993 Proceedings. Pepper Rodgers was head coach at Georgia Tech University.

Blocking the Wishbone

Jimmy Sharpe

The game is won in the trenches and, regardless of what offensive formation you use or believe in, that 18 inches of combat zone determines who will win the game. I am completely sold on offensive line play out of the Wishbone because of the improvement in our offensive line play.

We do several things differently at Virginia Tech that have helped our team improve overall. First, we are a true triple offense read football team. Contrary to what people think, we feel we are forced to read because we do not have people who can physically line up and knock folks off the football, and we have found that by using different blocking techniques involved in the read scheme, we are able to create a lot more problems for good defensive teams.

Our primary objective is to establish our fullback attack with our up-front people. We constantly try to sell our offensive line and FB on the fact that they are where it starts, that to be successful, our FB must average over four yards per carry. This year, our FB averaged 4.5. I feel we can achieve success more quickly with the Wishbone attack than any other offensive set. The first reason is the simplicity of the offense, the fact that you put the entire offense in at the beginning of the year and, with few exceptions, never change. Second, I feel that the players involved have a better understanding of the big picture, meaning a real feeling and understanding that it takes 11 people trying to win on every play. Third, because of the simplicity and improved understanding, I think players can better realize that the end result is the most important thing in football. It is not how pretty it looks, but it is getting the job done.

I mentioned that we do several things differently. First, our basic line splits a little wider than most Wishbone teams. Second, our FB runs a little tighter veer path than most (the FB's aiming point is the guard's outside hip). Third, for blocking assignments, we count all of our defenses from the inside out. And fourth, we feel we have simplified our basic blocking assignments and count system to the point where our players are not handicapped with an overabundance of assignments and recognitions.

We try to break the structure of our defenses down into categories of seven-man front, four-spoke defense, eight-man front, three deep, and some type of overshift or undershift. Because of the large variety of basic defenses and combination defenses, we have tried to further simplify and to sell our players on the fact that there are only six different fronts they will see. As the offensive line comes to the LOS, we require our offensive guard to identify the defense he sees. We tell our people that by recognizing what is directly in front of them, they can make the necessary call for the blocking scheme best suited for that particular defense.

As I have said, we have simple recognitions and rules, but we have a variety of blocking schemes or individual techniques that greatly enhance our players' ability to achieve the best end results. These are the rules for basic triple option play:

Onside tackle: Four techniques LBs, not there; first LB inside; stays alert for call.

Onside guard: Blocks number one. Stays alert for call.

Center: Blocks zero. Onside gap, back side LBs.

Offside guard: Blocks number one. Stays alert for call.

Offside tackle: Blocks number two, downfield. Stays alert for call.

As you can see, these are very simple. But now comes the part I think is so great about the Wishbone offense: the blocking schemes or techniques. The number one blocking scheme for the Wishbone or veer started with the veer block or, as we call it, the inside block (figure 1).

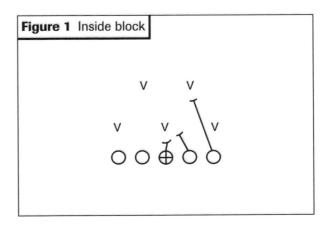

Figure 1 Inside block

In the past four years, with the defenses improving or becoming more cognizant of what the Wishbone teams are doing, the defensive folks began to play games with tackles and LBs and have almost nullified the pure inside block. This brought on the different blocking schemes in the Wishbone, and next came what we call the loop block (figure 2).

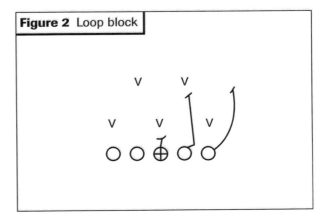

Figure 2 Loop block

With the loop block, the Wishbone people began to try to take advantage of the defensive reaction they knew the defensive tackle would make. We use the loop block and still read the defensive tackle. We worked long and hard with our QBs and offensive line on all of the blocking schemes so that we could have a high percentage of success in reading for the triple option.

Defenses continued to get smarter, to understand what the offensive folks were trying to do, and they countered by trying to play games with the defensive tackle and defensive five techniques by getting penetration upfield. This brought about the addition of another call by the Wishbone teams: the offensive guard had a help call, so that he now sealed for any inside penetration by the defensive tackle.

An important part of the loop block in reading the defensive tackle is that the offensive tackle must make solid contact with his inside shoulder pad, driving through the outside shoulder pad of the defensive tackle. He must be very careful not to avoid contact. If the defensive tackle makes a move inside, the offensive tackle continues on to pick up the LB. If the defensive tackle fights out, then the offensive tackle maintains contact and the QB gives the ball to the FB. This was a very successful blocking scheme and one we used quite a bit at Virginia Tech, one we used an awful lot at Alabama. But, again, the defensive coaches began to play games to destroy this blocking scheme. This brought about a blocking scheme that we call the "X-block" (figure 3).

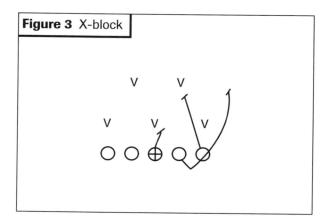

Figure 3 X-block

The X-block, by far, is our number two scheme against the 50 defense, and we have had tremendous success in eliminating tackles and also blocking LBs. The X-block tries to take advantage of a combination of an inside block, or pure veer block, with the tackle releasing inside the five technique. The offensive tackle tries to avoid contact, releasing inside for the

LB. At the same time, the offensive guard pulls around the offensive tackle, going outside the five technique to block the LB. Our QB still reads the defensive tackle as to whether to give the ball to the FB or not.

Our next basic blocking scheme is the plain old vanilla. By that, I mean a base block where everyone blocks numbers one and two (figure 4), and we either predetermine to hand off to the FB or predetermine to take the ball to the outside.

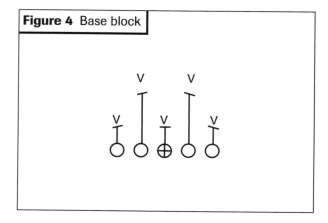

Figure 4 Base block

I honestly feel that these blocking techniques have proved very effective for Virginia Tech in the past two years and have, on occasion, enabled us to equalize an outstanding defensive player. In addition to these base techniques, I feel very strongly that in order to get the best out of the offensive linemen, one must give them extra tools or techniques, so that during the course of the game they can make adjustments at the LOS to do the most effective job.

What I am saying is that we have asked an onside guard to block a defensive tackle who has defensive position on him, or a tackle will take a guard's assignment and the guard will pull around to take the tackle's assignment, or the end will take either the guard's or tackle's assignment and the guard or tackle, depending on front, will take the end's assignment. We use color-call changes-of-assignments for the guard and tackle (figure 5).

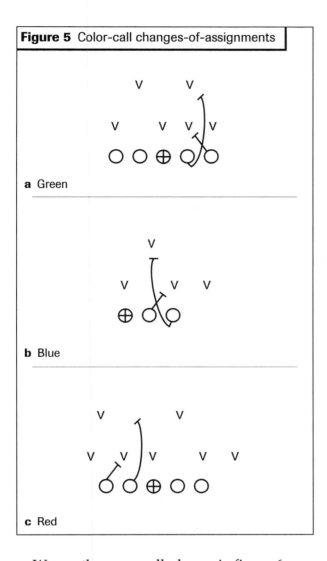

Figure 5 Color-call changes-of-assignments

a Green

b Blue

c Red

We use the swap call, shown in figure 6, any time an offensive end is taking either the guard's or tackle's assignment.

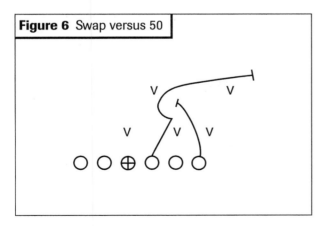

Figure 6 Swap versus 50

I honestly feel these extra tools have enabled us to get the most effective use out of our offensive line. As I said before, the players have become more involved in the big picture. Because of the simplicity of the offense, we spend 90 percent of our time working on techniques, recognizing defenses, and selling our youngsters on our primary objective of controlling the LOS. This brings us into the area of drills and those things we do to perfect these various techniques.

We start, like everyone else, with one-on-one drills and board drills, trying to get to where we just come off the ball reckless, cutting, and slashing—trying to make something happen.

We also use chutes and seven-man sled drills to increase our quickness and togetherness in our offensive charge. There are two drills I feel are essential in having a good offensive line. First is the old fashioned three-on-three drill, where the whole team is around and everyone is whooping and hollering, having a good time, and the offensive players are bragging on the offensive folks, and the defense is bragging on the defensive folks.

The other drill I think is a must if you are going to operate any type of true read offense is a full-speed read drill, where your offensive front, QB, and FB are going against the best defensive front you have. The thing I like about this is that not only are you working on different techniques, such as loop, X-block, inside block, etc., but also that your QB is getting the benefit of full-speed read, of recognizing in that split second when to give the ball to the FB and when to take the ball outside. And your FB can see, full speed, over and over, all of the different defensive reactions that are taking place, which I think makes him a better runner and certainly more effective as a blocker when the ball is taken outside. We continue to use the full-speed read drill even after the season starts.

The last area I would like to talk about is pass protection. We all know that Wishbone teams do not have a great reputation for throwing the football, but my belief is that you must throw the football at least 15 times per game. And when you throw, you have got to get the big play.

The pass protection of the offensive line is a must. We try to incorporate the same basic rules and techniques for our linemen that they have for the running game. We feel they can do a better job, again because of the simplicity of assignments and techniques. Our basic pass protection rules are that we let our line block down people and our faking backs are responsible for LBs. We think it is important in throwing the football that the entire team must sell the run. For this reason, we want everything to look like a run to the play side.

These are our rules for pass protection:

Onside tackle: Blocks over inside.

Onside guard: No one, double-teams the first man to the inside.

Center: Blocks over, back side.

Off Guard: Blocks man over, picks weak.

Back side tackle: Blocks over, picks weak.

We have found through these rules and techniques that we never have an offensive lineman to the play side giving away pass.

To tie in with our X-block and help against secondaries that do a good job keying off backs for pass or run, we also have had good success using what we call the "G-block" in pass protection (figure 7).

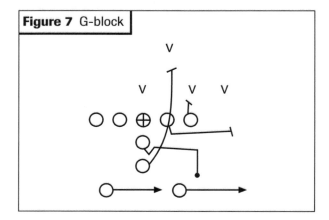

Figure 7 G-block

As I said in the beginning, there are a lot of ways to do things, a lot of techniques, a lot of offenses, but as I hope you can see, I am totally convinced that the results we have been able to achieve have come about by the things I have talked about.

1976 Proceedings. Jimmy Sharpe was head coach at Virginia Tech University.

Changing From Wishbone to Veer

Fred Akers

At Texas this year, we changed from the Wishbone to the Veer in order to take advantage of our great running back Earl Campbell. This also allowed us to spread around our key people in order to spread the defense. With the Veer, we are able to use more running passes and play-action passes, giving us more flexibility and versatility. Another advantage of

the Veer is that it gives you a fast north-and-south attack. We want our people headed toward the goal line, not the stands. And we were still able to use the option attack, which I believe is the best of all offenses.

On our inside option plays we used two types of blocking: the veer block and the zone block. With the veer block (figure 1) we were able to read the tackle, and with the zone block (figure 2) we could get a good predetermined running lane for the back inside the tackle. Our play side tackle in the zone block would put his head on the outside hip of the defensive tackle and drive. The play side guard would step to the tackle gap. If no slant, he would head straight upfield to block the LB. Our zone block is the easiest for our QBs to run.

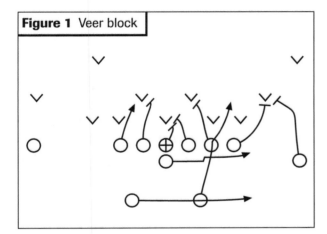

Figure 1 Veer block

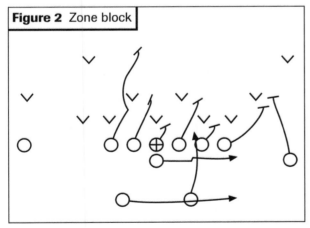

Figure 2 Zone block

Our backs were runners and not super blockers, so they loved this change where they didn't have to block as much. We do use the backs to block the tackles on the load play. We used the three-point stance with the linemen

for more versatility in the passing game, with a minimum 30-inch split—and the majority of the time using 36-inch splits. We used four running paths with our backs (figure 3) and slowed their approach to the line to enable them to cut and run any of these. This also gave us a north-south counter action attack.

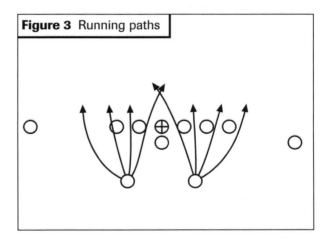

Figure 3 Running paths

20 Series Plays

On most of these, we use the base block and allow the back to read and cut to the hole (figure 4). The 20 is our cutback, where the back keys the noseguard.

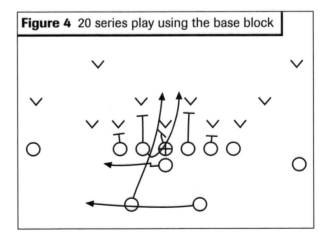

Figure 4 20 series play using the base block

Another block we used is the hi-lo block, where one lineman would dive behind the defensive man and we would push him over backward (figure 5). Figures 6 and 7 show the outside veer plays we run.

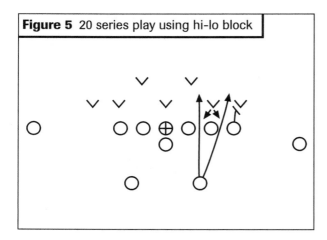

Figure 5 20 series play using hi-lo block

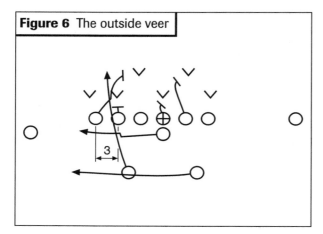

Figure 6 The outside veer

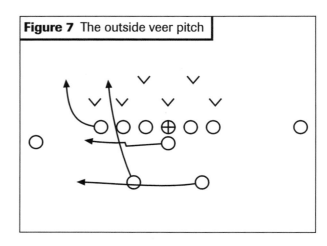

Figure 7 The outside veer pitch

On our counter option (figure 8), we do not fake a back. We reverse out our QB and sprint him down the line to read the end. On this, we also block with the flanker or split man. His technique is a three-point stance with his inside foot back. He drop-steps and goes for the LB.

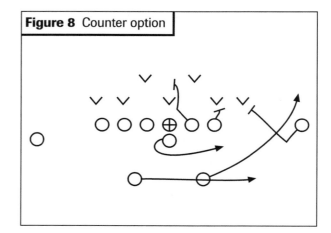

Figure 8 Counter option

1978 Proceedings. Fred Akers was head coach at the University of Texas.

Attacking Gaps With the Veer

Don Morton, Ross Hjelseth, and Pat Simmers

Run the football! Get excited about the four-yard play! These two statements pretty well summarize our offensive philosophy. We believe in the veer system as our means of moving and controlling the football. A strong offensive running game, combined with a fine defense, will lend itself toward a high degree of success against our opponents.

Contrary to many beliefs, the veer system does not require great speed at running back and QB. Rather, a combination of fine athletes in the offensive line and backfield, along with patience in play selection, seems to make up for any lack of speed.

A Simple System

An ingredient needed for successful offense is simplicity. Over the years we have tried to simplify our veer-option system. Our players will produce to the extent to which they learn, not to the extent to which we try to teach. By simplifying our system, we get closer to the point where the student-athlete learns.

Our first step in simplifying our offense was to sell out totally to split backs. Regardless of the alignment of our receivers (Twins, Pro, two tight ends, etc.), our running backs will always be four yards directly behind our guards. Alignment in split backs improves our backfield execution. In triple-option football, backfield execution is of extreme importance, and we want our backs in consistent relationship with one another. Our QB's confidence allows him to execute the triple-option reads, and his confidence is reinforced by consistent mesh techniques with the dive back

and a somewhat consistent relationship with the pitch back.

Another step taken to improve our execution was the requirement of consistent offensive line splits. All of our backfield aiming points depend upon the offensive line splits. It is critical that these splits are exact so that our mesh points and exchange zones are consistent for our QB. Figure 1 indicates the alignments for our offensive line and the position of our running backs.

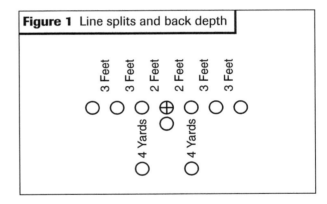

Figure 1 Line splits and back depth

For communication, we adopted a letter and number system for labeling responsibility gaps and alignments of the defensive players. Figure 2 (on page 116) illustrates this system as taught to our players.

Veer Series

The veer series is the backbone of the option system. It is a true flow dive-option sequence that includes triple-option reads for the QB as well as a called dive play. With the veer series, we are capable of attacking every gap in the defensive front with three plays:

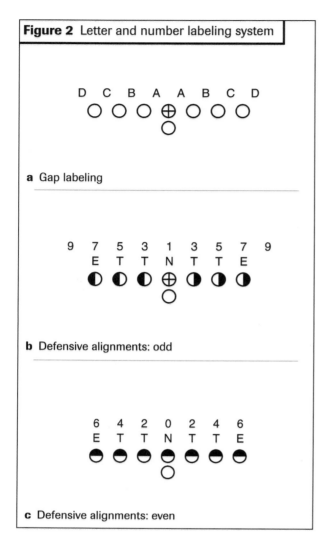

Figure 2 Letter and number labeling system

D C B A A B C D

a Gap labeling

9 7 5 3 1 3 5 7 9
E T T N T T E

b Defensive alignments: odd

6 4 2 0 2 4 6
E T T N T T E

c Defensive alignments: even

1. *Veer.* The outside veer threatens the off-tackle hole and allows the QB to also option a secondary defender for keep or pitch. There is a triple-option read for the QB.

2. *Zone option.* This is another triple-option play that may attack inside of the defensive tackle with the hard dive or allow the QB to option the defensive end for keep or pitch.

3. *Scoop.* The called dive play may hit at any point along the defensive front. This gives us the hard dive and cutback dive threat that we need to settle pursuit of the defense.

The veer series gives us an opportunity to get off on the ball with our offensive linemen and aggressively attack the gaps of a defense while forcing the defense to defend all three phases of an option attack. All three plays are designed to give the defender the same look, but, in fact, give our offense several means of attacking the defensive front.

Up front, we have sold out to the scoop or zone-blocking concept. We constantly struggle to keep it simple up front. We want our linemen to get off the ball and establish the LOS. In execution of the veer series versus the 5-2 defense, we use simple scoop blocking to control both a reading defensive front and a slanting defensive front. We must get movement up front, seal the inside, and create tracks for the running backs. The veer series epitomizes this philosophy.

Veer

The veer (figure 3) is a triple-option play that gets to the corner quickly. It gives us the opportunity to option a secondary defender instead of constantly blocking the secondary. It is especially good near the opponent's goal line because the secondary becomes more difficult to block with a veer release or stalk block.

We like to run the outside veer at either a four technique or an eagle tackle, as these situations allow our TE to combo block the defensive tackle and also get a good piece of the LB. If we cannot combo block the LB because of a five technique tackle, we depend upon cutting off the LB with movement from our double-team, allowing our guard to block the LB.

The QB triple-reads the outside veer. His first key is the defensive end. The mesh with the dive back takes place behind our offensive tackle, and it is critical that the QB stay on the LOS as he meets with the dive back at the mesh point. He keys the defensive end while meshing with the dive back and extends the mesh with the dive back into the LOS.

If the defensive end does not close to tackle the dive back, we hand off to the dive back. To guarantee a good exchange, the QB steps forward with the dive back as he hands off the ball. After the ball is handed off, the QB gathers himself and sprints by the defensive end into the secondary as though he actually has

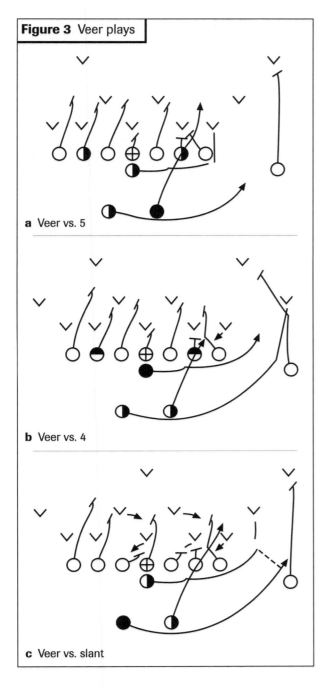

Figure 3 Veer plays

a Veer vs. 5

b Veer vs. 4

c Veer vs. slant

man chooses to defend the QB. After pitching the football, the QB should continue downfield to block a pursuing defensive player (figure 3c).

The dive back is responsible for establishing the mesh point with the QB. The dive back aims his dive route at the inside hip of the offensive tackle. As he meshes with the QB, we want the dive back to soft-squeeze the football. If the dive back is given the football, we encourage him to hug the block on the tackle and square his shoulders to the goal line as he breaks into the secondary. If the dive back does not get the football, he must give a great fake and get tackled.

The pitch back must sprint hard to get good pitch relationship with the QB. As he reaches this point, it is critical that he stay in phase so that the QB can pitch at any time. The flanker must read the secondary coverage and stalk block whichever secondary defender is defending a deep portion of an outside zone. We do not want to block the force man, as this is the player the QB will option for keep or pitch (figures 3b and 3c).

Versus a five technique, the TE is responsible for sealing the five technique and helping the tackle get movement off the LOS. He first takes a 45-degree step at the defensive tackle, reading the defender. His second step is upfield, sealing the defensive tackle. Versus a four technique, his responsibilities are to seal the defensive tackle and combo up to the LB. His first step remains a 45-degree angle, reading the foot of the defensive tackle. He wants to make contact on the play side shoulder of the defensive tackle, work his way to his hip, and push off from the defensive tackle's hip, which enables the offensive tackle to control the defensive tackle's play side arm. He then works straight upfield, walling the LB to the inside. If the defensive tackle slants (figure 3c), the TE is responsible for the play side LB. His first step remains the same, his second step is straight upfield. He tries to wall the play side LB to the inside, cutting him if necessary.

Versus a five technique, the play side tackle's responsibility is to get movement off the LOS. His first step is at the defensive tackle's play side number. Versus a four technique, he is

the football. If the defensive end tackles the dive back, the QB pulls the football from the back. As soon as the QB has pulled the ball, we want him to seat the ball in a good ballcarrying position and sprint into the secondary (figure 3b).

The QB will usually know from the secondary alignment whether there will be sky or cloud support. Regardless, the QB will only pitch the football when the secondary force responsible for movement and keeping the defensive tackle sealed after the TE combos off. His first step is at the play side number of the defensive tackle, beginning to get movement. When he feels the TE combo upfield, he should be conscious of working his hips around so he can control the play side arm of the defensive tackle. If the tackle slants, this man is his responsibility. He should step to the play side number of the defensive tackle, slide down, and double with the play side guard. He must keep the defensive tackle sealed.

Versus a five technique, the play side guard's responsibility is to cut the LB. He should take the maximum angle to the LB. The first step must be upfield. His assignment remains the same versus a four technique. He must be conscious of his maximum angle because the defensive tackle will not react to the double-team as quickly. If the defensive tackle slants (figure 3c), he will automatically run into the tackle. He locks on and double-teams with the offensive tackle.

When the noseguard is responsible for the play side "A" gap, the center must reach him. His first step is to the play side arm with his play side foot. He can stay high and run the noseguard into a pile created by the double-team. If the noseguard slants to the back side "A" gap (figure 3c), the center's responsibility is the back side LB. He steps to reach the noseguard; then, when the noseguard disappears, the center works upfield to the backfield LB.

Versus a noseguard who is responsible for the play side "A" gap, the guard will take a 45-degree step toward the noseguard, reading the defender's back side foot. When the noseguard disappears, the guard will take a maximum angle to the back side LB. If the noseguard is slanting to the back side "A" gap, the guard is responsible for him. He takes a 45-degree step at the noseguard. When the noseguard's foot moves toward him, the guard must get his helmet in front of the noseguard and work his hips around.

The back side tackle will release inside and is responsible for the tackle first and the fold end second. The split end will release inside and work from the safety to the corner.

Zone Option

We like to use the zone option to prevent teams from an aggressive five technique. The zone option (figure 4) is designed to take care of any defensive tackle technique but is especially quick-hitting with the dive handoff inside of the five technique, which will not allow our offensive tackle to reach the defensive tackle (figure 4a). Success with the dive inside of the

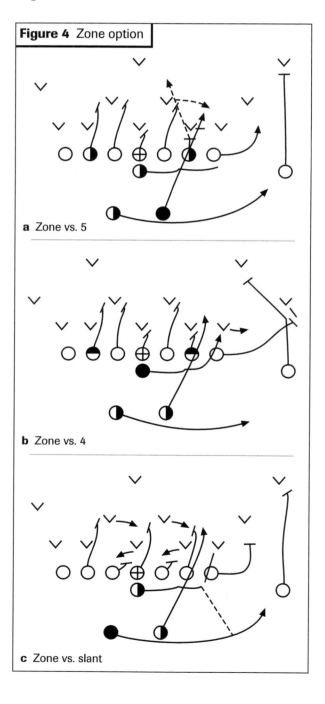

Figure 4 Zone option

a Zone vs. 5

b Zone vs. 4

c Zone vs. slant

five technique will eventually force the defense to change the defensive tackle's technique, thus allowing us to run our option game outside and get to the pitch.

For the QB, the zone option combines the mechanics of the inside veer and the outside veer in one play. The mesh takes place at the same point as on the outside veer. The defensive tackle is the QB's read for dive or keep, and the defensive end is the read for keep or pitch. The same mesh mechanics and coaching points that were used for the QB on the outside veer are also used on the zone option play.

As the QB receives the snap, he begins his key on the defensive tackle's movement. The QB's reads are quite simple. If the defensive tackle moves to the outside to avoid the reach block, the QB hands off the ball to the dive back, taking advantage of the gap inside of the five technique's stretch. With the handoff, we have a hard dive that hits quickly and is a track play to the goal line (figure 4a). What could be better! After the handoff, we want the QB to continue down the line and carry out his option fake.

If the defensive tackle does not stretch (four technique) or if the tackle uses his slant technique, the QB pulls the ball from the dive back. In these situations (figure 4b or 4c), we can now get to the end to option for keep or pitch.

The physical difficulty for the QB is in pulling from the dive back and getting ready to option the defensive end. If the defensive end commits to the pitch man, the QB keeps and carries into the secondary (figure 4b). If the defensive end takes the QB, the QB will pitch the ball (figure 4c).

The dive route is at the same point as on the outside veer, and again the dive back soft-squeezes the football while rushing with the QB. If given the football because of the five technique stretch, the ballcarrier stays on track, keeping wide of the noseguard and reacting to the block on the inside LB by our offensive guard. If that LB is pursuing hard to the outside track, the dive back bends back to the inside, making the LB overrun the play (figure 4a).

When the dive back does not get the football, he becomes a blocker, blocking the first wrong-

colored jersey that shows. He is especially conscious of getting to the free safety.

The pitch will occur sooner on the zone-option play than on the outside veer. Because of this, the pitch relationship must be attained sooner. The pitch back must read the secondary in order to follow our perimeter blocking versus corner or safety force. This must be done on the run and may force the back to alter his pitch relationship slightly (figures 4b and 4c).

Because this is a triple-option play, the receivers do not know whether they are blocking for quarterback keys or for the pitch back. Consequently, the receivers work as a team, reading the secondary force and then creating a running lane for the ballcarrier to find. Figure 4b shows the flanker and TE combining to create a running lane inside of a corner force situation. Figure 4c illustrates the receivers blocking safety force with the TE using his veer release technique and the flanker using his stalk technique. Effective perimeter blocking is one of the keys to option football. It is more effective when the receiver uses finesse as opposed to aggressiveness.

Versus a five technique, the play side tackle's responsibility is to reach the defensive tackle. He steps directly at the play side number of the defender, makes contact, establishes the LOS, and tries to get some backward movement. When the LOS is established, he works his hips around and reaches the five technique. He must maintain contact at all times. His responsibility is the same versus a four technique, only he makes sure the step is at the play side number, not lateral.

If the defensive tackle does slant, the offensive tackle is responsible for the play side LB. He steps directly at the defensive tackle's play side number. As he disappears, the offensive tackle continues upfield to the play side LB.

Versus a five technique, the play side guard is responsible for the play side LB. He takes a 45-degree step at the defensive tackle, reading the defensive tackle for a slant. When the defensive tackle stretches, the guard continues to the LB at a maximum angle. He wants to stay high if possible, because the ball might be given to the dive back. A four technique does not change his responsibility or his technique. It will probably be necessary to cut the LB, though, because the four technique will diminish the guard's maximum angle.

If the defensive tackle is slanting, the guard is responsible for blocking the eagle tackle. His first step is 45-degrees at the defensive tackle. The guard's helmet must cross in front of the defensive tackle to stop penetration, and then he gets his hips around to hook the defensive tackle.

The center is responsible for the noseguard where he has the play side "A" gap. On the snap, he will cut the noseguard's play side leg immediately. With the hard dive being a possibility, we cannot allow the noseguard to move down the LOS. If the noseguard slants to the back side "A" gap, the center must pop up and proceed downfield to the back side LB.

All other linemen's techniques, the back side guard, back side tackle, and the split end remain the same as they were for the outside veer.

Scoop

This predetermined hand-off dive complements the outside veer and zone option. It also gives us a quick-hitting counter play. The scoop dive (figure 5) fits into our play selection whenever the LBs are running or when the noseguard is making the play on the dive back on the zone option. We have no preference with the scoop in relation to defensive technique. The scoop is designed to attack any soft spot in the defensive front. The dive back simply finds the daylight created by the pursuing defense.

The QB's technique is changed somewhat from that used on the outside veer or zone. He will give the ball deeper to the dive back, allowing the dive back to make the dive cut easier. After the handoff, the QB continues the option fake down the line with the pitch back.

Against the 5-2 defense, the dive back reads the play side tackle and noseguard for his cut along the front. We encourage the dive back to read the alignments of these two players before the ball is snapped so that he can anticipate the cut.

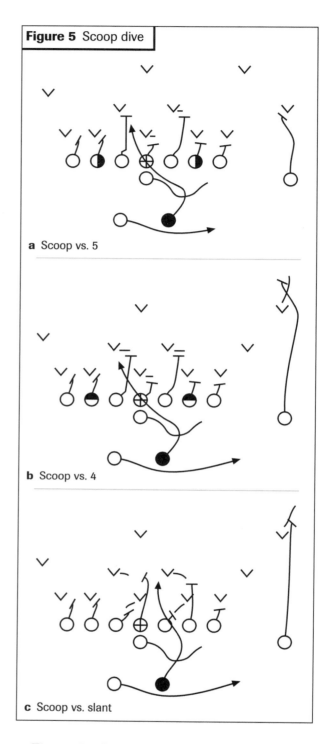

Figure 5 Scoop dive

a Scoop vs. 5

b Scoop vs. 4

c Scoop vs. slant

Figure 5a shows the cut the back will make against a five technique tackle with the noseguard working hard play side. As the dive back feels the pressure from the noseguard, he begins the cutback phase of his path and finds the first daylight on the back side. In figure 5a, the daylight is between the noseguard and the back side LB. Figure 5b illustrates the back making a cut similar to that in figure 5a, except that the back side LB is also flowing, so the dive back cuts behind the noseguard and the back side LB. Again, the ballcarrier finds the daylight created by the pursuing defensive front. The path in figure 5c is a straight cut upfield because the defense is using a slant technique by the defensive tackle. When the dive back sees the slant technique, he knows that the noseguard is usually going away from the play and daylight is play side instead of back side.

The pitch back simply runs his pitch route, carrying out the option fake with the QB. As he turns upfield after the fake pitch route, he blocks the first wrong-colored jersey.

The inside play gives the flanker an opportunity to adjust his split from the TE. This eliminates split keys for the opponents. His other assignment is to release upfield and get inside of the most dangerous secondary defender. As he does so, he reads the eyes of that defender in order to find out where the cut has been made and becomes a downfield blocker. He will get the block that means the difference between a good play and a great play!

The TE is responsible for the defensive end. If the defensive end is in a seven technique, the TE takes a short step with his play side foot at the defensive end, trying to make him stretch. He treats a six technique the same way but will be more conscious of a fire-in end. If the defensive end fires in, the TE must be able to stop penetration.

The play side tackle treats a five technique just like with the zone option, reading the defensive tackle and getting him to stretch. The four technique is also the same as with the zone option. The tackle must drive the defender off the ball. He cannot free the defensive tackle up inside. If he has a slant tackle on him, he treats it like a zone option again, but

it becomes a mandatory cut. We do not want the LB to push off of the offensive tackle to recover back to the inside.

The play side guard's techniques change drastically from those of the zone option. Versus a four or five technique, the guard takes his 45-degree step at the defensive tackle, reading his foot. When the foot does not appear, his second step is straight upfield. The second step enables us to get on the LB's back side shoulder and push him by the hole, which is ideal for the cutback. If the guard gets a slant tackle, we want him to wall the defensive tackle to the outside (figure 4c).

When a noseguard is responsible for the play side "A" gap, the center will try to reach him. He steps to the noseguard's play side shoulder. If the noseguard starts to stretch down the LOS, the center locks on him and rides him along the LOS. The center must eliminate any penetration so the ballcarrier can cut back. If the noseguard slants to the back side "A" gap, the center continues to the back side LB, just as with the zone option and veer plays.

Against a noseguard responsible for the play side "A" gap, the back side guard's responsibilities and techniques are just like the play side guard's. Using a 45-degree step, he reads the noseguard. His second step is straight upfield, and then he looks on the LB. If the noseguard slants to him, he will hook him just like he would on the zone option and the veer plays (figure 5c).

The back side tackle is responsible for his man at all times. If the defensive tackle is in a four or five technique, he will step inside and turn the defender out. If the defensive tackle slants, he must cut him immediately.

The split end's responsibilities are the same as the tackle's. He has man coverage at all times, turning out a six or seven technique and cutting a fire-in end.

1982 Summer Manual. Don Morton was head coach and Ross Hjelseth and Pat Simmers were assistant coaches at North Dakota State University.

Adapting the Veer

Bill Yeoman

Before we could determine what segment of the attack we were going to use, we first had to assess our own capabilities. First, we had an untried QB who had come off knee surgery. We had a quick offensive line that was unduly light, with one quality offensive athlete. We had a TE who was five feet, 10 inches and 185 pounds. Good quickness, adequate strength, but no bulk. We had three adequate wide receivers. Nothing was going to strike much fear in the hearts of any defense we played. Add to that the fact we had fired eight blanks the year before.

Any offense starts with the QB. We had to give him an opportunity to be successful, to first master the position mechanically then add the mental strain. Before we went any further, we had to determine what segments of our running attack would be best suited and what had the best chance of success.

Better Blocking

The two basic segments are the fast flow, or veer action, and the slower flow, or counter and counter-option action. We didn't feel we had sufficient strength to live with the counter and counter-option action, so we felt we had to make our fast-flow action work. Once this was settled, we realized this was possibly the higher risk part of our offense, so we wondered what might be done to ease that. The most obvious solution was to use the base block instead of the veer block and continue to read instead of using the veer block. As you can see in figure 1, this occupies everyone on the LOS and prevents the quick shot on the QB, which is the basis for a lot of concern about the option.

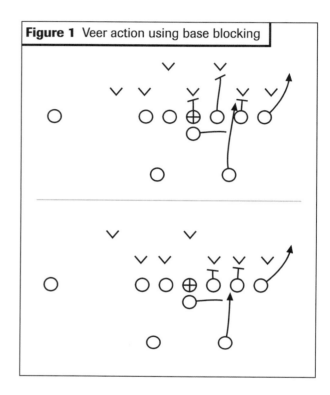

Figure 1 Veer action using base blocking

The coaching points for R and T were the same. Our guard and tackle had three ways of blocking the play: base, under, and zone (figure 2). Which one we used depended on the play of the defensive tackle. If we used base blocking (figure 2a), the guard and tackle counted off two-three and took their men wherever they went. If we used under (figure 2b), the guard blocked the tackle and released at an angle. The tackle released outside the tackle. If he was engaged by the defensive tackle as he released, he locked in, resulting in a double-team by the guard and tackle. If he was able to effect the release, he blocked the LB.

The zone block (figure 2c) is a little different in the release angle. Our guard takes a jab step toward the tackle parallel to the LOS. If the tackle slants down, our guard engages

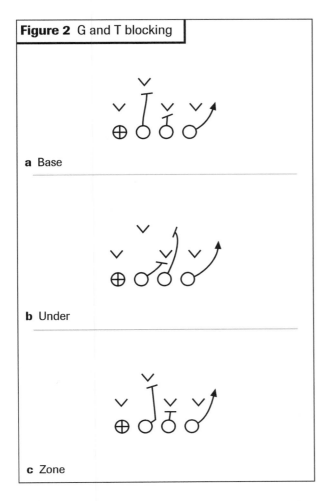

Figure 2 G and T blocking

a Base

b Under

c Zone

was whether or not he could get to the defensive end in order to effect an option. If, in his opinion, he could, then he would withdraw the ball from the fullback and option the end. If he didn't feel he could do this, then he would leave the ball in the fullback's stomach.

This type of blocking did leave a few loose ends once in a while, but provided a better opportunity to move the chains with an inexperienced QB.

The mechanics for the two set backs did not change. The only consideration was how much trouble the center was having with the noseguard. This might adjust the width of the dive. When a team used an even defense, we always blocked base.

The outside veer presented some problems. Our TE was five feet, 10 inches and weighed 185 pounds. He had excellent quickness and good strength but was limited bulkwise. Regardless, we still used the basic outside veer. The off-tackle play that we relied the most on was the G blocking of the outside veer (figure 3). It was very effective against the odd defense (figure 3b). We had the double-team on the defensive tackle, and the guard's pull sometimes had a softening effect on the end. Plus, his turning back on the LB was

him. If the tackle stays wide, the guard straightens up and blocks the LB. The offensive tackle drives through the outside number of the defensive tackle's jersey. If he becomes engaged with the defensive tackle, he continues with the block. If the defensive tackle slants to the inside, he continues and blocks the LB.

Another consideration made the base block on the inside veer a possibility. In reviewing film, it appeared to us as if most defenses gave the down linemen and back side LBs dive responsibility. More LBs seemed to overrun the dive, and we noticed the back running by more people who were not blocked.

Reading Adjustments

The QB's mechanics were the same as they always have been. The only adjustment was in his read. He still keyed the first man outside the offensive tackle, but his basic consideration

Figure 3 G blocking of the outside veer

a Even defense

b Odd defense

not a particularly difficult block. Running the G play against an even defense (figure 3a) presented too much of a problem for our TE, so it was never a consideration in our planning.

Effective Quick Pitch

The quickness of our TE did permit us to run the quick pitch very effectively (figure 4). The play averaged better than six yards per try both into and away from the TE. We used the quick pitch into the split end side on any kind of overshift or tight play by the defense.

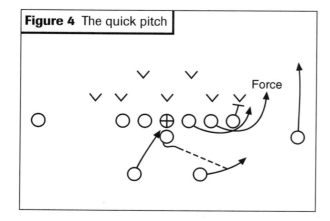

Figure 4 The quick pitch

The counter play was not used as much, nor was it as effective as it had been. Nevertheless, the area had to be threatened. Blocking the counter option and handing off to the dive back proved to be fairly effective (figure 5). The TE and flanker release. The tackle pulls and blocks the end. The guard zone blocks, and the center and back side guard scoop block.

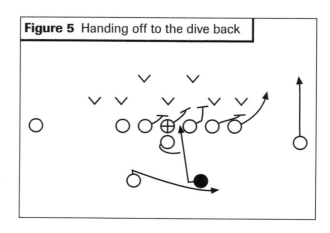

Figure 5 Handing off to the dive back

Against the even defense, the TE and flanker release as on the counter option. The onside guard releases outside the tackle as if to cut off the middle LB. The center reaches the front side tackle. This type of blocking seemed to precipitate a softer play by the defensive tackle than did the basic counter blocking.

Our draw play was the same except for the route of the back carrying the ball. Our guards had a difficult time stopping penetration, so we had to bring the back behind the QB.

Our passing game was, of necessity, very basic. By the time our TE learned to run a quick post, flat, quick out, and drag—plus have the QB find him—the season was over. All passing out of the running attack was the same as it has been. We did go back to some dropback action, and we were fortunate on occasion to have everyone covered so that our QB was forced to run. I have never been more grateful for the flexibility of our offense than I was this year.

1977 Proceedings. Bill Yeoman was head coach at the University of Houston.

Adding the Whirlybird for the Big Play

Bo Rein

With today's defensive schemes, the veer offense simply can't be as effective with the basics of the called dive, counter dive, counter option, and inside and outside veer. To continue moving the football effectively no matter what offensive scheme or combination is used, constant revisions must be made in blocking schemes, companion plays, line splits, formations, etc., to counteract the defense and its play recognition.

One answer in keeping the veer offense from split backs abreast with the changes in defensive thinking is our version of the crazy, whirlybird, or trap option. It is known by all these names. It is one complementary play that we can execute aggressively versus all defensive looks, although, like every outside play, it is better against some than others.

From split backs, this play is to the inside trap what the counter option is to the counter dive. Both series are necessities, but the advantage of the whirlybird option over the counter option is that it eliminates pursuit more effectively, essential in executing an option consistently. We borrowed the theory and blocking schemes from successful I teams a few years ago, and they complement our inside trap as effectively as they do theirs.

This play has served three primary functions in our offensive thinking. It has developed into our best big-play threat on the perimeter. It has kept our bread-and-butter plays as consistent as ever. Remarkably, it can handle almost all defensive schemes. The ball action and blocking pattern for the trap option is shown in figure 1.

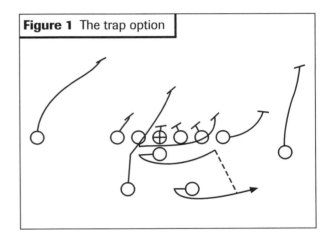

Figure 1 The trap option

Blocking Scheme

We block looks and do not have set rules on this play, so I will give a few examples of our schemes versus various fronts. Except for the pulling guard's technique, we are blocking our inside trap. Versus the 52 defense, the pulling guard seals the off-tackle area, isolating the defensive end. He reacts to three different looks. He overblocks the trap man if he closes (figure 2).

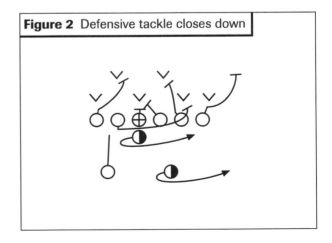

Figure 2 Defensive tackle closes down

He kicks him out if he jumps outside, and the QB ducks up inside (figure 3). Or if he crosses our tackle's face as he blocks inside (figure 4), the guard turns up inside and seals the LB or anyone else who shows. The center and onside guard and tackle simply veer block the 52 defense. The back side tackle executes a cutoff or a play side gap.

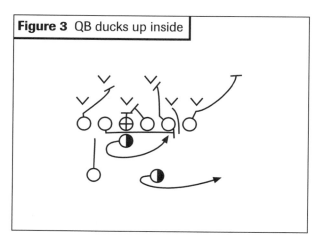

Figure 3 QB ducks up inside

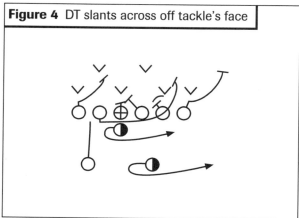

Figure 4 DT slants across off tackle's face

On even fronts, we trap the defensive tackle, so on the option we seal this area with our trapper and bring our front side tackle on the LB (figure 5). The tackle's technique is to pin the LB inside as the flow misdirects him. On all fronts but 52, the center and onside guard gap block. On the over-shifted front, we still have an option because of the extra blocker (figure 6).

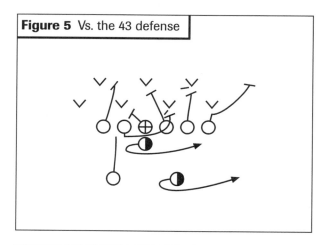

Figure 5 Vs. the 43 defense

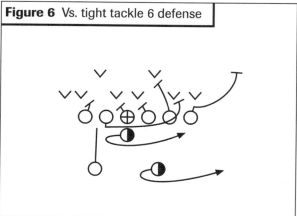

Figure 6 Vs. tight tackle 6 defense

The total scheme, coupled with the flow of the backs, does the following to the defense:

1. It isolates the option point consistently better than any option we've seen.

2. It slows LBs or counters the quick flowing scheme.

3. It provides a sure way of keeping a great noseguard from running down the play from behind.

4. It matches blockers with all forms of over-shifted defenses.

Backfield Action

The backfield action provides another plus in attacking the defense. The dive back attacks the LOS, aiming at the outside leg of the guard for two steps. This is important in creating flow. His assignment is to block any penetration in this area. If there is none, he should have a seam play side to run through and chop the first defender who crosses his path.

The QB takes his initial step at a 45-degree angle toward the dive back. He holds his position on this foot until the dive back clears. His second step is a balance step. When it plants, he pivots sharply and takes his third step at the defensive end. Then he simply accelerates, attacks the defensive end, and executes the option.

The pitch back takes two steps across the formation, starting with his near foot. Sloppy footwork results in too little flow. As the second step hits, he reverse pivots to the outside. He stays low and keeps the center of gravity low. This eliminates the possibility of falling down. Now he should get his head around quickly and sprint to maintain the pitch relationship with the QB.

The backfield action gives us the following three advantages:

1. It provides an option from split backs with great leverage on the QB (i.e., the defensive end can't play both the QB and run down the pitch).

2. It slows down a very active run support free safety with the misdirection.

3. It gives a softer force out of the secondary for the arc blocker (figure 7).

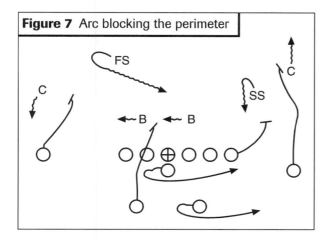

Figure 7 Arc blocking the perimeter

The techniques and assignments of the perimeter block are identical to the conventional counter option and inside veer but are easier because of the hesitation created for the initial force from the secondary. To the Pro set, the TE and flanker can block in normally (figure 8) or switch block (figure 9). To twins, the same situation exists (figure 10). To the back side, the split end can read the rotation and also have a softer block (figure 11).

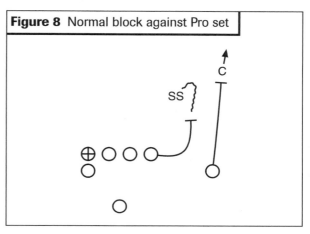

Figure 8 Normal block against Pro set

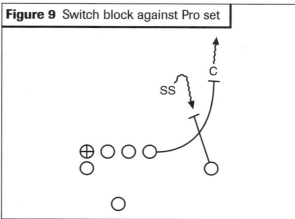

Figure 9 Switch block against Pro set

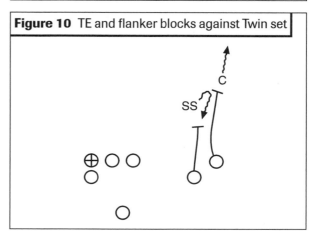

Figure 10 TE and flanker blocks against Twin set

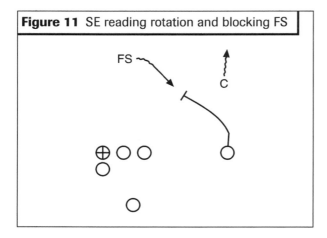

Figure 11 SE reading rotation and blocking FS

Problem Areas

I have listed many reasons why we like this option and why we incorporated it in our offensive scheme, but I want to mention the problem areas that can occur. Any time you run an option and the QB open-steps away from the point of attack, you must constantly watch for crashing defensive ends. The play loses its effectiveness if the backfield action is not precise or the backs align closer than five yards from the ball. Finally, there is no set coaching technique to drill the pulling guard. In one instance, he seals a down lineman; in another, he seals a LB; in yet another, he is forced to kick out a looping tackle and forces the QB to duck up inside.

Even with these problem areas in mind, this play was statistically our most effective outside option over a two-year period. Through play recognition, defenses did a better job of defending it this year, but the blocking pattern is sound and the action passes from this add a whole new dimension to keep the whirlybird flying for a good while!

1978 Summer Manual. Bo Rein was head coach at North Carolina State.

Blocking the Perimeter for the Veer

Larry Zierlein

There has been much discussion over the years concerning the veer offense. Offensive line play, backfield techniques, or the coordination of the two have been thoroughly covered. However, an area that seems often to be neglected is the all-important area of perimeter blocking. Breakdowns in this area appear to be quite common on all levels of football.

A tactic used by many teams in defensing the option is to take away the first two phases of the option and rely on their containing unit to defeat the blocks of the WRs and TE. This is often successful because of either the lack of ability to block or the receiver's lack of training in this area, usually the latter. In order for the offense to operate at maximum efficiency, the wideouts and TE must be able to block on the corner and give us room to run when we pitch the football.

We are fortunate at Houston to have receivers who are good blockers. Their efforts contributed to our average of 6.4 yards per carry on all our option plays during the 1978 season. Our primary option plays are the zone option, counter option, and trap option (figure 1).

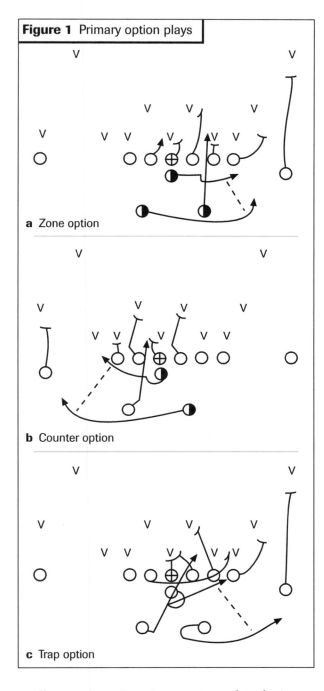

Figure 1 Primary option plays

a Zone option

b Counter option

c Trap option

The receivers' assignments and techniques are the same on all three option plays. Although the technique of each receiver varies, there are two rules common to each block:

1. Patience. Don't overcommit. Be under control!

2. Invite the defender to commit to a certain side when he goes for the ball-carrier.

To the two-receiver side, the TE will block the man responsible for the pitch and the flanker will block the defender responsible for the deep outside.

TE Technique Versus Invert

These are the coaching points for the TE technique versus invert:

1. The TE releases flat across the face of the DE by pushing off the inside foot and lead-stepping laterally with the outside foot. The second step is a crossover, and the third step reestablishes the initial position of the TE. By the third step, the TE will have read the secondary coverage and know if he is blocking the SS (invert) or the cornerback (roll) (figure 2).

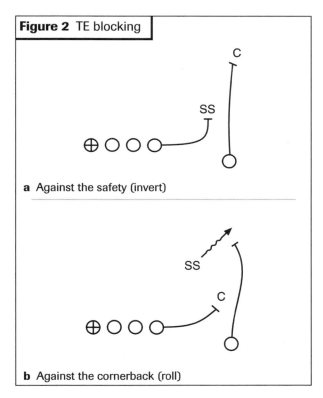

Figure 2 TE blocking

a Against the safety (invert)

b Against the cornerback (roll)

2. It is very important for the TE to keep his shoulders square with the LOS throughout his approach to the SS. He can accomplish this by pulling back with his inside arm as he releases and continuing to pull back as he approaches the SS. This serves two purposes: insuring the necessary squared-up position when the TE reaches the SS, and facilitating the TE's ability

to come back on the SS who comes hard to the inside in an attempt to make a big play.

3. He continues gaining width flat down the LOS until reaching a position in which his body is aligned with the outside number of the SS. This is the relative position to be maintained throughout the block. He does not start gaining ground upfield until he reaches this relative position. Gaining ground upfield too quickly is a common error and will result in a failure to maintain outside leverage on the SS when he goes for the pitch man.

4. After he has established the proper width, the TE can then begin gaining depth on an arc that allows for his maintaining outside leverage. He gains as much depth as possible before engaging the SS in order to give our pitch back more room to operate at the corner.

5. The arc block itself is not intended to knock the defender off his feet, but to occupy him long enough for the back to go past. By gaining outside leverage, the TE will accomplish one of the following: hook the defender so the back can run outside (figure 3) or make the SS fight to the outside in an effort to prevent being hooked, opening up an inside running lane (figure 4).

After engaging the SS, the TE continues to block on his outside number, then recoils until the defender has either been hooked or has been stretched to the sideline. To do this, the TE must operate from a good base with the tail down and head up. He hits up through the defender and not out at him. Overextension is one of the most common errors. It results in a

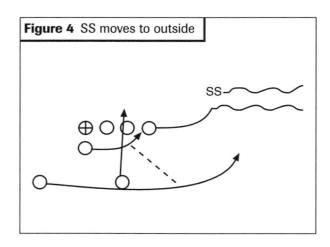

Figure 4 SS moves to outside

loss of balance. The advantage then goes to the defender because he can get rid of the TE and still have plenty of time to come up and make the tackle on or behind the LOS. (The relationship between the back and the TE dictates that the block be maintained longer than when the blocker comes from the backfield, as in the Wishbone.) The pressure is on the defender to get to the ballcarrier, so let him be the one to make the first commitment. He has to come through the TE to get to the ballcarrier. The TE does not have to go after the SS.

In summarizing the arc block versus the invert safety, these are the important points:

1. Release flat across the face of the defensive end.

2. Recognize the secondary coverage by the third step.

3. Gain width to the outside number of the SS before gaining depth downfield.

4. Stay under control with the shoulders square to the LOS.

5. Do not overextend. Let the defender come to you. Keep a good base and hit up through the defender and not out at him.

6. Maintain outside leverage and either hook the SS or stretch him to the sideline.

The above is the TE's technique in an ideal situation. Following are some defensive maneuvers that can cause problems for the TE, and how we try to cope with them. The first one occurs after the TE has established outside leverage and the defender tries to power through the blocker. The TE forgets about hit-

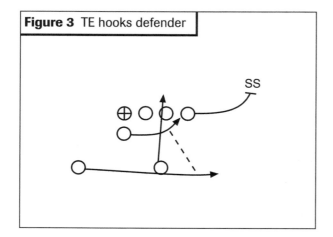

Figure 3 TE hooks defender

ting and recoiling, and meets force with force by exploding into the defender's outside number and locking on. Again, he keeps the shoulders square and either gets the defender hooked or stretches him to the sidelines. Hitting and recoiling versus this defensive maneuver will result in the TE's being driven back into the path of the ballcarrier.

The second one occurs on the snap of the ball, when the SS charges hard upfield (figure 5). A big defensive play can result if the TE doesn't make this block. As soon as he recognizes the hard charge, he turns his shoulders parallel to the sideline and throws his body across the path of the defender. In this instance, we hope to get the SS on the ground. Attempting to block him high will again result in the TE's being driven into the path of the ballcarrier.

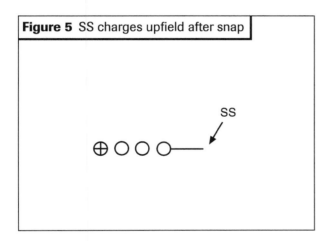

Figure 5 SS charges upfield after snap

The third situation occurs when the SS comes hard to the inside trying to get behind the TE. This is a defensive gamble, but an effective one if the TE is not prepared. If the TE is under control with his shoulders square and gets no wider than the defender's outside number, he will be able to seal the SS to the inside and allow the running back an outside lane (figure 6).

The fourth situation occurs immediately after the TE begins his arc release. The SS fakes inside, then comes to the outside. The natural reaction to the fake will usually result in the TE's losing outside leverage and then being forced to turn his shoulders parallel to the sideline in order to block the defender. The SS

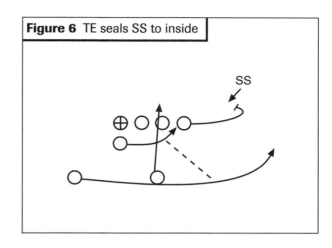

Figure 6 TE seals SS to inside

is not wide enough to allow the back to run inside of him, and the result is that the TE blocks him into the path of the ballcarrier. This can be a very effective defensive maneuver, and the TE must be drilled on it every day. The TE should remember this: Any time the defender tries to go inside the block, he runs the risk of being sealed to the inside and providing us with a big outside running lane, with the defensive pursuit having to go a long way to get to the ball if it is pitched. If the SS is coming inside, the TE has plenty of time to react and seal him on the inside. The TE doesn't have to react immediately to a possible inside fake. By delaying his reaction, he is in position to block the SS after the defender fakes and then attempts to come outside.

This must be drilled daily. It is a natural reaction to honor any fake. The TE must see this often so that he becomes accustomed to not reacting too quickly to the inside move.

The fifth situation occurs when the SS goes hard to the outside, then comes back inside into the path of the ballcarrier. This can be good against the TE who is conscious of getting outside leverage. The hard outside move by the SS forces the TE to turn his shoulders and run out of control if he is to get to the defender's outside number. This is exactly what the SS wants, because he can come inside the blocker into the path of the ballcarrier and probably not be touched by the TE because of his poor position.

In handling this situation, the TE should be aware of this fact: The SS is getting too wide and opening up an inside running lane any time he makes a move that forces the TE to turn his shoulders and get out of control in order to get to the defender's outside number. He should never get into a footrace with the SS. He should stay under control with his shoulders square, and when the SS tries to come back inside, the TE will be in position to apply an effective block (figure 7).

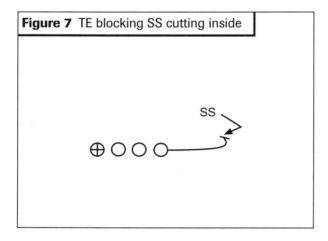

Figure 7 TE blocking SS cutting inside

If the SS gains ground upfield until he is even with the TE, only then would the TE turn his shoulders to the sideline and block the defender out, thereby giving us an inside running lane.

Again, he shouldn't get into a footrace with the SS. Any time the TE has to get out of control to block the outside number, the SS is getting too wide. Of course, the best play against a constant dose of this defensive technique is the dump pass to the TE (figure 8), but if an option play has been called, we have to be able to block the SS.

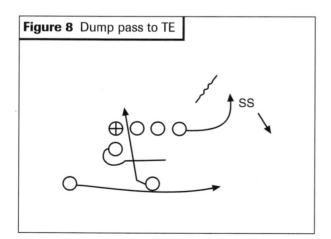

Figure 8 Dump pass to TE

Flanker Technique Versus the Invert

The flanker will block the defender responsible for the deep outside. Here are some coaching points:

1. The flanker drives off hard to make the defender think he is running a deep route. He runs at the outside shoulder in an attempt to widen the defender.

2. When the defender recognizes run and breaks down to come back to the ball, the flanker will also break down and align his nose with the defender's inside number. Since our ballcarriers have a tendency to head straight upfield after turning the corner rather than trying to get outside the flanker's block, we get inside position and try to create a lane between the flanker's block and the block of the TE (figure 9).

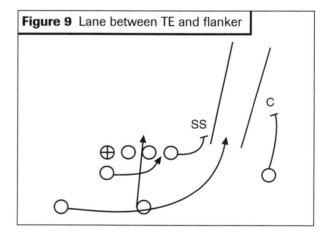

Figure 9 Lane between TE and flanker

3. From a broken down position with the head up, tail down, and the nose aligned with the defender's inside number, the flanker mirrors the movement of the defensive back but does not initiate contact. Making contact too early gives the defender time to defeat the block, then come up and make the tackle for a short gain.

4. When the defender commits and contact can no longer be avoided, the flanker locks on and takes him in the direction of his commitment (we hope our inside alignment will have

invited him to the outside). During contact, the flanker uses his forearms to keep a good blocking surface and really works his feet to stay on the defender. We continually preach against lazy feet in this phase of the block.

Note: We began by teaching the hit-and-recoil technique (much like offensive line pass blocking) to both WRs but found it required too much time and was a difficult technique to master. We have gone to the simpler method of locking on, accelerating the feet, and staying glued to the defender.

To summarize the flanker's block versus the deep outside defender, these are the important points:

1. Widen the defender by driving at his outside shoulder.

2. When the defender recognizes run, break down, assume inside number leverage, and mirror his movement. Delay contact as long as possible.

3. Do not commit too soon and do not overextend.

4. Invite the defender to get to the ballcarrier by going to the outside. When he commits, lock on with a good blocking surface, accelerate the feet, and hang on until the ballcarrier has passed.

TE Technique Versus Rolled-Up Corner

Here are the coaching points for the TE technique against the corner rolled up:

1. The TE releases flat across the face of the defensive end. By the third step, the TE will have read the coverage and know that he has to block the rolled-up corner.

2. After recognizing coverage, the TE turns his shoulders toward the sideline and approaches the cornerback from an inside-out relationship. To create a wider running lane, he must accelerate and get as much width as possible before engaging the cornerback. (The running lane is inside the block of the TE versus the rolled-up corner.)

3. Upon reaching the cornerback, the TE breaks down and aligns his nose with the opponent's inside number, inviting the defender to try to get to the ballcarrier by escaping the block to the upfield side.

4. The TE mirrors the movements of the cornerback, maintaining inside leverage. When the defender commits to the ballcarrier, the TE locks on and takes him in the direction he wants to go, ideally upfield. If he escapes to the downfield side, he has a chance to make the play on the ballcarrier, but if he tries to go around the upfield side and the TE locks on, he will be taken out of the play.

As with all perimeter blocks, the TE must not commit too soon. He should let the defender make the first move. Also, he should not react too quickly to an upfield move that could draw him out of position and allow the cornerback to come inside into the ballcarrier's path. The TE should be sure the cornerback is actually trying to come around upfield before committing to the block.

Flanker Technique Versus Rolled-Up Corner

The flanker recognizes the rolled-up corner either by alignment or after the ball is snapped. Regardless, his first priority is to release outside the cornerback on his way to blocking the deep outside defender. The outside release accomplishes two things:

1. It widens the cornerback, who is usually coached not to allow the outside release. This helps set up the TE's block and helps to widen the running lane.

2. It will probably also widen the deep outside defender and help the flanker establish inside position on his block.

Attaining inside position is made more difficult by the outside release. At times, the cornerback will simply not allow the outside release. If this happens, the flanker takes the inside release, but only after first widening the cornerback with the attempt of an outside release (figure 10).

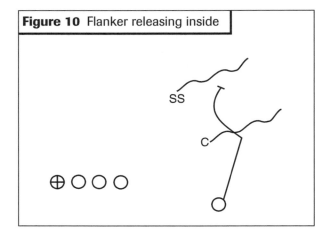

Figure 10 Flanker releasing inside

If he cannot attain inside position on the deep outside defender, the flanker gets outside-number leverage and uses the same techniques described before in blocking the deep defender.

TE and Flanker Versus Overshift

Another coverage that we see occasionally is the overshifted secondary. As shown in figure 11, the TE blocks the SS using the technique employed against the invert safety, and the flanker blocks the cornerback with the technique used by the split end versus the rolled-up corner. These techniques will be described in the following section on split end play. The FS is unblocked.

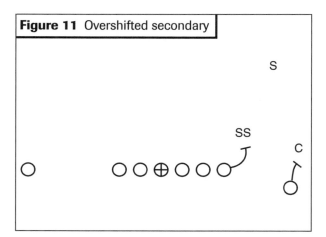

Figure 11 Overshifted secondary

Perimeter Blocking to the Split End Side

Despite the variety of defensive coverages, the split end will see basically two looks to his side. Either the cornerback will be rolled up to play the pitch, or he will be playing the deep outside and the pitch will either be taken from the LOS or by a secondary player, usually the FS.

If the cornerback is playing the deep outside, the split end will use the same technique the flanker uses to block the deep outside defender to the TE side. We like to counter him on the play-action passes. We have found that reading the coverage to determine whether the corner or safety has the pitch can be confusing and sometimes results in the split end's blocking neither the cornerback nor the safety.

The rolled-up cornerback with no deep pass responsibility presents a difficult block for the split end. Correct technique is extremely important due to the length of time the blocker must occupy the defender before the ballcarrier gets by. The running lane is inside the split end's block (figure 12).

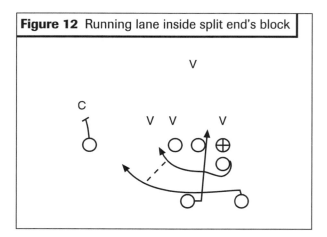

Figure 12 Running lane inside split end's block

These are the coaching points:

1. The split end comes off quickly but under control, and he establishes a position that puts him about two yards from the cornerback and directly between the defender and the

area where the ballcarrier will receive the ball if it is pitched. The first priority is to prevent the big hit—that is, the cornerback making the tackle at the same time the back receives the pitch. If that happens, the result is usually a fumble.

2. From a broken down position and with his nose aligned with the inside number of the cornerback, the split end mirrors the defender's movement. He does not initiate contact. He invites the defender to take an upfield route to get to the ballcarrier. He delays contact as long as possible, but maintains inside leverage.

3. When the defender commits to the ball or initiates contact, the split end locks on with a good blocking surface. Keeping a good base, he maintains contact until the ballcarrier has passed. Foot acceleration is important in order to stay glued to the defender.

The rolled-up corner can present the following problems to the split end. The first problem occurs when the defender comes hard inside when the ball is snapped. In a situation where the split end doesn't have time to station himself between the cornerback and the ballcarrier, the best he can hope for is to get his upper body across the front of the defender and drive him down the LOS to the inside. The ballcarrier will now most likely run outside the split end's block.

If we face a cornerback who does this very often, we will make the play-action pass in the hole an integral part of our game plan (figure 13).

The second problem occurs when the defender fakes upfield, then comes inside into the ballcarrier's path (figure 14). The split end should not react too quickly to an upfield

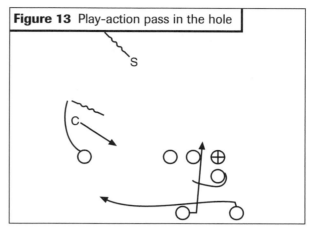

Figure 13 Play-action pass in the hole

Figure 14 Defender fakes upfield, moves inside

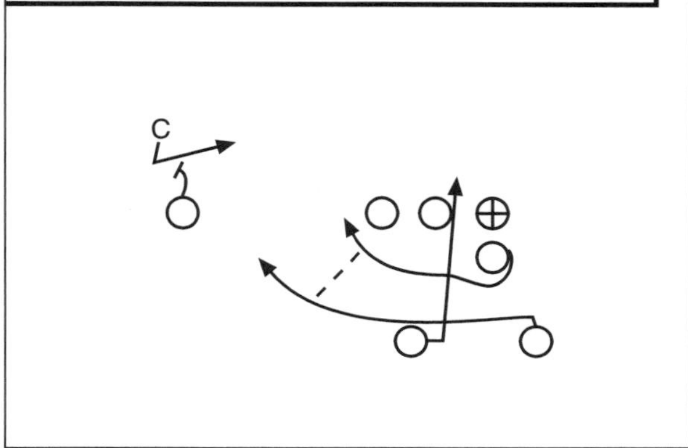

fake. He has time to react and block the defender if the cornerback commits to the upfield move. However, he will not be in position to stop the inside move if he reacts too quickly to the upfield fake.

As defenses evolve, new techniques of perimeter blocking will need to be developed and different problems will present themselves, but WRs and TEs must adjust to handle them. Perimeter blocking must be effective if the offense is to operate at maximum efficiency.

1979 Summer Manual. Larry Zierlein was assistant coach at the University of Houston.

The Option Package

Eddie Crowder

The option theory assumes that since, as the play begins, there are at least two alternatives for the offense, the defense cannot be right. This is the basic point the players must believe gives them an advantage over the defense if they execute properly.

The second consideration in the option attack is the use of the I formation. The I allows the offense to attack left or right, depending on the defensive adjustment. This is not possible if, for instance, you have a fullback behind the QB and one halfback behind one of the tackles.

The third point is an emphasis on execution. Regardless of what the offense is, the most important factor is the elimination of the self-defeating error. It is necessary to devote enough time to the perfection of our attack so we minimize assignment errors and fumbles.

The basic play in our option series is the FB dive. The FB aligns at a depth so that his hands are on the ground three yards from the ball. He takes a four-point stance. These considerations facilitate his getting to the LOS as quickly as possible. On the dive play, he hits approximately four feet from the ball. This is our aiming point rather than one associated with the guard because the guard will vary his split and we want the FB's angle to remain the same.

The other important consideration for the FB is to look at the defensive man in front of the guard. We ask him to avoid looking for the ball or at our blocker. This allows him to develop a natural reaction of breaking away from the defensive man. The QB steps to the FB with approximately a twelve-inch step on a 45-degree angle back. He places the ball to the FB's far hip, rides with him to the LOS, and then continues down the line carrying out an option fake (figure 1).

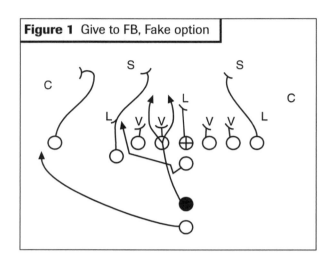

Figure 1 Give to FB, Fake option

We practice this play in every practice session by standing a large dummy in front of the offensive guard's position and placing a coach behind it to give the FB a reaction. As the FB receives the ball, the coach steps in one direction or the other without moving the dummy. The FB watches him and slides around the dummy to the opposite side, heading upfield again.

First is the double option, which comes off this play (figure 2). It is blocked by the center, guard, and tackle the same as the dive play. By virtue of this fact, we trust that the defense will respect the fake, which gives us an opportunity to isolate the outside man on the LOS, creating a two-on-one situation with our QB and tailback.

It is important to develop the "downfield option." As the QB completes his ride fake to the FB and drives to a point inside the defensive end, he turns up and runs with the ball when practical, but always retains the potential of making the pitchout to the trailing tailback.

Next is the triple option (figure 3), which the QB and FB execute in the same way as our dive play and double option only we add a third option, giving the ball to the FB. We

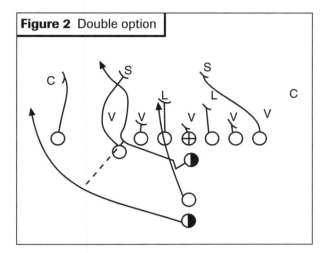

Figure 2 Double option

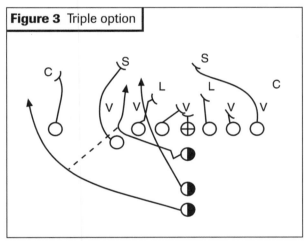

Figure 3 Triple option

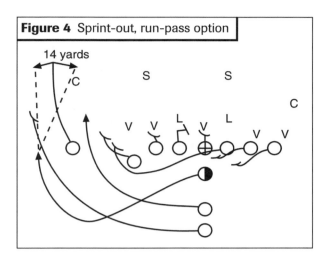

Figure 4 Sprint-out, run-pass option

14 yards

leave the second man on the LOS unblocked and have the QB "read" him. He turns his eyes directly to this man while stabbing the ball to the far hip of the FB. If this man does not close on the FB, the QB leaves it with the FB. If he closes, the QB withdraws the ball and executes the double option.

The sprint-out, run-pass option (figure 4) is also part of our basic option package. This play is run first and pass second. It is important for the QB to practice sprinting while holding the ball in throwing position. This allows him to execute a basic sweep play with the option to fire to our split end if the defense reacts aggressively so that we cannot gain yardage through the run.

The slotback blocks the outside man on the LOS by starting with the intent of hooking him from the position of alignment one yard off the LOS and one yard outside our tackle. As the slotback moves out to hook his outside leg, if the outside man comes across the slotback's face, the blocker makes contact, keeps his balance, and drives him out.

The FB starts on a course parallel to the LOS, swinging a natural arc that will take him across the line three to four yards outside our slotback. He blocks the first man who comes to his arc from the inside. If a defensive man comes through inside the slotback, the FB chops him down. If not, he continues his arc downfield. He must never veer from his arc to block anybody who comes across his face or is to his outside.

The tailback runs a course parallel to the LOS, crossing the line six to eight yards outside our slotback. He blocks the first man outside the FB arc. If any man comes across his face, he must turn him out with the same type of block described for the slotback. This allows the QB to run inside any man forcing his way upfield to contain.

The QB action was described in the basic information at the start of this play. The most important factor for the QB is to continue to sprint, trying to run with the ball unless forced to throw as a result of the defense acting up. In this case, the wide receiver is almost always open.

1973 Proceedings. Eddie Crowder was offensive coordinator at the University of Colorado.

Four Options for More Yards

Jim Carlen

Our running offense is built around four option plays: counter option, down-the-line option, triple option, and outside veer option. These options contributed nearly 30 percent of our total rushing offense this past season and averaged 6.2 yards per attempt.

The Counter Option

The counter option (figure 1) was probably the most consistent play in our offense. When our QB kept the ball, we averaged 6.8 yards. When our QB pitched the ball, we averaged 7.6 yards. We have run this play from numerous formations and with various motions. We motion to run the play in order to get away from pressing secondary coverages and create loose corners.

The dive back's alignment should be four yards deep. His takeoff point (TOP) is the foot of the center. He should drive to his TOP and carry his fake into the hole. He should stay on

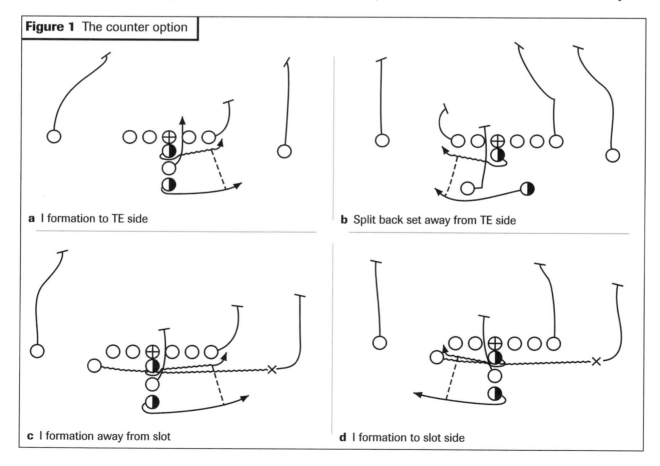

Figure 1 The counter option

a I formation to TE side

b Split back set away from TE side

c I formation away from slot

d I formation to slot side

his side of the center and hit any inside LB (to keep him from helping on the pitch) or QB or any noseguard slanting to his side.

From the I formation, the pitch back's alignment should be six and one-half yards deep. In divide backfield, his alignment should be four yards deep. The big difference between the I and divide counter options is the pitch back's relationship with the QB. In order for us to get approximately the same pitch relationship with our QB, we require the I back to take a jab step away from the play side and the divide back to push off quickly to the play side. The ideal pitch relationship is five and one-half yards from the QB and four yards in front of the QB.

The most difficult technique that the QB must execute on the counter option is to turn his back to the LOS and find his key before he starts down the line on the attack. The QB must spin quickly on his off foot, getting shoulder pads and headgear square with the sideline. He must locate his key, letting the dive back do the faking. After locating his key, he should attack the key's inside shoulder and execute the option. When running the counter option to the two-man side, the QB must realize that he is unprotected and that his key can get to him a lot quicker than if running to the three-man side. He must get around quickly and be ready for quick pressure.

If a defensive man is down a tackle, he should use a reverse block. Against an even defense, the guard should place his head in the middle of the defensive man. The TE should make an outside release and block the defensive man responsible for covering the flat. The flanker must release off the LOS and make the secondary believe the play is going to be a pass. His blocking responsibility is the defensive man covering the deep outside zone.

The Down-the-Line Option

We like to run the down-the-line option (figure 2, p. 140) against defenses whose LBs are not respecting the inside fake on our counter option play. We bring our TE, slotback, or split end down inside to cut off fast-moving LBs. Like the counter option, we run the down-the-line option from numerous formations and with various motions.

The FB's depth should be four yards. On the snap, the FB pushes off to the sideline and reads the block of the outside receiver. He should always block the outside man unless the wide receiver fails to crack. The FB should never let the outside man beat him to the inside. To block, we teach a FB to put his headgear on the widest man's headgear and destroy him. We have found this block to be much more effective than attempting to cut the outside leg.

The pitch back's depth in the I should be six and one-half yards. The pitch back should take a jab step with the offside foot and get his numbers over the opposite foot. This jab step has two purposes: influence LB movement and allow the FB to get out in front far enough so as not to interfere with the pitch. After the jab step, the pitch back should push off to the sideline and get in a good pitch relationship with the QB. If the ball is pitched, the pitch back should get in the FB's hip pocket and cut off his block. If the QB keeps the ball, the pitch back should turn upfield and keep the pitch relationship.

The QB should make the counter move opposite the play side with his head and shoulders in order to influence the LBs and let the FB clear the pitch. After the counter move, the QB should push off the opposite foot and attack the key as quickly as possible. If for some reason the QB cannot get down the LOS to his key, he should turn up inside and run. He should never pitch off of any defensive man except his key.

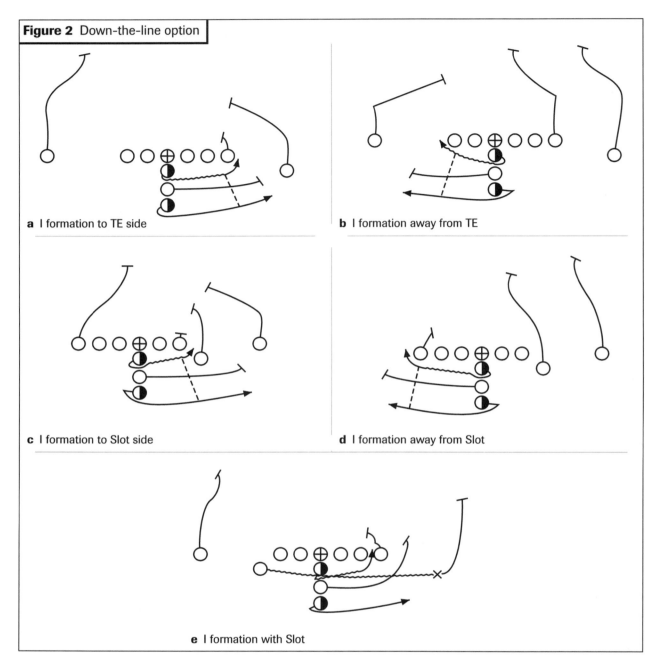

Figure 2 Down-the-line option

a I formation to TE side

b I formation away from TE

c I formation to Slot side

d I formation away from Slot

e I formation with Slot

Against a 52 defense, the TE should read the depth of the LB and either combo with the tackle if the LB is deep or double with the tackle if the LB is tight. Against an even defense or eagle, the TE has the option to release inside to the LB (figure 3a and 3b) or release around (figure 3c).

Against a 52 defense with the LB deep, the onside guard should ensure the onside tackle is blocked (figure 3a).

The Triple Option

Figure 4 shows two ways to run the triple option to the TE side (a) and away from the TE (b).

The dive back's TOP is the guard/tackle gap. He should never leave his TOP until the ball is given to him or pulled by the QB. If the ball is given to him, he should wrap it up with both hands. He should keep his head up and run outside of his tackle's block. If the ball is pulled,

Figure 3 TE and G options

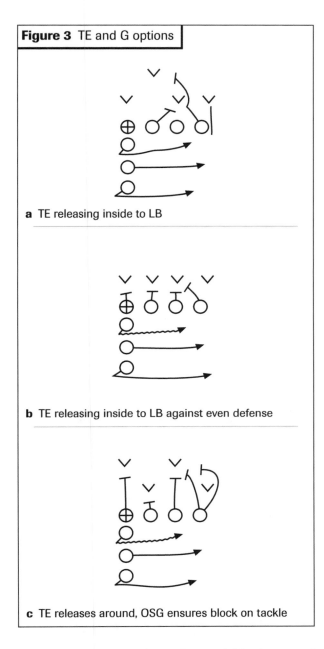

a TE releasing inside to LB

b TE releasing inside to LB against even defense

c TE releases around, OSG ensures block on tackle

Figure 4 The triple option

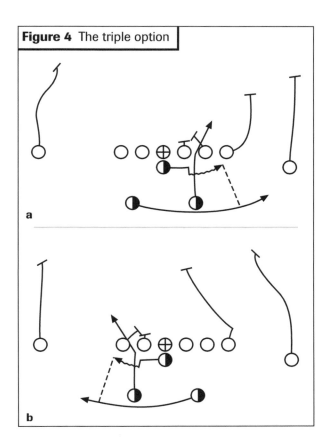

a

b

he should stay on his TOP and block one of three people: if the key keeps his position or attacks the dive back, he blocks the key; if the key disappears inside, he blocks the first man to show on his path (most likely a LB from the inside); if no one shows in his path, he blocks the free safety.

The pitch back's first assignment is to push off to the sideline without a false step and catch the QB. He should get into a good pitch rela-

tionship with the QB (five and one-half yards deep and three yards in front). The pitch back must anticipate the pitch if he is getting quick force from the strong safety. We want him to hit the seam quickly and run off the TE's block. If the QB turns upfield, the pitch back must turn upfield and keep the pitch relationship.

The QB's mechanics of running the triple option will determine how successful it is. On the snap, the QB takes an open step and places the ball on the hip of the dive back, looking at his first key (first man on or outside the offensive tackle). If the key makes a definite move outside, the QB jabs the ball into the dive back's pocket. If the key does anything else, the QB should pull the ball, work up into the line, and attack the inside leg of his second key. The pitch should be soft but firm and should be made end over end by turning the palm out and the thumb under. The QB should always steal a look as the ball is pitched. He should never pitch the ball off his first key.

The Outside Veer

Figure 5 shows the outside veer play.

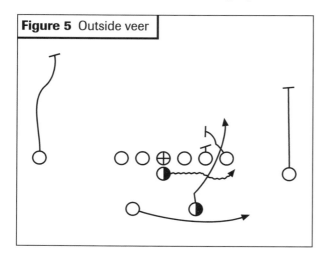

Figure 5 Outside veer

1974 Proceedings. Jim Carlen was head coach at Texas Tech University.

The fullback's TOP should be the outside foot of the offensive tackle. His first step is a six-inch jab step up with his inside foot and then a push off to his TOP. He must keep his head up and cut off the TE's block as close as possible, keeping his shoulders down.

The pitch back should push off to the sideline, catch up with the QB, and get into a good pitch relationship. The QB's assignment is basically the same as in the triple option except that the dive back hits one hole wider. He should work up into the line and key the defensive man on the end of the LOS. If his key's head disappears inside, the QB should pull the ball and turn upfield. If the key does anything else, the QB should give the ball to the fullback.

The onside tackle should cut his split down from three feet to two feet.

The Essential Dive Option

Doug Carter

An integral part of our running game is the option. We presently use three forms of the option: dive, lead, and trap.

The dive option is the only option we take into every game. We also use the trap and lead options but don't always feature them. Like all of our plays, we try to make them as simple as possible, especially the dive option. We ask our QB to make only one read. We don't read the triple. By reading only one player, we don't need the countless reps it takes to perfect the triple.

Occasionally, we have a bad play, but usually we have a big one to counteract it. The dive off the dive option has been a productive play for us. This is a predetermined give that, over the past two years, has averaged over six yards a carry and four yards or more 54 percent of the time.

First and foremost, we try to make all assignments simple. We don't want our players thinking, only reacting. Through simplification, we can cut down on missed assignments and forced errors.

The Dive Option

Figure 1 shows four ways to run the dive option. The keys and assignments are:

- Tight end: Junction release and block support CP. If load block is called, block DE; versus support blitz, automatic load.
- Front side tackle: Number two area scoop. CP tighten split, give DT alignments call; hard zone scoop with FSG.
- Front side guard: Number one area, hard zone scoop with FST; CP listen for DT alignment call.

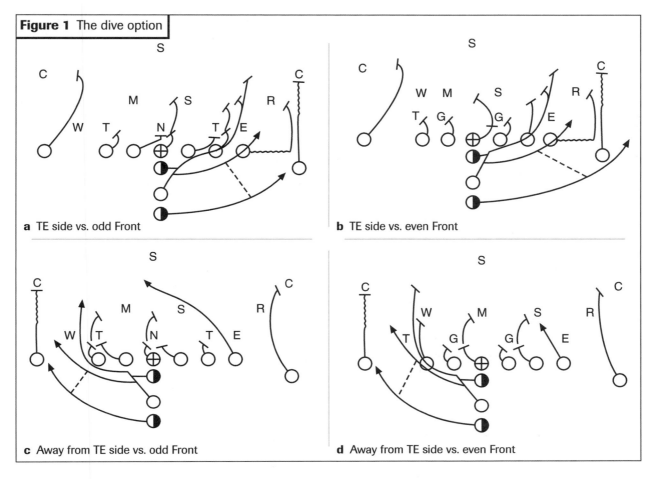

Figure 1 The dive option

a TE side vs. odd Front

b TE side vs. even Front

c Away from TE side vs. odd Front

d Away from TE side vs. even Front

- Center: Scoop zero area.
- Back side guard: Versus nose, scoop zero area; versus even from seal DG.
- GST: Seal tackle area.
- Fullback: Fake dive. Aiming point is play side hip of guard. Keep head up; after fake, flatten out and look FSLB to FS.
- Tailback: Lead step and turn shoulders to play call side. Sprint to a point 10 yards outside of Y's alignment. CP keep pitch relationship if QB turns up.
- Quarterback: Fake dive and option EMOLOS and CP. Work downhill; don't belly back.
- X: Block outside one-third.
- Z: Block outside one-third CP read corner to FS; versus hard corner, lock up; versus man, run off.

The front side tackle and guard must at least maintain the LOS. When possible, they should get positive movement. This allows the QB to work downhill. The scoop should be hard and aggressive. The tackle works from the DT's breast plate to armpit. If the DT goes straight ahead or inside, the tackle comes off the LB and cuts. If the DT slants play side, the tackle stays locked up.

The FSG steps flat enough to enable him to get his far elbow and hat past the DT's hip. If the hip comes straight ahead or toward him, he initiates a scoop. If the hip goes away, he makes a hard climb to LB. The guard should place his play side hand on the FST's hip. He will now be close enough to initiate a scoop, keeping low, and the OT can judge when to come off the DT. The most important thing to remember is if the DT is in the gray area, we would rather both players stay on the DT than both come off for the LB. Defensive tackles make plays for losses, so if we miss the LB, we'll probably still get positive yardage.

The FB must make a great fake and get involved. After the fake, the FB flattens out and checks FSLB. If he is taken care of, the FB continues on track and looks for the FS trying to fill the alley. When we can get our FB to the FS, we'll usually have a big play.

The QB takes the ball to the EMOLOS. When possible, he runs downhill, he doesn't belly back. If you belly back, pursuit usually catches you. If outnumbered to the play side, we reverse it and run the other way.

The tailback always wants to get outside after receiving a pitch. He comes inside only when forced. He should always keep the proper pitch relationship with the QB. If QB turns up, so does he. If we can get the pitch off downfield, it will usually result in a home run.

The TE on the junction release should take an open step, then cross over and gauge support's attack angle. He continues flat until we get our outside eye caught up with the rover's inside eye, then turns up, being careful not to overrun him.

If rover supports quicker than anticipated, the only alternative is to kick the rover out. If this happens, TB must turn up. We always prefer to log the rover. On contact, we want to work high through the outside breastplate of the rover. Don't overextend, mirror the rover. It should be like playing man-on-man defense. Just stay in his way.

One variation of this play develops with our TE's blocking scheme. We can load the TE on the DE and option the rover. This load scheme (figure 2) can be called in the huddle, or the TE has the option of loading if he feels he is unable to get a sufficient junction block. The TE has a rule: automatic load versus rover blitz.

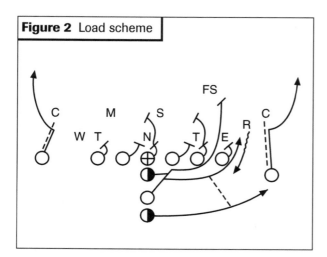

Figure 2 Load scheme

Versus a switch call by the defense, we try to read it and load the DE (figure 3). A switch occurs when the DE and rover switch responsibilities. By his second step, the TE will be able to determine if a switch is taking place. It takes some reps, but he will be able to lock up on the DE. When a switch occurs, the FB must flatten out and try to cut the rover.

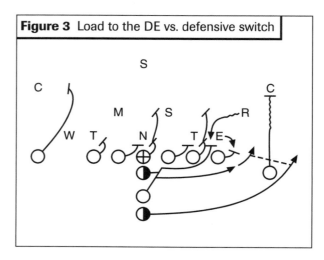

Figure 3 Load to the DE vs. defensive switch

The play side receiver reads the play side corner. If the corner doesn't give ground on the snap, the receiver continues up and blocks him (figure 4a). He stays high, doesn't cut, and mirrors him. If the corner gives ground on the snap, the receiver alters course to intersect the FS's angle of attack and block him (figure 4b).

Versus hard corner, the receiver locks up. He stays high and aggressive, trying to gain inside position (figure 5). We lock up on hard corners so the TE isn't required to read coverages that change on the snap. If he reads man coverage then runs off, he pretends he is running a fade and is the primary receiver (figure 6). All options are good versus tight if you can get the ball pitched.

Anyone can run the dive option. We don't spend more time on it than we do any other play. Yet more big plays can be attributed to it than to any other. For the past few years, we've had an option QB. But we'll run this play year in and year out even when our QBs aren't as adept at running it. The option limits the man coverage we'll see, which in turn limits the blitz.

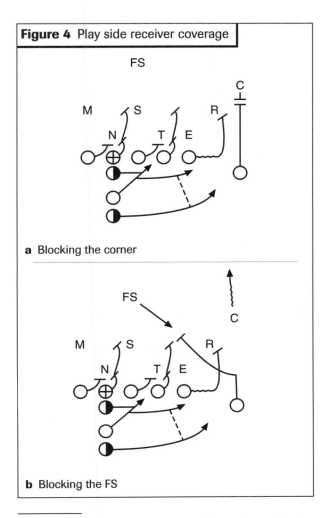

Figure 4 Play side receiver coverage

a Blocking the corner

b Blocking the FS

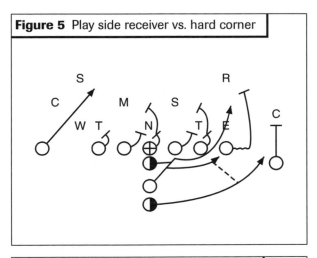

Figure 5 Play side receiver vs. hard corner

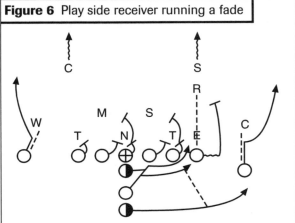

Figure 6 Play side receiver running a fade

1990 Summer Manual. Doug Carter is offensive line coach at Eastern Kentucky University.

The Freeze Option Game

Dick MacPherson

As we entered our planning stages for the 1985 season, we felt very strongly, as a staff, that we needed option football to improve our offensive productivity. Listed below are the most significant reasons for our commitment to the option.

1. It was the best way for us to get the football outside the perimeter of the defense. It has become increasingly difficult to establish a sweep or toss play as an outside play. However, the option gave us a chance to get our skill people at running back and QB loose in the open field.

2. You do not need dominant offensive linemen to have success in an option offense. The finesse and deception of option football allows you the luxury of not having to knock people off the ball on every snap. You can read some

defenders rather than blocking them. Also, the angle blocks and double-teams of option football help your linemen.

3. You can make the defense play assignment football by defending the option on every play. We felt the defense would assign a man to the dive, QB, and pitch phases of our option on both sides of our formation. This made defenders play assignment football rather than reaction football.

4. The option helps pass offense dramatically because of the defensive structures to be faced. Not only did our rushing totals improve tremendously, our option offense broke nine team and individual school passing records. This success can be attributed to the types of defenses we saw to stop the option: eight-man blitzes, two-deep zones, and TE rotated coverages.

Our Option Philosophy

Before our staff talked about any specific option play or style of option, we felt it was critical to develop an option philosophy in which we all could believe. If times got tough, we felt we would need to have a strong basis and belief for what we were doing, one our coaches and players totally understood and believed in. When that was accomplished, deciding on the specific plays in our offense was relatively easy. Our philosophy included these components:

1. Make the defense constrict on the fullback. Establish the fullback game inside.

2. Use multiple formations and motions to run the same options.

3. Find a flank. This concept means that we will try to determine which side of these formations are the 11 softest flanks in which to attack the perimeter with our option game.

4. Use the option from the I formation to allow the speed backs at tailback to catch the pitch and run outside, and the fullback to be the inside runner.

5. Use a play-action pass off all our options.

6. Employ the dropback game to prevent defenses from ganging up on the option game.

Last season, we were a multiple option team. We ran 10 different styles of options. We usually had three or four option types per game. The heart and soul of our option attack was the freeze option series that was established at Wichita State and refined and popularized at East Carolina. This series gave us the inside fullback game we wanted, with an excellent option game complementing it. As defenses adjusted to take away our freeze option, we would immediately go to the other complementary options in our package that were available because of the way the freeze option was taken away. We feel you need multiple option styles.

Establishing the Fullback Inside

The first way we would run the FB inside would be with the tight FB dive (figure 1). It is a quick-hitting play in which the FB can run off the block of the offensive center versus the 5-2 defense. It is a base blocking concept up front.

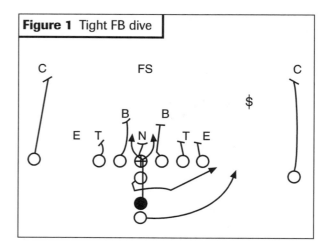

Figure 1 Tight FB dive

FB dive mechanics

■ QB: Steps back off the midline and stretches the ball back to the FB. He gathers his second step and hands off the ball to the FB. He continues the option fake off the football until he gets to the outside leg of the guard, then attacks downhill.

■ FB: Takes a lead step and runs the midline. He runs off the block of the center. Once he makes the cut, he gets his shoulders square.

■ TB: Freezes on the snap of the ball. Once the QB's second step hits the ground, he sprints into pitch relationship.

The second and most compatible method of running the FB is the FB trap off the tight dive action (figure 2). Realize the backfield mechanics are the same as the tight dive, except the FB must now get in phase inside the trapping guard.

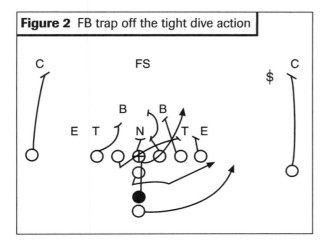

Figure 2 FB trap off the tight dive action

The Freeze Option

The option play that was the most frequent play of our option series was the freeze option. It became the heart and soul of our offense. It is a play that can be run both to the TE side (figure 3a) and the SE side (figure 3b).

Freeze Option Rules

■ Onside tackle: inside for LB.

■ Onside guard: down on nose.

■ Center: slams nose and blocks "A" gap back side.

■ Offside guard: pulls and reads the tackle area; fights to get to LB.

■ Offside tackle: gap seals hinge.

■ TE: for the option toward, he blocks primary run support; for the option away, he gap seals the hinge.

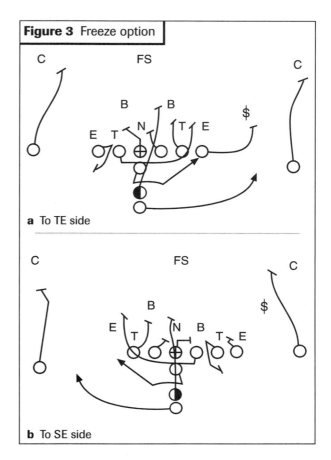

Figure 3 Freeze option

a To TE side

b To SE side

■ Split end: for the option away, he blocks the inside number of the near halfback; for the option toward, he blocks primary run support.

■ Flanker: for the option toward, he blocks nonprimary run support; for the option away, he blocks the inside number of the near halfback.

■ Fullback: runs through the midline of the center; he gets a great mesh and drives to the back side linebacker.

■ QB: steps back off the midline; stretches the ball back to the FB; gathers his second step and rides the FB to his front hip; stays off the ball until the outside leg of the guard, then drives downhill and options the number three man.

■ TB: Freezes on the snap. When the QB's second step hits the ground, he sprints to pitch relationship, keeping a four-yard-by-four-yard relationship with the QB.

Use of Formations

While studying the defensive structures you will face, it will become apparent that the use of multiple formations and motions can provide you with definite advantages in attacking the perimeter with the freeze option series. For example, in figure 4 linemen's and backs' rules are consistent, regardless of the formation. In the Twins formation (figure 5), only the receivers must adjust blocking schemes.

The motion can change the defensive support system of certain coverages, which can give you an advantage in the perimeter without changes for your people up front.

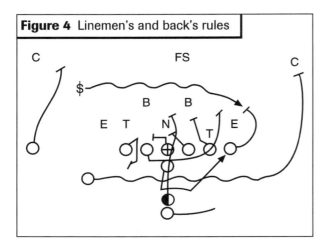

Figure 4 Linemen's and back's rules

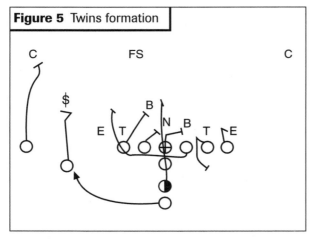

Figure 5 Twins formation

Use of the Play-Action Pass

The importance of the play-action pass off the option action must be noted (figure 6). It is crucial that the defensive support people be placed in a pass-run bind in order to slow down their option support.

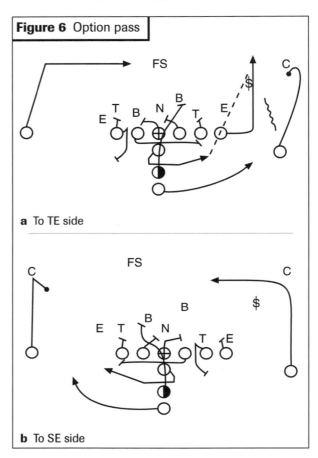

Figure 6 Option pass

a To TE side

b To SE side

In summary, during the 1985 season, our players were able to execute and thoroughly understand these simple concepts of option football. This confidence and understanding of the system had a lot to do with our offensive success.

1986 Summer Manual. Dick MacPherson was head coach at Syracuse University.

The I Option Package

Jimmy Satterfield

Our offensive package consists of six basic elements:

1. **Power game** (sweep, isolation, FB base)
2. **Trap game** (FB, TB)
3. **Option game** (inside, counter, load)
4. **Play pass** (option, bootleg, sprint)
5. **Dropback** (three-step, five-step, seven-step)
6. **Screens, draws, delays, reverses**

This article will focus on our option game. In order for the option to be successful from the I, we must establish the FB inside with base plays and traps. We feel we then have a chance to run the inside option.

When we call an option, we expect to have a big play. We sell our players and coaches on this and work very hard for everyone to execute his block in order to break the play.

Inside Option

Our inside option scheme includes the veer scheme, loop scheme, and base scheme.

Figure 1 shows our veer scheme. Here are coaching points for the veer scheme:

- ■ FB: Hand at four yards. Takeoff point is inside guard's hip.
- ■ QB: Reaches FB deep and reads tackle. If he keeps the ball, he runs to the DE and pitches on the run.
- ■ TB: Gets in pitch position approximately one yard deep and four yards wide. He gets the pitch going downhill.

Each offensive lineman has a specific technique that he must use on each blocking scheme. The defensive tackles' alignment will usually determine which blocking scheme we will use.

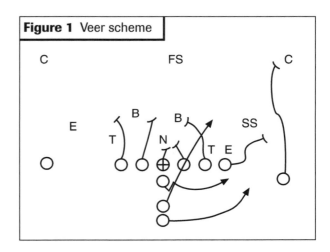

Figure 1 Veer scheme

Figure 2 shows our loop scheme. These are the coaching points:

- ■ Offensive backs block the same as in the veer scheme.
- ■ On guard and tackle block LB to free safety.

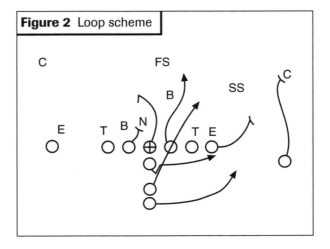

Figure 2 Loop scheme

Figure 3 shows our base scheme. These are the coaching points:

- FB: Takeoff point changes to gap. He blocks LB to FS.
- QB: Reaches FB deep and fakes. No read. He pulls and runs ball to end.
- TB: Same.
- Off guard: Blocks LB to FS.

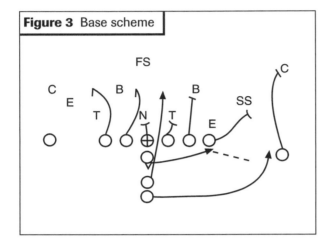

Figure 3 Base scheme

Counter Option

Figure 4 shows our counter option. These are the coaching points:

- FB: Takeoff point gap; he makes a good fake and blocks LB.
- QB: Reaches FB deep arm ride; after a three-step reverse, he runs to end or SS.
- TE: Checks DE and arc blocks SS. If the end stunts, the TE blocks him.

This is a basic scheme we use in running the counter option. We have used a variety of schemes over the years: trap option, guard lead, tackle lead, etc. We have also had some success running the counter option off the sweep fake.

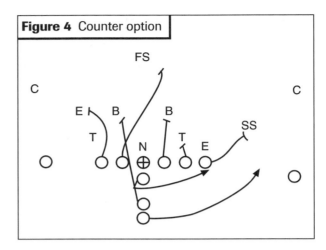

Figure 4 Counter option

Sweep Option

Figure 5 shows the sweep option. These are the coaching points:

- FB: Fake sweep and block the DT.
- QB: Fake sweep, hide ball from LB, and option end.
- TB: Fake sweep, get in pitch position.

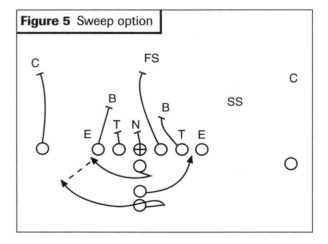

Figure 5 Sweep option

Loaded Option

Figure 6 shows our loaded option. These are the coaching points:

- FB: Takeoff point ends inside foot; block LB to FS.
- QB: Reverse out, run ball to SS, and pitch or keep on run.
- TB: Get in good pitch position.

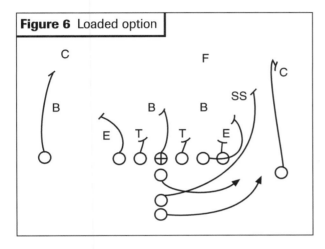

Figure 6 Loaded option

Figure 7 shows our loaded option G scheme. These are the coaching points:

- For the FB, QB, and TB, assignments are the same as for the loaded option.
- For on guard: load DE.

This is a general outline of our option game. We have used several different variations, formations, and types of motion to run the option. We feel that options work best for us when we don't try to force them and we have patience.

Often, we are asked how many times we pass, run the option, etc. We do not predeter-

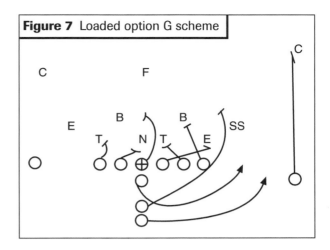

Figure 7 Loaded option G scheme

mine how often we will run a specific play each game. We try to call plays dictated by what the defense gives us. Sideline decisions and play selection are a vital key to our offensive success. We ran the following plays in the 1988 national championship game:

Power game—21 plays (sweep, three; FB base 18)

Trap game—five plays

Option game—12 plays (inside, five; counter, five; load two)

Sprint draw run—seven plays

Play pass—10 plays (bootleg three; sprint draw four; option three)

Dropback—four plays

Quick pass—two plays

Total—62 plays for 355 yards

Obviously, we have a lot of offense. Each week we try to determine which parts we will major in and try to get maximum repetition on them. We also sell our coaches and players on taking whatever amount of quality time is necessary to get the job done.

1989 Proceedings. Jimmy Satterfield was head coach at Furman University, Greenville, SC.

PART III

The Passing Game

Part III—The Passing Game

The Pass Protection System

Homer Smith

Our offensive staff, led by Bruce Tarbox, believes that protection assignments for all of our pass plays can and should begin with one system for identifying defenders and, further, that assignments for screen passes and draw runs can begin with the same system.

Pass Protection

An onside and an offside are established by the number-name of the play. The center is considered a part of the offside unit and a defender over him is an offside target. The offside targets are not counted but are grouped as a picture of four potential rushers. The onside targets are counted one, two, three, four, with the guard and tackle assigned to numbers one and two. Figure 1 shows four defenses with offside targets blackened and onside numbered.

Different from conventional pass protection systems is the application of one identification system to all passes and the concept of grouping

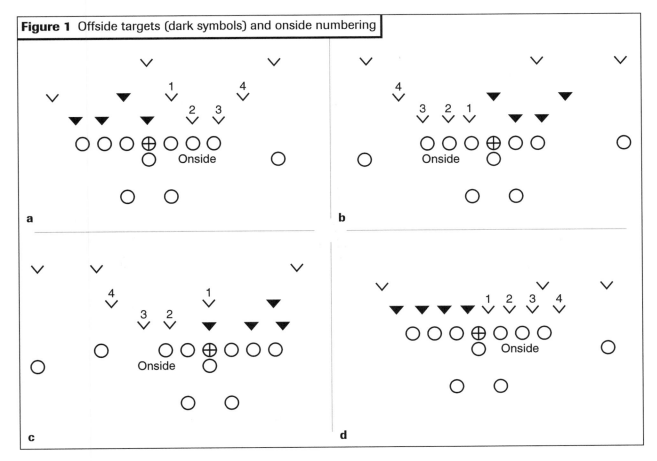

Figure 1 Offside targets (dark symbols) and onside numbering

offside defenders into a picture. We keep the two-receiver side as the onside on all dropback passes, believing that it is difficult to rush four defenders over the onside but not over the offside, and wanting solid protection where the biggest rush problem exists. This is different, as is our system for varying assignments to get either more or fewer blockers or to change targets by using code words that the QB can communicate.

Basically, the onside is the side of the play. With our dropback passes, however, the onside is always the two-receiver side. It is a simple matter to identify a primary receiver. By having the two-receiver side as the onside, we keep four potential blockers on the side with the greatest chance of facing four rushers. If a fourth man rushes on the two-receiver side, it is much easier to make him pay a price because the tight end can catch a short pass behind the rush.

Figure 2 shows four-man rushes to each side, with the offside rush being blocked and the onside beaten by the pass pattern. The backs find it helpful to know that they are always assigned to the outside defender in the grouping on the one-receiver side when needed as complementary receivers. This defender is least likely to rush, so we can have our cake and eat it, too.

Blocking techniques vary with the type of pass being thrown, of course. Figure 3 shows three plays in which the right guard is on the onside and is assigned to number one but where three different blocking techniques could be employed.

The dropback problem is simple. Referring to the second diagram in figure 3, somewhat more aggressiveness can be applied with the back faking outside of the guard. Referring to the third diagram in figure 3, the guard is asked to protect onside and then allow for bootleg movement toward the offside. Sorting out number one as the target is just a start for a guard.

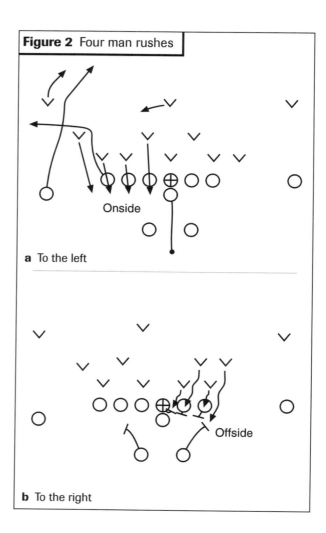

Figure 2 Four man rushes

a To the left

b To the right

Offside Blocking

With the one system for identifying onside and offside defenders established, it is not confusing to learn a short list of variations. Each variation has a code-word name and is defined simply and positively in terms of exactly what a blocker or a group of blockers does.

Uncovered

When we want to handle the four-man rushing threats on the offside with just three blockers, we call for either *uncovered* or *hinge* blocking. With uncovered blocking specified, the center, offside guard, and offside tackle

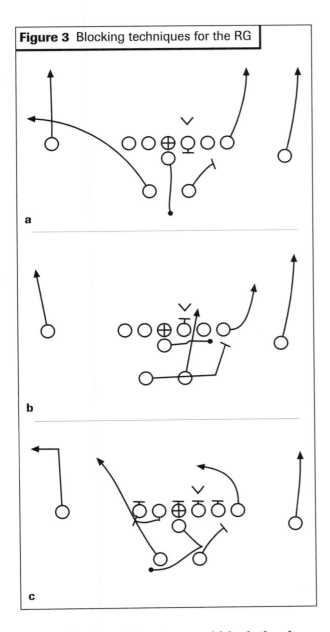

Figure 3 Blocking techniques for the RG

a

b

c

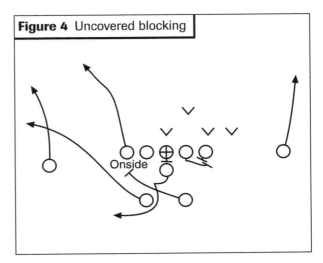

Figure 4 Uncovered blocking

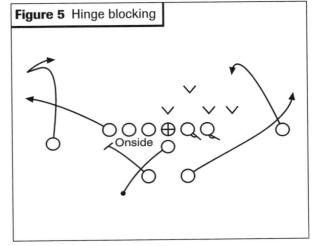

Figure 5 Hinge blocking

Mike

The offside tight end blocks the outside man in the four-man rushing threat. Mike is implied in many plays (figure 6).

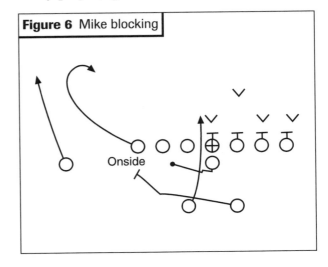

Figure 6 Mike blocking

watch the four defenders and block the three who rush. The man with the linebacker over him checks the linebacker and if the LB does not rush, steps out to take the defensive end (figure 4).

Hinge

The center, offside guard, and offside tackle watch the four defenders and swing or hinge out to take the three who rush. Both men must watch the linebacker because if he rushes, they cannot hinge (figure 5).

Sierra

The offside back does what the offside end does in Mike—he blocks the outside man in the four-man rushing threat. Sierra blocking (figure 7) is usually called in the huddle, but it can be implied in a play.

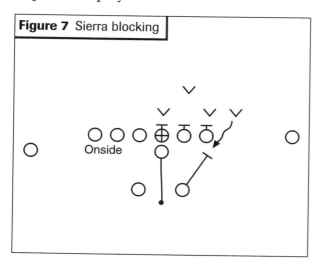

Figure 7 Sierra blocking

Big-on-Big

When assigning a back to the end man on the line, Sierra protection would have him blocking a big lineman while one of his own big linemen checks a linebacker. The solution is to call for a big man to block a big man (figure 8).

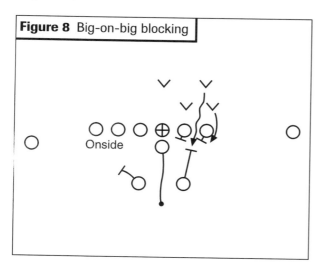

Figure 8 Big-on-big blocking

Alpha

When a back can be used to block a linebacker over the center or over an onside lineman, the

blockers to the offside of that linebacker can block away. This obviously enables us to get four blockers on the offside four-man rushing threat while releasing the offside TE (figure 9).

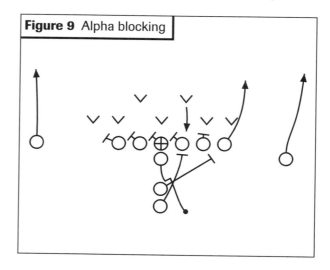

Figure 9 Alpha blocking

Onside Blocking

Romeo

All blockers think of reaching toward the onside to stop a fourth defender who rushes over the onside three blockers (figure 10). (This assignment requires combo blocking technique to deny penetration.) This cannot be used with uncovered or hinge protection.

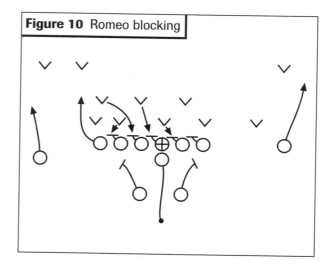

Figure 10 Romeo blocking

Down

The tight end on the onside blocks to his inside because a fourth defender threatens to rush to

the inside (figure 11). This is used when Romeo protection cannot be used because only three blockers are available on the offside.

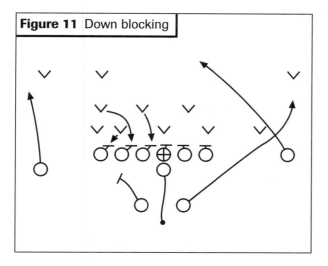

Figure 11 Down blocking

Shoulders

This can be a call or an assumption. Throughout pass protection, linemen close their shoulders while they wait to see which defender comes to the inside and which to the outside. The shoulders technique gets its toughest tests in the defensive maneuvers diagramed (figure 12).

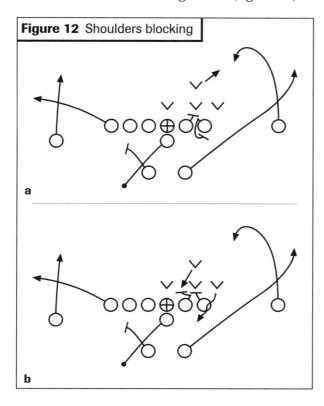

Figure 12 Shoulders blocking

Check

An onside lineman with a linebacker on him checks to be sure the linebacker is not rushing and then helps another lineman (figure 13).

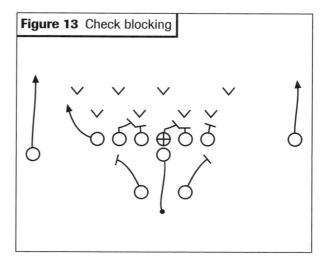

Figure 13 Check blocking

Area

There are two defenders outside of an offensive player. The offensive player takes the one who threatens the play. The word means exactly what it does in running offense (figure 14).

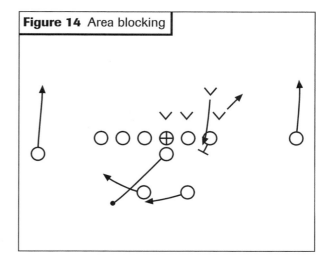

Figure 14 Area blocking

Rush

A fourth defender is rushing from the outside on the onside. This implies that the pass pattern must beat the extra man (figure 15).

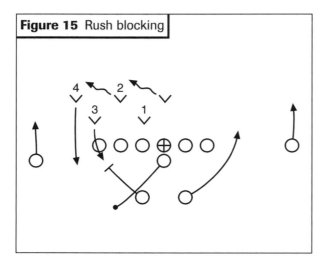

Figure 15 Rush blocking

Blitz

A defensive back is an extra man in the inside rush. Blitz means to stop the blitzer by blocking toward the inside and to make any unblocked man come from the outside (figure 16).

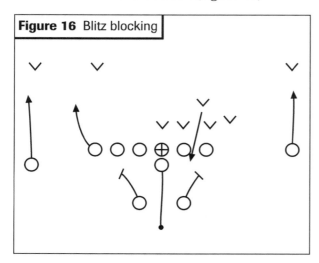

Figure 16 Blitz blocking

These are a lot of words. If we did not standardize words this way, however, we would have to use sentences and paragraphs to explain what must be done in pass protection. The words listed can be used in huddle calls, LOS communications, or in discussions of plays and defenses.

Visioning

The key to pass protection is vision. A blocker must find the man to whom he is assigned, look for cross charge or linebacker run-through possibilities, communicate with other blockers if necessary, and use his eyes. Most pass protection failures are a result of poor visioning.

When defenders attempt to surprise blockers, the blockers must hold relative positions in the blocking front. Assignments are by area for purposes of picking up cross charges and linebacker run-throughs. Blockers close shoulder pads to deny penetration and then block the defenders who rush on their respective sides.

Special Adjustments

Overshifted seven-man fronts present special problems. We do not want to recount the outside defenders because inside defenders jump one way or another. Our solution is to block standard and overshifted defenses the same, helping ourselves with romeo and gap calls where possible. Figure 17 shows two problems and our blocking solutions.

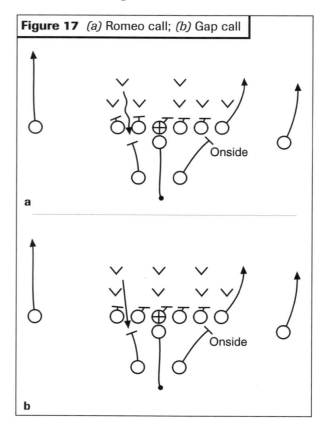

Figure 17 *(a)* Romeo call; *(b)* Gap call

The eight-man front, which threatens four rushers over three onside blockers, requires the romeo call or a gap call on passes that necessitate hinge or uncovered blocking on the offside. Figure 17 shows both calls with plays that require them.

A number three lined up over the tackle calls for big-on-big blocking. The man assigned to number three watches both LBs and takes the most dangerous. A romeo or gap call is possible.

Launch Points

There are essentially six spots from which the ball will be launched. We have more than six pass actions, but for blocking purposes, just the six points need to be defined. Passes with fake option plays are thrown close to the LOS, approximately behind a tackle. Halfback passes and sprint-outs are thrown well outside of the blockers. When we fake run action and then move to a side, the movement of the quarterback is delayed. This needs to be distinguished from the action where the quarterback moves away from the center, showing pass. Bootleg passes move the quarterback to a side, but with extreme delay. Dropbacks and certain play actions leave the quarterback directly behind the center. Figure 18 shows the six launch points.

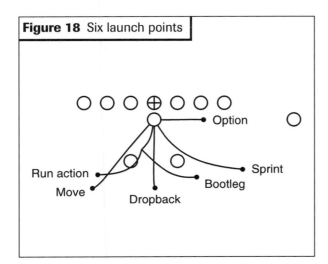

Figure 18 Six launch points

Screens

Screens, like draws, require more than learning assignments. The following material is essentially what we require players to understand. As in most aspects of football, understanding is like a good computer program that is ready to fit and relate any information it receives.

A screen is first a pass. A pass play is called, an action is protected, and a pattern is run. Everything done in pass protection blocking against a defense is done in a screen play, because it is first a pass play. At a point, the screen blocking unit—both guards and the center—breaks to the outside, and the pattern runners wheel around to block for a play that is trying to get to the outside. Blockers start after two seconds, after two quick but good pass protection blows, then break off together with the first man pulling the other two. (I have used Huey, Dewey, and Louie from Donald Duck movies as an example of men in good formation for screen blocking.) Moving, waiting for a "go" call from the receiver, starting downfield with proper timing, obeying rules that say you cannot block downfield until the ball is in the air—these things are not difficult. For the receiver, sneaking out without giving the play away is difficult, but can be learned. The problem is to stop a rusher completely with one blow and then fake losing him.

What is really difficult about a screen is calling it properly while having an accurate prediction of defensive vulnerability. It needs a space between rushers and defenders. How many defenders rush and drop off is not primarily important. It is how they rush and drop, and how much space is created. We search for the space in scouting and during game action. Figure 19 shows one defensive end going with a receiver and another holding a shallow position awaiting counter action. Is there a space to set up a screen? Everyone can help determine whether or not there is.

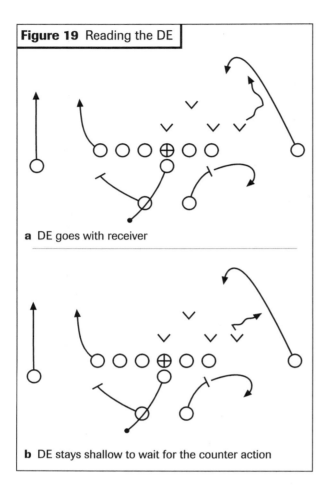

Figure 19 Reading the DE

a DE goes with receiver

b DE stays shallow to wait for the counter action

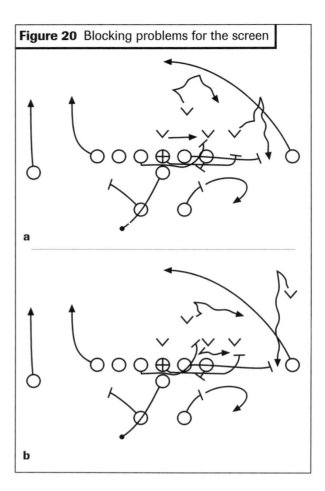

Figure 20 Blocking problems for the screen

a

b

The next most difficult thing is exchanging the ball. The quarterback's enacting of the pass play must pull rushers; the blocking by those who break off must leave no hint of a screen. In moving down the line, the blockers must look to the outside, straight ahead, and to the inside in order of their places in line. They are protecting a reception point not unlike the way pass blockers protect a passer's launch point. Nothing can come between them, the receiver is behind them, and unless more than four defenders are collapsing on the reception point, the ball exchange should be made. Figure 20 shows the most common blocking problems.

After experiencing dozens of screen plays, scouting an opponent, practicing, and visioning the defense before the snap, a screen blocking unit will be as confident as a pass protection unit.

Blocks by downfield receivers should be aimed high (since the receivers cannot be certain where the ballcarrier will go) and executed with speed. Get to a defender by the shortest and fastest route! On hearing "Go," the three-man unit sprints out, looking to the outside, straight ahead, and inside. Blocks are high. Everyone, including the ballcarrier, tries to get the ball to the outside.

With these points, players should be able to coach themselves on screen plays. As on draws, players are asked to coach themselves as a way of demonstrating their potential in mastery and self-correction. The only situation in which they do not have a chance to execute the screen is when a defender gets between the passer and the receiver, smells the screen, and backs off into the play. To prepare for this, players practice the discipline of not going downfield before the "go" call, and the QB practices the discipline in preventing lost yardage. The QB is making decisions from the time he says "hut." He can make a regular pass play, he can execute the screen, he can throw the ball away or run a QB draw, he can use the back not involved in the screen as a target, he can do something before he gets thrown for a loss.

Draws

Like screens, draws lend themselves more to understanding than to memorizing assignments. The idea is to fake the pass as much as possible to get the rushers rushing and the pass droppers dropping! In assignments, the blocking is onside/offside, the same as it is in pass plays; in execution, the blocking is different in that we never want two linemen teamed on one defender. We will always have a blocker for each of seven targets: four on the offside and three on the onside. Understanding this takes care of many of the questions players ordinarily have about our draw plays.

The next challenge is to understand points of attack (figure 21) and blocking timing and technique. The blocker at the point of attack takes a man over him either way or takes a man in the gap to the inside. Other blockers keep their men away from the point of attack if they can, but keep them covered if they cannot. Turn a defender away from the point or keep him covered. Whether he is a lineman or a linebacker, turn him away from the point or keep him covered.

Against the split LB look, a call must be made to get either the guard or the tackle to step around. Step-around blocking should be used freely because it results in better protection of the point of attack against pinching and in better timing of blocks on LBs. Technique is dictated by knowledge of where the ball is going and feeling of when it will arrive at the points where blocks are executed.

Our square block tells the blocker and the runner that the ball can go either way. Because the play is slow hitting, a square block should never spill a defender to a side. Other blocks used are the standard gap and wall, the shoul-

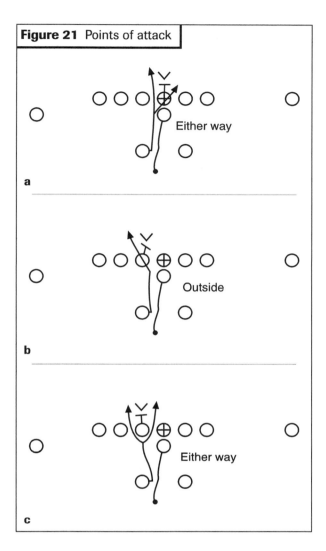

Figure 21 Points of attack

der with timing on either a lineman or a linebacker, and area where there is a cross charge possibility from the perimeter.

The play can be run from split backs or I backs. In order to have seven blockers with split backs, the tight receiver must block on the onside; with I backs, the fullback will block the third man. On the offside, with split backs, one back serves as the fourth blocker; with the I, there must be a tight receiver. Figure 22 illustrates these points. The key is to remember that we want seven blockers: three onside, four offside.

Next, we move to the assignments for the two receivers not involved in the seven-man blocking unit. A spread man does not attempt to block. He is run outside of the man on him and deep, taking advantage of a chance to threaten the defender deep. An offside tight

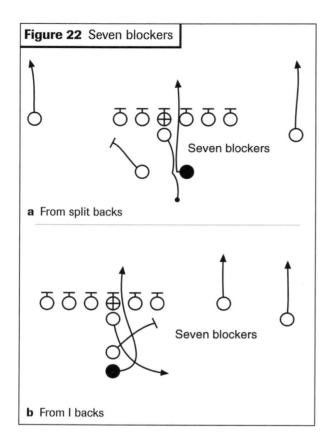

Figure 22 Seven blockers

Seven blockers

a From split backs

Seven blockers

b From I backs

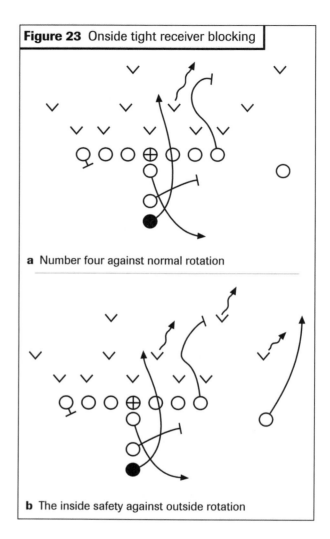

Figure 23 Onside tight receiver blocking

a Number four against normal rotation

b The inside safety against outside rotation

receiver (from a split formation) influences the inside linebacker and blocks the safety.

An onside tight receiver (from an I formation) influences the inside LB and then helps all he can. Figure 23 shows him blocking number four against normal rotation and the inside safety against outside rotation.

When it is not clear who is to block whom, the players are to think pass protection. Problems are solved in the same way. The section on pass protection headed "special problems" applies to draw plays. The draw is blocked like a pass: The same seven defenders must be stopped. If eight defenders rush, the same man is left unblocked.

Summary

The simplification of having just the one system for identifying defenders in no way restricts us. Pass protection, screens, and draws work because players understand what is going on around them. Having one system is a steadying factor, a solid foundation upon which to learn.

1977 Summer Manual. Homer Smith was head football coach at the U.S. Military Academy. Smith is offensive coordinator at the University of Arizona.

The Multidimensional Passing Game

Steve Logan

The following is a brief discussion of the purpose and utilization of the five basic packages We use to attack defenses. It is important to this discussion to bear in mind that our philosophy is throw first, then run.

We begin our installation of the passing game with our *three-step drop* package. We have 10 different three-step route packages accessible to the QB at the LOS. We train our QB to use certain route combinations versus certain coverage looks. This gives us easy completions, allows us to control the coverages we see, and, more important, allows our offensive linemen to cut the defensive linemen in an aggressive manner. The three-step is used extensively in our coming out and going in offense.

The next installation is our *five-step* game, which is very extensive in terms of number of routes and protection schemes. We will generally release receivers with this package and read the whole field. This will be a hot throw for the QB versus the blitz. This is how we attempt to move the chains with a 10- to 12-yard route thrown on rhythm. The pass protection here is, again, very aggressive. We want the fight to be on the LOS with the expectation that the ball will be gone in 2.5 to 2.9 seconds.

The last dropback package installed will be the *seven-step*. When we use this method, we employ a seven-man protection that will double-team a defense's three best pass rushers. We think we can extend the routes to the 16- to 18-yard depth now. It will take 3.5 to 3.9 seconds to get the ball thrown, so that is why we double-team the pass rush. Many times we will employ a half-field package for the QB to work with. The trade-off is that we lose control of some of the underneath coverage, but this can be overcome by the depth of the routes, those routes being deep in cuts, deep comebacks, or deep choices. We will use this method in third-and-long situations, expected blitz situations, or anytime we are experiencing protection problems.

The next category is the *play-action pass*, which includes the nakeds. This is the single best way to throw the football. This method of throwing the ball will strip underneath coverage, give you a high completion percentage, help your run game, move the QB, and help your offensive line. We spend most of our time researching and designing play-action passes. We may throw only 10 to 12 out of an average of 38 throws per game, but this package sustains every other facet of our offense. The other critical element in this package is that we will double-team the five tech rusher or the three tech rusher in an aggressive run blocking manner. This is an early down call for us, usually coupled with an audible. We have found through experience that we can and will throw play actions into exactly the looks that we desire.

The last category, but by no means the least important, is our *sprint pass*. Here again, we want to move the QB away from pressure. We can employ 10- to 12-yard routes or go to extended routes. It is always wise to utilize the sprint when you have been sacked or pressured. We will again utilize three different types of sprint protection to enhance our offensive line's aggressiveness.

In a discussion of the passing game, it is impossible to ignore the teaching and training of the QB. I would submit the following for consideration, as I have found these items very constructive in the development of a QB.

1. Never take a sack. This is the single worst thing that can happen to an offense from a functional as well as a morale standpoint. Learn how to throw the ball away.

2. The QB must throw against the blitz every day. Throwing under pressure is not natural and must be rehearsed over and over.

3. Set up a quality protection system so your QB is assured he will never get a free rusher in his face. We also convince the QB that he can take a five-step hit-and-throw drop and get the ball gone before any outside rusher can sack him.

4. Know where your hot receiver is, presnap.

5. During skeleton drills, take a five-receiver route and have your QB progress normally, then backward through the progression. Debrief your QB after each throw; ask him what he saw.

6. Encourage spontaneity in a veteran QB who knows your system, but discourage spontaneity in a new or young QB.

7. Study great players on film. It is important to emulate men who have taken the QB position and made it an art form: Dan Marino, John Elway, Joe Montana, Steve Young, Troy Aikman.

8. Separation from the LOS is the single most important fundamental to be achieved in the making of a QB. On a three-step drop, we separate four yards and release the ball 1.9 seconds after the snap. We try to get seven-and-a-half yards in 1.6 seconds from snap to hit of the fifth step. Our seven-step drop is 10 yards deep in 1.9 seconds from snap to the hit of the seventh step. Again, the separation drill is rehearsed over and over until this becomes a subconscious activity for the QB.

1996 Summer Manual. Steve Logan is head coach at East Carolina University in Greenville, NC.

The Flare-Flood Offense

Mike White and Roger Theder

The passing game and all other phases of football change from year to year, as well as game to game. Our knowledge, research, and interest in the pass game began in 1968, when several of my staff and I were members of John Ralston's staff at Stanford University. It became obvious to us at that time that in order to be successful at Stanford, we had to understand and be able to utilize the forward pass to win in the Pacific 8 Conference.

As with the veer offense, the pass offense of today must have a total foolproof concept relative to making decisions in attacking all types of defenses. In every aspect of our passing attack, we want our QB to be confident he is armed with the decision-making mechanisms. This can be accomplished through the structure of the pattern and/or the after-snap reaction and subsequent decision that the defense forces us to make.

We feel there are certain advantages to putting the ball in the air. Reasons why we throw:

1. Can beat the best in our conference

2. Knowledge of this offense

3. Few pass offenses today, causing a lack of defensive preparedness

4. Ability to recruit the skilled athletes

5. Facilitates easy off-season development

6. Excellent catch-up and two-minute offense

7. Advantageous in tiring defenses (pass rush, etc.)

8. Weather and synthetic turf advantage

9. Less injury factor, can practice game situations often

10. Psychological advantage: big-play offense

11. Learn from 26 other teams

In offensive football, it is our belief that "you must be known for something." This belief has never changed, and we want to be known as a team that throws, and thus forces defenses to try to stop our passing attack. Because of this philosophy, we feel the key is to be a high-percentage, low-interception, ball-control offense. This does not necessarily mean we will throw the football 40 or 50 times a game, but however many passes we throw, we will strive for this percentage, interception, and control philosophy.

As in all areas of football, you learn through the things you do, and these first two years weren't easy. Yet we have never questioned this philosophy of pass offense or the use of it as a weapon. Our great enlightenment has been just how to reach the end result of winning with this philosophy.

Become Goal-Oriented

Last season, we became a goal-oriented program. It is easy to do this in a pass offense because it is a statistic-oriented offense. We could now say after a game that we either did or did not accomplish these goals. As an example, our offensive staff came up with these goals for each game and made a chart that we examined each week (see table, page 168).

Also, with the cooperation of his players, each individual coach in his respective area set some goals, examined them each week, and placed them on a chart. These are the key result areas for our QBs, receivers, and running backs:

QBs

1. Yards passing each week: 250.
2. Interceptions: less than one per game.
3. Completion percentage each week: 55 percent.
4. Sacks: less than one per game.
5. Two first downs per drive 55 percent of the time.

6. Two long scoring drives (75 yards).
7. Key third down conversions 55 percent or better.

Receivers and running backs

1. Never allow a ball to be intercepted.
2. No mental errors.
3. No penalties.
4. Three big plays (25+ yards) per game.
5. Great play!

Based on these goals, awards were given and decal bears placed on our helmets each Monday for excellent and consistent performances. We have never been great believers in placing awards on our helmets as a motivational device, but it worked hand-in-hand with our goal system, and we are convinced it had a positive effect on our squad.

Must Have Total Package

When discussing the pass offense, most coaches make their biggest mistake by not going to the total pass package. If you are going to throw, do it all! By this, I mean we must have the complete pass package, so that people can't feel California is all dropback, all sprint-out, or all action pass. We feel we made this error in the past by trying to go to a total sprint-out game a year ago and losing sight of the total pass package idea.

Coaches are afraid to go into this total package because of the coaching aspects involved with varieties of patterns, actions, and protection. It is our belief that one complements the other and forces defenses to prepare for the various ways we are able to protect and throw the football. We do not feel a team can throw the ball only from directly behind the center but must also sprint and roll to change the throwing spot. It requires more coaching time, but it is necessary in keeping defenses off balance. We are convinced a total package is the key. This is California's total pass package:

1. Dropback (60-70-80)
2. Sprint-out (51-59)

California Offensive Goals

Goal	Florida	SJS	Army	Illinois	Oregon	OSU	UCLA	USC	Washington	WSU	Stanford

450 yards per game
   225 passing
   225 running											

Make first down on each possession											
Three long scoring drives of 60 yards or more											

Key third down plays
   3rd and 2: 100%
   3rd and 3–4: 75%
   3rd and 5–10: 50%
   3rd and 11+: 25%											

Score inside 30-yard line											
Always score inside the 10-yard line											
Be a violent downfield blocking team											
Outscore opponents in the first quarter											
27 points per game											
1.5 interceptions per game											
59% completion rate per game											
1.5 sacks per game											
1.5 fumbles per game											

3. Quick (90)

4. Delays (SE-flanker-TE-FB-RB)

5. Play action (P.23 B1-P.38-P.34 wag)

6. Short yardage (51 roll)

7. Draw (dropback-sprint-roll)

8. Screen (dropback shift and str.-quick-roll)

If you are going to develop this offense, the key to its success is the man under the center and your ability as a coach to evaluate his strengths and weaknesses. You must place emphasis where his strengths lie and give that phase of the pass offense major attention. The formula is simple: a total commitment from both the QB and his coach to do what it takes to be successful.

QB Must Understand Defense

Our QB is the most important guy, and he must understand defense and its relevance to our flare-flood pass. He must understand what a defense is trying to do so that he can take advantage of a defense before the snap, or have enough knowledge or experience to take advantage of the defense after the snap. This is the key and where our development begins. Our QB's other two primary functions are the game plan itself and the use of our automatic system.

We devised a simple system that can easily be understood by QBs based on these defenses. The chart in figure 1 has helped us to educate our QBs without referring to defensive people by name initially. We do not necessarily care who the people are or how they got in these critical areas, but merely the fact that these areas must each be attacked with the pass. Once our QB gains this knowledge, we can begin to name coverages and show how these zones are covered.

The defensive trends of alignment and multiple coverage have caused this system to evolve. In the area of man-to-man and blitz coverage, we feel this is more readily understood after mastering this zone concept. The hot receiver principle applies to blitzing defenses and will not be cov-

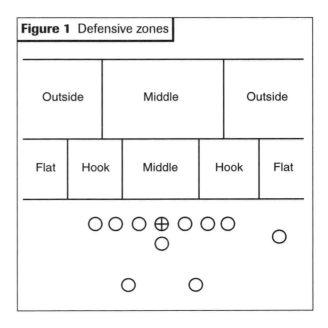

Figure 1 Defensive zones

ered in this lecture. Our flare-flood pass package adapts easily to man-to-man coverage.

This pass offense will attack four areas: deep, medium, short, and behind the LOS. The old pass ratio was four-four-three and lent itself to a flare control system. Now we continually face ratios of four-five-two and three-four-three, and we must begin by having total understanding of the five underneath principles.

It is our belief that a well-disciplined five underneath defense will have well-coached people and be in the five short zones we have discussed. We must attack these alleys and lanes in order to be successful. The attackable alley is 12-17 yards behind the LBs and in front of the safeties, and the attackable lane splits the area between the five short zone coverage people. These defensive people must be affected with a flare control principle to open the alleys and lanes and allow the QB to throw successfully.

Attacking Zone Coverages

There are various ways to prepare your QB on the field through drills many of us use. We have selected a few basic ones to get this young QB ready, and we have a progression that we use (figure 2). Very quickly, our system is to:

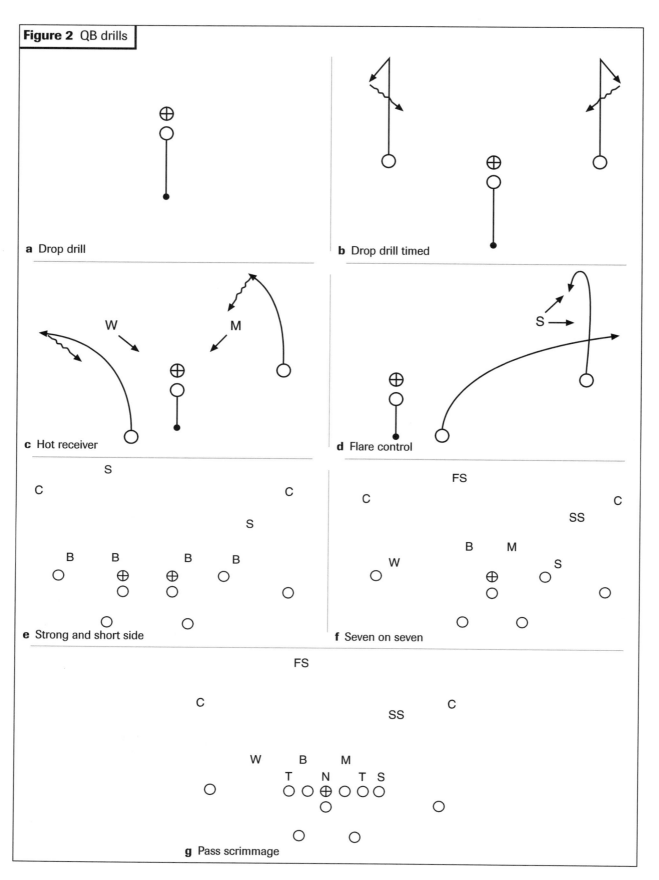

Figure 2 QB drills

a Drop drill

b Drop drill timed

c Hot receiver

d Flare control

e Strong and short side

f Seven on seven

g Pass scrimmage

1. teach the two-, five-, and seven-step drop (figure 2a);

2. time the two-, five-, and seven-step drop and throw (figure 2b);

3. teach the hot receiver principle with an executed blitz and throw (figure 2c);

4. throw individual patterns;

5. teach flare control with one underneath LB (figure 2d);

6. work a strong side drill (figure 2e);

7. execute our seven-on-seven drill (figure 2f); and

8. pass scrimmage (figure 2g).

We have now become such strong believers in teaching this zone principle of flare-flood control that once the fundamentals are taught, we immediately go to this three-on-two attack.

The QB and receivers must understand that we are placing three quick receivers in two zones to outnumber the defense and allow us to be successful (figure 3). The pattern number is immaterial, but the flood idea is now executed.

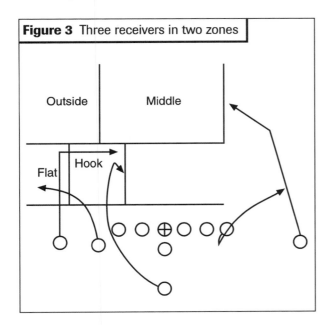

Figure 3 Three receivers in two zones

In attacking the five-under defense, we have found that the outside flat zone is the area most changeable. Because of this, our quarterback begins the attack in the hook zone, where the pass can more easily be thrown. The lead short side underneath pattern is the IN. The split end

and FB will now exploit the short side hook area, and the RB will control the flat zone.

A receiver is placed in the deep alley and a back in the short alley on the isolated LB. This package forces the LB to make his decision, and he is also affected as the near back comes out. We hope to create movement to open the lane or cause the LB to stop his drop, thus opening the split end as the primary receiver.

This package handles the blitz or the zone concept, as the FB must be alert for his blocking assignment to be blitzing.

We have the mirrored play to the strong side through the use of our TE, flanker, and FB. The weak side flood has been the most effective because of the drop of the strong LBs, who have a tendency to favor the TE side.

The hook area may also be exploited through the flood attack where the outside LB is isolated in this zone. In this package, the QB should throw the out if it is open because of coverage and alignment (figure 4).

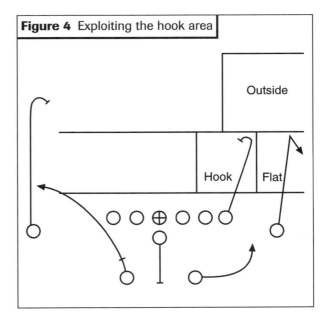

Figure 4 Exploiting the hook area

In the five short zone coverage, the ball will be thrown to the TE or FB based on LB drop and angle. We do not feel you will ever put two defenders in this hook area.

As in the IN package, we have the mirror of this pattern to the short side. Before showing how to attack the flat underneath zone, let me get into our principle of attacking the three-deep zones. When confronted with the three-deep coverage, this deep area will not be our primary area of attack. Most teams tend to show a high percentage of the two-deep coverage, and now the lead pass is our double streak or double Z (figure 5).

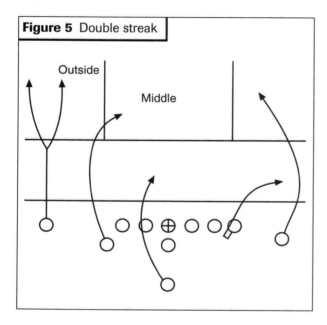

Figure 5 Double streak

The deep flood idea is to place two receivers in these two deep zones covered by one defender. The primary attack is the dropback, but the sprint-out is an excellent way to beat this coverage. Often, a formation variation or motion will dictate a coverage and help the QB's initial read. Pressure is now on the safety to make a decision and favor the WR or RB. Should the underneath coverage get deep enough to be a factor, the FB delay is built in, and the FB will catch the ball in the short alley moving upfield.

When confronted with the three-deep zones covered, the TE is coached to hook up, and now the flare-flood package once again is effected in the hook area. As mentioned, the toughest area to predict is the flat zone, yet teams become very consistent with their corner play as a game progresses. Immediate pressure must be placed on the flat coverage man through the bench pattern or sprint corner pattern. In the bench pattern, the talents of our WR and FB are used. This pattern is most effective when attacking the five under, two-deep defense.

In each of these patterns, the flat coverage defender must make an immediate decision, and the QB can determine the primary receiver and throw the completion.

The final package is the very effective sprint-out series (figure 6). In this package, the QB is given all the weapons to make correct decisions based on coverage and the application of the flare-flood attack.

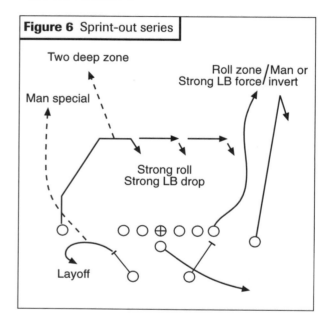

Figure 6 Sprint-out series

The strong feeling here is that in this package, the defense will dictate immediately the primary, or the QB decision will be made after the snap. Here, the entire field is attacked and the back side becomes our flare-flood combination. The number one choice is the strong side out to our flanker. Secondly, the TE is our primary if coverage doubles on the flanker out pattern, and only a hook coverage defender can take this pattern away.

The QB being forced to come to the back side would only happen because the defense overmoved the underneath zone and placed more than one defender in the middle, hook, or strong flat zones. The split end in pattern and RB hook becomes the primary. This one package was probably our most successful and consistent gainer in 1974. There are various combinations off this strong sprint-out attack you can utilize to keep the defense off balance.

1975 Proceedings. Mike White was head coach and Roger Theder was offensive coordinator at the University of California. White is an assistant coach with the St. Louis Rams.

The Diversified Pass Attack

Larry Smith and Linde Infante

We have three main goals: have a consistent winning program, earn invitations to bowl games, and gain national prestige. Our offensive objectives are to score as often and as quickly as possible, outscore the opponent in every game, and make individual speed, quickness, and ability to make big plays top priorities.

Offensive Approach

Our offensive theory begins with having a sound but diversified running attack, sound in the fact that our runs will be limited in number and diversified because of formation variations. Second, we want to have a passing game based on high percentage of completion with the potential for big plays. Third, we want to use motion and formation variations to force assignment problems, limit coverages, and disguise basic passes and runs. Fourth, we want to move the football even when we do not score, in order to gain field position and keep our defense out of a hole. Fifth, we want to play error-free football, both mentally and physically. Finally, we want to have a sound kicking game that will give field position and ultimately a Tulane score.

In our passing game, we seek to give the QB all he can handle. We use the whole field and look to destroy all tendencies each week. We call 40-45 passes per game and try to use all six eligible receivers. We use formations, shifts, and motion to create zone or man-coverage weaknesses. Our QB throws the ball off of every possible action-sprint, half-sprint, pocket, shotgun, and all types of play action. This prevents the defense from establishing rush lanes. We strive to have an individually simple communication system of formations, motions, runs, and passes, and go into each game with audibles by the QB and reads by the receivers.

We use draws and lots of screens to complement our passing game. Finally, we want to have fun.

Calling Formations

Our system is made up of a series of descriptive terms. The only part of our formations that will always be the same is our interior five linemen. We do not flop our guards and tackles. Our right guard and tackle are always right and our left guard and tackle are always left.

The first term in our call system, if not right or left, will indicate a change of position for backs other than the I. If the first term is right or left, the backs will line up in the I. When lining up in positions other than the I, we will shift from the I, if possible. We will always shift on the first sound by the QB. If running a play on the first sound from a formation other than the I, we will not shift but line up in the called formation.

The call that will always be made is a direction, right or left. This places our TE to the called side and our SE to the opposite side. If no position change is indicated to our flanker, he will go to the called side. This directional call will also place our backs to the proper side in formations other than the I. Following the directional call will be terms to change the position of our WRs and TE.

Each position has a group of terms that move the players from their normal positions. In the following sections, we describe the terms to change the positions of our backs, WRs, and TE.

Flanker Motion

In calling our three basic flanker motions, we call the formation as it will appear at the snap of the ball, not where the flanker lines up prior to the motion. The three basic motions are: Zac, where the flanker goes across the formation (figure 1a); Zing, where the flanker comes in from an outside position but does not cross the formation (figure 1b); and Zoom, where the flanker lines up behind the QB and motions out to his position (figure 1c).

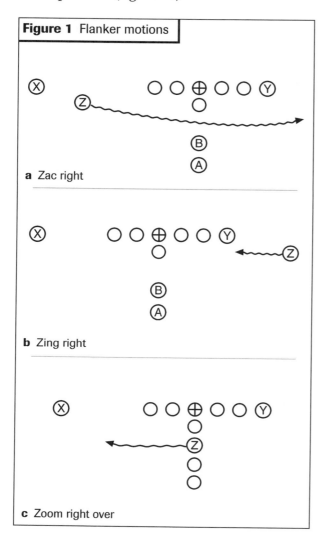

Figure 1 Flanker motions

a Zac right

b Zing right

c Zoom right over

Backfield Motion

Any backfield motion will be called to the TE by the word "motion" and away from the TE by the word "fly." To indicate which back is in motion, we label our TB "A" and our FB "B" (figure 2).

If we want our TE in motion, we use the word "Tim." It will simply be called "Tim right" or " Tim left" (figure 3). The TE lines up behind the QB and goes in motion to the called side.

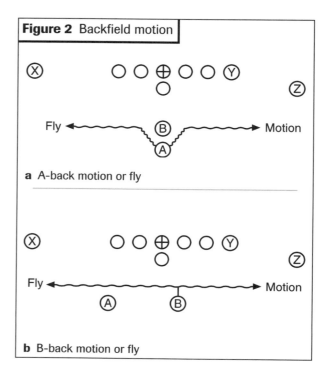

Figure 2 Backfield motion

a A-back motion or fly

b B-back motion or fly

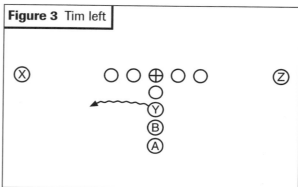

Figure 3 Tim left

Note: All motions will start on the QB's heel movement unless otherwise predetermined.

Passing Series

In our passing series, as in our running series, we will group our passes according to what the QB does. To indicate direction in all of our pure passing series (50 through 90), a number precedes the series number. The number "one" indicates a pass called to the left and "two" indicates a pass called to the right. This follows the odd and even principle of our numbering system.

The 50 Series

Our 50 series indicates a full sprint pass (QB breaking contain) with both backs blocking to the play side. As stated above, a one or two will be called first to indicate a sprint left or right. We can sprint to or away from our TE.

The last number called in this series will always be zero because we will call the pattern or route to be run by its name; for example, left over 250 X out. See figure 4 for another example.

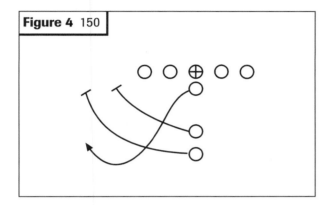

Figure 4 150

Our receivers must know if they are front side or back side. The front side will run the called route or pattern. Any receiver on the back side will run a cross.

The 60 Series

Our 60 series (figure 5) is a half-sprint series with the QB setting up behind the tackle to the called side. Our front side back is scat (no blocking assignment), and the back side back blocks to the play side. Direction is indicated by the numbers one for left and two for right, as in the other pass series. The last number indicates the pattern for the receivers. If we wish to run a special pattern that is not numbered, the last number is zero, and we call the pattern by name.

If we call a numbered pattern, our TE must know if he is front side or back side. If he is back side and the only receiver that side, he will block through the end man on the line and run a streak up the boundary. If he is back side and the inside receiver, he will set back and block for three counts, then run a delay. If the TE is front side, he will run the pattern called.

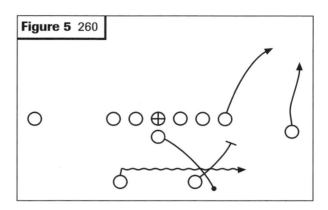

Figure 5 260

The 70 Series

Our 70 series (figure 6) is a straight dropback series with the QB setting up seven to nine yards deep behind the center. It also indicates split flow by our backs. We indicate the front side with the numbers one and two, as in other passing series. Both of our backs have blocking assignments, but one or both may be in the pattern if their assignments do not blitz. The last number indicates the pattern. If the last number is zero, the pattern is called by name.

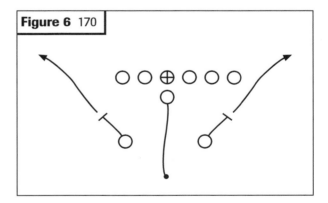

Figure 6 170

The 80 Series

In our 80 series (figure 7), the QB half-sprints to the area behind the tackle, as in the 60 series. The difference is that now the backs are in split flow (one on either side of the QB). The 80 series is blocked the same as the 70 series, except we now protect the area behind the front side tackle. The front side will be indicated by the numbers one or two. The last number indicates the pattern for our receivers. As in the 60 and 70 series, if the last number is zero, we call the pattern by name. Both backs have blocking assignments but may be in the pattern if their assignments don't blitz.

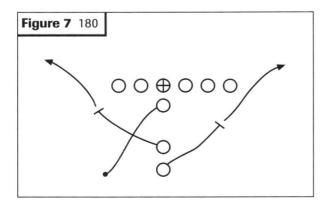

Figure 7 180

The 90 Series

The 90 series (figure 8) indicates a three-step drop by the QB. Our WRs run mirrored routes (same on both sides). Our backs block the ends if they rush or run flat if they drop. As in our other passing series, one and two indicate direction for our line. We always call this series to our TE, although we may throw the ball in either direction. Both WRs run the route or pattern called. The TE takes an inside release and works straight upfield.

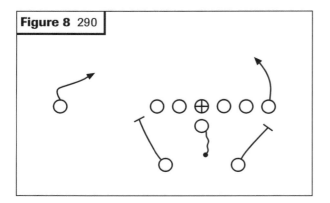

Figure 8 290

Offensive Diversity

At Tulane we feel that one of the most important weapons an offensive team can have is diversification. We also feel that by diversifying our sets, we neutralize one of offensive football's biggest enemies, play recognition. Although we may run the same basic pass with the same reads from week to week, we will go to any

extreme to change in some way how it appears to the defense. We do this through the use of motion, shifts, and substitution of personnel.

Because a large part of our offensive output comes from the passing game, we go to great lengths to make our pass offense as diversified as possible while maintaining consistency. We use many forms of protection and have the QB throw the ball from any position on the field. We feel strongly that this is one of the reasons for the degree of success we have had.

Since diversification is the cornerstone of our offensive philosophy, it is a predominant thought in virtually every play or pass we develop. Seldom, if ever, will we draw up a pass that does not have the flexibility to adjust after the snap to best attack the defense at that particular time.

We feel that pass patterns must be versatile enough to be adjusted to attack five basic coverages, which make up about 80 percent of the pass coverages in college football today. As a general rule, we assume the pass must be effective versus all forms of three-deep zone, basic forms of two-deep, man with a FS, man with no FS, and man with a safety blitz.

We feel that if we can design a pattern that will put receivers in the weakest areas of these coverages, then we have a pass that has an excellent chance of success when it leaves the huddle. Pass patterns that are good versus one or two coverages but not good against others makes play calling strictly a guessing game and in many cases will place your QB in a position where he does not have a chance for success.

Quarterback Reads and Keys

Before we discuss a particular pass, a brief description of what we expect of our QBs may be in order. First and most important, it is not what the coach knows about pass patterns and secondary play that is important. All of us are capable of drawing long lines on a piece of paper indicating a receiver in an open area. What is important is what the man under the center knows. You can design the most elaborate pass in football, but if the man pulling the trigger insists on throwing the ball into the teeth of the coverage, his and your chances of success are slim. So our first job is to make sure the QB has a firm knowledge of secondary coverages. He must first learn to recognize them and then know their strengths and weaknesses. If he knows the coverage and where its weakness is, and the pass is designed to place a receiver in that weak area, your pass has a great chance of success.

We give our QB and receivers as many tools as possible for reading coverages. We get a presnap read from the alignment of the safeties, corners, and positions of other defenders, but we never assume that a presnap read will hold up. In many cases, what receivers or QBs see prior to the snap will be what they get, but they continue their reads and keys up and through the first 10 to 12 yards of their routes. In other cases, the coverage will be disguised so that what type it is cannot be determined until after the snap. This is why it is important for your pass pattern to have the capability of adjusting itself after the snap.

To eliminate confusion as to what the coverage is, or as a double check of what is seen prior to the snap, we give each of our receivers and QBs a key to help them distinguish what type of coverage they are facing. As a general rule, our outside receivers key the outside defensive backs. Our inside receiver and QB key what we refer to as the square (figure 9).

The square is a hypothetical area in the middle of the field roughly 15 to 25 yards deep. Its outside edges are about three yards inside the hash mark. This is the area that our inside receiver and QB focus on when in a basic pocket-type pass. We feel this is the area one of the safeties will occupy on any form of three-deep or FS coverage. If both the safeties remain outside this area, we feel safe to assume it is a form of two-deep coverage.

To illustrate how reading the square is used in our pocket-passing attack, along with the other keys for our wide receivers, we will take one of our basic patterns, break it down into various parts to illustrate our versatility in route adjustment, then put it back together and see how it works versus the various basic coverages we mentioned earlier. Figure 10 shows one of our basic patterns with the called pattern illustrated by the solid lines and the possible adjustments shown by the broken lines.

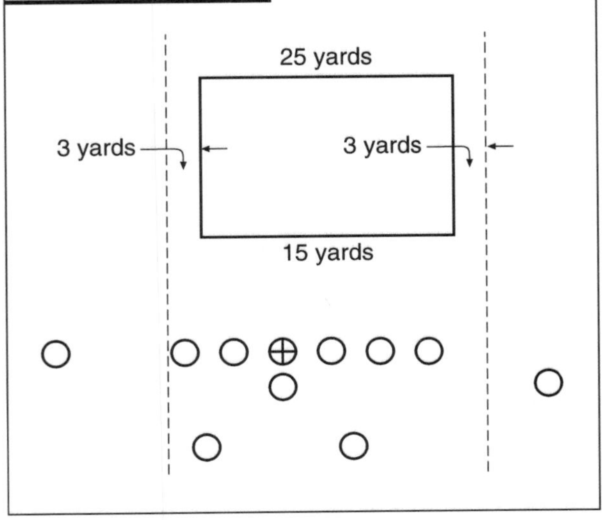

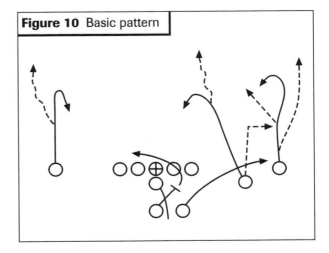

Figure 10 Basic pattern

At first glance, it might look complicated, but no one person has more than three options or potential routes to run.

Our running backs have it simple. Our front side back has no blocking assignment. If not in motion, he runs a flat route. If a safety blitz occurs, he will stop and pick up the blitz. If in motion (either back), he runs to the spot where our widest receiver lines up and stops on the LOS facing the QB. The remaining back (back not in motion, back side back if no motion, or tailback in the I) has a blocking assignment that he checks before running a drag out the back side of the formation.

Figure 11 shows some of the possible looks created by changing our backfield alignment.

Figure 9 The square

25 yards

3 yards

3 yards

15 yards

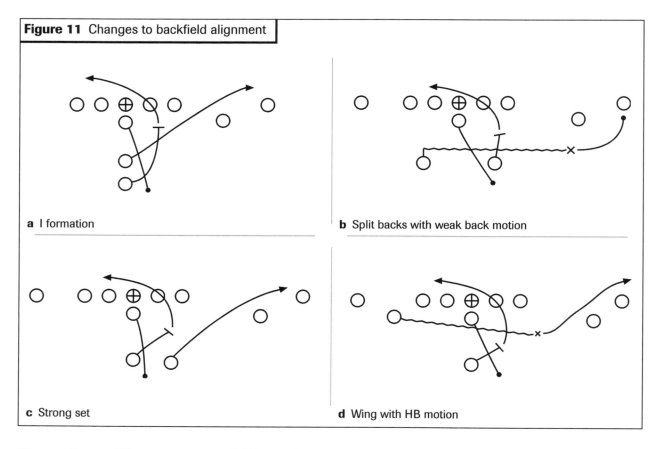

Figure 11 Changes to backfield alignment

a I formation

b Split backs with weak back motion

c Strong set

d Wing with HB motion

Receiver Routes and Reads

To help us maintain our versatility, we teach our receivers their routes and reads by the position they occupy in a particular formation. We refer to them as the outside receiver (WR to the two-receiver side), the inside receiver (the inside receiver to the two-receiver side), and the short side receiver (receiver to the one-receiver side).

Our outside receiver keys the corner to his side. If the corner backs up either in a zone or man technique, our wideout runs a hook. If he feels the corner is playing a zone as he retreats, then the receiver works to beat the first underneath coverage. If he is retreating in a man technique, the emphasis is on beating the corner. If the corner squats or jams the WR, he then works to get by either inside or outside and runs a streak four to six yards from the sideline. The only other situation we ask our outside receiver to be alert for is the safety blitz. If this occurs, he runs a post, breaking at eight yards (figure 12).

The inside receiver, who could be our TE, SE, or flanker, reads the square through the defender on him. If either safety runs into the square, the inside receiver runs a hook. He uses the same thinking regarding man or zone techniques. Versus zone, he beats the underneath coverage; versus man, he beats the man covering him. If one appears in the square, he runs what we call the middle idle. In this route, he works to get himself 15 to 18 yards deep to his side of the square. He wants to be under control and ready to go catch the ball wherever in that general area it is thrown. Like the WR, he has a safety blitz key. If the safety on his side blitzes, he runs an out at 12 yards. The thinking here is that on a safety blitz, the remaining safety will be in an inside technique and will in most cases give you the out (figure 13).

The short side receiver (receiver on the one-receiver side) keys the corner to his side. If the corner retreats, he runs the hook using the same principles as the WR, beating the man-on-man coverages and the underneath coverages versus

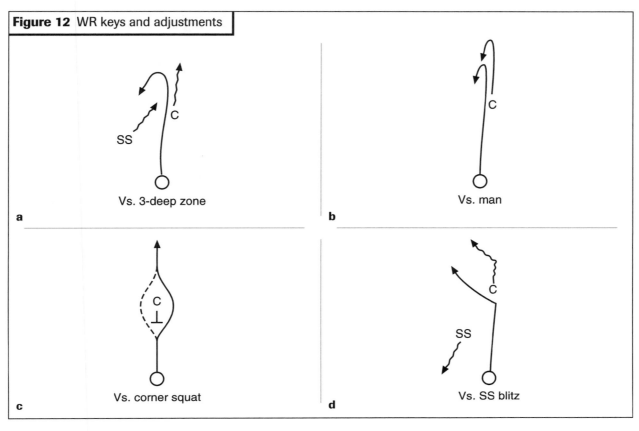

Figure 12 WR keys and adjustments

a Vs. 3-deep zone

b Vs. man

c Vs. corner squat

d Vs. SS blitz

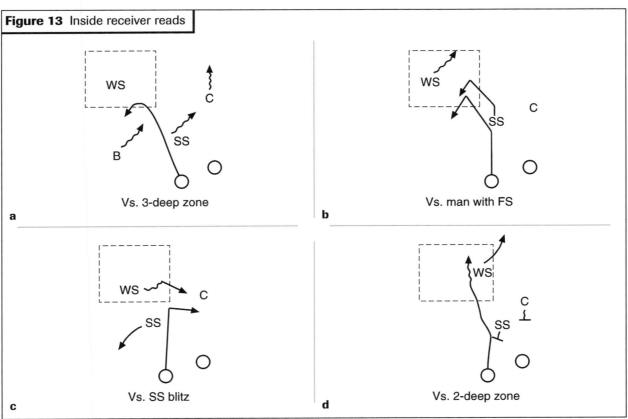

Figure 13 Inside receiver reads

a Vs. 3-deep zone

b Vs. man with FS

c Vs. SS blitz

d Vs. 2-deep zone

zone techniques. If the corner squats, he runs what we refer to as the idle. He gets by the corner as soon as possible and works to an area 15 to 18 yards deep behind the corner and about four yards from the sideline. Versus a weak safety blitz, we ask our short side receiver to run a 12-yard out (figure 14).

There are many cases where our short side receiver is our TE. Because of his tight position, the fact that he will generally be held up, and the difference in mobility, we give him only one route to run. He works his way off the line and runs a flag, working to beat the corner on his side.

By using all these keys and route adjustments, we feel that in most cases we will have someone working in the weakest area of the coverage a high percentage of the time. Now it is up to the QB to work the weakness of the defense. To get him aimed in the right direction, we first get a presnap read, which, in most cases, will at least narrow down the coverage possibilities to two or three. From there on we read the square.

QB Coverage Rules

When using the square as a guide to coverage weakness, the QB follows these rules:

- When either safety shows in the square, work from the inside receiver to the outside receiver on the two-receiver side. The third option is the back.
- When neither of the safeties shows in the square, work from the square to the short side receiver to the back.
- Versus the safety blitz, work from the out to the post on the two-receiver side.

Putting each of the segments together, we now have a pattern that will adjust itself in such a manner as to have one or more receivers in the most vulnerable areas of each of the basic coverages mentioned. Another advantage of this type of adjustment is that as coverages change from down to down, so does the appearance of the pattern. To the defense, it might appear as though we had called as many as five different passes when in reality it has only been one.

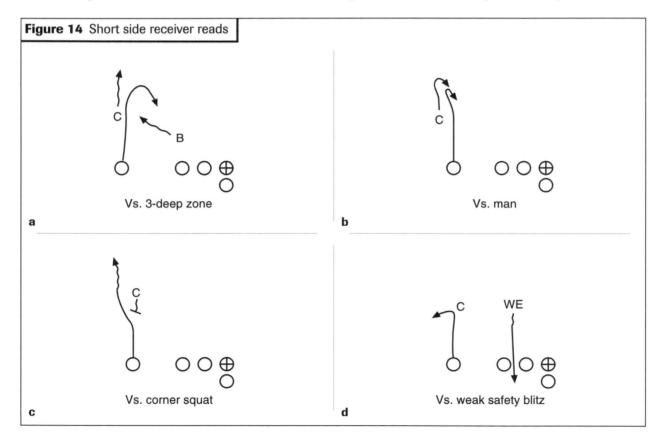

Figure 14 Short side receiver reads

a   Vs. 3-deep zone

b   Vs. man

c   Vs. corner squat

d   Vs. weak safety blitz

Figures 15-18 illustrate how this particular pattern adjusts to the weakness of a coverage. Figure 15 shows the basic pattern against three-deep zone coverage. The QB looks from inside receiver to outside receiver to back. When the defense shows man coverage with a FS, the QB also looks from inside receiver to outside receiver to back (figure 16). Against the two-deep coverage, the QB looks from inside receiver to short side receiver to back on the short side (figure 17). If the defense comes with a strong safety blitz, the QB quickly looks from inside receiver to outside receiver (figure 18).

As you can see, by using a few WR keys on certain individuals and by using the square as a tool to determine the weakness of the coverage, we are able, in most cases, to have people

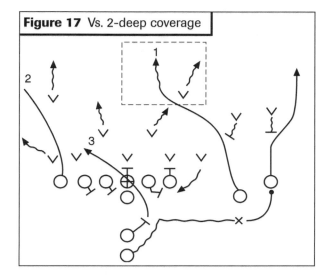

Figure 17 Vs. 2-deep coverage

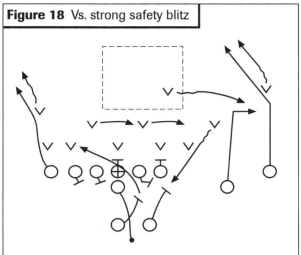

Figure 18 Vs. strong safety blitz

in the open area or working the weakness of the secondary. This is one pattern with just the basic coaching points, for time and space do not permit an in-depth discussion about techniques, but I believe you can see how, with a few adjustments, patterns take on a totally different appearance to the defense. For WRs and QBs, the reads are the same in all the examples.

In conclusion, versatility and diversification are the keys to what success we have had throwing the ball. We feel strongly that with the continued use of keys, area reads, and route adjustments, we can continue to maintain our flexibility, have people in the right places at the right times, keep a high percentage of completion, and take what the defense gives up.

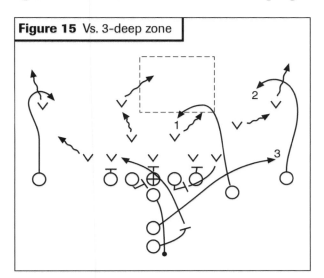

Figure 15 Vs. 3-deep zone

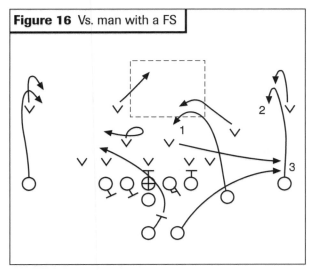

Figure 16 Vs. man with a FS

1980 Proceedings. Larry Smith was head coach and Linde Infante was an assistant coach at Tulane University. Smith is head coach at the University of Missouri.

The Quick Passing Game

Billy Joe

The quick passing game is always the first part of our offense that is introduced to our teams at the start of spring and fall practice. It is the foundation for all of our other passing schemes; it is our DNA, the building block of our total offense. In 1996, our passing offense finished the year ranked number one statistically in all of Black College Football in total passing yards (2,978) and average passing yards per game (270.7). Without question, the quick passing game produced many of those yards.

There are many reasons why I like the quick game. The quick game can interface with any coverage in any situation, irrespective of down, hash mark, field position, or time remaining on the clock. I am aware of no other passing game that accommodates all phases and varieties of the game and keeps defensive coaches awake all night trying to develop schemes that will confuse offensive coaches.

I will discuss and diagram four of our quick patterns and routes and demonstrate how they interact and impact on the most frequently seen coverages that we encounter throughout the season (figure 1). These are the four routes on our passing tree:

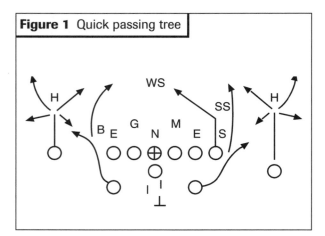

Figure 1 Quick passing tree

1. Quick slant
2. Quick out
3. Quick hitch
4. Quick fade

These routes combined with other receivers' routes comprise a pattern. When wide receivers on opposite sides of the center run the same routes, we call them mirror patterns. They, of course, will make coverages balance up.

The quick slant (figure 2) is designed primarily to work against coverage that is loose and soft to the inside. Many of our receivers have had excellent 40-yard speed. As a result, many coverages we see are what we call a cover 6 (a three-deep zone/strong safety rotate variety).

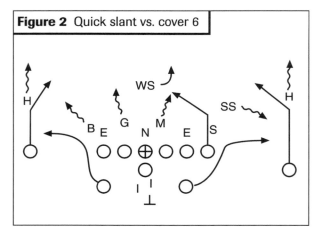

Figure 2 Quick slant vs. cover 6

Our game plan will indicate who the primary and secondary receivers are on the field. Defensive secondary personnel deployment will dictate the quarterback's read progression. We attempt to put receivers in all passing zones. Thus, defenses are unable to double up or rotate without revealing obvious holes in their coverage. The quick slant pattern versus cover 6 will allow the receiver to catch a short pass. He can then use his run-after-catch ability. I have seen many short slants go long distance because of the receiver's elusiveness and maneuverability. The quarterback must throw the ball immediately after his third step. Most of our problems occur when the quarterback holds onto the ball too long and causes the receiver to run past his receiving zone and into underneath coverage. When that happens, the quarterback must pull the ball down and improvise by using his athletic talent to prevent a negative play.

The quick slant also is effective versus cover 0 (figure 3). Cover 0 is basically a four-deep prevent-type coverage. Cover 0 puts extreme pressure on the underneath coverage by the linebackers. It is used currently with a very popular 4-3 scheme up front. The big-play capability is not there because of four defensive back personnel playing one-quarter of the field deep, as opposed to cover 6, with three defensive backs playing one-third of the field deep.

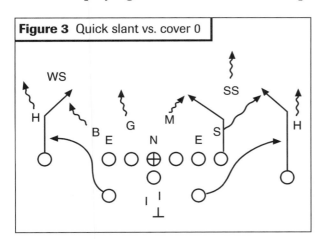

Figure 3 Quick slant vs. cover 0

We ask our quarterback to read the safeties first to rule in or out corners rolling up and "squatting down" on our wide cuts. The second read is on the outside linebacker's drop, to determine if a lay-off is necessary for our backs in the flat. Our third read is on the middle linebacker. If he dogs, we may have in our game plan for that week to throw to the tight end on a quick pop. We tell our wide receivers to push upfield six yards and break inside at a comfortable angle, quickly looking for the ball. We will throw the quick slant pattern against

any alignment by the defensive corner that is slightly outside of our receivers on or near the line of scrimmage. We must know that we can get an inside relationship (position) on the corner before we call such a pattern. Then our other concern is where the underneath coverage is. The quick out is a pattern that is made to order for any coverages or deployments that will allow your wide receivers to get an outside relationship without impediment.

Figure 4 illustrates our quick out pattern versus cover 1. Always remember, the quick out can be thrown anywhere on the field if you have a cushion. A loose cover 1 is designed to take away the quick slant, thus giving you the quick out. Cover 1 is man-to-man coverage on all receivers on or near the line of scrimmage, with the weak safety playing free. The quarterback must take a pre-snap look (PSL) to determine which defender or side of the formation he wants to throw to. If there is an obvious mismatch, the game plan will inform the quarterback where to pass the football. A basic rule of thumb is to read the defensive backs for wide receiver passes and read the linebackers for running back passes.

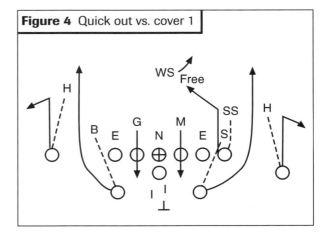

Figure 4 Quick out vs. cover 1

The course of our wide receivers on the quick out is to push upfield as fast as possible for six yards, then quickly snap the head around to the outside while bringing the route back one yard toward the line of scrimmage. Our offense has experienced a lot of success with this pattern against cover 1 because of the run-after-catch potential. Defensive backs and linebackers are locked on their respective assignments. Such an arrangement doesn't permit room for error by the defensive back covering the reception. Only the weak safety is in a position to make the open field tackle if the covering secondary falters. The open field tackle by the weak safety is his worst nightmare against a shake-and-bake (stick-and-go) receiver.

The quick hitch (figure 5) can be utilized similarly to the quick out and quick slant, although the quick hitch pattern provides another dimension. It is an easier pass for the quarterback and a very simple route for the receiver. We call this pattern more often than any of the other quick patterns. We will call the quick hitch if we are not sure if the defensive back is taking away the quick slant or quick out. But it is imperative that we know there is a cushion.

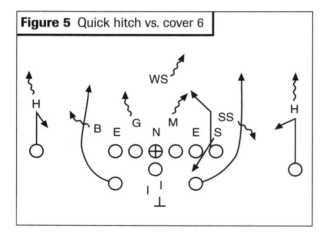

Figure 5 Quick hitch vs. cover 6

Our receivers also like this pattern because it allows them to get the ball in their hands as soon as possible so they may begin their vertical push upfield. Your quarterback must be very efficient with coverage recognition versus brackets and rotation concepts. He will have exceptionally good games if he can master these coverages. The quick slant, quick out, and quick hitch are excellent versus brackets, rotations, and double coverages. Cover 3 is a form of a man/zone bracket on our tight end (figure 6).

Against cover 3, quite naturally, our quarterback's recognition and reads will dictate that he avoids the tight end and throws elsewhere. In this situation, we prefer the quarterback to throw quicks to the strong side be-

cause the strong wide receiver will be singled up in many cases. Cover 4 and 7 are a form of weak side man/zone rotation (figure 7). Our quarterback is instructed to throw strong side to our wide receiver. If the wide receiver pass is not there, the quarterback must then read progressively from outside to the inside—that is, wide receiver first, tight end second, and fullback third.

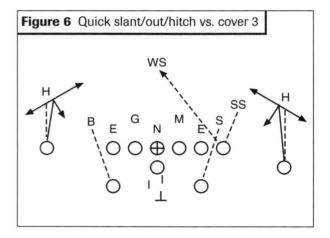

Figure 6 Quick slant/out/hitch vs. cover 3

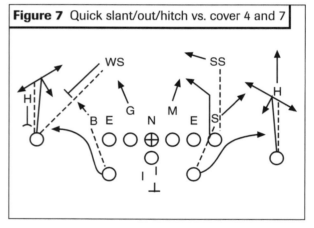

Figure 7 Quick slant/out/hitch vs. cover 4 and 7

Cover 5 (figure 8) is a form of strong side man/zone double-up. This coverage is designed to take your strong side wide receiver out of the game. It will force you to throw away from perhaps your most prolific receiver. Your weak side receivers, however, will be licking their chops. They know the ball will be thrown in their direction. They also know the secondary is vulnerable to a big play because there are few defensive players deployed weak side. Needless to say, we don't see this coverage much during the course of a season.

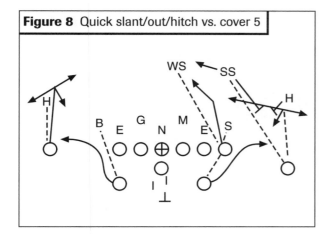

Figure 8 Quick slant/out/hitch vs. cover 5

The quick fade pattern requires pressure from the corners in order to have a high success rate. We will call this pattern when it is obvious the defense is attempting to take away the quick slant, out, and hitch. This pattern is best against cover 9.

Cover 9 usually is accompanied by all-out dogs and with all receivers manned up. We ask our receivers to bend (fade) their routes toward the sidelines and locate the ball. We ask the quarterback not to be in a hurry to pass. The quarterback must judge the bend, speed, and position the receiver has on the defender before releasing the ball. In some situations, we instruct the quarterback to take a one-step drop and release the ball to a certain position on the field.

The quick fade has been the most successful pattern against many dog-oriented predicaments, especially on the goal line (figure 9).

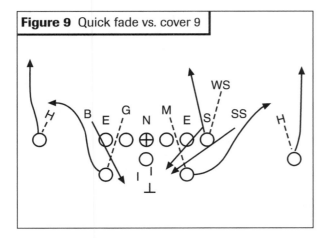

Figure 9 Quick fade vs. cover 9

Bump-and-run is the most prevalent cover technique used against our team in cover 9. If the bump-and-run is coming from the outside in, don't further exacerbate the problem by fading out. We ask our receivers to use an inside release and then bend (fade) toward the sideline.

We get the most in-out bump-and-run coverage against half coverage. Cover 2 is half coverage in the deep secondary with zone coverage underneath. Cover 8 is similar to cover 2 in the deep secondary, with the exception of having man coverage underneath (figure 10). These coverages can be very effective versus your quick game if you don't have a tight end or a slot man who can keep the safeties honest by getting down the hole.

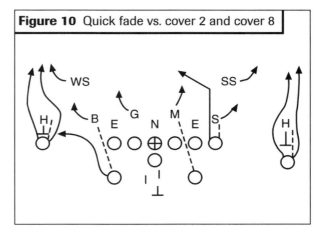

Figure 10 Quick fade vs. cover 2 and cover 8

We will use a variety of formations to stretch the defense. We have discovered motion; stemming and shifting will also provide enough deception from unique but irregular defensive coverages.

In closing, the quick package can cover all coverages. The success of our offensive attack is attributed to our quick game. It has contributed immensely to our overall team success. However, it is definitely not a cure-all for the many looks you will encounter. It is meant to accompany your total offensive scheme so you may present a balanced game plan every weekend.

1997 Summer Manual. Billy Joe is head football coach at Florida A&M University at Tallahassee.

Passing From the Wishbone

Fisher DeBerry

People win for you, not X's and O's, size, or formations. At the academy, our Wishbone offense has gotten a lot of attention, but I assure you the foundation of our program is pride and attitude in executing the fundamentals of the game, and doing the little things correctly so the big things will happen. My basic coaching philosophy is that I sincerely believe you win more consistently with good defense and a sound kicking game. We really spend a lot of practice time on the fundamentals of blocking and tackling and kicking.

At the academy, we believe in option football and prefer the Wishbone structure. For a while, the Wishbone seemed almost extinct, but now it seems to be resurging some. There are several reasons why we run the Wishbone offense:

1. It is a run-oriented offense. I believe your chances of winning consistently are better if you rush the football.

2. The option attack suits our personnel at the academy because of the limited time we have with our players. Also, we don't believe you have to have big physical folks to execute our schemes.

3. It is an offense predicated on precision, execution, and repetition. Our players are oriented this way, and we think you get better through repetition.

4. The Wishbone is unique in our pass-oriented league. It forces defensive teams to switch gears, and it is a tough offense to get ready for in a week's preparation.

5. We have had success with it and have been one of the top rushing teams in the country the last four years, so our players really believe in it. That is probably our most important reason.

6. Finally, the Wishbone is a team-oriented offense, and the team concept we believe in so strongly is richly enhanced. The offense forces everyone to be a complete player and teaches unselfishness, which I really believe is the underlying reason our team has been successful. Our players don't care who gets the credit as long as the team is successful.

We are committed to the option. This is our bread and butter. However, to gain the real benefits of the option, you must read it. Therefore, the majority of our practice time constitutes reading, seeing, and reacting to a multitude of defensive schemes.

At the academy we take great pride in our ability to throw the football. In contrast to what many people say, I think the Wishbone formation is a great throwing formation because it creates one-on-one coverage. In most defensive schemes versus the option, the secondary is required to get involved in run support. To defend a balanced attack like the Wishbone, the defense must stay balanced and commit nine players to the run to have everyone accounted for. Therefore, there are only two left to defend the pass. These are the odds people look for in the Pro passing attack.

Being an old secondary coach, I always felt the toughest passing game to defend was play action. Therefore, the philosophy of our pass game is to make it look like the base option play is in development. We refer to it as the down-the-line game and the throwback game, which we think, in most instances, will draw man-to-man coverage to either action. We think the best time to throw is in a run-down situation. We hope, by using the Wishbone, you won't find yourself in many long-yardage situations.

If we do throw, we have done our homework and will break the Bone. We spend a lot of practice time throwing the ball, which our players really like. We do a lot of one-on-one challenge drills in practice, with outside and team pass drills and our two-minute offense. Fifty-five percent of practice time is allotted to passing.

Another reason we like passing from the Wishbone is that it requires only one or two basic pass protections. So, through much repetition and just doing minimal things, our efficiency improves in protection like it does in the option run game.

I would like to show you our basic front side routes from two of our basic sets, as well as some of our back side routes and our basic "turnback" protection.

Our two basic Wishbone formations are "Right" and "Left," depending on which side the tight end is on, and "Right" and "Left Split" using two split ends (figure 1).

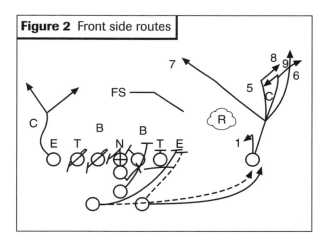

Figure 2 Front side routes

In our back side pass game (figure 3), we call the routes 40s (Right) and 50s (Left) and add the name of the route we want to run—40 flag, for example. After the mesh, our QB takes two steps down the LOS and three steps back. If we should get rover fire, we are outnumbered in our protection, so the front side receiver runs a hot route.

Post wheel cross (figure 4) is a read route that gives the QB three options. The first read is off

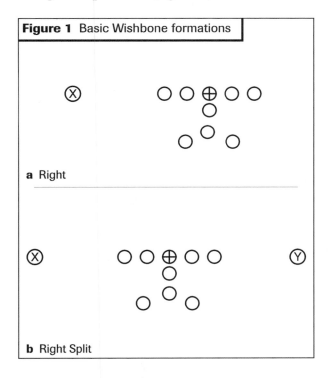

Figure 1 Basic Wishbone formations

a Right

b Right Split

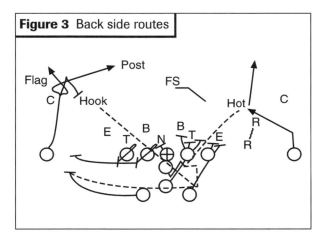

Figure 3 Back side routes

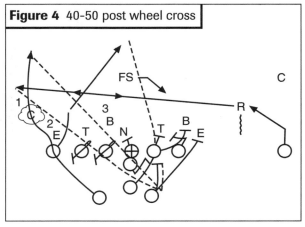

Figure 4 40-50 post wheel cross

We call our front side play-action passes 40s (Right) and 50s (Left) (figure 2). We add a number to designate the route. The quarterback makes a good mesh with the FB to get secondary to commit to run. The QB reads the secondary's development.

the CB to the outside LB to the crossing receiver off the weak inside LB.

The halfback pass (figure 5) gives us a fourth option from our base play. This has been a very good play for us and really can put pressure on the perimeter of the defense when executed properly. The HB reads the corner support for run or pass.

These are just a few things we do from the Bone. I believe that if you can effectively pass from the Wishbone, you will be amazed how your run game will improve, and that is what we want the pass game to do for us—to take some pressure off the run game.

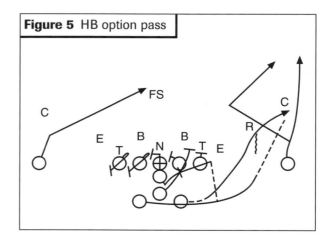

Figure 5 HB option pass

1986 Proceedings. Fisher DeBerry is head coach at the U.S. Air Force Academy.

Passing to Complement the Veer

Bill Yeoman

We are run-oriented, but we feel it is imperative to throw effectively. To increase effectiveness, we feel our passing must be very simple and unsophisticated, to permit the most repetition and understanding. We feel also that we must encounter a minimum number of defenses. Based on this, all our throwing comes out of the running game or flow action. This puts most of the defenses we play into a normal rotation. Our QB needs to worry only about a corner, safety, or linebacker force. With this kind of secondary play against us, we do not key defensive people. We watch only our receivers and try to throw the ball to one of them in the open.

Our passing game can best be divided into four basic concepts: one-man routes to the flanker side, one-man routes to the split end side, two-man routes to the flanker side, and two-man routes to the split end side.

Timing, as everyone knows, is extremely important in the passing game. In our situation, we are concerned more with timing as it relates to the depth or vertical seams. Our basic routes involve movement straight up the field, as opposed to curls, outs, drags, etc. The simplicity of the cut, we hope, will result in better execution and increased effectiveness of the passing game.

I would first like to consider the one-man cut to the flanker side. Our backfield is that of the outside veer, coupled with the onside guard pulling to protect the QB.

A brief description of the mechanics of those involved in the play, save the QB and flanker, might be appropriate at this time. The onside guard pulls with enough depth to clear the tackle and end. He must be prepared to engage the DE with his inside shoulder should the end come aggressively. But he would prefer to pull across the face of the end and be prepared to come back on him from the outside should he not take the fake of the FB and QB ride. If the end does tackle the FB, the guard picks up either a linebacker or someone in the secondary if the QB is not able to throw and has to run.

The tackle and end assignments are rather obvious. They double-team the defensive tackle as on the outside veer.

The QB executes the outside veer, realizing his ride with the FB can be longer and more pronounced because his offensive guard protects him from pressure by the end. We feel that if the play is to have any chance of success, the QB must be able to stay close to the LOS.

The critical parts of the play are the understanding of the coverage by the flanker and the QB and the timing of the throw. The timing I refer to is the time from the snap of the ball until the QB is ready to deliver the ball. The spot is designated by an X in figure 1.

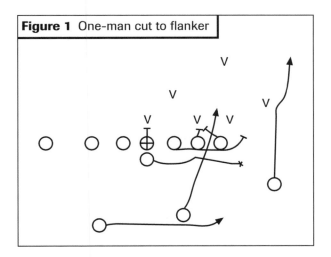

Figure 1 One-man cut to flanker

We hope the basic execution of our offense will limit the coverages used by the defense and make recognition of the coverage not too difficult. For purposes of discussion, I'll mention only those defenses used most by our opponents last year: the two-deep zone, two-deep man, and normal rotation with safety or corner force. Since the two-deep zone presents the same recognition problems as the normal rotation or cover 1 with the corner force, I'll

lump those two together. With this in mind, the flanker has to recognize and react to the two-deep zone, two-deep man, and cover 1 with a safety force. It would also help if the QB understood what was going on.

The first critical point of the flanker's route is to get off the LOS with all the speed he can muster. If he does this, the coverage will establish itself very quickly. If the cornerback doesn't give ground quickly but instead tries to engage the flanker and funnel him inside, the flanker knows that it is a zone with a cloud force. Then his main consideration is to make sure he cannot be covered by the safety. He must fight his way to the outside of the cornerback and get to the vertical seam between the corner and safety (figure 2). He wants to get there when the QB reaches the point where he is ready to deliver the ball.

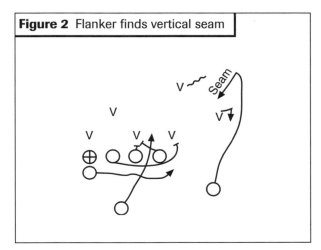

Figure 2 Flanker finds vertical seam

If the flanker bursts off the LOS and the cornerback turns his shoulders, gets underneath the receiver, and begins to run with the receiver, our flanker immediately knows he is in two-deep man and will lay back his ears and run for his life, knowing the chances of the ball being thrown to him are very slim. As the QB gets to his delivery point and sees the corner running with the receiver, he becomes more interested in running the ball and optioning off of the first odd-colored jersey (see figure 3). We do not like to have a pass play where the option of running the ball is not available.

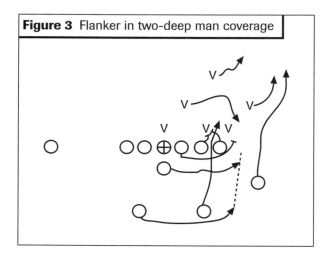

Figure 3 Flanker in two-deep man coverage

The only other situation we saw last year was the cover 1 with a safety force. This coverage shows itself quickly with the flow of the play and, we hope, the speed with which the flanker leaves the LOS. If the flanker sees the cornerback pedaling to maintain a cushion between himself and the receiver and it is obvious that he has deep outside responsibility, the flanker drives him as deep as he can. Then, when the flanker feels that the QB has reached the delivery point, he jabs his outside foot in the ground and turns in to receive the ball (figure 4).

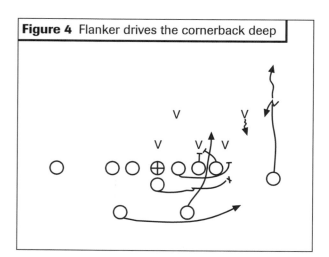

Figure 4 Flanker drives the cornerback deep

As you can see, there are no intricate maneuvers as far as the flanker is concerned, just an abbreviated understanding of three coverage responsibilities by the secondary man in front of him. The restricted learning process gives us the opportunity for more repetitions, which should help in execution. So much for the one-man cut to the flanker side.

All of the learning points for the split end on his one-man cut are identical to those of the flanker on his side (figure 5). The only thing that changes is the backfield action. Going to the split end side, we use our delayed option, or 70 series. The QB takes one step back, then comes down the line to get to delivery point X. To get him there, we have the halfback attack the end man on the LOS and roll block him. The FB maintains a pitch position similar to that of the RB going the other way. The potential coverages are the same on the split end side as on the flanker side, so the reaction and read of our split end is the same as that of the flanker.

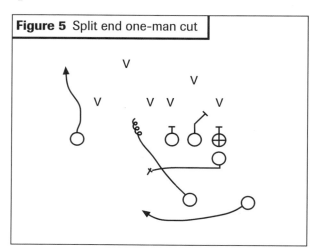

Figure 5 Split end one-man cut

On the two-man cut to the flanker side, the flanker does exactly as he does on the one-man cut in every respect. He, however, is not the primary receiver. The primary receiver is the TE. His route is the same as the flanker's, generally straight up the field. We use three backfield actions (figure 6) in throwing the two man out.

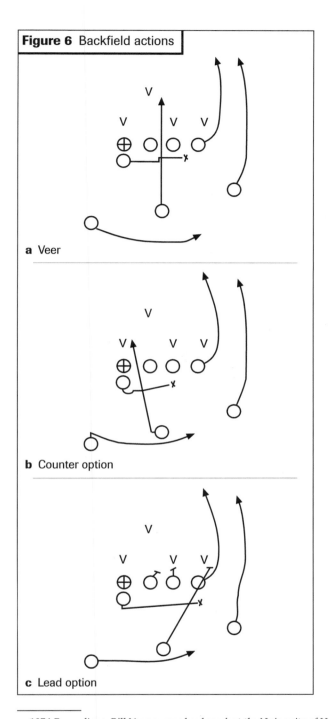

Figure 6 Backfield actions

a Veer

b Counter option

c Lead option

The spot indicated by X is the delivery point, so the time taken from the snap of the ball through the fake to point X is the time the TE has to get to the seam between the LB and DE and inside of the safety. As the TE releases from the LOS, he wants to appear as if he is trying to block the force man in the secondary. As he makes his move, he can see whether it is a sky or cloud force. If it is a cloud force, he does not concern himself with the safety but concentrates on getting between the DE and LB at the proper time. If he reads sky force, then in addition to getting between the LB and DE, he must get inside the safety to protect the throw. This is not a long, difficult throw nor a complicated route, but timing is most important. Should the pass route be covered, the QB still has the option to run.

Our two-man cuts to the split end side have never thrilled us that much because we are committed to pass. We throw the two-man cut out of two basic backfield actions, the flow and draw, and have as our basic cut the curl and flat.

As with most teams who throw a lot, we have several routes available to the split end, with companion routes for the HB. We also call the TE into the pass cut, but when we do, the protection on the back side gets to be a problem.

Our passing attack certainly isn't complicated, but since our split end averaged 20.6 yards per catch, our TE 19.5 per catch, and our flanker 16 yards per catch, it was fairly effective.

1974 Proceedings. Bill Yeoman was head coach at the University of Houston.

Passing With Bootleg Action

Frank Kush

For years, our bread-and-butter series has been the power sweep and the accompanying bootleg pass patterns. Our sweeping game probably illustrates our offensive thinking better than anything else we do. We believe in simplicity, repetition, and execution.

We start with simplicity, something I understand the most! Basically, our outside game consists of a double-team at the point of attack and everyone else trying to get around the corner. Repetition comes from devoting a certain amount of time each day on our drills, rather than long periods one day and none the next. Execution comes as a result of simplicity and repetition.

Each spring, we start with our sweeping game as our primary offense. Basically, it is a power series and, as a result, we feel that we can teach some toughness to our players, especially our backs. Our wingbacks and running backs, who usually have excellent speed, must learn to double-team or block one-on-one. We really feel that toughness can be taught, and this particular series is very conducive to our toughness program.

In the right 121 (figure 1), we double-team with the TE and wingback, pull the offside guard, and lead with the FB. The HB makes his cut off of the FB's block. For the left 121 (figure 2), the WB double-teams with the tackle; the rest is the same.

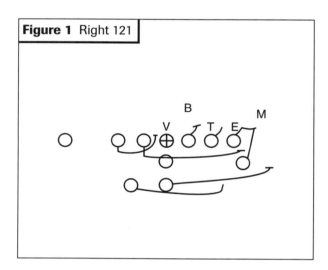

Figure 1 Right 121

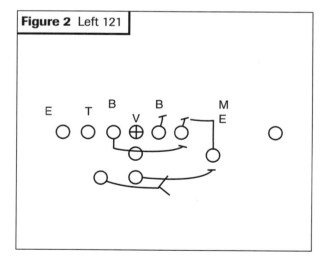

Figure 2 Left 121

Our backs are required to block and, as a result, become just a little tougher. Like all other sweeping teams, we can pull both of our guards or keep them in according to a simple call: sweep—both guards pull; solid—both guards stay in (figure 3). Also, we can hand off the ball to the HB as we do in our sweeps, or toss and have the QB lead as we do in the solid call.

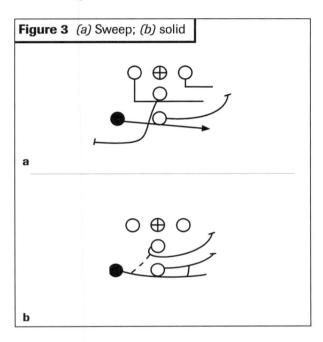

Figure 3 *(a)* Sweep; *(b)* solid

a

b

Our passing philosophy from the bootleg is considered part of the running game. The bootleg pass is called off our sweep action. We can run the pass from any formation. This particular play pass has proven very successful against both zone and man-to-man coverages.

Blocking protection is simple (figure 4). We number in from the outside, one-two-three. The outside tackle has two, the guard three, and the pulling guard, one. The FB picks up the three man over the pulling guard, and the offside tackle has two. Our HB picks up one.

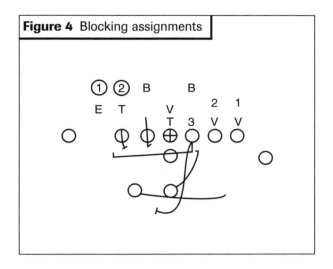

Figure 4 Blocking assignments

Our onside protection is aggressive, with the center helping toward the pass side. One thing we do is call solid blocking against stunting or hard-charging teams. By calling solid, we keep the guard in and replace this block with the FB. The basic pattern is shown in figure 5.

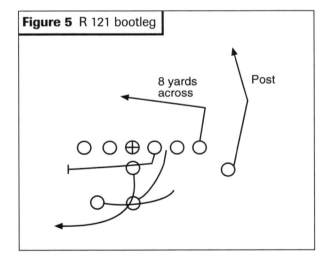

Figure 5 R 121 bootleg

8 yards across

Post

In the R 121 bootleg, the primary receiver is the across man (TE), especially when the LB keys and pursues with backs or guards. The end should go down four yards, then across to a point eight yards deep over the middle, reading the LB. The alternate route is quick across (figure 6). Figure 7 shows the various individual patterns to the split end.

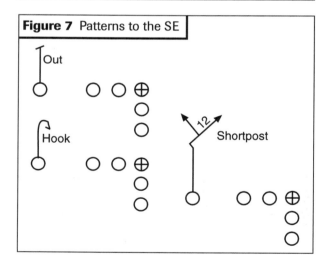

Figure 6 R 121 bootleg TE quick across

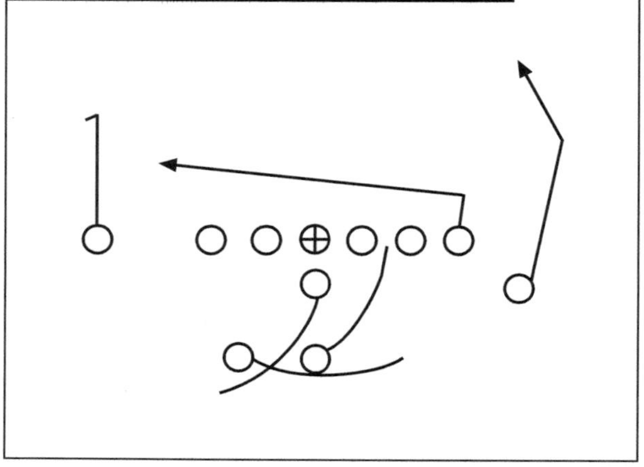

Figure 7 Patterns to the SE

The split end runs a short post if the three-deep safety is covering deep middle, rotating with flow, and the defensive HB is playing outside. The split end runs a deep post if the four-deep safety is rotating and the four-deep FS attempts to pick up the WB or end coming across. From a slot set, the patterns are the same for the WB and SE. Figure 8 shows the TE's individual routes. Figure 9 shows the angle flag designed to beat the HB. The TE uses

the flat pattern when the DE is responsible for the flat HB dropping off deep or rotating (figure 10).

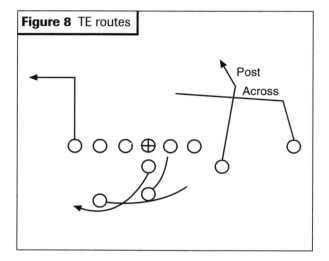

Figure 8 TE routes

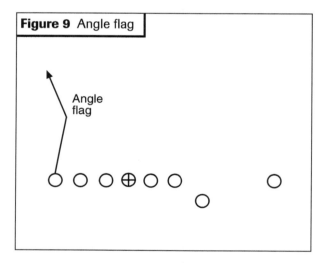

Figure 9 Angle flag

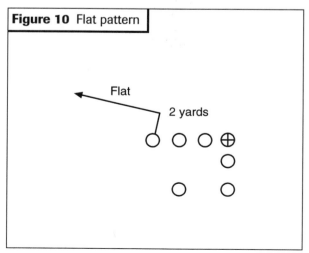

Figure 10 Flat pattern

The post pattern is used to beat the HB versus a rotating or man-to-man secondary. Some of our most effective screens have come out of this bootleg pass. When screening right to the HB, we call solid blocking and fake the bootleg pass, then screen to the HB (figure 11). When screening left to the FB (solid), we fake the bootleg and hit the screen to the FB (figure 12).

Figure 11 Screen right to HB

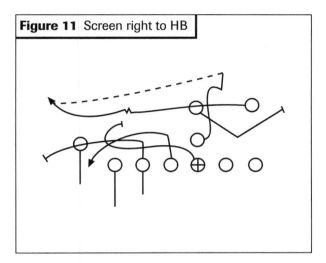

Figure 12 Screen left to FB

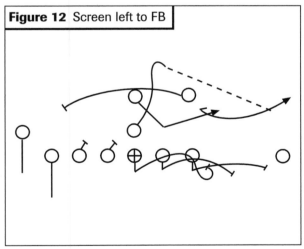

Two other plays that have been successful off the bootleg action are throwbacks—one to the QB from the HB and the other off the bootleg fake thrown back to the HB (figure 13).

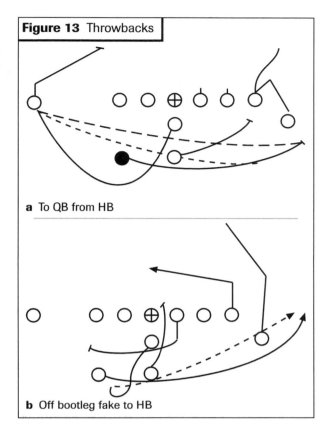

Figure 13 Throwbacks

a To QB from HB

b Off bootleg fake to HB

One other maneuver is the third man out (figure 14). We can get our FB in the flat quickly. This play is good on the goal line, where the opponent is more likely to be in man coverage.

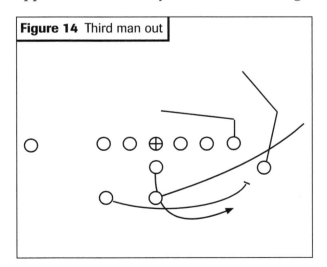

Figure 14 Third man out

1971 Proceedings. Frank Kush was head coach at Arizona State University.

Building a Passing Series From Basic Sets

Larry Kehres

We have tried to follow the adage that offensive planning should begin with player evaluation, progress to formation identification, and culminate with the selection of the best plays to use with the players and formation.

We had tremendous talent at the skill positions entering this season. Our offensive line was a question mark with four new starters. The offensive staff determined that we should rely even more heavily on our pass offense and skill players to lead the way. We dropped our Power I short-yardage and goal line attack, deciding instead to refine our passing game and attempt to use it more effectively as we moved into scoring position.

We felt that our offensive line could be more effective pass blocking than in power-oriented running schemes, even in short-yardage and goal line situations. Having a veteran QB made the decision to stress the passing game seem logical. We also believed that our defense would be effective in limiting the rushing offense of our opponents.

Simply put, we felt that if we could get into games where both teams were passing frequently, we would maximize our chance to win. Our defense lived up to its potential by limiting opponents to 54 rushing yards per game during the regular season and performing well in the play-offs.

Formation selection was based on returning talent. We determined that a two-back, flexed TE, two-WR formation would be our basic look (figure 1). This was supplemented with a one-back, four-receiver formation (figure 2). Out of both sets, we used motion approximately 50 percent of the time.

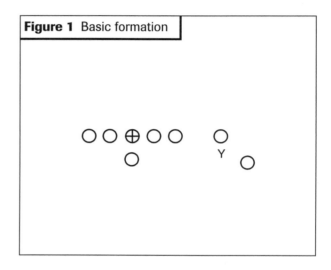

Figure 1 Basic formation

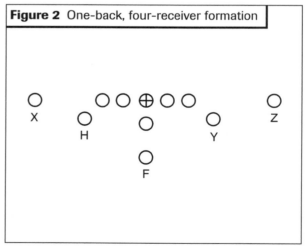

Figure 2 One-back, four-receiver formation

These basic sets were complemented by a Trips formation from the one-back (figure 3) and also by a tackle-over set from our two-back look (figure 4).

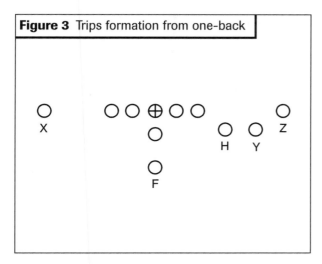

Figure 3 Trips formation from one-back

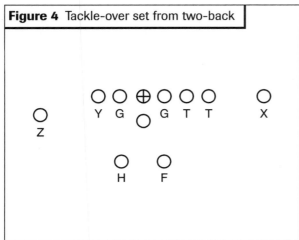

Figure 4 Tackle-over set from two-back

This combination of two-back and one-back formations enabled us to use our talent at WR, yet we could pose the threat of the run and maximize the blitz protection of the defense.

Play selection was based on our decision that our players dictated a pass-first and run-second offensive system. We felt it was imperative to allow our QB to throw from several areas: the pocket, the tackle box, outside the containment of the defense, and from an area just behind the LOS in a quick-throw series.

We continued to use a five-step, dropback scheme and complemented it with the lead draw, which has been a part of our offense for years. We selected a bootleg action to allow the

QB to throw from the tackle box and complemented it with the counter gap. We continue using a form of a sprint action that we have used for years. This play action comes off the outside veer play. Although we used the outside veer run infrequently, the ability to get the QB outside to throw was an invaluable component of our offense.

We occasionally used a very quick play action that involved a quick reverse pivot and counter dive fake. Usually, we were looking for a quick hitch (versus three-deep zone) or a quick fade (versus two-deep zone). This counter dive pass was complemented by running the counter dive, which we used nearly exclusively in short-yardage and goal line situations. If we determined that the counter dive fake would not influence the defense, we substituted a three-step drop.

Primary Patterns

We use four basic patterns in our five-step drop scheme. These patterns are very basic and are best versus three-deep zone or man-to-man defenses. The first is a strong side triangular pattern (figure 5). The QB reads the flat defender and delivers the ball to Y, if open. If Y is not open, the QB delivers the ball to Z in the curl. If the ILB has dropped under the curl, the QB goes to F on a six-yard hook.

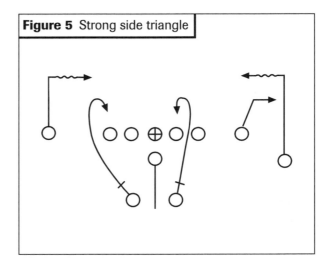

Figure 5 Strong side triangle

The second pattern involves a triangle of receivers in the middle of the field (figure 6). The QB reads the weak side inside linebacker. If the linebacker stays weak, the QB will go to Y or F based on the drop of the strong inside linebacker. If the weak linebacker drops under the middle hook, the QB will go to H.

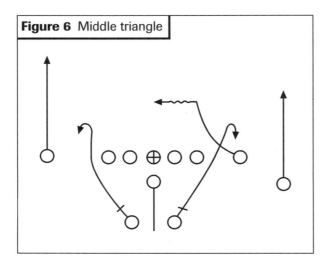

Figure 6 Middle triangle

The third pattern features a triangle of receivers on the weak side of the formation (figure 7). The QB reads the weak side flat defender. If the flat defender defends H, the QB goes to X. If the weak inside linebacker drops under the hook, Y provides an outlet in the six-yard hook zone.

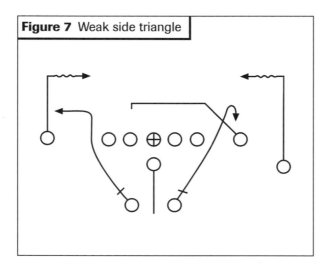

Figure 7 Weak side triangle

The fourth basic pattern in our five-step dropback is the out (figure 8). We run this to both the strong and weak side of the forma-

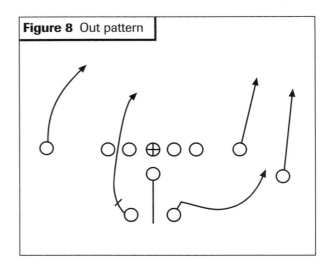

Figure 8 Out pattern

tion. The QB reads the flat defender and goes to Z or F. The TE finds the seam between the inside linebacker and the outside backer. He works away from pressure, providing a third choice.

These four patterns are adjusted versus two-deep zone coverage, allowing the receivers the option of working into the holes between the corners and safeties, and giving the TE the option of working between the safeties. We make many other adjustments to our dropback patterns based on defensive tendencies, individual defensive skills, and our own unique skills. For example, it was necessary to extend the depth of the routes and use a seven-step drop at times this season.

The lead draw complements our dropback passing very well. Our offensive linemen find that protecting the QB is aided by the frequent use of the draw. We believe that we can produce more yardage with the draw than with a run, which would require more aggressive blocking and more movement by the offensive linemen on the defensive linemen. We run the draw early and often.

Screens

We have developed three screens that complement our dropback passing game. Our screen from the two-back set (figure 9) involves both backs flaring with the guard and tackle leading the blocking. The center goes to the side of the QB's first choice. The back on the side away from the call checks blitz before flaring. From the one-back set, we screen to the split end sliding in behind the LOS and to the back working behind the LOS and near the tackle area on either side.

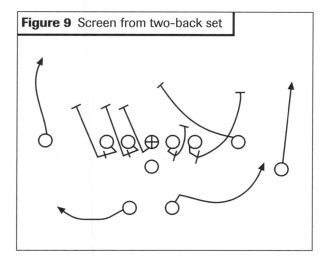

Figure 9 Screen from two-back set

The bootleg action has been a tremendous plus for us the last two years. In 1991, we struggled with dropback pass protection. Needing to rely more on play-action passing, we felt that moving the QB quickly to the right and left after a cheap play fake seemed to stabilize our protection. We developed this action from both two-back and one-back formations (figure 10).

The QB progresses from the flat route to the crossing receiver to the 18-yard comeback, and finally to the back side receiver, who is working the back side curl in the middle third underneath the FS. At times, F provides an outlet receiver if our protection has broken down.

This pattern has been very productive. We have featured the quick throw to the flat or the cross. The protection enables us to block six defenders, and we generally have good angles. The fake is not dramatic; the emphasis is on holding the inside linebackers enough to allow the crossing receiver to clear. The bootleg action has been very effective as we near the goal line. The counter gap has been our second most productive run. It is necessary to use this play enough to keep the threat of the run present.

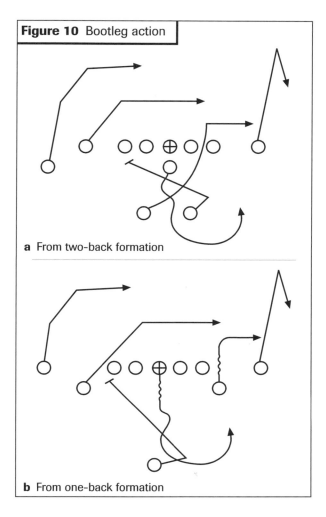

Figure 10 Bootleg action

a From two-back formation

b From one-back formation

Sprint Action

The necessity to get the QB outside the defensive rush has led us to continue to use the outside veer pass (figure 11).

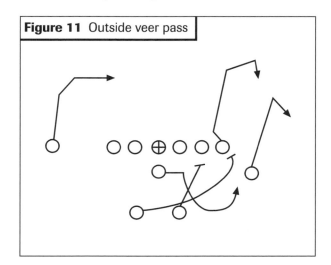

Figure 11 Outside veer pass

The action provides a zone blocking scheme for the offensive line. The running backs can secure the containment. The 18-yard comeback can be converted to a takeoff should the corner's coverage dictate. The TE aligns tight and works into the seam between the inside and outside backers. The split end works the post.

In order to better guarantee the QB can get to the corner, we move the tackle to the play side and use the TE on back side protection. If the back side rush is strong, we will sprint and screen back to the TE. This screen has been very effective.

We use our sprint action to run the TE on a cross with the split end running a square in and the flanker running a post.

Bootlegs

The decision to stress the passing game in short-yardage and goal line situations paid tremendous dividends. A minimum of 10 minutes each day was used to practice our passing game from the 15-yard line and closer.

The bootleg pass (figure 12) has been our most successful passing action near the goal line. We threw 25 touchdowns out of the boot, and 16 were distances of 10 yards or less. We had success with our regular pattern, and several adjustments also were real good. The first adjustment involved a crossing route by X and Z (figure 13).

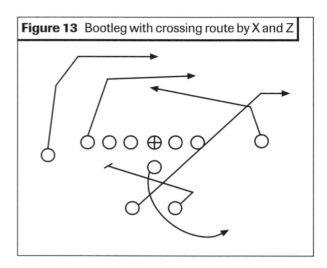

Figure 13 Bootleg with crossing route by X and Z

This adjustment to the pattern gave the QB three receivers moving with him to the play side. We want the receivers at three different depths. The split end (X) slices through the defense at LB depth. If the deep backs are flowing with the crossing routes of Y and Z, then X will continue into the far third of the field. The split end will stop in a hole in the defense if the deep backs have stayed in their zones.

A second adjustment to the pattern has X and Z align on the play side and both cross away from the roll of the QB (figure 14).

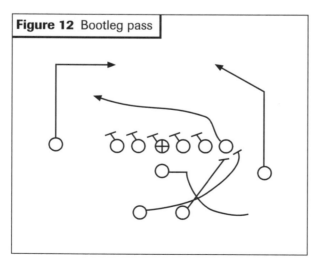

Figure 12 Bootleg pass

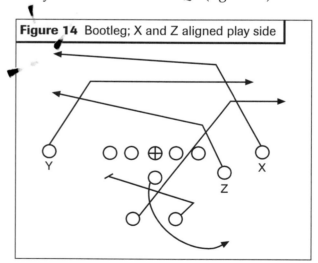

Figure 14 Bootleg; X and Z aligned play side

This double crossing action gives the QB a great spread of receivers. The first choice is the receiver in the flat; the second choice is the crossing TE (Y). However, if both are covered, the QB has the two wide receivers crossing at shallow and deep depths. This is particularly effective if the QB's movement is stopped by defensive pressure off the corner. As the QB stops his movement to the right, assuming his receivers moving to the right are covered, he is able to work with his receivers moving to the left.

A third adjustment can be effective when defenders are playing tough man-to-man (figure 15). The back side receivers begin to cross toward the roll of the QB, then reverse direction and move away. Anticipating this reverse, the QB looks first to the receiver in the flat; if he does not make the throw to the flat, he immediately stops and looks for his receivers breaking away.

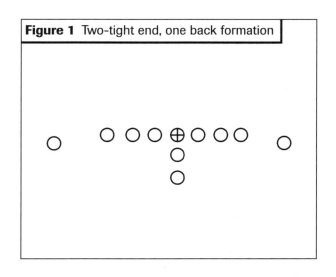

Figure 15 Bootleg with reverse direction

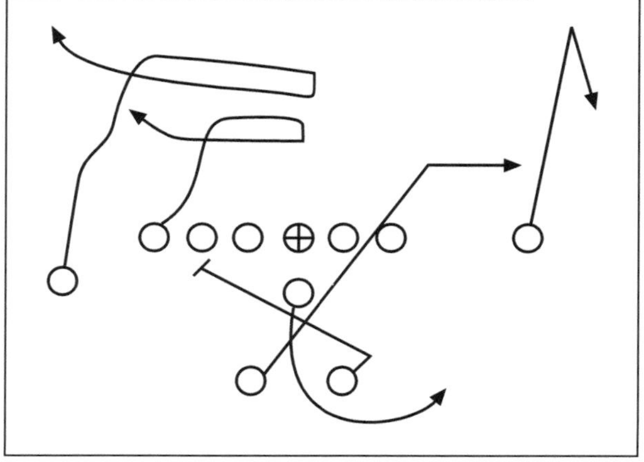

This action is effective for us in a few limited situations. Of course, any adjustments can be effective if players are capable of making them successful.

1994 Proceedings. Larry Kehres is head coach at Mount Union College.

Passing From a One-Back Set

Bob Griffin

Success in this game and in everything we do in life depends upon our ability to both cooperate and compete. As coaches, we must strive continually to enhance and emphasize this ability of our team through the systems we choose to employ.

We will always attempt to keep in mind that you win with people. The people available to us will be a major factor in our deciding what we will do on both offense and defense, and also how we will do it. Once we've made our decisions, we will continue to remind our team that players, not plays, win football games. In our attempt to get the best people on the field and best utilize their talents, we settled on the "two-tight end, one-back" attack (figure 1).

Figure 1 Two-tight end, one back formation

Impact of New Formation

Over an 11-game schedule, one of our tight ends caught 74 passes, a new I-AA record. The other tight end caught 53 passes through nine games prior to being injured early in the 10th game. Both were catching the ball at a record or near-record pace by I-AA standards. Our healthy tight end and eventual I-AA all-American, Brian Forster, went on to key our quarterfinal victory over a fine Richmond football team by catching 18 passes for 252 yards.

The Two-Tight End, One-Back Attack

The information given below outlines our philosophy behind the "two-tight end, one-back" formation, the personnel needed, and the different components of the attack.

Philosophy of Attack

1. Pass is primary.
2. Attack the whole field.
3. Field position is irrelevant.
4. Every down-and-distance is a passing situation.
5. Draw and screen are essential complements. They improve pass protection as well as complementing overall attack.
6. Take the run when it is given; otherwise pass.

Personnel Qualifications and Developmental Emphases

1. Get a quality quarterback. He must be an above-average thrower and a good decision maker.
2. Get two quality tight ends who have receiving ability, courage, great running ability and speed, and blocking ability.
3. Get two quality wideouts who have receiving ability, good speed, and blocking ability.
4. Develop an effective pass-blocking front line that has the size and quick feet, competitiveness, ability to think and

adjust, and speed and quickness to be successful.
5. Get a quality running back who has exceptional running ability, blocking ability, and receiving ability. Size is helpful, but not essential.

Components of the Attack

1. Three-step drop.
2. Five- and seven-step drop.
3. Full sprint.
4. Play action.
5. Running game: dive, trap, cutback, belly (best weak side), C.T. or counter, pitch, or toss.
6. Screens: running back, tight end, or double screen.
7. Draw: base draw, trap draw, or quarterback draw.
8. Special plays.

Implementing the Attack

I will attempt to illustrate some specific examples of the way in which we implement the actual attack.

The *three-step drop* (preread, drop, confirm or key) can be used versus normal zones with soft corner play (for example, 86-87 key flat defender; figure 2); versus man-to-man with pressure and 5 under man-to-man (for example, 80-81 go to tight end; figure 3); and versus 5 cover (hard corner) with two deep (for example, 88-89; figure 4).

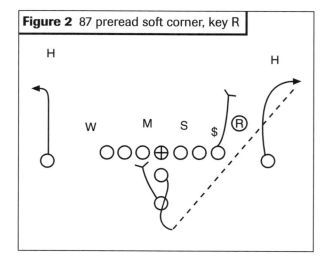

Figure 2 87 preread soft corner, key R

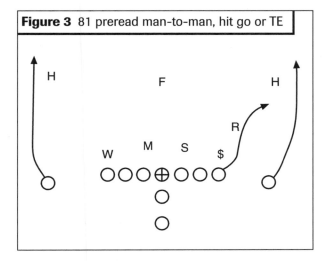

Figure 3 81 preread man-to-man, hit go or TE

Figure 4 89 preread hard corner and 2 deep

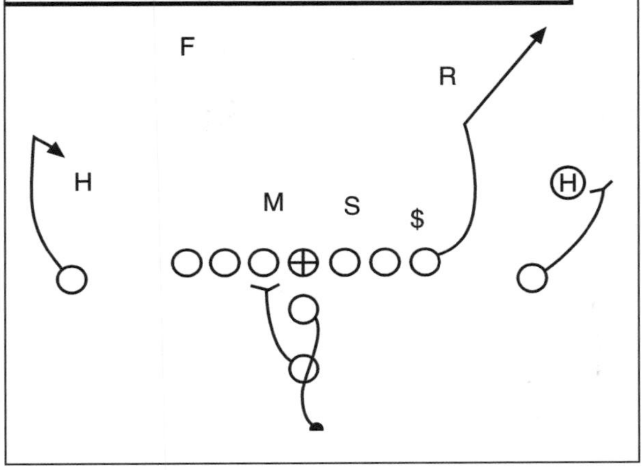

For the *five-step drop* and *seven-step drop*, the same format is developed as that listed for the three-step drop (figure 5).

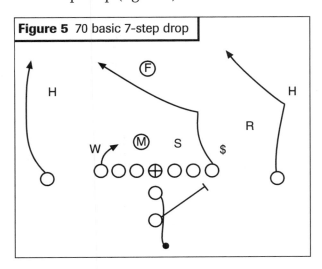

Figure 5 70 basic 7-step drop

The *full sprint keep action* is used primarily versus pressure (figure 6).

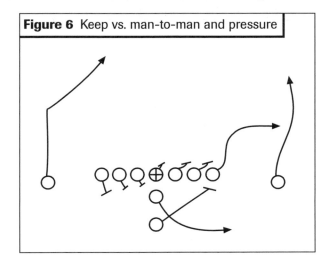

Figure 6 Keep vs. man-to-man and pressure

The *play action* provides misdirection and pressure on the defensive perimeter (figure 7).

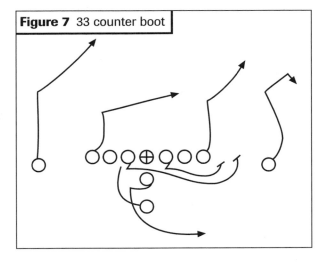

Figure 7 33 counter boot

The attempt here was to expose you to the philosophy and the actual mechanics of the "two-tight end, one-back" set as used in 1984 at the University of Rhode Island. I hope it has helped to stimulate your thinking as it relates to the planning and development of your own attack, as well as given you some insight into ours.

1985 Proceedings. Bob Griffin was head coach at the University of Rhode Island.

Attacking With an H Back

Joe Tiller and Larry Korpitz

Since 1986, we have finished as high as second in passing offense, fourth in total offense, and third in scoring offense. We'll always have a chance to be rated in the top 20 in these three categories, but it is our ability to control the ball at critical times that concerns us. For this reason, we are always researching ways to add an element of power football to our offense.

Although we've been able to achieve a measurable degree of success using just one back, we are not blessed with outstanding foot speed at running back that will allow us to consistently get to the corner. We also find that we need to even up the numbers in the running game to give us a chance at blocking all of the defenders aligned to stop the run. And at the TE position, our personnel are considered to be undersized.

To integrate the type of receiver at the TE position we want in our attack, we find that we often have to sacrifice size for speed. When faced with these limitations, we began to look for ways to run power football out of our one-back formations and settled on inserting another TE into the offense. We wanted to get in a position to run the football effectively to complement our one-back passing attack. The extra TE (or H back) was our solution to solving this dilemma.

We maintained most of our original formations, but we employed an extra TE in our Heavy formation and two extra TEs in what we refer to as our Jumbo formation. We had been doing this since 1986, but only in our goal line package. We now incorporate this combination of personnel in all situations and at any place on the field. We've found that defenses are not nearly as quick to change personnel as they had been because of their concern about matching up with our people.

Although our emphasis has been primarily in the running game, we also throw play-action passes and most of our short drop game from these formations. As with most coaching staffs, our emphasis in the future will be determined by the personnel we have coming into our program. But let's take a look at our two-back attack with just one back.

Running Scheme

First, our inside sprint play employs zone blocking to the play side but can be vulnerable from the back side. We eliminated the back side squeeze on the ball by incorporating our Heavy Doubles formation and blocking the back side with our H back (figure 1).

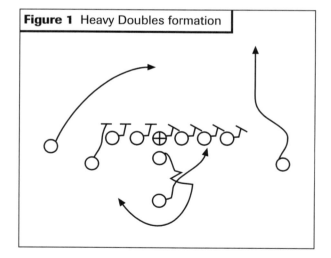

Figure 1 Heavy Doubles formation

We also needed a way to eliminate pressure coming from the outside in the form of a rover or SS (or LB overhang) blitz. We next went to our Jumbo Ace formation, employed strong side motion, and eliminated the overhang problem (figure 2).

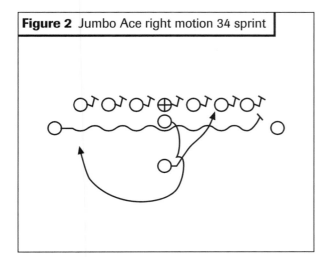

Figure 2 Jumbo Ace right motion 34 sprint

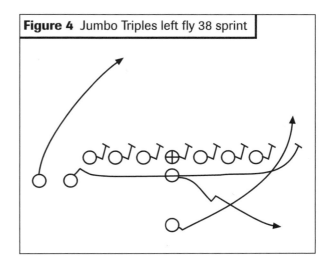

Figure 4 Jumbo Triples left fly 38 sprint

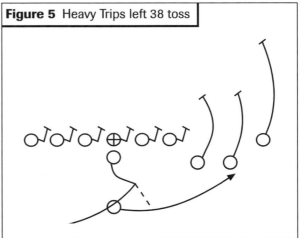

Figure 5 Heavy Trips left 38 toss

Since we employ three WRs the majority of the time, we sometimes find ourselves in a physical mismatch when running off the edge of the formation. For this reason, we again use our H back and now match up against more physical defenders. Our Heavy Doubles formation gives us what we are looking for to the open side (figure 3). With our Jumbo formation, we add a physical blocker into the mix when running to the strong, or closed, side (figure 4).

One of our most effective formations is the Trips alignment, and again we get the physical matchup we want by aligning in our Heavy Trips formation and tossing the ball (figure 5). However, we still didn't have a true lead-back power play. We worked this play into our attack by teaching the power O play with the back side guard pulling and our H back as lead blocker. This play brings numbers at the de-

fense and allows you to run off a double-team. It is a play we can go to when we want to run the ball regardless of the defense's alignments (figure 6).

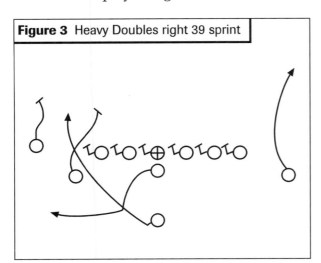

Figure 3 Heavy Doubles right 39 sprint

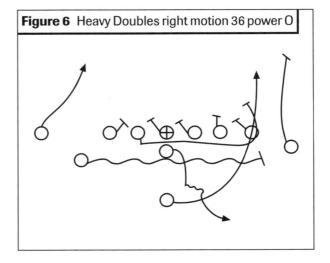

Figure 6 Heavy Doubles right motion 36 power O

Passing Schemes

The passing segment of our two-back attack with just one back includes play-action passes developed from the run game just described. At the end, I've included a dropback pass we run from our Heavy and Jumbo alignments. The power O play-action pass uses the success of the run to influence the near safety and play side linebackers.

The secondary force determines which of two routes we use with this play. Against a team that run supports with its play side safety, we will plan the power pass with the play side TE (safeties key on run support) blocking down like he would on the run play power O. We simply run the play side WR (Z) on a skinny post. The Z must get inside leverage on his defender and push vertically, gaining separation from the run support safety. To occupy the back side safety, our back side receiver runs a post corner, moving at the back side defender to gain his attention.

This scheme assures us maximum protection, allowing our QB the time necessary to make a good ball fake and gain depth and separation from the LOS. We emphasize that the QB get back and align properly at his target to ensure an accurate throw. Heavy Doubles motion and Jumbo Ace motion power pass are illustrated in figures 7 and 8.

Figure 7 Heavy Doubles motion 336 power pass

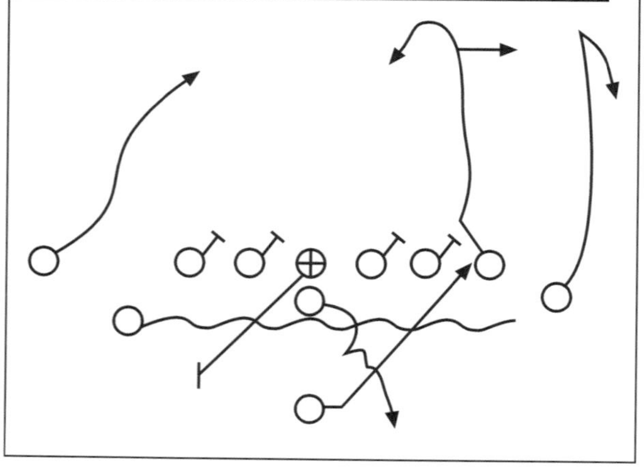

Figure 8 Jumbo Ace motion 336 power pass

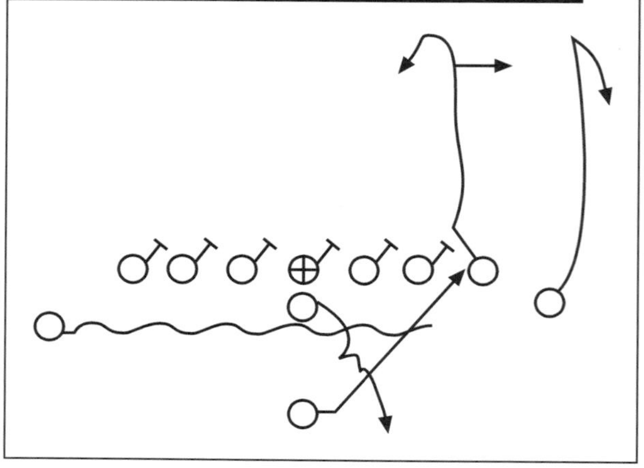

When facing a team that supports the run with underneath defenders (linebackers, strong safety, roll corners), we will alter our routes on power pass. The power O play-action fake will influence the underneath pass coverage and allow us to exploit the flat curl areas. Against this defensive scheme, we will inside release the TE on an option route, giving him the responsibility of finding the vacated zone. In this scheme, the Z takes an outside release and runs an 18-yard comeback, and the back side receiver runs a post, trying to replace the middle safety if he is influenced by the run fake. When running this play out of a true two TE formation, the back side TE blocks to help guarantee a more solid protection scheme.

In this section, I will describe a couple of ways we run our naked bootleg play off of our inside sprint run play. The success of our inside sprint run play is necessary to influence backer flow and allow us to successfully misdirect the defense with our naked play-action pass. We can add the letter "O" to the end of the call to alert the offside guard to pull play side, to help protect the QB versus an outside backer blitz or a wide defensive end, containing the bootleg.

Naked Bootleg

Our QB has the option of adding an O call at the LOS based upon defensive alignments. We plan our nakeds weekly based on the ways (formations and motions) we plan to run the inside sprint. The ball mechanics of the QB must be identical in executing both plays (the run and naked pass). The QB deliberately flashes the ball—with ball and arms extended—allowing the defense to see the ball placed in the TB's pocket. We hope this ball-handling technique influences the flow of the backers and secondary in the naked and run game, allows better and bigger cutback lanes in the run game, and allows for better misdirection in the play action.

A coaching point for the QB following his fake is that he must quickly get his head and shoulders around while gaining depth and width. He must be ready to trigger the ball to the flat (the number one receiver) when that zone is vacated.

Our QB has a consistent progression on our naked play action:

1. He runs when not contained because the containment has been fooled by the run fake or is trying to cover the flat.

2. The flat route is the first pass progression, and the quickest and easiest to complete.

3. He stays aware of the drag by the back side receiver, or TE. The TE's job is to get behind the underneath coverage and across the field into the QB's vision. If the QB is contained, the receiver should settle down against zone coverage at 10 to 15 yards in depth. If the QB breaks the containment and continues outside, the drag route should continue across, maintaining a good relationship with the QB in his vision.

4. The last progression is the back side post, and this occurs only when there is a number two receiver back side. Figure 9 illustrates two variations of our naked play action.

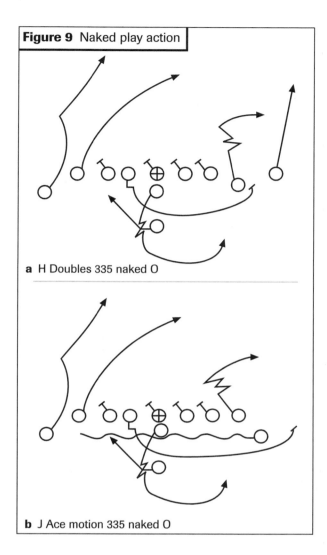

Figure 9 Naked play action

a H Doubles 335 naked O

b J Ace motion 335 naked O

Naked Pin

A variation to the naked play action we use when trying to make a big play or pick up a first down in a short-yardage situation is our naked pin O. Again, we have a number of different ways to run pin O. What pin O describes is the technique of our play side flat receiver eliminating his route and having him block down, pinning the contain defender. This allows our QB to break containment and adds time, allowing him to throw the ball up the field. Different situations will dictate to him which progressions to follow. In certain situations, he thinks to throw the ball up the field, looking for the home run. In other situations, he thinks to run and pick up the first down. The pin by the H back or TE should assure the O guard the opportunity to lead the QB to the outside. On the QB's command of "run," the guard should turn upfield, blocking the first different-colored jersey with the QB on his hip. Figure 10 illustrates a couple of ways we have used the pin O scheme.

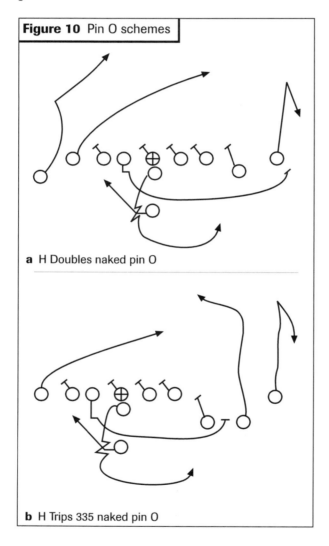

Figure 10 Pin O schemes

a H Doubles naked pin O

b H Trips 335 naked pin O

Dropback

The final pass in this presentation is not a play-action pass but a dropback incorporating our Heavy and Jumbo schemes. It is necessary in

our style of play to incorporate our basic 90 passing game within this scheme. This package allows us to empty our backfield and still maintain maximum pass protection.

In the huddle, the QB makes a call that keeps the H back in for protection and slides the protection away from him. This puts the QB in a situation we refer to as a "no-brainer," allowing him to disregard his blitz keys. Our most successful play from this scheme is our Z option play. We use this play when we are assured that our motion will create a coverage mismatch with our Z receiver. Figure 11 illustrates two ways to run this dropback 90 pass play with our Heavy and Jumbo personnel. In this case, the progression our QB follows is (1) adjustment to motion, (2) uncovered (if the defense adjusts but leaves someone uncovered), (3) call route (Z option), and (4) back side route when applicable.

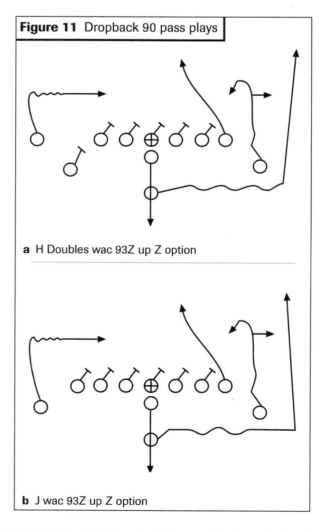

Figure 11 Dropback 90 pass plays

a H Doubles wac 93Z up Z option

b J wac 93Z up Z option

1994 Proceedings. Joe Tiller was head coach and Larry Korpitz was offensive coordinator at the University of Wyoming. Tiller is now head coach at Purdue University.

Using Motion in the Passing Game

Darrel "Mouse" Davis

By stealing some ideas from Glen Dobbs, borrowing a formation from Tiger Ellison, and evolving our own approach over the past 12 years, we have had some excellent success with the passing game.

In developing our offensive approach, we believe in establishing offensive goals to shoot for on a game and season basis. Our game-by-game offensive goals include the following:

1. No more than 1.5 sacks per game. This and goal number two we carry over from game to game. We threw the ball 461 times this past season and had six games in which we realized this goal.

2. No more than 1.5 interceptions. We realized this goal in six games.

3. Make a first down on each possession. We were perfect in this goal only once during the season. In that game, we had 681 yards of total offense. This is an excellent example of what reaching this goal can accomplish.

4. Score 27 points a game. We accomplished this in eight of 11 games and ended up fifth in the nation in scoring.

5. Attain 60 percent completion per game. Much of the success we have in this area is tied not only to our quarterback's ability to throw but also to our receivers' ability to catch. Therefore, we keep two percentages in this area: quarterback completion percentage, which equals the total drops by the receiver as completed, and actual completion percentage. We think this increases our receivers' concentration on receiving.

6. Outscore the opponent in the first quarter. We think our offense is different enough to give us a decided jump in getting to our opponent early, and we want to take full advantage of this.

7. No less than 75 plays per game. We average 79.4 plays per game and have a goal of never being under 75. We were under 70 plays once and lost the game.

8. No less than 370 yards of total offense per game. We set our goal at a combined total of from 370 to 500 yards of offense per game. We were under the minimum 370 only twice this past year, and in one of those games we had 368 total yards. We were over 500 yards on three occasions.

9. Season percentage of interceptions at 5 percent or less. We reduced this percentage from 9 percent in 1974 to just under 6 percent in 1975.

10. Score inside the 30-yard line 90 percent of the time. Score inside the 10-yard line 100 percent of the time.

11. Score by quarters. Our philosophy may differ from most in this area. We plan to have the game out of reach by the fourth quarter and establish our goals with this in mind. Our scoring goals by quarter for the 1975 season were 90 points in the first quarter, 90 points in the second quarter, 70 points in the third quarter, and 50 points in the fourth quarter. Our actual scores by quarter were 86 points in the first quarter, 125 points in the second quarter, 84 points in the third quarter, and 71 points in the fourth quarter.

12. No less than 15 yards gained per reception. In 1974, we made 14.6 yards per reception and set a goal of 15 yards per reception in 1975. In 1975, we actually finished with an average of 16.5 yards per reception.

We establish an overall team goal of finishing number one in the nation in total offense and pass offense. We did finish number one in both categories in 1975, with 5,196 yards of total offense and 3,979 yards passing.

Basic Sprint-Out Attack

Our basic approach to offense is to attack the defensive perimeter. We hang our hat on the sprint-out and sprint-out-and-set passing games. We feel it is necessary also to include a dropback passing game in the total passing attack.

We make our system of communication as understandable as possible, with a minimum of numbers. The first thing we state is our formation. If we are going to run from a Double-Slot (which we do over 90 percent of the time), we eliminate the formation call. Our next call is our motion (figure 1). Any call starting with "R" is going right; the longer and/or stronger the word, the longer the motion. Naturally, "L" is for left. We believe our motion calls give us the greatest flexibility and are absolutely necessary to avoid giving tendencies with the length-of-motion run. Our basic set and spacings are found in figure 2.

We use words to describe our patterns in the belief that there will be fewer errors and better carryover from year to year in remembering, thereby speeding up learning. We break our passing game into packages. This article will cover our scramble series with some of the

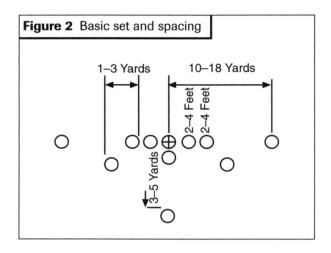

Figure 2 Basic set and spacing

variations off our basic pattern. We number the defensive men as is shown in figure 3. We start by keying the number four man and throwing away from him. The basic pattern we run when keying number four is shown in figure 4.

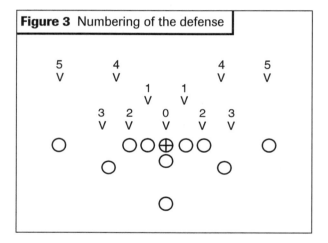

Figure 3 Numbering of the defense

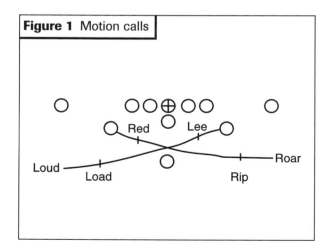

Figure 1 Motion calls

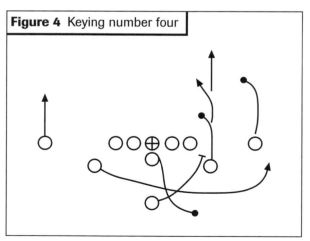

Figure 4 Keying number four

The onside patterns are as follows:

■ Split end: Runs a 7-12 yard curl depending on the drop of the linebackers in the undercoverage. Uses the general principle of keeping an open passing lane between him and the quarterback.

■ Motion back: If running rip motion, he continues on the snap of the ball to a depth of five yards immediately in back of the outside hip of the split end; he turns and makes a square corner upfield. If running roar motion, he hangs 001-002 and releases in a straight line upfield over the spot where the outside hip of the split was at the snap.

■ Onside slot: Reads the first linebacker to the inside. If he blitzes, slot screams "Hot" and looks for the ball over the inside shoulder. If the linebacker drops into the coverage, the slot does one of two things: he hooks and slides to open a passing lane between him and the quarterback or runs a post or go pattern to stretch the deep coverage. We vary this by opponent.

■ Quarterback: Keeps his eyes on the number four man from the first step. He takes his first step at a deep enough angle that he could run in back of a right halfback lined up in a full house backfield. If the number four man does anything other than move toward the LOS, he goes immediately to the corner and keys him, as he has become the number four man. The quarterback's job is to throw away from the number four man and avoid the undercoverage. He will throw this pattern on his fifth or seventh step off the right foot on the run. (If going left, it will be the sixth or eighth step.)

■ Fullback: Blocks number three. If number three drops into the coverage, he looks back to his inside and helps on the first wrong-colored jersey to show. We use a variety of techniques for our fullback to block the number three, all dictated by how the number three man is playing.

■ Offside end: Occupies the deep outside zone and is aware of setting up any defensive man playing on him.

If the pattern breaks down and the undercoverage has taken the short and intermediate patterns and the quarterback has gotten beyond his seventh step and is either scrambling or set (in which case he throws off his left foot), we break our pattern as follows:

■ Onside end: Breaks from his curl pattern through the deep middle safety area. If he recognizes the coverage as man, he starts his break through the deep safety and on recognition flattens his pattern to a straight line to the goal line.

■ Motion back: Breaks from his pattern, which is run off the outside hip of the split end on a streak. The only reasons he would vary from a straight line are to increase the distance between him and a defensive man he has on his hip or to break in front of a defensive safety rolling so quickly to the outside deep third that it is to advantage to break in front of him.

■ Onside slot: No change in pattern.

Figure 5 shows our method of identifying the pass zone we desire to attack. Depending on the coverage, we make reference to the area we will target. We believe a good passing attack should be able to control the depth of the pocket zone (depth of undercoverage) to 12-17 yards. If the linebackers are consistently getting deeper drops, you should have good success with short and delay passing. We also believe if teams consistently give maximum coverage (six under, three deep), we must have the ability to run with the quarterback at the corner.

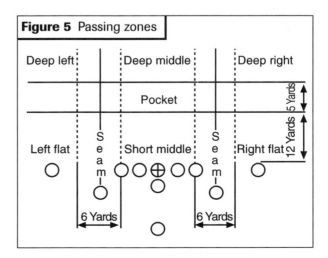

Figure 5 Passing zones

If we find invert coverage (figure 6), we read the number four and throw away from him. If he is found in position "A," the quarterback throws to the motion back. If he is in position "B," the quarterback throws to the split end.

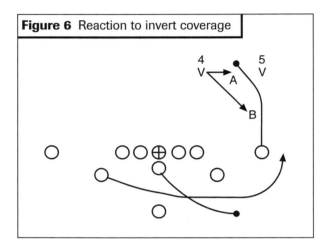

Figure 6 Reaction to invert coverage

Figure 7 shows a drill we call "key four" that we use in the first stage of teaching. We make it an easy read for the quarterback by flying to the motion back or the split end. We progress by allowing the number four man any option in an attempt to confuse the read.

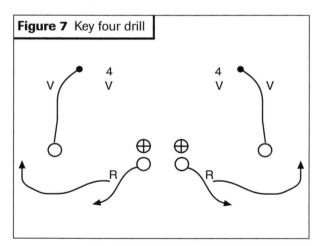

Figure 7 Key four drill

Figure 8 shows the corner roll and what the quarterback reads if the inside man does anything but come forward. He immediately reads the corner as number four. If number four rolls to position "A," the quarterback throws to the motion back. If he is found in position "B," the quarterback throws to the split end.

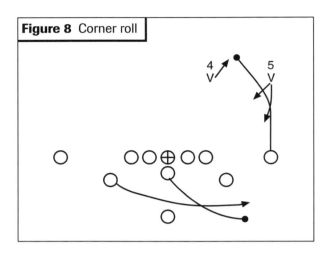

Figure 8 Corner roll

Figure 9 shows the drill we use to develop the quarterback's ability to read the corner roll. We then progress to the inside safety, giving a visual signal to the corner to indicate invert or corner roll coverage. We call this drill "key four-five."

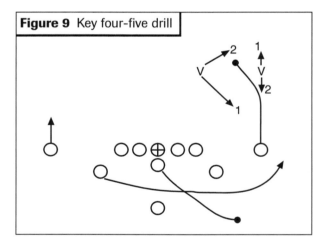

Figure 9 Key four-five drill

By following these same progressions, it is relatively simple to coach the necessary reactions for attacking all the coverages the quarterback may see.

Off this basic pattern, it is possible to attack breakdowns in coverage by giving constant patterns to the two people not involved in the called pattern. Figure 10 illustrates a post or flag pattern by the onside slot; the remaining onside receivers run hooks. This pattern is called basically to take advantage of a breakdown in coverage and is not a read pattern for the quarterback.

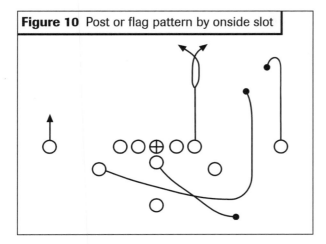

Figure 10 Post or flag pattern by onside slot

The next portion of our basic attack is coming back away from the direction of motion. We tell our split end he has the freedom to break his pattern away from the individual defensive man on him or to break into an open area in zone coverage. We tell the end he must make his break slightly before or as he enters the pocket zone depth. Figure 11 illustrates the split end's movements depending on the location of the defensive man.

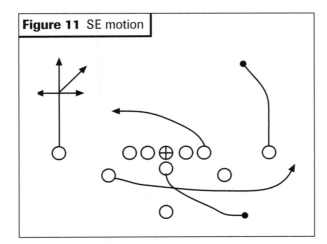

Figure 11 SE motion

On this pattern, the quarterback reads the same man as the split end and anticipates the break of the receiver. The quarterback will throw the pattern off the fifth to the ninth step, depending on the break and depth of the receivers.

The offside slot runs his safety valve pattern off the linebacker in the coverage. He may also be the hot receiver in this pattern.

We run a variety of screens off these two actions. First, we run a screen to the offside split end that involves only a change in blocking for the offside tackle (figure 12). We run a screen to the fullback onside as shown in figure 13. We run a screen to both the onside and offside to the onside slotback, as shown in figure 14.

Another variation of our screen game is to sprint away from motion and run the screen back to the motion back, as shown in figure 15. We also run a middle screen (figure 16) to the onside slot—and to our fullback.

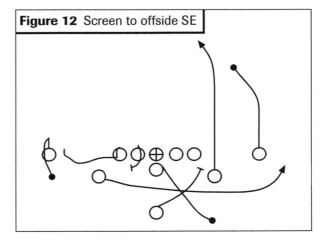

Figure 12 Screen to offside SE

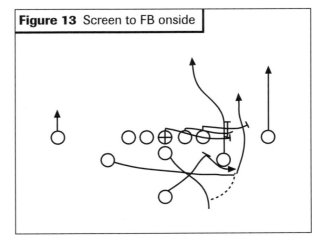

Figure 13 Screen to FB onside

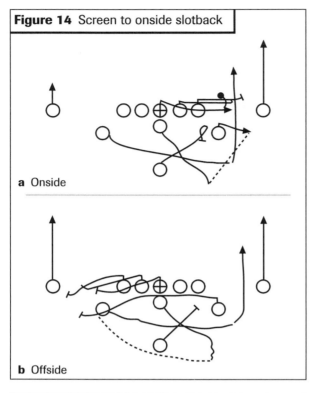

Figure 14 Screen to onside slotback

a Onside

b Offside

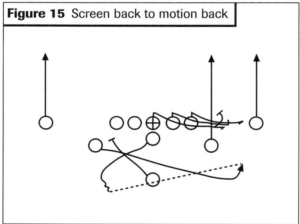

Figure 15 Screen back to motion back

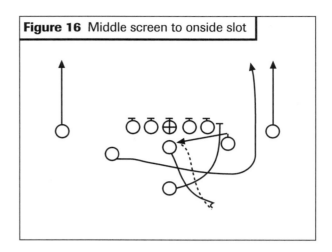

Figure 16 Middle screen to onside slot

We run a no-motion package passing attack that has been outstanding for us. In closing, I believe the basic reason for success in the passing game is belief in the passing game. If you base your attack on it, you must spend the necessary time to be successful with it. If it is to supplement a running attack, recognize that. It seems to me the teams that have the most problems moving the football are those not noted for any one phase of offense. We feel we will realize the greatest success with a sound plan to attack any defense, a commitment to that plan, and the best players available to execute the plan.

1976 Summer Manual. Darrel Davis is head coach at Portland State University.

Adjusting Pass Patterns

LaVell Edwards

We are committed to the forward pass as our means of offensive football. Our passing attack is basically five-fold:

1. We try to protect the passer at all times. Our efforts are to devise schemes that will protect the passer, leaving little to chance.

2. We control the football with the forward pass. We emphasize throwing the ball downfield, but we also emphasize the short and intermediate passing game.

3. We run to set up the pass, and we pass to set up the run. We run the draw to slow down the hard upfield pass rush and run wide to take advantage of the soft corners, who are more concerned about pass coverage than about run support.

4. We always strive to take advantage of what the defense gives us. We guard against being greedy and going for the long ball if it's not there, or forcing the ball into coverage. We try to execute and be patient and attack the inherent weaknesses in any defensive scheme.

5. We always try to KISS it. The acronym, as I'm sure you all know, is "Keep It Simple, Stupid." We try to show the defensive team as many different looks as we possibly can while still running the same routes and plays over and over again.

My focus today is on the specific adjustments that we make during particular pass patterns. For the sake of clarity, let me define two terms for you. A *pass route* is the route run by an individual. A *pass pattern* is the total package of pass routes run by the various receivers.

We feel that the halfback in our offense must be a versatile athlete who can block, run, and catch the football. He must also be smart and alert, as we give him a number of pattern adjustments. For example, figure 1 shows our HB read option from our basic formation. Note that he aligns as wide as possible, often directly behind the offensive tackle or at least splitting the inside leg of the tackle. We also have him in a two-point stance, as we do with our wide receivers. His width allows him to release better into the pass pattern, and his stance allows him to see the linebackers and coverages a little better.

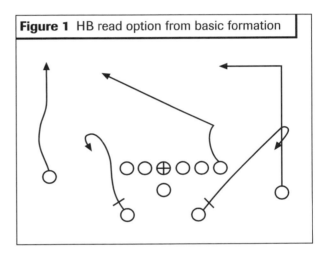

Figure 1 HB read option from basic formation

We realize that the takeoff of the backs and receivers is not as explosive. However, in our specific situation, we are willing to make a trade-off. We feel it is extremely important to recognize coverage, and we work hard on our get-off from a two-point stance to compensate for what we may lack in explosiveness.

Figure 1 illustrates how we attempt to vertically stretch a defense. The single WR runs a fly with an outside release. The inside of the two receivers runs six to eight yards upfield from an inside release, then plants and aims for a point 15-17 yards downfield in an area that, we hope, has been vacated by the single receiver. The outside receiver on the two-receiver side runs a 20-yard in route. The pattern is a weak side flood or dig pattern; however, this 20-yard in route is crucial for us in man-to-man coverage. There is a large void area because most of the coverage is weak, and this route, if run properly, should be good for a 20-yard advantage in man-to-man coverage. The FB runs an arrow, again to help facilitate the 20-yard in to the outside receiver. The QB's progression is to the HB, to the crossing route, and to the clearing route, in that order.

As the primary receiver, the HB has to be able to make the appropriate reads. If the defense is in a 3-4 alignment and the weak outside and weak inside linebackers drop in a strong invert coverage, then he finds an open area approximately six yards deep. Splitting the two linebackers, he turns and readies himself to catch the football (figure 2). If they have some type of weak roll coverage or two-deep five-under zone coverage with the outside linebacker rushing, then he finds a hole between the corner in the weak flat and the weak inside linebacker's drop (figure 3).

Please remember our original premise that the pass protection is solid. Thus, in this scheme, the left guard would block the rushing LB.

If the defense is in some type of man-to-man coverage, then the HB releases hard, using pressure in an attempt to get as close as he can to the defender. He is allowed to go either inside or outside, depending on the position of the defender.

Figure 4 shows the HB's route versus a man with FS coverage and the weak outside LB on a blitz. If the inside LB rushes, the only change is that the HB must now run his route versus the weak outside LB rather than the inside LB. This same adjustment applies in any man-to-man coverage, regardless of whether the defense has one or two safeties free (two-deep, four-under man). As illustrated, there is a lot of field to work with versus man coverage, as everyone has cleared out of the area.

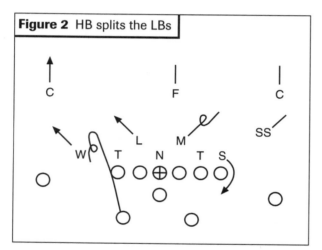

Figure 2 HB splits the LBs

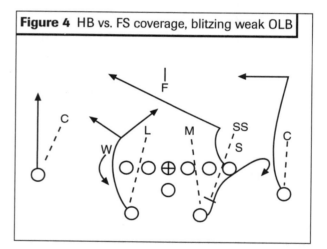

Figure 4 HB vs. FS coverage, blitzing weak OLB

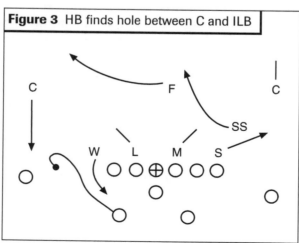

Figure 3 HB finds hole between C and ILB

Man blitz coverage presents the problem of pass protection if the defense decides to rush both weak outside and inside LBs at the snap and chooses to cover the HB with the FS (figure 5). In this situation, the HB breaks hard on a shallow flat right along the LOS and, we hope, the FS has a long way to go to tackle him. If he misses, a big play unfolds. We immediately throw the ball utilizing the hot principle, as the QB knows that there will be a defender unblocked and that the HB will look immediately. He must deliver the ball before the defender reaches the HB.

Figure 5 HB covered by FS

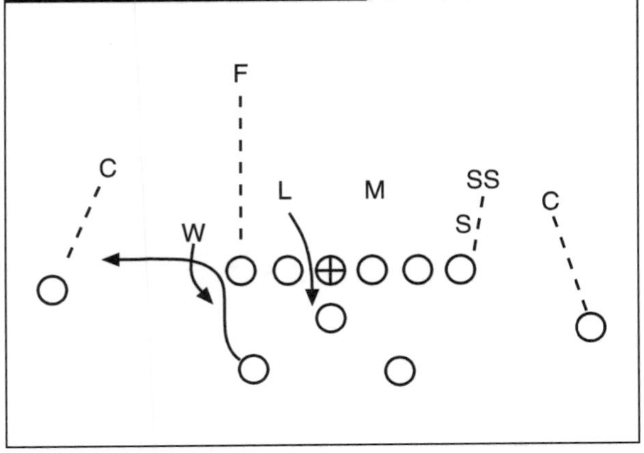

If the defense chooses to take away the HB by squeezing him on his route with both weak LBs (figure 6), the read then goes to the inside double receiver, who should find a hole on his intermediate route.

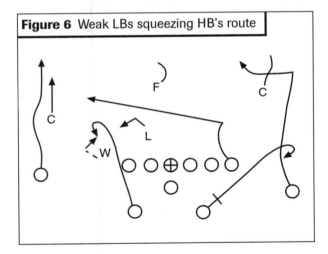

Figure 6 Weak LBs squeezing HB's route

It would be ideal if we saw only a straight 34 defense; unfortunately, this isn't the case. The reduced front and 43 front also are popular defensive fronts that need to be dealt with. Again, the critical factor is the pass protection. Figure 7 outlines a reduced front off of a 34 front.

If we decide to block the center to the strong side and allow the HB to block the weak inside LB if he rushes, then the hot principle is the read. The HB has no blocking assignment but releases, watching the LB. If the LB rushes, he turns outside immediately along the LOS, expecting the FS to cover him (figure 8). If the LB

drops, then he finds a void between the weak flat coverage and the weak inside LB. Figure 9 shows a weak roll, which, along with two-deep coverage, can usually be expected with this front.

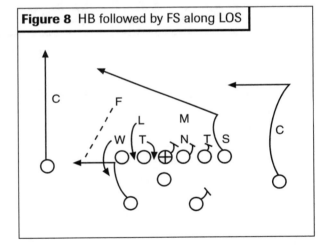

Figure 7 Reduced front off 34 front

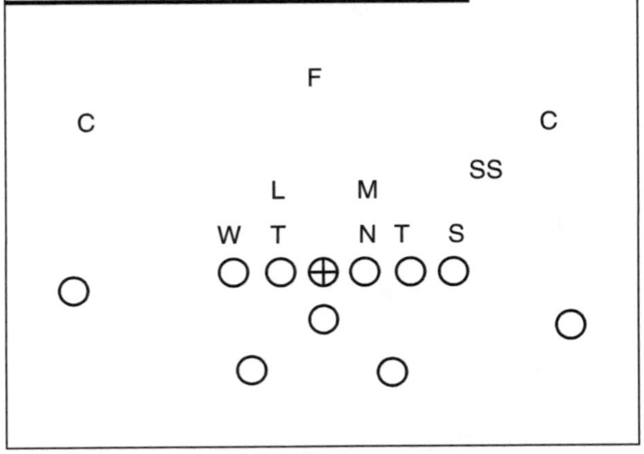

Figure 8 HB followed by FS along LOS

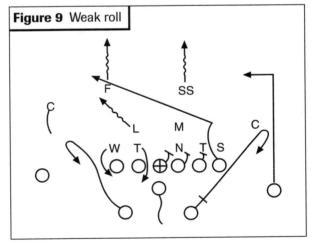

Figure 9 Weak roll

If we decide to block the center to the weak side, then the HB knows that he does not have a blocking assignment. If the weak inside backer rushes, the HB does not have to flatten his route at the LOS, but rather can run his regular route, usually against the FS (the route will be deeper and with more technique), knowing that if he beats the FS, he could possibly score (figure 10).

We hope we have discussed enough coverages to give you a feel for our adjustment philosophy. This pass pattern has been a good one for us and allows us a good pattern, regardless of the type of defense we anticipate or encounter.

Figure 10 HB runs regular route against FS

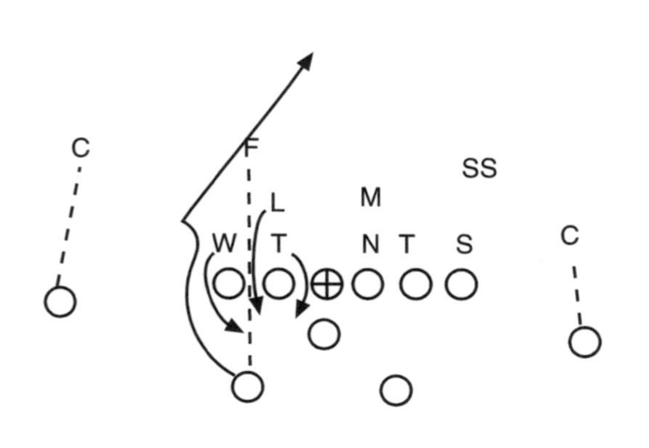

1985 Proceedings. LaVell Edwards is head coach at Brigham Young University.

Spreading the Defense

Jim Wacker

A few years ago, when I would speak at different clinics, it was about veer option football. We ran that offense for 19 years and had a tremendous amount of success during that time, winning four national championships at the Division II level. But I still believe in the veer and in the option. If you are going to base your offense on the run, that is still the way to go.

In the 1988 season, we had a lot of disappointment and did not execute well offensively, so we decided to make a drastic change. At that time, we decided to go to the one-back offense, spread receivers out all over the field, and throw the football first and run it second. A lot of people thought I was crazy, and I'm not sure they weren't right. But we have had a lot of fun, and it has opened up new vistas as far as studying the game of football is concerned.

Once again, I want to stress that I am only sharing some ideas. Like I said, I probably have a lot more questions that I do answers, but I will be open and honest with you as to what we are trying to do at TCU with our passing attack.

Why go to the "one-back, no-back" passing attack? The first reason is simply that it is a formation made for the passing game. The more you can spread out the defense, the easier it is to throw the ball. There are several reasons for this. The first, and maybe the most important, is that it is easier to read blitz when you are in a one-back or no-back formation. If the defense has to cover four or five receivers on the line of scrimmage, that means the maximum that they can bring is either six or seven. If our quarterback does a good job recognizing a blitz, we should minimize the number of sacks and have a chance of really putting a lot of points on the board.

When they blitz you in the "one-back, no-back," they turn the game into high-stakes poker. As long as you have a good trigger man, you've got a good chance of making the scoreboard explode.

The second reason we like to spread the defense is because it opens routes for short, horizontal patterns. The simplest pattern in the world is to run four or five receivers, stop them all at seven yards, and throw to the guy who looks open. You spread them out in the Trips formation on the hash, with three wide receivers to the field and two into the short side. In the middle of the field, you can go two and two or three and two, but the defense is forced to go out and cover them.

Obviously, it is important to throw any time you have an uncovered receiver, and we motion to get to the no-back offense a lot of times in order to take advantage of mistakes by the defense. If they make a mistake and we get an uncovered receiver, it's the shortest, quickest, easiest throw in football. We have had some of those turn into really big plays for us. The following are some examples of the short passing game from the one-back and no-back formations.

Figure 1 is a Pro-right formation with fly motion, which puts our "B" back in motion toward the tight end. We then run five step routes for a quick horizontal stretch and the quarterback throws to the guy he thinks is going to be the most open. If they blitz, obviously, he can go to any one of the five receivers because it is a three-step route. We will run this same route with corner routes by the number two receiver to one side and the number three receiver to the other. This now puts a vertical stretch on the defense as well.

In figure 2, three receivers are on stop routes and the two inside receivers are on corner routes. It is excellent against cover 2 or one free, and you can really burn the defense with a deep corner as long as the quarterback has time. Of course, if he is feeling pressure, he will take it to one of the short stops underneath. Both of these routes are excellent against the blitz because the quarterback can unload the ball in a hurry.

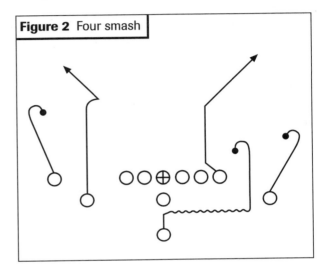

Figure 2 Four smash

The second big advantage of spreading the defense is to use the philosophy of putting receivers "low, high, and take the top off the coverage." We structure a lot of our passing game around this particular principle. An example would be 84 stretch (figure 3).

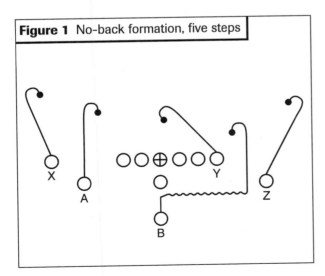

Figure 1 No-back formation, five steps

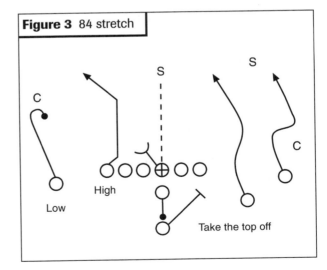

Figure 3 84 stretch

In 84 stretch, you simply read the corner. If the corner plays under the corner route, the quarterback hits the stop. If the corner plays the stop, he throws high to the tight end on the corner route. If we see the free safety breaking off the hash trying to help on the corner, we tell the quarterback to read stretch, and he will look to the pole route by our slotback.

This same principle can be incorporated into a number of different formations and different patterns. When you are trying to attack any kind of zone coverage, I think it is always good to think "low, high, and take the top off the coverage."

Figure 4 is an example of 334, a vertical stretch pattern. On our 334 pattern, we run two receivers down the hash marks and two receivers deep down the sideline and basically key the free safety. If he plays in the deep middle, we should be able to hit the A-back underneath as he is running a jump route down near the hash mark.

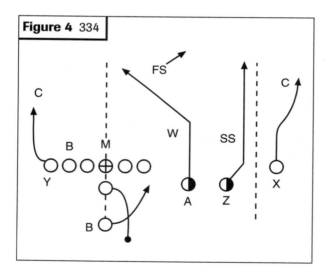

Figure 4 334

If the free safety jumps the A-back, we will take a shot at our Z, who is running the far hash. If either corner overlaps, we will throw to one of the wide receivers on the outside. If they are playing a lot of man-to-man, we will again try to hit the A-back against one free, but we will try to check out of this pattern if they blitz. Another very effective complementary route is to run the B-back on either a flat, an option, or a delay, depending on linebacker under-coverage.

We employ this same principle from Pro formation in the middle of the field. Now we have two receivers on either side of the quarterback running the verticals. This means our X and Z run the deep routes down the sidelines, and our Y (tight end) and our slotback run the verticals down the hash marks. Again we fake 34 or 35 action and throw quickly if the play side tight end opens early, or we look back to the number two inside receiver if the free safety jumps the play side route. The entire one-back passing attack is designed around this vertical stretch principle, and everything else works itself under that big umbrella.

Another version of the vertical stretch is 334 switch (figure 5). Again we run four verticals. If the play side tight end opens early, we throw him the ball. If he doesn't open, we can throw either to the flanker in the side pocket on the strong side or we can look for throwback. If we look for throwback, the X is running the hash mark and the slotback is running the wheel down the sideline. Both of these are option routes.

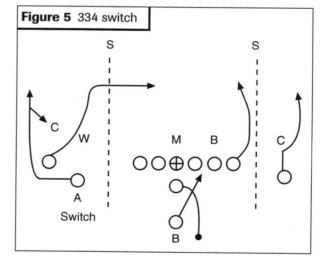

Figure 5 334 switch

If it is cover 3, the X receiver will run deep down the hash, look for the ball, and try to catch it in the seam between the free safety and the corner. If it is cover 2, he will set the route down at about 15 to 18 yards and look for a throwing window inside of the Will linebacker.

The A-back also runs an option. If it is man-to-man coverage, he will either take the top off the coverage, running hard up the sideline, or he will "set it down" on his wheel pattern. The 34-35 play-action ties in well because it looks exactly like a zone dive, our base running play. The quarterback then simply reads the coverage and tries to find the open receiver.

Another way that we work "low, high, and take the top off the coverage" is with our curl and spear route (figure 6). This is a five-step pattern, and the quarterback will now read the Will linebacker. If he cushions the curl, we will throw to the slotback on the spear. If he works through to cover the spear, we will throw to X on the curl.

The tight end will run a post pattern across the face of the free safety in order to keep him out of the curl area. If the free safety tries to rob the curl to X, we will throw the post to the tight end. We will also sometimes motion the B-back toward the tight end and then run him on a quick spear to uncover the strong side curl pattern. This would put us in a no-back formation, and the quarterback can read the same pattern to either side.

The "low, high, and take the top off the coverage" concept can be developed throughout the entire passing game. If you are using

Figure 6 Curl and spear

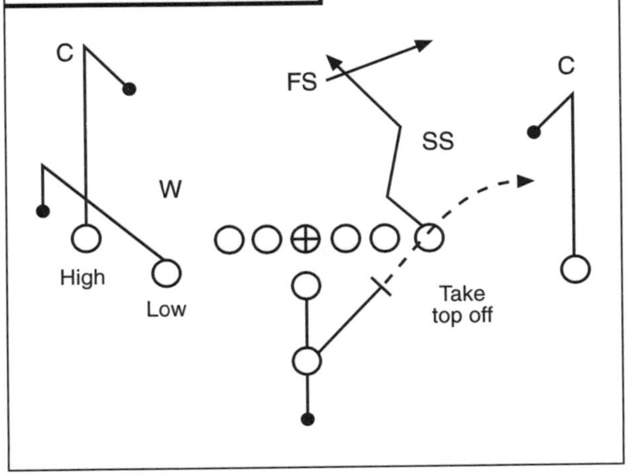

this concept against zone coverage, the receivers always work to find a throwing lane inside of the linebackers. If it is man-to-man coverage, the receivers turn the pattern into a runaway, which means they simply run their patterns across the field. Running away from the nearest defender, who is covering them, is the easiest pattern to hit against man coverage. This has been an easy rule for our receivers to remember.

1992 Proceedings. Jim Wacker was head coach at Texas Christian University in Ft. Worth, TX.

Passing to Win

Steve Spurrier

I am a firm believer in the "Seven Steps to Success" developed by Georgia Tech's athletic director, Dr. Homer Rice. They are:

1. Make a commitment.
2. Set a target date to achieve your goal.
3. Assemble the ingredients to be successful.
4. Give of yourself.
5. Visualize your goal being accomplished.
6. Believe it will happen.

7. Expect your goals to happen.

Our practice time involves about 75 percent passing and 25 percent running. Sometimes I think we spend too much time on the running game. We work on new run plays each week that usually don't gain many yards or never get called. Our lead draw play has been our best run since I've been an offensive coordinator or head coach the past eight years.

During two-a-days, we throw at both practices. We believe our QBs will not get sore arms if they are using the proper throwing motion.

Throwing a football is a natural throwing motion that should not require a QB to ice his arm after practice or games.

Our offensive philosophy here is to use the pass to set up the run. We pass first and run second. One coach commented that we treat first down as if it were third and long. Actually, we try to throw on first down with some type of play-action hoping for a 15-20 yard gain, but we are content with a 6-8 yard gain. Our offensive talent is such that we have a much better chance of throwing an eight-yard completion than running for eight yards.

Also, we have tried very hard to eliminate the bad things (sacks, interceptions, and penalties) that go along with 45 pass attempts per game. Our interception percentage was only four percent, and we lost only 15 yards per game in sacks.

Our passing statistics say we gain 7.8 yards every pass attempt, and our run statistics say we gain 3.3 yards every running attempt. So, obviously, as the play caller, I call more passes than runs.

The three most important aspects of any successful passing team are:

1. Can they control the ball?
2. Can they make first downs?
3. Can they stay on the field?

Our sprint draw passing probably looks like just about everyone's, but I think one reason we've had so much success is that we throw to the TB more than other teams. We believe that in any good passing attack the backs should catch as many passes as the wide receivers. We also release our wide receivers on an inside angle when running the post and middle route, which is different from most teams.

Our preference for throwing against a 3-deep zone would be the wide field curl. The preference for a Z-deep zone would be the short-field corner. If the coverage takes away the wide receivers, we try to immediately find the TB and get rid of the ball. Figure 1 shows our wide field curl against a 3-deep zone. We try to hit Z or Y, then back to TB.

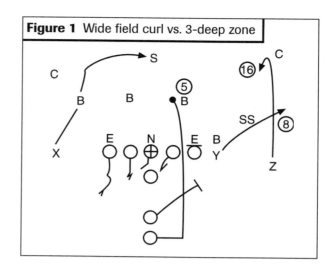

Figure 1 Wide field curl vs. 3-deep zone

Figure 2 shows our short-field corner against a Z-deep zone. We try to hit X or Y, then back to TB. Figure 3 shows our middle route against a 3-deep zone. We look for Z if no safety deep, then X, then Y or TB. Since all four receivers are in view, this is not all that difficult for the QB.

Our protection scheme, and the results, has been so good over the years that we continue with the basic turn-back protection principles. When expecting blitz, we like to get into a twin formation and throw Z a post or corner route (figure 4). This protecting gives us a chance to block eight rushers.

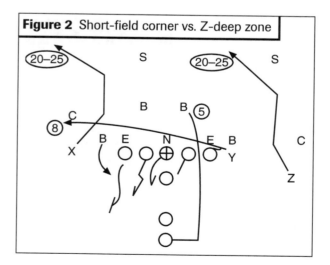

Figure 2 Short-field corner vs. Z-deep zone

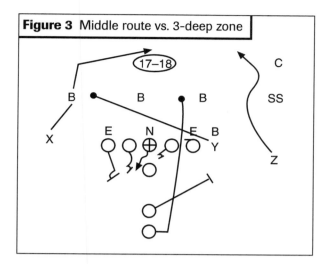

Figure 3 Middle route vs. 3-deep zone

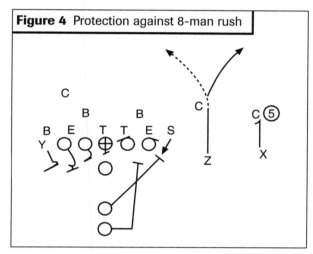

Figure 4 Protection against 8-man rush

These are a couple of our patterns against a 3-deep zone and a 2-deep zone. Again we want to throw curls against 3-deep (figure 6) and corners against 2-deep (figure 7).

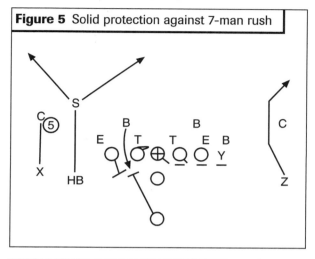

Figure 5 Solid protection against 7-man rush

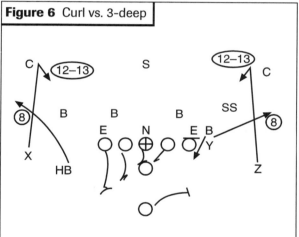

Figure 6 Curl vs. 3-deep

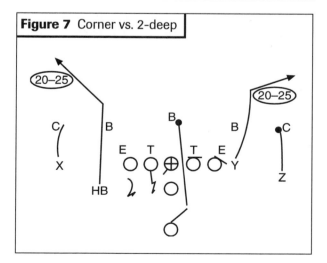

Figure 7 Corner vs. 2-deep

The other protection from the one-back formation is our solid protection (figure 5). This is designed to handle seven rushers. The center must bump towards the four-man rush side. The one-back is responsible for the weak outside LB. This protection is needed when teams rush two LBs from either side. It also gives you the maximum protection as a one-back formation.

In our one-back passing game, we use two protections. Our slide protection is designed for only four rushers but can protect three from each side. It is the same as sprint draw protection to the offensive line. The one-back has a double read from the inside LB to the outside LB. This protection is designed to get four receivers out quickly with no blocking responsibilities.

If we get eight rushers when in a one-back formation, we go to the 3-deep pass and the offensive line blocks the inside gap area, the back goes weak, and Y also blocks inside (figure 8). We allow the wide rushers to come free, expecting the ball to be already thrown.

To have a highly successful offense, it must appear complicated to the opponent but must be simple for the coaches to teach and easy for the players to learn.

We don't throw 45 times a game to run up our passing statistics. We do it to help us win games. We have a system that reduces sacks, penalties, and interceptions and gives Duke University its best chance to be competitive and continue to have winning seasons.

Figure 8 3-deep pass

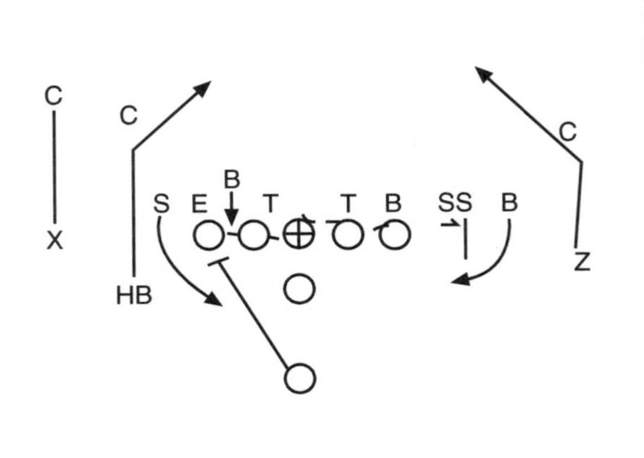

1989 Proceedings. Steve Spurrier was head coach at Duke University. Spurrier is head coach at Florida.

Striking With a Strong-Side Screen

Darryl Rogers

The strong side screen is a simple screen that is compatible with our overall passing game. It offers a change up, at times limits the rush, and its base pattern makeup is identical to our dropback game. The most difficult aspect of this screen (or any screen) is to create the illusion that the play is a regular dropback pass.

Quarterback

We attempt to accomplish this illusion by first emphasizing the QB's action (figure 1) and, as on all pass plays, we are primarily concerned with what he does with his eyes and his feet. On the snap, he is to rivet and lock his eyes on a specific member of the defense (for example, the inside LB) until his right foot hits the ground the fourth time. At this time, he is to stop and stay stationary for one full count; then, and

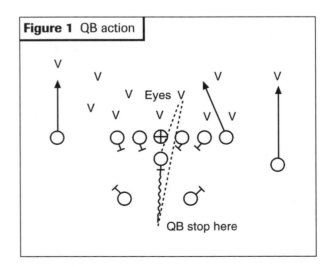

Figure 1 QB action

only then, will he continue to retreat looking to his screen back, delivering the ball if the back is open, throwing the ball away if the back is covered.

This stopping action of the QB is extremely important and is to be timed up with the offensive center and guard action, for they should begin their release and lateral movement only after this stop. Due to various schemes and covers, the ball will actually be thrown downfield if certain situations leave receivers uncovered, so what we have here really is two separate passes: the regular dropback and the screen.

Screen Back

For the screen back, the relationship with the pulling guard has great importance, as does blitz pickup responsibility. If the screen back's LB does not blitz, the screen back steps inside his tackle (versus an outside rush) and immediately locks his eyes on the onside guard. When the guard pulls (and not before), the back should pull and stay inside and back of the guard, maintaining this position while looking for the ball on his outside shoulder. When the ball is released by the QB, the back yells "GO" to signal the linemen to turn upfield (figure 2).

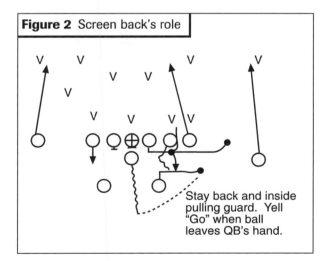

Figure 2 Screen back's role

Stay back and inside pulling guard. Yell "Go" when ball leaves QB's hand.

If the screen back gets a blitz from his assigned LB, he steps up to deliver a solid pass-protection block (figure 3). We prefer to block the blitzer to the inside, but many times the rush is so wide this is not possible, and in this case an inside out chip block is permissible. The problem when the LB blitzes is to get the correct

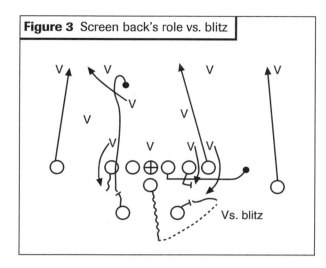

Figure 3 Screen back's role vs. blitz

Vs. blitz

relationship with the pulling guard, as the tendency is for the back to get too far outside the guard. This problem can be helped by having the back come off of the chip block a bit slow to give the guard time to get in front.

Offside Back

The offside back has blitz responsibility on his side, plus block responsibility on his inside LB. If his LB blitzes, he blocks inside out with a pass protection technique. No blitz, he gets an inside position or blocks tough on the inside LB.

Tight End

The TE is responsible for the first LB to his inside. If the LB goes man on him, the TE will run him across the field. If the LB hangs or goes zone, the TE works for an outside in position so he can cut him off (figure 4). On occasion, we instruct the TE to block tough on his LB if it's predetermined that the ball will be thrown back of the LOS.

Wide Receivers

The wide receivers run a route away from the striking point if the corners go man (figure 5). If the coverage is zone, the wide receivers push the corners and then stalk block the corners. Versus a corner roll or two-deep defense (zone), it will be ruled as a zone.

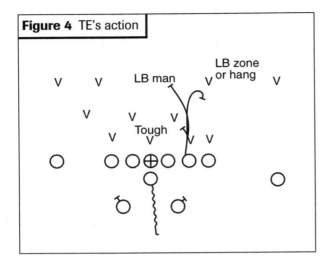

Figure 4 TE's action

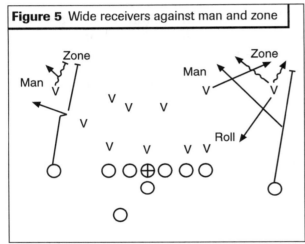

Figure 5 Wide receivers against man and zone

Center and Guards

The center pass blocks until the QB hangs up, then pulls to the play side and is responsible to the inside, then up. The strong guard pass

1979 Proceedings. Darryl Rogers was head coach at Michigan State.

blocks until the QB hangs up, then pulls to the play side and is responsible to the outside, then up. This guard junction blocks his man, meaning he blocks the man's outside hip with his inside shoulder no matter where the man is unless his man forces hard; then the guard kicks out. The weak guard pass blocks until the QB hangs up, then pulls to the play side and is responsible for any trailer near the screen back, then upfield.

Tackles

The tackles execute regular pass blocks and cut at the last moment if the rush dictates (figure 6).

Routes and blocking assignments will change depending on the various fronts and covers that are presented, but basically this is our strong side screen and the fundamental points that we use in teaching the play.

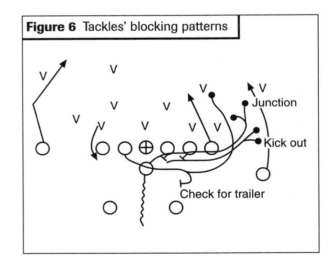

Figure 6 Tackles' blocking patterns

Adding the Action Pass

Herb Deromedi

This football program built its reputation by emphasizing a strong defense and commitment to the running game. However, in order to balance an offensive attack, coordinating the running game with the play-action pass can bring excellent results.

A strong running game can be advantageous to a football team for

1. ball control,
2. short-yardage and goal line situations,
3. the ability to perform in adverse conditions, and
4. the opportunities it provides for the "action pass."

Briefly, a ball-control offense enables your team to keep the opponent's offense off the field, rest your defense, frustrate the opponent, and use the clock to your advantage. A strong running attack has proven beneficial in short-yardage and/or goal line situations when defenses load up, and it takes away the ability to spread a secondary vertically.

The ability to run the ball can become a necessity when weather conditions (wind, rain, field, etc.) make passing ineffective. Finally, when an opponent concentrates on stopping the run, the opportunity to throw the play-action pass can be an effective weapon.

As we prepare our play-action pass package, we emphasize these coaching points:

1. If a running play is good in our offense, we want to design a play-action pass to supplement it. The play does not necessarily mean that the quarterback must throw the ball, but passes to running backs and receivers can and should be considered.

2. Factors such as down and distance, field position, score, and time on the clock dictate when the action pass is most effective. Throw when the defense anticipates a run. Throw when your self-scouting shows that you are a running team.

3. Sell the fake in order to get the defense to react to the run. This may mean involving your offensive line, ballcarriers, quarterback, or receivers.

4. Time the route of a receiver so that he is open when the passer is ready to throw the football. How many times have you seen a receiver break open too soon, only to have the defender recover before the ball arrives on target?

5. Initially, put the play-action pass against air (no defense). Work out the details of technique and timing, but practice all play-action passes versus the defense in run down-and-distance situations.

To illustrate, I have selected several basic running plays in our offense, along with a corresponding pass play that we use (figures 1, 2, and 3).

In closing, although these plays are basic, they were effective for our program. I am confident that with a little imagination and work, you can complement your running game with the play-action pass.

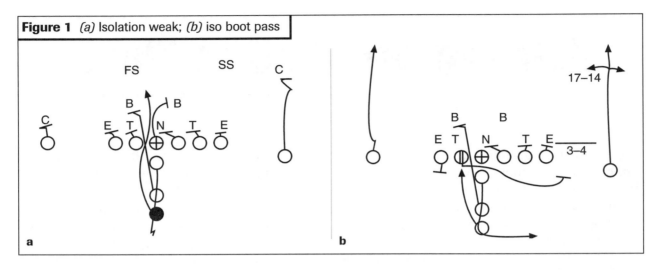

Figure 1 *(a)* Isolation weak; *(b)* iso boot pass

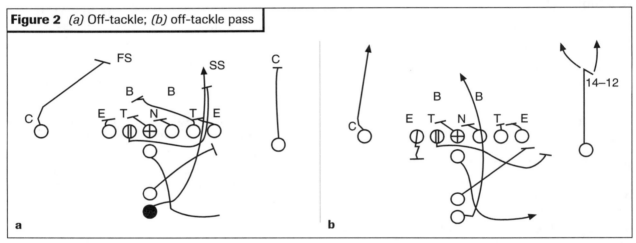

Figure 2 *(a)* Off-tackle; *(b)* off-tackle pass

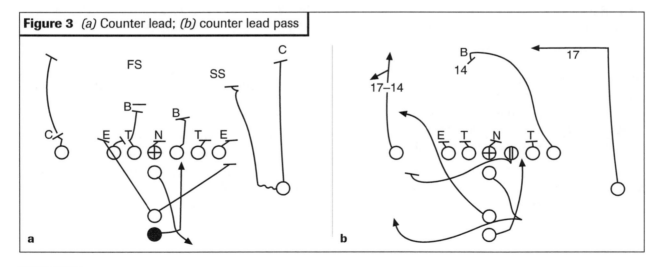

Figure 3 *(a)* Counter lead; *(b)* counter lead pass

1991 Proceedings. Herb Deromedi was head coach at Central Michigan University. He is athletic director at Central Michigan.

Moving the Pocket

Rich Brooks

At Oregon, we strive to develop a balanced offense. This year, we came as close as any team I have had in my 13 years at Oregon. In the Pacific-10, we finished second in passing offense, third in rushing offense, second in total offense, and first in scoring. We feel good about this balance and believe our play-action passing game was an integral reason for our success.

The play-action pass has contributed to our success in two distinct ways. First, the run fake holds the underneath coverage from getting quick, deep drops that would take away our medium-range passing game. Second, the pass after a run fake eliminates some aggressiveness from the run support.

This has put our offensive line in a more successful position to run and pass block. Our play-action passing game does not allow defenses to pin their ears back and take away our running game.

The success we had with our play-action attack on first down and in obvious running situations has enabled us to keep defenses guessing and, consequently, gain an advantage with both our run and pass in these situations.

We develop our play-action passes from our running game. The four play-action passes I have chosen to explain come off of three running plays: the counter, cut, and slice.

Counter Strong

In blocking for the counter strong play (figure 1), the onside tackle and TE will combo block the DE and offside linebacker. The onside guard will angle block to the offside. The center will angle block to the offside. The offside guard will pull and trap the first man past the offensive tackle. The offside tackle will pull through the four-five hole for the onside linebacker.

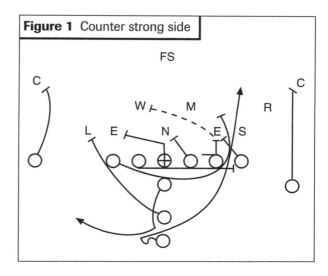

Figure 1 Counter strong side

The QB opens offside and hands deep to the tailback. He then boots away from the call. The tailback will skip step away from the call and take an outside handoff. He will then run to daylight. The fullback will fill for the offside pulling tackle. The flanker and split end block the cornerbacks to their sides.

We have two play-action passes off of the counter play. First is the waggle pass, which attacks the strong side.

Waggle Pass

For the waggle pass (figure 2), we use an aggressive man blocking scheme for the entire line. Our linemen will step aggressively at their assignments, trying to sell the run fake.

The QB reverse pivots at six o'clock, fakes an outside handoff, and boots around the end, attacking the perimeter. The quarterback should take his time on the fake and allow the play to develop. He can pull up if the contain forces him to. The QB will key the rover to the strong flat. His reading progression is: fullback, tight end, flanker, split end, all on the run.

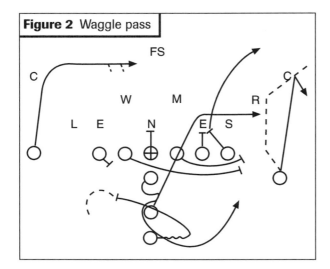

Figure 2 Waggle pass

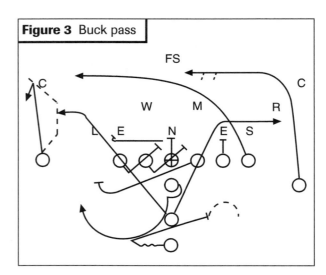

Figure 3 Buck pass

The tailback will skip step sideways toward the direction of the call. He will fake the counter handoff and check to see if the weak inside or outside linebacker dogs. If neither dogs, he will continue on his path and run the back side screen. The fullback will drive through the play side "B" gap and run a five-yard flat pattern.

The tight end will slam release inside and push upfield to a depth of 15 yards, then angle behind the cornerback, being sure to never come underneath him. The tight end should try to stretch the cornerback as much as possible against any three-deep or man coverage. Versus any two-deep coverage, the tight end will still push to his 15 yard depth, but then he will turn out and sit on the hash, being sure not to drift to the sideline.

Versus any three-deep or man coverage, the flanker will run a 20-yard comeback along the sideline. Versus any two-deep coverage, he will run a corner route away from the safety. The split end will do a 16-18 yard deep in route, finding the open void versus zone coverage or continue to cross the field versus man coverage.

Buck Pass

The second play that comes off of our counter play is the buck pass (figure 3). This is a weak side attacking play.

We will use an aggressive man blocking scheme that looks like our counter play with cross pulling of our guards.

The quarterback will use the same procedure he used in the waggle pass. The difference is that he will key the weak side outside linebacker to the weak flat, and his reading progression is fullback, split end, tight end, flanker, and then run. The quarterback must be ready to pull up quickly and deliver the pass. The contain or force will come much faster from the weak side.

The tailback will skip step toward the direction of the call and fake the handoff. He will check strong side middle backer to outside backer, then check to see if the rover is blitzing. If none of these people rush, he will continue on his path and run the back side screen. The fullback will also do as he did on the waggle pass but run through the weak side "EB" gap.

The tight end will release inside and angle 20 yards deep to the opposite hash. Once he reaches the hash, he will flatten out and run toward the sideline. This pattern is not affected by coverage. The flanker will run a 16-18 yard in route. He will find the open void versus zone coverage or continue to cross the field versus man coverage. This is the same as the split end did on the waggle pass. The split end will run a 20-yard comeback route versus three-deep or man coverage. He will run the corner route versus any two-deep coverage.

Cut and Cut Pass

In the cut play (figure 4), the entire offensive line will use a man blocking scheme. The QB

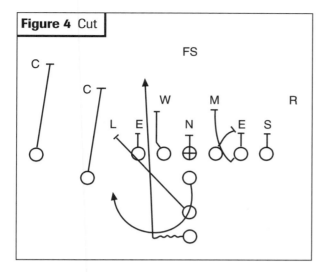

Figure 4 Cut

reverse pivots at six o'clock and hands deep to the tailback. The tailback will skip step square to LOS, receive the handoff, and run to daylight. The fullback will lead step at the inside foot of the tackle and kick out the end man on the LOS. The flanker and split end will each block the cornerback to his side.

The cut pass (figure 5) comes from our weak side cut play. This action has helped us run off tackle to the weak side.

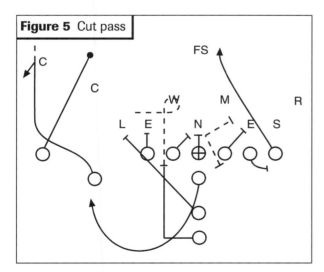

Figure 5 Cut pass

We use an aggressive man blocking scheme on the play side and an area blocking scheme to the offside. The quarterback reverse pivots at six o'clock and fakes the handoff on his third step. He will continue on his path, bootlegging to the side of the call. He will key the free safety to rover and strong outside one-third. His

reading progression is split end, flanker, tailback, run.

The tailback will fake the cut handoff and check the weak inside backer to the outside backer, then leak. The fullback will lead step one foot outside the end man on the LOS and cut him down. The fullback must attack his assignment and not allow penetration.

The tight end will slam release inside and push to the pole between the uprights. He will not look until 33 yards downfield. Versus three-deep or man coverage, the flanker will run a bench route, breaking toward the sideline at 15 yards deep. Versus any two-deep coverage, he will continue running up the sideline and not break out at 15 yards. The split end will run a 14-yard stop route. This pattern will not be affected by coverage.

This play is run from Twin formation. The backs need to be in the backfield for the run fake and blocking purposes.

Slice and Play Pass

In the slice play (figure 6), the onside tight end, tackle, guard, and center will use a man blocking scheme. The offside guard and tackle will block number one and number two on the LOS, respectively.

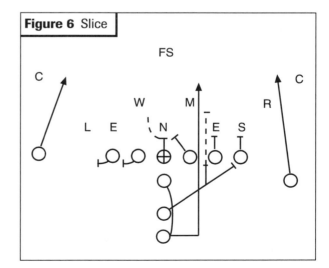

Figure 6 Slice

The QB open steps at six o'clock and hands off deep to the tailback, then boots away from the call. The tailback will skip step in the direction of the call, receive the handoff, and run to daylight. The fullback will take a lateral step and key the block on the defensive end. He will block the first linebacker head up to or outside the guard. The flanker and split end will block the cornerbacks to their sides.

The last play action comes off of our slice running play. This gives us a fake that affects the middle of the defense. For the play pass (figure 7), protection on the play side is an aggressive man blocking scheme, while the back side is an area blocking scheme.

The quarterback reverse pivots at six o'clock and fakes the handoff deep to the tailback. He

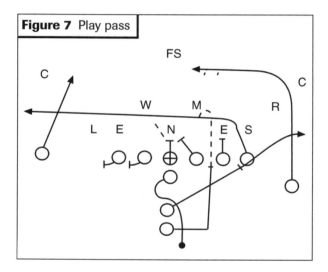

Figure 7 Play pass

drops back and sets up at seven yards behind the onside guard. He will key the free safety to rover and then the strong hook. His reading progression will change depending on man or zone coverage. Versus man coverage, his read is split end, tight end, flanker to fullback. In zone coverage, his read is split end, flanker, tailback to tight end.

The tailback will skip step square to the LOS and fake the slice. He will block the second linebacker from outside in, then leak over the football. The fullback will lead step to the outside leg of the tackle and block the first linebacker from outside in. If the LB doesn't rush, the fullback will run a five-yard flat pattern.

The tight end will take an inside release and drag across the field, gaining ground to a depth of six yards on the opposite sideline. Versus zone coverage, the flanker will run a 16-18 yard in pattern, trying to find open void; versus man coverage, he will continue across the field. The split end will push up the field, aiming at the middle pole between the uprights. He will not look until 33 yards deep. He will try to stretch the middle one-third coverage.

These four play actions can be given any combination of receiver routes. We found changes necessary due to defenses playing our routes on a given play action.

1990 Proceedings. Rich Brooks was head coach at the University of Oregon. Brooks is assistant head coach of the Atlanta Falcons.

Inserting the Play-Action Pass

Gary Moeller

Michigan football is based on good defense and ball-control offense. We want to eliminate mistakes and attempt to force our opponents into mistakes and turnovers. However, we feel the passing game must be an important part of our ball-control offense.

Since we are primarily a running team, we use a play-action fake to control the defensive coverage. We have three basic play-action passes. Our favorite action comes off our off-tackle play (sprint draw). The other actions are option and bootleg. Last year, we ran the off-tackle play more than 200 times, so we use this play-action for the major part of our passing game. We reverse out on our off-tackle play and also on our pass action. We like the reverse pivot (run and pass) because it hides the ball from the defenders, freezing them for a fraction of a second.

Cover the Field

Many play-action passes do not allow you to attack the complete field. To us, this is a top priority in setting up any attack. We do not want to always roll right and throw right, allowing the defense to flood LBs. We must be able to throw to all areas, so the defense has to cover the entire field. I would like to illustrate how we cover most of the field with our four basic passes.

Flanker Out

In the flanker-out play (figure 1), the flanker drives hard to a depth of 12 yards and works back to 10 yards. The comeback allows him to maintain body position on the defensive HB.

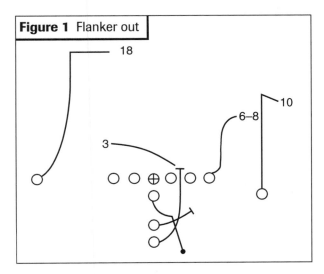

Figure 1 Flanker out

The TE takes an outside release and works six to eight yards deep, at the same time working away from the LB. If the strong safety is in this area, the TE hooks up right next to him. This will hold the SS inside, while our QB throws to the flanker. (The TE must find the void versus zone.) If he reads man-to-man, the TE drives up five yards and breaks sharply to the flat.

The split end runs a square in at a depth of 18 yards, working opposite the Mike or inside linebacker. He finds the void unless it is man, then breaks it off sharp and stays on the move.

The tailback blocks the inside LB if he blitzes. If the inside LB does not blitz, the TB flare controls the Mike LB. We want him to get three yards over the LOS and on the outside of our offensive tackle. We do not want too much depth by the TB; we would rather throw for a three-yard gain and then allow our back to run with the ball. The TB will also be more secure catching the ball knowing he will not get hit just as he catches. Many of our patterns require the TB to flare control underneath coverage in various areas along the LOS.

The QB will take a prealignment key to help him determine who will cover the front side flat. If the SS has the flat, the QB will read his drop and either throw to the flanker or the TE (figure 2).

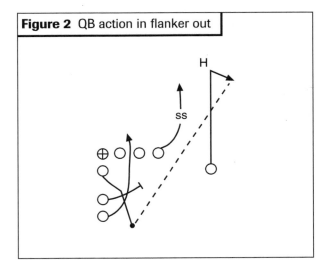

Figure 2 QB action in flanker out

If the flanker's cornerback rolls up, the flanker runs a seam route and the QB can go to the flanker or back to his SE or TB. This route requires a lot of timing by the QB and flanker. We throw it every day against air.

Flanker Square In

The flanker square in (figure 3) is the second pattern in our play-action series. This pattern allows us to throw to the front side hook or curl zone.

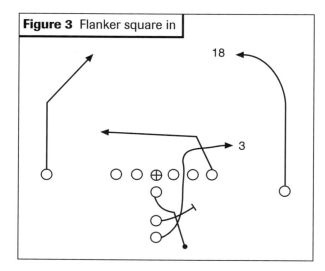

Figure 3 Flanker square in

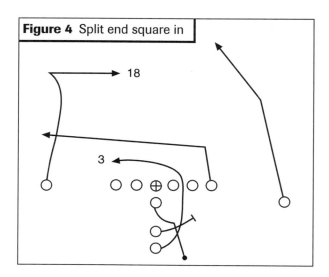

Figure 4 Split end square in

The flanker starts a post cut and then squares to a depth of 18 yards behind the SS and front side LB. As the flanker comes across the formation, he finds the hole in the defense and settles into this void.

The TE runs a crossing pattern at a depth of five yards. He works past the LBs as quickly as possible. If he has man coverage, he drives upfield and breaks off sharply at five yards. Our TE is a primary receiver when he runs a crossing pattern, and he must always be ready for the ball.

The SE runs a post pattern. He must get deep as fast as he can and get behind the FS. The TB runs a flare control pattern to the side of our flanker on the inside LB. This is the same type of route that he ran in the flanker-out pattern, except to the other side of the formation.

The QB takes a prealignment read to find the defender responsible for the middle one-third of the field. When he is set after the snap, he must check the SE for the post. He will then go to the flanker if the post is covered. If the underneath coverage has dropped deep and covered the flanker square in, the QB must dump off the ball to the TB.

Split End Square In

This third pass in our play-action package is very similar to the flanker square. The split end square in (figure 4) has the same basic reads for the QB, except to the opposite side of the formation. We now have two patterns similar in reads, making it easier for our QB to execute.

The flanker runs a post route through the middle one-third of the field. He drives hard to get behind all defenders quickly. The TE runs a crossing pattern as he did in the flanker square in.

The SE runs a square in pattern at a depth of 18 yards. He must find the hole in the coverage, working opposite the Mike LB. As he drives off the deep coverage, he must snap his head around to find the location of the Mike LB.

As with the flanker square in pattern, the prealignment read should tell the QB who will be the middle one-third defender. After the snap, he must confirm this defender and check the flanker post route. If the post route is covered, the QB will go to the SE. If the LBs have deep drops, he then dumps the ball to the TB. Some coverages will leave the TE open, and when our QB feels this, he gives the ball to the TE.

Split End Out

The split end out pattern (figure 5) is the fourth and final pass in our basic play-action passes. It is also a big pattern in forcing the defense to take honest drops. In other words, it forces the defense to cover the entire field. This pass allows us to throw in the complete opposite direction of our play-action fake.

The flanker runs the flanker square in route, and we throw back to him only if the SE and TE are covered. The TE runs a crossing route to a depth of five yards and controls the weak flat.

The SE runs a comeback out to a depth of 20 yards, then back to 17 yards. This route should appear to the defensive back as though the SE

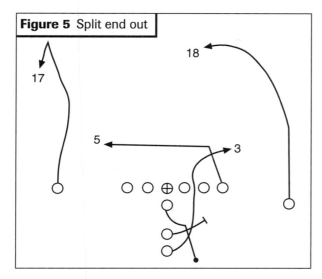

Figure 5 Split end out

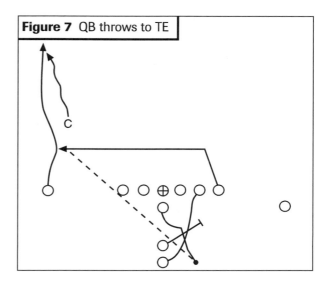

Figure 7 QB throws to TE

is running a deep route. If the cornerback rolls up in the flat and we get four-two deep coverage, the SE runs a seam route.

The QB must take a prealignment read to find out who is responsible for the weak side flat. After the snap, he must confirm this read and throw opposite the flat defender. It is a high-low read, hitting the SE if the weak defender doesn't get depth (figure 6). If he gets good depth, then the QB will hit the TE (figure 7).

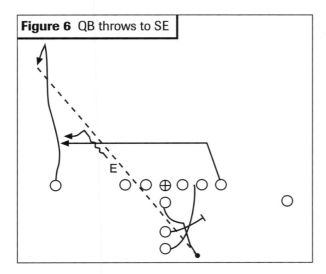

Figure 6 QB throws to SE

As I indicated earlier, the important thing about any attack is that it must cover the entire field. If you chart the play-action attack we just discussed, you will find the field is covered and the defense is forced to take honest drops.

Another important factor in the passing game is that we do not want the reads very difficult for our QB. It is hard for any QB to set in a pocket and throw a route under pressure. So the sooner he makes a decision as to where he should throw, the more effectively he will throw. We feel our high-low read theory for the QB is as simple as we can make it. It is very easy for a coach to diagram and think of a number of pass routes, and sometimes we all become too creative. The secret to a good passing attack is the same as to a good running attack: good technique. Maybe a more important secret is repetition; the more your QB repeats these passes, the better chance he has to become good. If you do add extra passes to your attack for a particular opponent, don't give your QB a lot of thinking. Make it simple.

1982 Summer Manual. Gary Moeller was assistant coach at the University of Michigan. Moeller is an assistant coach with the Detroit Lions.

Establishing Quarterback Consistency

Sam Rutigliano

The selection of a quarterback to someday lead a team to the Super Bowl is a crapshoot. Ron Wolf, general manager of the Green Bay Packers, was quoted, "Everyone wants to apply science to the selection, but it's more seat-of-the-pants than science. A quarterback is like a tea bag—you don't know what you have until you put him in hot water."

In times of crisis, think of players, not plays. For example, the Chicago Bulls were playing in the seventh and final game of the NBA championship. Only seconds left to play. Only one shot left on the clock, the final shot of the game to win or lose. Everyone in the arena—fans, coaches, officials, and the opposing players—knows that Michael Jordan is going to get the ball to take that final shot.

It is the final drive, less than two minutes to go. The Denver Broncos are behind and must score a touchdown to win. John Elway is directing his team down the field. During this final drive, Elway is looking for playmakers who will make plays under pressure. In times of crisis, when the game is on the line, think of Elway or Jordan because consistency confirms authenticity.

The quarterback needs to be instinctual. When he starts thinking about the whole process, the why and how, the quarterback loses the flow he needs. Commitment is the key ingredient, the crucial key to peak performance. Quarterbacks do not compete with others, only with themselves. For them, the goals are dreams with deadlines. Failures or setbacks are treated only as stepping stones. Putting in the hours is necessary to succeed, but peak performers know that working long is much less important than working smart.

Great quarterbacks are spontaneous, creative, and thrive on the critical third down game-winning play. Joe Montana, calm amid the chaos, flawlessly directed his offense, saving the best for when the stakes were highest. Quarterbacks are inquisitive and acquisitive; they want to know everything. They operate successfully under pressure because they know what they are doing. Pressure is when you get squeezed on the outside, you find out what you are made of on the inside.

For the quarterback, reading defenses is fundamental. The quarterback must see the defense in slow motion. Reading defense is an instinctive ability. Repetition is the mother of learning. The quarterback sees, perceives, and then acts. The quarterback must understand that somebody has to be in a certain area on every play. A good quarterback must have a clear awareness of defenses and what they are trying to do. If you don't read defenses well, you are not going to be healthy or a very good quarterback.

Bill Walsh, the Hall of Fame coach of the San Francisco 49ers, held a "bad situation" practice period where he told his quarterback Joe Montana to see, perceive, act, and throw to the third receiver in his read progression. Create the game situation in practice and the quarterback will react through rote memory. Brian Sipe, the 1980 NFL MVP and architect of the 1980 Cleveland Brown's Kardiac Kids, engineered drives that decided 13 of our 16 games in the final two minutes of play. Brian had the innate ability to concentrate in the pocket and look downfield, focused on his progression of reads with the bullets flying all around him.

Blanton Collier was a highly successful head coach of the Cleveland Browns. Coach Collier had an interesting theory that your eyes lead your body and you see what you are looking for. Coach Collier believed that your margin of error would increase or decrease in direct proportion to the size of the target. A smaller target reduces the margin of error. You begin by insisting the passer select a smaller target, a small part of the receiver's body, his chest, shoulder, head, or hip. Focus your eyes on the target before the arm action starts and watch it until after the ball leaves the hand. Once the passing progression for the quarterback is set, look at the target and throw.

Many quarterback coaches believe the passer actually throws with his feet. The quarterback positions his feet as he sets in the pocket. Setting his feet gives him the base, balance, and rhythm in his release. It is compared to the golf swing or batting stance in baseball. The quarterback is drilled in footwork daily. In the three-step drop in the quick passing game, the quarterback is positioned approximately four to five yards behind the center. The quarterback also practices his footwork in the five-step drop, and that has the quarterback positioned seven to eight yards behind the center. The offensive linemen know exactly where the quarterback is at all times. Also, the quarterback is timed on both drops daily.

Even though an understanding of the various strategies and theories is basic to intelligent reading and play calling, many other factors that must be considered and understood. Before discussing them, I want to emphasize that, in the final analysis, the basic objective of the quarterback is to call the right play and score. Select the play that the defense least expects, and at the same time, take advantage of the weaknesses of the anticipated defense. Even though most quarterbacks are directed to call plays coming from the sideline, the quarterback's responsibility is to not call a bad play where the defense has outnumbered the offense and has the advantage. The quarterback never audibles out of a good play to a better play. That's why the quarterback must have a thorough knowledge of the opponent's defenses and weaknesses, as well as a complete understanding of his own offense and personnel.

The acid test is the final drive in a football game when you must score a game-winning field goal or touchdown in your last possession. Winning quarterbacks have an end zone mindset. They must know everything about their opponent's coverages, and above all, the reason to anticipate tactical situations. They must have the visual picture. The quarterback must be ready to exploit a defense and find its weaknesses. On the final drive, communication is intense. The quarterback must use the clock and preserve time. He must orchestrate the audibles, field position, and down and distance. Everything is understood, and there is no misunderstanding. The quarterback must be audacious and a risk taker. This is no time to play it safe. No one wins by statistics.

You have lies, damn lies, and statistics. This final drive reveals the quarterback's ultimate confidence as he leads his team to a win. Your approach in this situation, and ability to win consistently will ultimately get you to the Super Bowl and the ring.

1999 Summer Manual. Sam Rutigliano is head coach at Liberty University, Lynchburg, VA.

Drilling for Quarterback Improvement

Dave Arslanian

Two good reasons Weber State has consistently been one of the top passing teams in the nation for the past 10 years are the *system* and the *people*. Credit outstanding coaches who have contributed to the development of our offensive system. The execution of the system by talented young men has contributed to some outstanding accomplishments.

The system contributes a great deal to our success, but the most critical factor is the *people*—the coaches and players. As with any system, specific fundamentals and techniques must be properly performed to achieve the desired results. Over the years, we developed a comprehensive list of personal qualities, basic fundamentals, and specific techniques necessary for our system to function.

We constantly evaluate and update our system. Part of that evaluation has to do with the qualities, fundamentals, and techniques. Some things change as we find better ways to do things, but most of them are constant. The key, then, is the emphasis and the teaching methods used by the coaches, and the execution and quality repetitions performed by the players.

The key is the discipline that comes from quality repetition of each drill. With that in mind, let's discuss the topic of this article, and the one position that determines the effectiveness of our system more than any other position: the quarterback.

We have drills that relate to the development of personal qualities, basic fundamentals, and specific techniques for playing QB in our system. It would take a book to adequately explain all of the drills we use to develop our QB in each category. What I will do is list everything that fits into each category, and then explain some of the drills we use within each category.

Every drill relates directly to a specific quality, fundamental, or technique necessary for proper execution of our system. Also, I do not claim credit for the origination of any of these drills, but rather credit them to the coaches through the years who have influenced my thinking on QB play.

Personal Qualities

We recruit QBs with these qualities and then work to maximize them when the young man joins our program.

1. Leadership and responsibility. He must be a leader and must assume the responsibility that goes along with being a team leader.

2. Winning attitude. He must be willing and able to do what it takes to win. There will be setbacks, but he must have the attitude that his ability and the next play will get things going.

3. Hard worker. He must be the hardest worker on the team. He must be the first one on the practice field and the last to leave.

4. Knowledge of the offense. He must be a student of the game and must know the offense better than anyone else.

5. Confidence. He must radiate confidence. He must believe in himself, and his teammates must believe in him.

6. Loyalty. He must be able to take the public adulation as well as the criticism, always giving his teammates credit for successes and never passing along the blame for failures. He must *always* support his teammates and coaches 100 percent.

7. Arm and athletic ability. He must develop his arm strength and accuracy by throw-

ing every day and developing his God-given athletic ability to its utmost through hard work and dedication. Our QB must have a strong, accurate arm, and he must be one of the best athletes on the team.

Basic Fundamentals

Within each basic fundamental, we have specific techniques that make up that fundamental. Space does not allow me to list all of the techniques, but the following is a complete list of our basic fundamentals:

1. Huddle procedure and play calling
2. LOS procedure
3. QB and center exchange
4. QB and ballcarrier exchange
5. QB and ballcarrier faking
6. Short passes (1-3 steps)
7. Intermediate passes (5 steps)
8. Deep passes (7 steps)
9. Play-action passes
10. Passing
11. Running with the ball
12. Loose ball
13. Reading coverages
14. Two-minute offense
15. No-huddle offense
16. Goal line offense
17. Coming out offense
18. Preparation

The following are specific drills and the areas they improve and emphasize.

Chalk Talk Drills

Chalk talk drills assist in knowledge development, leadership, and confidence. The QB conducts these sessions. He is expected to get on the chalkboard and thoroughly explain items such as specific patterns versus specific defenses, the weekly play list, and the weekly audible list. During the season, the play list is determined by Tuesday, and on Thursday the QB conducts the position meeting by listing on the chalkboard, from memory, all plays on the play list.

The QB then diagrams each pass play versus the expected coverages and discusses the reading progression and necessary audibles. He then fields questions and is expected to be able to provide clear and concise answers.

Run the Show Drill

The run the show drill assists in huddle procedure and play calling, LOS procedure, leadership, and confidence.

Conducted in the classroom with the QBs, this drill is used in the early stages of development for our young quarterbacks and as a review for our veterans. It is used at the beginning of spring football and fall camp.

One QB gets up in front of the group and simulates receiving the play from the sideline, approaching the huddle, calling the play, breaking the huddle, approaching the LOS, and using the cadence and/or audible.

The important factors are: the QB receiving the play away from the huddle, stepping to the huddle with confidence, and standing arm's length from the front line; and speaking to the entire unit with confidence and self-assurance. Remember: how you receive the play and how you present the play play a major part in the ultimate success of the play. Radiate confidence.

The QB breaks the huddle and briskly approaches the LOS with confidence. Eye focus at LOS is LT to RT, RT to LT. Tap center on butt and get under him. Use audible or just the cadence.

Warm-Up Drills

Warm-up drills assist in player warm-up, arm development, footwork, throwing fundamentals, and techniques for basic passes. This drill is used daily as a warm-up before practice but also is used at certain times as an intense workout. Remember: Always stretch the shoulder muscles first!

1. Bull pen pitch: Throw like a pitcher in the bull pen. Loosen up the whole body: shoulder, arm, hips, etc. Note: From this point on, always aim at a target. Throw each pass with a purpose. Hit a target.

2. Spread legs and follow through: With legs spread wide and feet planted on the ground, throw the ball and follow through by touching the grass between your legs.

3. Face north/face south: Keeping feet together and planted, turn hips and shoulders in direction of throw and throw using good motion (release and follow through).

4. Left knee/right knee/both knees: Drop the ball, pick it up quickly, release the ball quickly. Emphasize quickness with the ball, but also good motion, follow-through, and accuracy.

5. High release: With feet together and planted on the ground, face your partner and hold the ball high above your head with a straight (stiff) arm. Throw the ball with only the wrist, keeping the arm straight, really flipping the ball (like a basketball shot) with a snap of the wrist. The palm of the hand should face the ground after snapping the wrist, and the arm is still straight, high overhead. (You should only be five yards apart for this drill.)

6. Fade and throw: Fade to the right and throw off the right foot. Fade to the right and throw off the left foot. Fade to the left and throw off the left foot. Fade to the left and throw off the right foot. Take two or three steps to perform this drill and develop a feel for throwing off balance.

7. Step—throw—freeze: Just to emphasize the follow-through.

8. Three-step drop: Face each other. Face north/face south. Execute a three-step drop and throw. Hit and throw (hit your third step and throw). Remember to step slightly in the hole when throwing across your body.

9. Five-step drop: Face each other. Face north/face south. Execute a five-step drop and throw. Hit and throw on half, gather and throw on half.

Dan Fouts' Mental Imagery Drill

The mental imagery drill assists with knowledge development, reading progression, vision, and footwork.

One QB throws the ball; three other QBs are used as receivers. Each pass pattern is constructed on the field with the QBs positioned as the receivers at the appropriate spots on the field where the ball would be thrown.

For example, if the pattern has a flat, curl, and post, then a QB (receiver) is positioned at each of those spots. The coach stands behind the QB throwing the ball and signals to the receiver he wants the ball thrown to. As the QB takes his drop, the designated receiver puts his hands up for the pass, and the QB sets and throws to that receiver. For best results, the receiver should put his hands up during the QB's drop, as it relates to the reading progression.

This drill can also be used by one QB and no receivers by putting towels on the field in place of the receivers. The QB rehearses his reading progression, sets up, and hits different towels. This drill is a great way for a QB to work out on his own during the off-season and summer.

Scout Skelly Drill

The scout skelly drill assists knowledge development, reading coverages, reading progression, and vision.

Receivers and the QB work together versus a scout secondary. Everything is done from the LOS. The coverage is explained, the secondary drops to the coverage as the receivers execute the pattern, and the QB throws to the appropriate receiver. This is a very simple basic drill, but each pattern is executed versus each coverage, and all details are thoroughly covered. It is then reviewed on video the next day before practice.

Pressure Drill

The pressure drill builds confidence, concentration, footwork, and throwing fundamentals under pressure.

Incorporate the pressure drill with other throwing drills when the QB must concentrate on specific assignments, fundamentals, etc. Two or three people line up on the LOS with hand-held shields. As the QB drops to pass, the shield holders approach as rushing defensive linemen or as a collapsing pocket, and then one, two, or three strike the QB after he releases the ball.

Do not interfere with the throwing motion or prohibit the QB from proper follow-through, but mainly harass after the throw. Condition him to be able to take a hit, still concentrate on his assignment, and execute his fundamentals and techniques. Make sure his throwing motion is not interfered with and helmets and pads are kept clear of his throwing hand!

Route Review Drill

The route review drill reviews fundamentals and techniques of specific routes (especially footwork). This is a very simple but vitally important drill for taking a specific route and going through in a very precise, exact, and disciplined manner the fundamentals and techniques for executing that particular route and pass. It is simply a throw-and-catch session with QBs and receivers, with both the QB coach and the receivers coach providing detailed instruction on each route and pass. Video is very helpful, but the most important aspects are slowing it down, getting it right, and taking advantage of the teach-and-rehearse method used by the coaches and players.

Shuffle and Throw Drill

The shuffle and throw drill works concentration, footwork, throwing fundamentals under pressure, and avoiding pressure.

This is similar to the pressure drill with three rushers, only now the QB feels the pressure and shuffles right or left, or steps up in the pocket and throws. It can be used with other throwing drills or in and of itself. It can also be used without rushers; the coach signals which way to shuffle and throw.

Be an Actor Drill

The be an actor drill practices play-action pass faking and throwing. This is similar to the route review drill, only using play-action fakes and passes. Position the other QBs as the defenders you are trying to fake, so they can be critical of the ball handling and the deception techniques being used by the QB and ball-carrier.

In summary, I hope you can use some of these drills to help in the development of your QB, and that this presentation stimulated your thoughts in developing drills that relate specifically to your system. Remember, your system is important, but even more important is a statement made by coaches through the years: "It's not so much what you do, but *how* you do it, *when* you do it, and *who* you do it with that makes the difference."

1991 Summer Manual. Dave Arslanian was head coach at Weber State University. Arslanian is head coach at Utah State University.

Training Quarterbacks to Read Coverages

Steve Axman

A young QB's introduction to the world of attacking college defenses is often a rude awakening. Two deep, three deep, combo, blitz, man under, drop end, rush end, gap control, nickel, brackets, and on and on.

Against multiplicity and disguise of both front and coverage, a coach must have a starting point from which to help a QB develop a basis of understanding of fronts, coverages, and their subsequent interrelation. Used to be, a coach could simply start with the concept of odd seven- and even eight-man fronts, and their related coverages. However, the increased usage of nickel and even dime personnel has all but shattered those basic teaching constructs.

Is it an overshifted, odd front look? Or is it truly an even eight-man front? If coaches debate the true front/coverage structure of a specific defensive look, then how can a young QB be expected to understand such design intricacies?

He can and he must if he is ever to operate the mechanics of leading an offense against today's multifaceted defenses. The young QB needs a place to start. The coach needs a place to start, so that as the young QB begins to develop, there is always a foundation of understanding and learning from which to draw when he sees that strange, new defensive look.

Where does one start? One starts by helping the QB understand that rarely does a front and a coverage design exist without an interrelation to one another. Fronts and coverages, coverages and fronts are almost always related to one another. One rarely exists without the other complementing it, to help produce a coordinated defensive package of deep coverage, curl/flat zone coverage, underneath coverage, perimeter support, and gap control fronts.

An understanding of the interrelation of fronts to coverages and coverages to fronts can help produce what are fairly reliable indicators in the effort to attack defenses with run, option, and pass packages. A defense may do a great job of disguising. However, a thorough knowledge of front and coverage structure can provide an edge in the recognition of such concepts as what the coverage is, who and where is the "A" gap defender, who is the curl-flat zone defender, etc.

In understanding the designs of the wide variety of fronts that he may see, the QB must understand the concepts of gap control. In its most basic form, gap control defense relates to the assigning of seven front defenders to the seven gaps of a right and left Pro offensive formation.

With few exceptions, gap control defense allows for one front defender (usually an outside linebacker) to be a flat or curl-flat zone

defender to one side or the other (figure 1). This is in addition to his perimeter support responsibilities.

In figure 1, the overshifted, reduced front 5-2 alignment allows for the TE side outside linebacker to be that curl-flat zone, perimeter support defender. It is the understanding of the nature of such a front and/or the related coverage that will give us reliable information from which to effectively attack the defensive structure at hand.

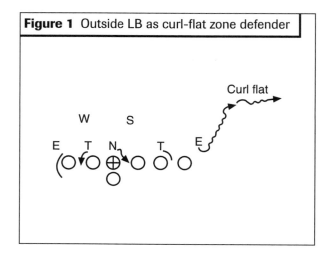

Figure 1 Outside LB as curl-flat zone defender

Many varieties of coverages exist. Structurally, however, we define for our QBs five basic families of coverage:

1. Three-deep, four-under zone
2. Two-deep, five-under zone
3. Man free
4. Two-deep, man-under
5. Blitz man (three- or four-deep)

Three-deep zone, of which strong safety invert, or sky, is the most common, is a strong-oriented coverage (1-1/2 deep defenders strong, and 1-1/2 defenders weak) that is usually easily recognizable. A FS aligns in the middle of the formation. (When the ball is on the hash, however, he can initially align on the hash in a two-deep alignment to give a two-deep look.)

Two corners are aligned deep (usually seven yards plus). The most distinguishing three-deep sky defender alignment is usually the inverted strong safety to the field/formation side (figure 2).

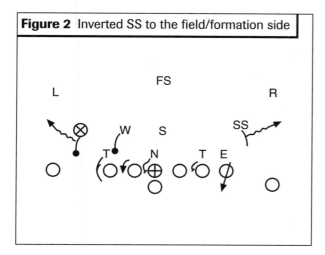

Figure 2 Inverted SS to the field/formation side

As figure 2 shows, the three-deep, strong-oriented coverage provides a curl-flat zone, perimeter support defender to the field/formation side in the form of the strong safety. (Field and/or formation strength is, of course, relative to how an offense lines up in formations. For the purpose of basic simplicity, we always start our explanations to our QBs in relation to a Pro formation with strength set to the field.) Therefore, the front must provide a flat zone-support defender to the weak side of the formation.

To accomplish this, the front should also work (angle/slant) weak to provide a contain defender, to allow for such a drop-type outside linebacker. In this way, the coverage and perimeter support can be balanced to both sides.

Therefore, the three-deep, strong-oriented coverage allows us to reliably predict that

1. the weak side outside linebacker is the drop outside linebacker;

2. the front will work weak in its gap-control efforts to provide a contain defender weak (the weak DT);

3. the defensive line's "A" gap defender, if there is one (the noseguard), will work weak to the weak "A" gap (the left side of figure 2); and

4. the rush outside linebacker will come from the formation/field side.

Besides the middle attitude alignment of the FS and the often obvious inverted SS alignment, here are some other helpful indicators that the coverage is three-deep zone (sky):

1. Weak corner off seven-plus yards. The weak corner is usually in more of an isolated, one-on-one attitude due to his being away from the formation side. As a result, he usually displays less effort to disguise.

2. Weak outside linebacker aligns off LOS. In essence, the weak outside linebacker cheats his alignment to enable a better, quicker drop in his flat-curl zone pass responsibilities. Such alignment cheating may happen late, just prior to the snap of the ball.

3. Defensive linemen shade weak. An Okie noseguard's alignment shades weak, to best control the weak "A" gap. The strong side Okie DT aligns head up or on an inside shade, to best control the "B" gap. The weak side Okie DT is in a heavy contain alignment.

Two-deep zone, even though there are two balanced secondary defenders to each side, is treated as a weak-oriented coverage. Field and formation considerations force two-deep coverages to get additional curl zone coverage from the strength-field side of the front lest there be definite coverage weaknesses left open to exploit (figure 3).

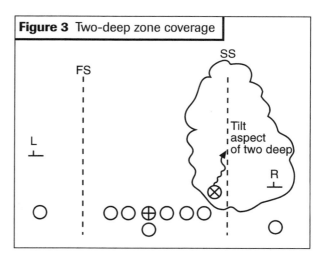

Figure 3 Two-deep zone coverage

Yet it is a tilted umbrella coverage structure in that two short zone defenders cover the curl and flat zones under a half-field safety aligning near, or on, the hash to the formation/field side.

Two-deep is most often recognizable by the fact that there are two deep defenders rather than the three of three-deep. The two safeties may do their best to disguise the look. However, by the snap of the ball, there will usually be two safeties aligned on the hashes.

In two-deep, the emphasis of the coverage structure is that the main perimeter support defender is weak, away from the field/formation side. Therefore, the front must provide a curl zone defender to the strong/field side of the formation. To accomplish this, the front must also work strong to provide a contain defender to allow for such a drop-type outside linebacker, so that the coverage and the perimeter support can be balanced to both sides, as seen in figure 4.

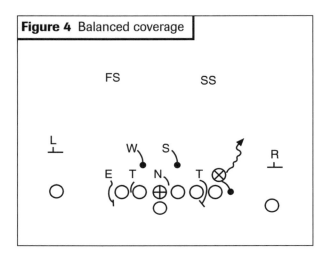

Figure 4 Balanced coverage

We feel that it is the squatted weak corner defender that allows us to reliably predict that:

1. the strong side outside linebacker is the drop linebacker;

2. the front will probably work strong in its gap-control efforts, to provide a contain defender strong (the same DT);

3. the defensive line's "A" gap defender, if there is one (the noseguard), will work strong to the strong "A" gap (the right side of figure 4); and

4. the rush outside linebacker will come from the weak short side.

Besides the squatted weak corner and the safeties aligned on the hashes, here are some other indicators that the coverage is a two-deep zone:

1. Reduced (eagle) alignment weak (figure 5). A reduced front is the one that has already worked (shifted) its way to the TE formation strength by its reduced (eagle) alignment. The reduced alignment almost always goes hand in hand with a squatted two-deep weak corner.

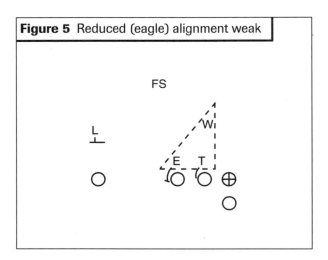

Figure 5 Reduced (eagle) alignment weak

2. Less than a reduced (eagle) look (figure 6). A reduced front in which the weak side of the formation shows even less than a reduced (eagle) look is almost always associated with a two-deep, squatted corner look. As shown in figure 6, the overshifted look is often associated with overloaded front's strong side. As a result of the overload, we can reliably predict that the "A" gap defender will be away from the overload and that the drop end or linebacker will come from the overloaded side to produce the two-deep tilt aspect of the coverage.

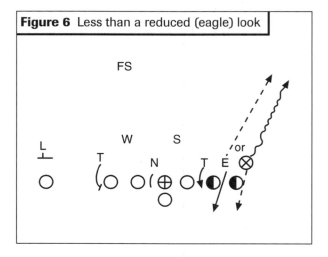

Figure 6 Less than a reduced (eagle) look

3. Drop outside linebacker walks out on spread set (figure 7). To a formation side spread set alignment, the strong side outside linebacker will probably walk out on, or to, the inside receiver in the tilt coverage concept.

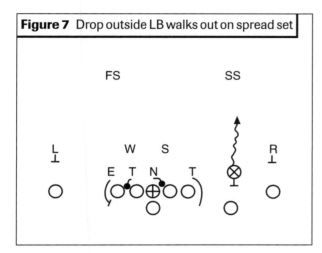

Figure 7 Drop outside LB walks out on spread set

Two-deep, man-under coverage necessitates a coverage structure designation of its own, even though it so thoroughly derived from what may look like two-deep zone. Two-deep zone is pure zone, with a structure of two deep halves or coverage safeties and five-under short zone coverage defenders. Two-deep, man-under plays normal two-deep halves or zone coverage safeties, but the five-under coverage defenders are all manned to specific receivers (figure 8).

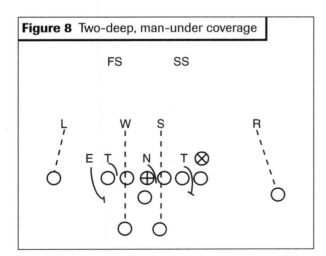

Figure 8 Two-deep, man-under coverage

The similarities of two-deep zone and two-deep, man-under are structurally important for a QB to understand. Two-deep, man-under is still treated as a weak-oriented coverage that is tilted strong. The main perimeter support defender is weak away from the field/formation side.

The front must provide a man coverage defender to the field/formation side (usually the strong side outside linebacker) to cover the TE type receiver. The front must work strong to provide such a drop and man the outside linebacker so that the coverage can man up on all five potential receivers, and so that the perimeter support can be balanced to both sides. In addition, two-deep, man-under reliably allows us to predict:

1. that the front will probably work strong in its gap-control efforts to provide a contain defender strong (the strong DT),
2. where the defensive line's "A" gap (the right side of figure 8) will be, and
3. that the rush outside linebacker will come from the weak/short side.

Reduced (eagle) type fronts and drop outside linebackers aligned out on spread set receivers also relate to the similarities of two-deep zone; two-deep, man-under; and their related front structures. It is the man-under play and looks of the under coverage that the QB must understand in relation to their very important differences.

The following are some of the indicators that the coverage is two-deep, man-under:

1. Inside-out corner alignments (figure 9). Showing man rather than head up to outside zone look. Actually, this may take the form of a tight man or bump coverage alignment.

2. Strong side outside linebacker aligns on TE showing man rather than a more normal zone alignment. The defender might align head up, inside out, or in a tough, bump-type alignment (figure 10).

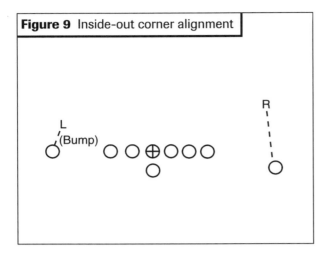

Figure 9 Inside-out corner alignment

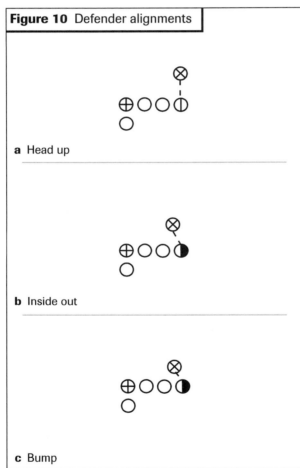

Figure 10 Defender alignments

a Head up

b Inside out

c Bump

Man-free coverage has many uses. By design, it allows for the rush of five front defenders while manning on up to five receivers with a FS left to play center field. In its most common use, the front will bring the two outside LBs and man the inside LBs on the backs (figure 11).

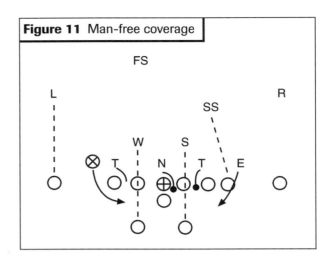

Figure 11 Man-free coverage

Versus man-free, we are thinking two rush outside LBs. The "A" gap defender will probably work to strength away from the short corner, weak side rush of the weak outside LB, and weak side DT. Note that man free usually brings both outside LBs to create the five-man front rush due to the need for contain rush assignments, since both corners are in a man coverage mode.

Man free certainly has much more varied use than was mentioned. Multiple fronts and motions will often tip the hand of man free and expose its structure, due to the man aspect of coverage. Sometimes varied formations will show that LBs other than the onside LBs are the rushing front defenders. For this reason, we must analyze the front as well as the coverage to determine who is the "A" gap defender and to what side the "A" gap defender and the front are working.

Following are some indicators of man free coverage:

1. The FS is midfield (figure 12). The FS will usually try to play center field to back up all man coverage play. He may not initially align in the center of the field. However, on the snap of the ball, he will usually quickly work there.

2. Three-across man look of the two corners and SS. The inside-out seven- to eight-yard deep configuration is often a giveaway.

3. The SS aligns on the TE (figure 13). Along with the FS in center field, this is often man free's biggest giveaway. The coverage can disguise three-deep sky very well. However, it's hard to disguise an inverted sky SS look when his assignment is (inside-out) man.

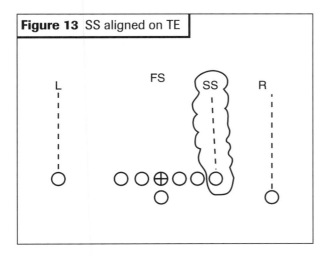

Figure 12 FS aligned at midfield

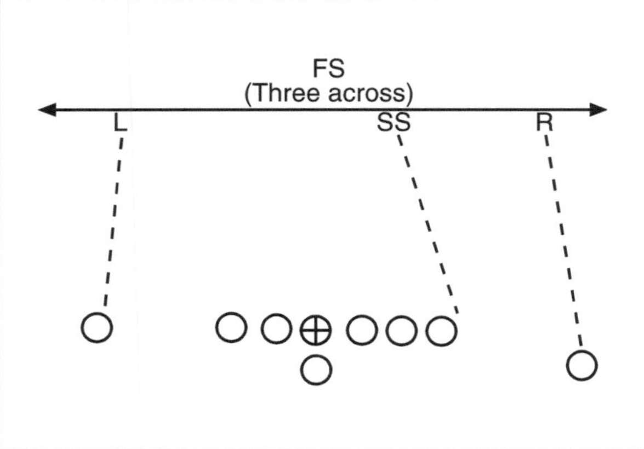

FS
(Three across)

L   SS   R

Figure 13 SS aligned on TE

FS   SS   R

L

4. Inside-outside corner alignments show man, rather than a head up to outside zone look.

Blitz coverage is man-up coverage to cover for a blitz! Here comes pressure! The QB and receivers must recognize it if it is to be handled and beaten. Blitz coverage has its own set of rules, as does the design of the blitz rush of the front and secondary. Our concerns are no longer necessarily such concepts as which way the front will work, who and where is the "A" gap defender, or who the drop and rush end or outside LBs are. On a blitz, the defense is gambling, relying on surprise, disorder, and

pressure to disrupt the offensive design it is facing.

We break down blitz coverage into two categories: four-across and three-across blitz man, in relation to the number of defensive backs being used to cover and/or blitz. With four-across blitz man, we are expecting up to a seven-man blitz rush from the defensive front.

The following are some of the indicators that the coverage is four-across blitz man:

1. The FS is aligned to cover first receiver out of backfield (or, simply, the second receiver to the weak side). Even with disguise, he usually works to a seven- to eight-yard deep man alignment by the snap of the ball.

2. Four-across man alignment look of the two corners and the two safeties.

With three-across blitz man, we are expecting up to an eight-man blitz rush. The major concern is a fourth potential rusher from the secondary to one side of the formation or the other. This might entail a weak corner blitz, FS blitz or weak, SS blitz, or even a possible strong corner blitz (figure 14).

In addition to some of the normal man look indicators, some of the indicators that the coverage is three-across blitz are

1. cheated alignments of the corners or the safeties to put them in blitz position,

2. a three-across man alignment look of the nonblitzing defensive backs, and

3. the cheating of the FS or SS to man cover for the blitzing corner or SS, as shown in figure 14.

This is only a beginning. It is a start, a foundation, in the effort to help the QB understand the interrelation of front and coverage structure. Such an understanding is a must if a QB is to successfully attack a specific coverage and its related front, or a front and its related coverage.

Figure 14 Three-across blitzes: *(a)* weak corner blitz; *(b)* FS blitz; *(c)* SS blitz; *(d)* strong corner blitz

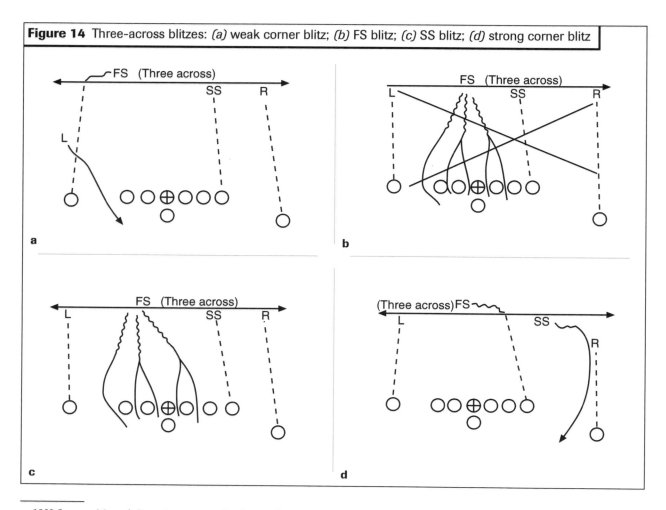

1989 Summer Manual. Steve Axman was offensive coordinator at UCLA. Axman is an assistant coach at the University of Washington.

Developing the Winning Quarterback

Bill Snyder

I seriously doubt that any other single position on a football team can have as significant an impact on the success of a program as the QB. Seldom is any other position as visible and certainly none is given more responsibility. We ask and expect so much in terms of leadership, poise, decision-making, and execution—at times, more than we should realistically expect. It truly requires a special person to accept and handle that responsibility. And let us all remember that a quality QB requires a very special and unique approach in working with him.

We have all identified traits we feel are important for successful players at each individual position. Those traits most desirable and necessary for a QB to possess include the following:

1. Being a good person. The value of character has never changed.
2. Responsibility. You can depend on responsible people.
3. A winning attitude. An ingredient you can't always understand, but you know it's there.
4. Ability to be a decision maker. This takes courage.
5. Toughness, mental and physical.
6. Confidence in himself and in the program.
7. Poise.
8. Dedication to preparation.
9. Ability to throw accurately.
10. Ability to provide proper direction.

To me, the responsibility of coaching this position lies in the ability to identify and develop these traits. There is absolutely no value in just listing those things you prefer in a QB and hoping you recruit someone who fits the mold. Even if you are fortunate enough to have one who possesses many of these traits, it should be understood that they must be adapted and developed into a college situation, an ever-changing environment at best.

The development process, then, is continuous, never taking anything for granted. I think it all begins with caring about and for the young people you work with. We are all conscious of the tremendous opportunity we have to mold the minds, attitudes, and lives of those we work with. It is not just an opportunity; it is a responsibility.

One of the most valuable tools in accepting and working at this responsibility for us has been a minimeeting concept: meeting with the QBs for brief (10 to 15 minutes) planned sessions on a regular basis throughout the year, discussing one and only one topic each session.

Topics for our minimeetings include: handling responsibility, confidence, self-esteem, decision making, toughness, poise, the thinking QB, on- and off-the-field leadership, loyalty, discipline, communication with coaches and players, goal planning, positive thinking, shaping attitudes, dedication and preparation, time management, relaxation, visual imagery, handling defeat and victory, what it takes to be successful, and developing meaningful relationships.

We discuss these and many other areas, not just once, but repeatedly. If you are willing to share ideas (yours and theirs), a feeling of honesty and mutual trust will prevail without disrupting the coach-player relationship. They want direction and discipline. They want to know what you expect of them. They want to know that you truly care about them and their development as individuals, not just as football players. These sessions are planned just like you plan your practice schedule. It is part of the routine.

Your relationship with your QBs is of extreme importance to the total concept of a successful program. If it is important to them that you respect and care about them as individuals—and it is—then you must be able to approach them with conversation about issues other than football. You must be able to sit down and ask about their ambitions, their feelings, their backgrounds, their futures, etc. You have to make time for them. If you care about them, you will.

Quarterbacking Philosophy

I want to present several execution skills of quarterbacking, all of which are very basic to most of you, and at the same time, often overlooked in the training of those we work with. But before doing so, let me mention a few vital, philosophical points that have benefited our approach to QB development.

Involve Them All

Make all QBs prepare for each game and each situation. I realize you cannot get five or six QBs physically and mentally prepared to play winning football each week. Time doesn't allow for that. And you can't give more than two of them enough field repetition to feel comfortable with their execution. But you can give them just as much mental preparation.

The important thing is to make the number two, three, and four QBs understand that every single thing that they do in the way of preparation is money in the bank. It's preparation for the future, it's being ready when the time comes, it's guarding against failure. You have to sell young QBs on this. A redshirt freshman must study, work, learn, and prepare just as diligently as your number one. You need to follow through to see that that happens. I have learned this the hard way. Test them, require just as much time for them.

Two wonderful examples of this took place, one in the 1983 season, when our number two QB, Tom Grogan, actually finished second in passing efficiency in the Big Ten behind Chuck Long, our number one QB. The other was in the 1985 season, when our number two QB, Mark Viasic, led Chuck and the Big Ten in passing efficiency the first three games of the season. Tom Grogan and Mark Viasic prepared themselves just as thoroughly as Chuck did.

Don't be afraid to do what he feels comfortable with. If he likes something, it's for a reason. He will execute it better. If he doesn't like something that you are hung up on, it's probably because he doesn't feel as though he can execute it well enough.

Train to Audible

Your QB can execute an audible system effectively if you believe in it and if you work at it. If you don't put him in the position to make audible decisions frequently every day, he will not develop the confidence to make proper decisions. Assuming that we are intelligent enough not to present a complex system, I think audible execution is no more difficult for your QBs than the execution of receiver selection.

In fact, the other 10 positions have a far more difficult time and need the exposure in practice as much as the QB. Your QB knows before he changes a play at the LOS what that play will be. He has time to visualize his role in the execution of the audible.

No other position has that luxury. They have come out of the huddle, taken an alignment, decided whom to block and how, or what route to run, etc., all within a comfortable, unrushed time span. Then the QB changes the play, and they have only 10 seconds to readjust all of their thinking. They have to experience this every day.

From day one, we introduce as much as 80 percent of our offense as audibles. They get used to hearing audibles. We may never use all the audibles, but the kids get used to reacting to play changes at the LOS.

One of the most meaningful drills our QBs do is a film drill. They put the projector on slow motion and let it run, trying to identify each defense as it appears and select (call out) an audible to a run or pass that fits that defensive scheme. If they can't make a decision or misread the defense, they run it back. As they improve their recognition of defenses and play selection over a period of weeks or months, they progress to accelerating the speed of the projector. This is a functional drill and develops an intense concentration in film viewing. Film study of defensive reaction to a QB's line of vision and throwing motion can be an excellent coaching tool on how and why these techniques can be used. You don't want to make him afraid to make decisions. It takes too long to develop that ability.

Move the Pocket

Give your QBs a chance against the rush. If the defense knows that your QB will set up nine yards deep directly behind the center every time you are to throw, he is in trouble. Offensive linemen lose the edge, and defensive linemen begin to ignore rush lanes and attack in ways a blocker doesn't expect. That's when you invite all kinds of stunts.

If your package includes sprints, pull up sprints, bootleg, play action, etc., as well as various depths of dropback passes, your QBs will have a better chance. Don't put them in predictable situations or positions.

Study your statistics. Nine percent of the passes we call (1 of 11) do not get thrown. We do not treat that as a negative. A flush can be as effective as any play in football if you work on it, just as you would any pass play. Defenses have trouble when a QB bounces outside and away from the rush and presents a threat to run or throw and has time to do either. Defenses don't work on that enough. It can be an offensive advantage. Big plays can come from potentially bad plays if you drill on it.

Go Deep

Be a threat to throw the ball downfield. It only takes one. We sometimes get so taken in with the possession passing game that we never threaten the vertical dimension of the field with the pass. We look at the deep ball as a very low-percentage pass, and who wants to spend much time practicing the low-percentage pass plays? To me, throwing the deep routes is no different than throwing the short passes. They both require time and practice. The more you work on them, the higher the completion percentage is normally going to be.

Fundamental Skills

Sometimes we can teach a QB too much about technique and not enough about when and where to throw the ball, and how to keep it away from the opponents. When it is necessary to teach the fundamentals basic to throwing the ball effectively, we stress the following two areas and the accompanying coaching points.

Setting Up to Throw

Properly setting up to throw is the basis of a quick release. We emphasize these points:

1. Shorten stride on next-to-last step to come under control.
2. Plant the foot parallel to the LOS or perpendicular to the throwing lane if you know exactly to whom and where you are throwing.
3. Plant on instep over a slightly bent knee.
4. Keep your shoulders forward; don't let your hips or shoulders come back over the plant foot.

5. Set the ball on your ear simultaneously with the plant by jamming the ball and shoulder up into the top hand.
6. Gather: pull the front foot back under your shoulder as you pop up into throwing position.
7. Point the front shoulder, hip, and lead foot at the target (throwing lane).
8. Lock your hips and cock your shoulders and throwing arm.
9. Eliminate short choppy steps just before you set up. They waste time.
10. Don't shuffle or edge toward LOS unless forced to scramble (this just puts you closer to defenders).
11. The plant, set, and gather should occur simultaneously.

Throwing Motion

Don't ever believe for a minute that your way of throwing the football is the only way. Don't change a throwing motion that gets the desired results. Improve it, but don't try to reconstruct it.

As mentioned previously, if a QB's throwing motion is getting results, don't try to rebuild it. Develop it instead. We emphasize the following points:

1. Push off instep of back foot.
2. Take a short lead step, pointing shoulder, toe, and knee of lead foot at the target (throwing lane) where you will throw ball, not where receiver is.
3. Transfer weight forward over lead step. (QB may shuffle step on long or high-velocity passes.)
4. Rotate shoulders and hips toward target.
5. Keep both hands on ball until you start shoulder rotation forward.
6. Keep throwing elbow parallel to ground or higher, and ahead of the hand.
7. Pull forward with the back hip.
8. Pull on ball with triceps and elbow as you start the ball forward.

Obviously, just as important as how a QB throws is *where* he throws. Accuracy is the execution of three simple concepts: throw the ball to the receiver and away from the defender; throw the ball to a spot where the receiver must continue to run to (attack) the ball, not allowing the defender to close on him or the ball; and versus zone coverage, keep the ball in the open area an equal distance from each defender in the area of the throw.

Volumes can be written about QB development, and neither time nor space would allow that here. A final point on QWB leadership. QBs gain respect by being tough. They gain confidence and enhance their leadership by being tough. Stress it! Talk to them about it.

1986 Summer Manual. Bill Snyder was offensive coordinator at the University of Iowa, Iowa City. He is head coach at Kansas State.

Breaking Down Pass Protection Techniques

Merv Johnson

For many years our passing game consisted of sprint out and play action passes. This simplified our pass protection because we could use the same techniques that our running game required. However, we found it increasingly difficult to get first down on obvious passing downs and in come-from-behind situations. The defense had to defend only 1/3 of the field versus the sprint out. With the dropback pass, they were more concerned sideline to sideline.

However, we wanted to retain our old sprint passing game. Against certain defensive adjustments and heavy inside blitzes, it had been awfully good to us. We also had enjoyed success with our play-action passes and felt we needed them to compliment our running game. So we incorporated these passing games into our pass protection.

Stance

Here was our first major problem. Having always been a fire-out, running football team first and a passing team second, we utilized the four-point stance. Because we did not want to become any less a threat with the run, we felt we should retain the four-point stance.

We modified our stance by putting only moderate weight on our hands and widening our feet slightly. The stance looks like the one used by our defensive linemen. By taking a short jab step forward with the right foot and dropping his tail, a lineman can set fairly quickly. Because the four-point stance limited our linemen's ability to set quickly, we added the pre-shift position with our LOS. This gives us the advantage of throwing with linemen in the up position.

Sprint Pass Protection

Most of our blocking and linemen's rules are split-T in nature. We count the defense and use fire-out blocking. Consequently, we tried to apply our basic count system to all our pass protection rules. We count from the ball to the outside. We give each lineman a rule and an alternate responsibility in each type of protection. The technique he uses and his alternate responsibility depends on the series and pass called (i.e., sprint out, dropback with or without maximum protection, play action, etc.).

On our sprint pass protection (figure 1), we get outside the defensive containment and hold

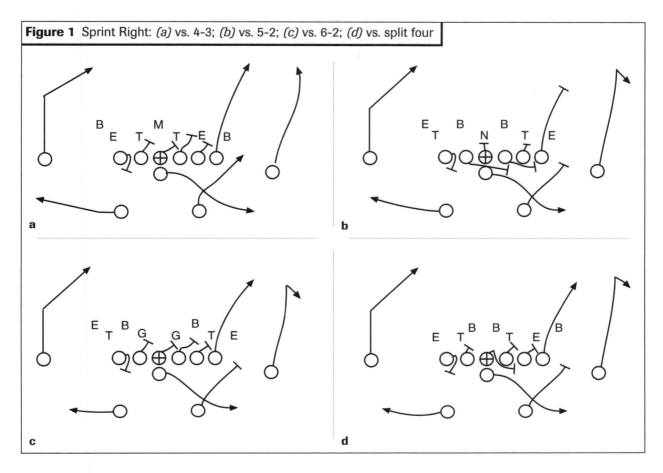

Figure 1 Sprint Right: *(a)* vs. 4-3; *(b)* vs. 5-2; *(c)* vs. 6-2; *(d)* vs. split four

the ball until a receiver opens in a one-on-one situation. Or we take advantage of a weak defensive adjust at the corner and get the ball to a receiver in a hurry. In either case, backside side protection is of little concern.

Basic Sprint Protection Rules

Onside End: if not in pattern, aggressively block end man on line.

Onside Tackle: aggressively block 2 or outside.

Onside Guard: slide with center; clean up the on tackle's block.

Center: aggressively block noseman; call and block slide toward.

Backside Guard: semi-aggressively block 1; clean up center's block.

Backside Tackle: block 2 or outside using dropback techniques.

Fullback or Halfback: roll block first defender outside onside tackler's block.

Line splits do not vary from our running game rules of 2 to 2 1/2 feet for guards and 3 feet for tackles. The exception is the onside guard versus an even defensive front. He cuts his normal split in half because he and the center will slide block. This reduces the center's responsibility.

The QB action shows pass immediately so anyone defending a LB can go almost immediately to his alternate responsibility. A reading defensive lineman reacts upfield rapidly as he pursues or contains, putting a premium on the blocker's ability to out-quick and intercept him.

The onside tackle and TE, if he blocks, have similar techniques. They lead the defender according to his width. They aim for his outside hip with their faces and inside shoulders, trying to shoot to and through the hip-thigh area into a running, scrambling, cut-off block.

The blocker delivers a blow with the head gear and shoulder while trying to run with the defender and ground his hands as late as possible. By stepping with the inside foot first in quick, crossover fashion, we engage the defender at a much better angle of strength and can maintain a much more forceful blocking surface. If we step near-foot first, we get so flat and stretched out that the defensive player can easily run through the attempted block. On a removed block, it is even more important that the blocker keep his head up, eyes on target, and "look his lick in."

With the slide versus an even defense, the guard must use enough lead to protect the area between him and his tackle. However with no apparent blitz, he should not slide so flat that he places an impossible task on his center. His block is a simple lead, cut-off block on the down lineman over him if he reads quickly or stunts outside, or on the LB if he blitzes. For a LB, the guard makes a half-speed pull to the outside while checking the LB for the blitz. If no LB blitz occurs, he slides outside and prepares to help the onside tackle with his block.

The center uses a lead, cut-off block if covered by a noseman. If the zero man is a LB at normal depth or there is no zero man, the center slides in the direction of the sprint out. He is responsible for the area between him and the onside guard. If no one is there, he continues to slide, helping the guard or acting as cleanup man to the end of the LOS. He then turns and looks back inside.

When covered on the line, the backside guard uses a controlled aggressive block on the defender. He needs to be alert to fall off and pick up any LB firing between him and his center. He will pull, checking the LB while maneuvering into position to help the center with the noseguard.

The backside tackle steps to the inside quickly with depth and looks for any penetration between him and the backside guard. If there is none, he turns to the outside and engages the first defender in much the same technique he uses in our dropback protection.

The FB or halfback, if we go to his side, sprints at a point two yards in front of the end man in the line. He adjusts to the defender's reaction and attempts to throw through the defender's outside knee with his front elbow,

making contact on the knee with the back of his shoulder. He rolls three times. This extremely effective block is hard for an end to combat. If the end tries to get low to meet the blocker, he can't maneuver or react, and if he plays soft the blocker gets into his legs and rolls him down. If our TE or tackle engages the end man, the back controls his charge so that he can get outside and roll the man up once the lineman loses contact.

Dropback Pass Protection

The dropback part of our pass protection is an area we find most difficult to teach. As I mentioned, we can tie in our sprint and play pass techniques with those of our running game. However the dropback has created a whole new set of techniques, ones that require almost as much practice time as is devoted to our more aggressive blocking skills (figure 2).

To keep our assignments simple, we follow the same rules we have for our sprint out protection. We man the defense as much as possible; we do not use area responsibility or do a lot of switching off. All these variations require precious practice time. If a lineman knows, without reservation, a defender is his, he can react better to meeting the challenge. Certain stack or tandem alignments may force the two adjacent blockers into an area responsibility.

Basic Dropback Rules

Tackles: block 2 or outside

Guards: block 1. End line rush or solid depending if the back stays in and blocks.

Center: block 0. End line rush from least protected side (or solid) depending on backs' assignments.

Backs: if not in pattern block first outside tackle your side.

The guard's and center's basic techniques are the same. If covered by a down lineman, he sets as quickly as possible. He should not get more

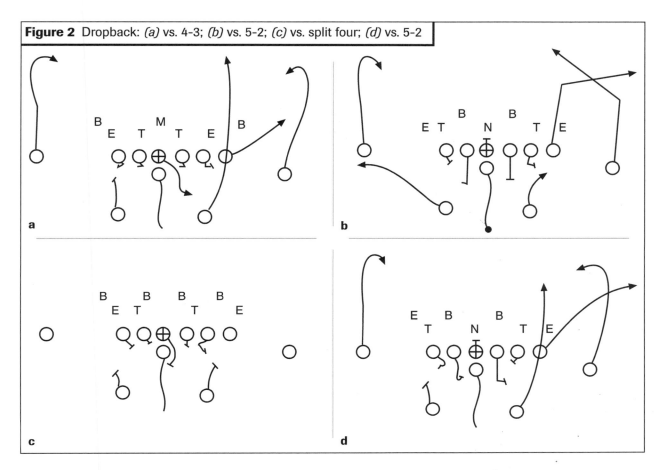

Figure 2 Dropback: *(a)* vs. 4-3; *(b)* vs. 5-2; *(c)* vs. split four; *(d)* vs. 5-2

than one foot deep because if he sets deeper, he tends to drift and can't stop a big defender. The biggest point for the two positions is for the blocker to slide to a true head-up position and take on the defender with feet and shoulders parallel to the LOS. If we engage a defender and have to drop step, we are beat every time. He will either bull his way through the side of the back foot or pull himself around the other side.

The blocker should set himself to meet the defender with tail low, back straight, and feet and fists moving with short choppy action. His fists should be under his chin with his elbows tucked at his sides. He engages the defender with a short upward blow delivered with his headgear and forearms. He strives to strike the defensive man in the upper chest. We ask him to bounce off the defender as he neutralizes his charge and reset quickly to engage him again. Once the defender commits in a rush direction, we drive him in an aggressive running block with the head across.

If LBs cover the center or guards, they should get two to three yards deep immediately. They watch the LB for a blitz through any hole and meet him. The blocker attains this depth so that he doesn't get caught up in the adjacent linemen's block. If this occurs, he can't react to the LB's rush somewhere other than straight ahead, and he won't get into position to engage a defensive end if this becomes his responsibility. Even if his responsibility is to stay solid inside, the depth will keep the adjacent blockers working in front of him, and he can best decide who to help and when. He engages the defender the same way as he did the down lineman depending on whether the rusher is coming to meet him or trying to go around.

The tackle's block should be easier to master than the guard's. In college football, the defender will normally be to the tackle's outside, depending on down and distance, how sprint-out conscious the defense is, etc. The tackle sets himself quickly, facing slightly to the outside.

He normally will set one to three feet deep depending on the defender's width. He should give the defender only the outside rush and be in position to take that away. By alignment, he should discourage the defensive man from going inside. If the defender comes to the blocker, he engages him with much the same technique as the guard and center used. He should try to make contact with his head in the rusher's outside armpit. This keeps the blocker's head and outside arm free and should keep the defender from grabbing and pulling himself outside. Whenever the defender chooses to charge, the blocker should drive on him with a running shoulder block.

When backs are required to stay in and block, their responsibility is the same as sprint out: first man outside your tackle's block. They set up and use the same techniques as the offensive tackle.

For the most part, linemen use these techniques on all dropback passes. Occasionally we let a lineman cut a defender, but only as a last resort. If a big, strong, reckless individual is physically beating him, our blocker may use this technique. He sets with slightly more depth and shoots between and through the defender's legs in an all-out scramble to keep him from getting back up. This should be used only once, and it usually will slow this individual to where the conventional technique can be employed. It has to surprise the defender, however, or he can avoid contact with the blocker rather easily.

Play Pass Protection

Play pass refers to a pass off a play fake with the action or backfield flow continuing the same way as the original move. The linemen's responsibility is similar to sprint out protection except we need to secure the backside as the QB usually will be delayed or may even pull up.

Play Pass Blocking Rules

Onside End: block one or inside if not in pattern.

Onside Tackle: block two or outside aggressively.

Onside Guard: block one or step solid.

Center: block 0; backside rush.

Offside guard: block one; backside rush

Offside tackle: block two or outside.

The onside linemen lead knowing that the defenders will react upfield and to the outside. However, they must be controlled enough so the man can't stunt inside them. If one is a LB, the guard steps to him in a quick, low manner then turns and looks at the center's block.

The center or backside guard blocks a down lineman as aggressively as possible. Against a LB, they work backside almost like they do on the dropback pass. The backside tackle blocks with the same technique he employs in a sprint out.

The backs execute the play we are faking with the blocking back performing his exact same assignment. The back who would normally have the ball makes a good fake and looks for a defender who may have worked away from one of our linemen.

Misdirection Pass Protection

Misdirections are passes where a play is faked to one side and the QB rolls back to the other. These patterns are extremely effective and are of a great concern to most defensive schemes. Protection on these passes is probably the most difficult thing we have to execute. It requires great discipline and quickness on the part of each blocker.

Misdirection Blocking Rules

Onside Tackle: block two or outside as aggressively as possible.

Onside Guard: block one or step solid.

Center: block noseman or one away.

Backside Guard: pull for end line rush.

Backside Tackle: block two or outside as aggressively as possible.

The onside tackle and guard and the center use absolutely no lead. They semi-aggressively establish perfect contact then gain a block through second effort, scramble, and the help of the backfield fake. The backside tackle executes almost the same technique as the linemen.

The pulling guard pulls as he would in a short trap so as not to interfere with QB action. Once past the center, he quickly goes two yards deep and locates the end man on the defensive line. He prepares to make a running shoulder block with his front shoulder. If the end crashes, it becomes a trap with the QB having to step up inside the block. If the end hangs or rushes slowly, the guard hooks him. If the end has dropped off to cover a receiver, the guard comes to the line outside his tackle's block ready to help him inside or lead the QB downfield.

The backs fake the play called and stay alert for LB rushes, missed blocks, etc.

1970 Summer Manual. Merv Johnson was a head coach at the University of Arkansas.

Defending the Passer

Don Powell

We throw an average of 30 times a game at Kansas State. About 20 of these will be dropback or cup passes. We use rollout to help the protections and, of course, utilize play-action passes, screens, and draws. There are definite times that everyone must be able to throw; it's late, you are behind, third and long, two minute situations, etc. To throw, you must be able to protect!

We feel that you do well with what you work on. Fifty percent of our practice time is devoted to the passing game. This is not only 50 percent of our individual techniques and group work, but team practice also.

Our linemen come to the LOS in an up position. When a dropback pass is called, they cheat their alignment back off the ball so that their front toes are on the center's heel. This gives us a crucial bit of additional distance from the rushers, enabling us to see dogs better. The linemen also cut down their splits somewhat. On obvious passing downs, we always throw from the up position, as we feel we can protect easier from the preshift position.

In order of rank, we teach the following to insure good dropback pass protection:

1. Set technique.
2. High press position.
3. In front.
4. Hit and double fist.
5. Chop.
6. Reverse (tackles only).
7. Fire out change-up and reset.
8. Stunts.
9. Full speed.
10. Big Bertha.

Set Technique

This is most important, and we must do it every day in our scheme of protection. From an up position, we cheat off the ball with our weight mentally on the outside foot. On the snap, we take an inside step first and then even up with an outside step. Keep the weight forward. If covered by a LB, continue to set back just a bit deeper. This enables the uncovered linemen to help out on escaping defenders and/or to pick up ends. In case of dogs, it helps us to switch men on the dog or go underneath for the LB in case of man protection. If throwing from a down position in our normal stance, we take a short jab step forward with our back foot to even up our feet and then shuffle back.

Our tackles set in the high press, an ape-like position with feet spread slightly, weight low, head up, and elbows in. They must be ready to slide either right or left and to catch a straight-ahead charge. The tackles shuffle to maintain an in-front position and do not hop when shuffling. Keep one foot on the ground when sliding; keep feet apart and moving. The tackles' set can be open versus an outside defender. Guards and centers must set more squarely to the LOS. Keep legs bent, maintain balance, and be under control for proper sliding.

We combine the set drill with our agility drills. Give them a snap count; have them set, shuffle right and left quickly on hand signals, and then cover. Our tackles cover flat on command until they find the ball. Center and guards cover like a punt.

High Press Position

We use this term for football position or blocking position for pass protection. Players can mentally see this high press position, and it helps particularly with the younger players. We want the rump down, feet chugging, knees bent, and elbows in to ribs with both fists in front of the body. With elbows in, it is hard for the hands to come outside the body's plane. The face should be up with the feet shoulder-width apart. Weight should be on the toes.

In Front

We try to mirror the defender's move and stay in front of him, with our bodies between him and the QB. If we set properly, pick up stunts, and stay in front, we feel we can get the pass off. We say protect the passer for a five-count, but he should throw the ball between 2.5 and three seconds. If you can stay in front well, you can protect. The drill we use is to have a defender rush, changing directions quickly right and left. No contact is allowed. Half of the time, we also have the offensive player put his hands behind his back while doing the in-front drill.

Overanxiousness and aggressiveness can get you into trouble. The pass protector should be relaxed and extend his body to an upright position. Keep legs bent. Take all inside fakes. Do not think in terms of a certain shoulder. Be eyeball to eyeball; the position is directly between the rusher and the passer. Keep him head up. Give ground grudgingly. Stay lower than the defender. It is like a basketball player in man-to-man defense staying between his man and the basket.

Hit and Double Fist

Once set, if the rusher tries to run over us, we hit him. Our technique is to drive him squarely in the chest with both fists. His body weight and force will keep our blockers' hands in. While making contact with the rusher, we drive with the top of the hat. Once we stop his charge, we push off and reset. If we do not hit the man squarely and stop his charge, we are in trouble. Generally, if a rusher gets to the side or can get his hands on us, we get beat. Cardinal rule here is to hit squarely, stop his charge, and do not let him get hold of you. Do not overextend while hitting him in the chest; absorb him. Use the legs in the contact. Hit on the rise. Shove off while recoiling. Regain fundamental position quickly and begin again. Do not be pushed into an upright position; straighten the rusher up. We use the two-man butt drill to teach this technique.

1. Form two lines of blockers two yards apart. One defensive man is placed facing the blockers. Coach's command is "set-go."

2. On "set" command, the two blockers and defensive players start rapid short steps.

3. On "go" command, the defensive man moves laterally to a position directly in front of a blocker. He then moves into the blocker high, with his face up. Once the blocker stops the defender's charge, the defender backs off a yard and re-

peats the procedure with the next blocker.

4. The blocker moves laterally with the defensive man, keeping him in front.

5. The hitter steps with his inside foot from a good football position, butting the defensive man in the numbers with the top of his hat. Simultaneously, he rolls his tail and lifts his legs on contact, driving the defensive man back and resetting, ready to hit again.

6. On "ready-ready-ready" command, the defensive man jumps between the blockers, facing the coach with all three men moving their feet rapidly in short choppy steps.

7. Coach gives cover call and all men cover.

Chop

As a change-up, we allow our men to chop a rusher. We set, fake up, and chop him at the knees. Once he's down, we either have to roll on his legs or get up quicker. We never chop a guy who is quicker than we are. Generally, it is the long-legged rusher we chop. We also chop as a last resort if a guy is whipping us. Use a quick-set explode with a body block, driving the head to the side the rusher is moving. Explode from a low position and fight through to maintain contact. Shoot an elbow in front and a knee behind. If the blocker misses, he should be prepared to leg whip. We use this technique on some quick over-the-middle passes.

Reverse (Tackles Only)

Most defensive ends in a 4-3 have contain responsibilities and generally rush outside. Once they get to our hip, with no chance of coming back inside, we drop-step, reverse shoulders, and run the rusher on past the QB. We practice this with a full speed rush. It is fairly easy to master and is a valuable technique.

Fire Out

If we are having trouble with a rusher, as a change-up we will fire out and stick the defender below the chin, a block similar to an onside tackle's technique on sprint-outs. After hitting hard and square, we now reset and use normal techniques.

Stunts

From the first practice, we look daily at stunt situations. Basically, one man keys the LB and shouts his direction. Remember, the man with the LB responsibility must set a bit deeper to negotiate underneath in case of man protection. If the defense uses zone protection, we will switch men.

Stunts, if anticipated on every down, can be picked up with very few busts. We work very hard on the opponent's favorite dogs. We also frequently practice "dirty dozen" dogs that have given us problems in the past.

Full Speed

When in pads, we go full speed twice daily versus our first-string defense. We do not chop and mainly stay in front. Keep plenty of distance between players to avoid pileups and injuries.

Big Bertha

Big Bertha is a 350-pound bag with a rope on either side, hung on a U-frame with chains. Using snap counts and proper sets, we swing the bag laterally with the offensive player in front of it. A man behind the dummy pushes forward occasionally, and we butt it. Its weight plus momentum makes blockers butt it square and hard—or be knocked down. The drill combines setting, in front, butting, and resetting. We cover to end the drill. Keep its duration for each man around 10 seconds.

Play Action Protection

We execute our onside play action protection in a manner that gives the impression of a run. As blockers fire out, they're slightly higher and hit rushers below the chin. Sustain contact at all cost. Keep control and do not overextend on first contact. Be aware of the scrimmage line and do not get caught downfield. Know exactly where the ball is to be thrown from and keep working for position between the rusher and the passer.

Draw Protection

We set as on normal pass protection, but we give the defender one way to go. If he doesn't come, we will go after him. On our quick draw, the tackles set, and once the defenders are by them, we release quickly upfield. Finesse is important in pressuring the rusher the way he wants to go.

Nutcracker

On quick passes, we use the aggressive face block through the groin of the defender. It is important to explode and drive through and up, to prevent the defender from recovering balance and getting his hands up. Second effort is vital.

To successfully dropback protect, you need big linemen with quick feet. A time-conscious QB is very important. We use a buzzer in most of our drills. The QB must set and throw on time. If the receivers are covered, the QB throws the ball away or scrambles. We do our best to build pride in protecting the passer, and we honor the offensive line whenever possible. One of our offensive game objectives is to not have a QB drop. When we make this objective, our head coach, Vince Gibson, lets everyone know it. Our guards must be our best protectors, since their men generally have two avenues of rush, whereas the tackles, by setting inside, only have the outside avenue of rush to contend with.

Our linemen know who the best rushers are. We know each week who we will help on if one of our linemen frees up. They know exactly where the QB will throw from. Through film study, we know our opponent's favorite rushing techniques and his strengths and weaknesses.

Have pride in being the best pass protectors in the league. Work hard on your techniques and weaknesses. All should strive for perfection and be satisfied only with no QB drops. Vary the snap count to upset the rusher's rhythm. This is done by using a quick count and some late counts. The late counts generally makes the defense show any dog intentions. The protectors must vary their blocking techniques. Don't get into predictable patterns of protection.

In conclusion, common faults of pass protection are not setting properly, overextension in hitting, not staying square in the middle, and not keeping their hands off you.

1972 Summer Manual. Don Powell was an assistant coach at Kansas State University.

Blocking for the Drop-Back Pass

Jack Little

The first thing we are interested in as we start talking to our squad about pass protection is acquainting them with the area they are to protect. We do this by making a diagram showing the area they must protect if we are to have a good passing attack (figure 1).

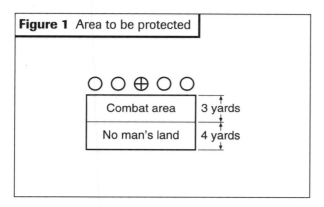

Figure 1 Area to be protected

The area from tackle to tackle and three yards deep is what we refer to as the "combat area," the area where we would like all combat to take place. We like to make our first contact with the defensive rusher as near to the LOS as possible. We have several techniques we can use; but if at all possible, we want our linemen to set on the LOS, thus eliminating the defensive rusher from getting a full head of steam before we contact him. If the defensive rusher chooses not to penetrate, we definitely do not want to go after him. As long as he is not a threat to our passer, we will leave him be.

The reason we allow three yards and make contact on or as near as possible to the LOS is to allow our protectors to give a little ground, if needed, and to shuffle to an inside position, inviting rushers to the outside and closing on them again before they get into no-man's-land. If

we make contact on the LOS and give a yard each time, we can contest rushers three times before they penetrate no-man's-land. This generally gives us enough time to get the ball in the air.

The next four yards are what we refer to as "no-man's-land." We think it ideal if our passer drops back seven yards, then shuffles forward five or six. Naturally, if he is going to throw from five to six yards deep, we would like to have this area clear of all rushers. Of course, this is what we are striving for and working toward, but, due to individual breakdowns from time to time, we don't always have the passer completely protected. Most of our passes are timed and should be thrown fairly quickly. However, there are times when the receiver is covered or one of our linemen breaks down on his assignment, forcing the passer to leave no-man's-land. We tell our pass protectors to stay with their blocks until they definitely see the ball has been thrown. To ease up on pass protection because you thought the pass had been thrown is a cardinal sin. Even if we lose contact with the rusher, we scramble after him until we are sure the ball has been thrown or until the play has been whistled dead. We want to have the best protection possible for our passer, and we are willing to study our mistakes, work hard, and make any sacrifice necessary to have good pass protection.

In teaching pass protection, we feel there are certain fundamentals that are necessary, the most important being to set quickly. In order to be a good pass protector, you must be able to set quickly. This means getting into a blocking position as quickly as possible. If we take our time in getting set, the defensive rusher will have us on our backs before we can move.

Getting set quickly and being in place is referred to as a good fundamental pass blocking position, or "set position." A good set position requires the head to be up with the eyes on the rusher. If we duck our heads or turn to one side, we do not feel that we can do an adequate job of protecting our passer. We feel that the head should definitely be up, eyes on the target. Other fundamentals of the set position are to have the back straight in a semisquat position, arms hanging and feet shuffling. The weight must be carried low in order to meet the pressure of the defensive man. The arms must be ready to move quickly but are not held up in a rigid position. The feet continuously move, to be ready for a change in direction or fake by the rusher. We always respect an inside fake but never take an outside fake. This covers the fundamentals of the set position.

Going into the techniques that we use in protecting our passer, we are faced with three different rushes, plus individual techniques on the part of each potential rusher, and games or stunts that may involve two or more players. The three types of rushing that we must be ready for are inside, outside, and head-on (figure 2).

If we have a defensive man aligned inside, we want to shuffle to the inside as quickly as possible. In doing this, we want to make contact with our inside shoulders and have our hips to the inside. We feel that in doing this, we force the rusher to come through the strong part of our protection. If we can keep our heads up and our shoulders square with our hips to the inside, we feel this is the best possible technique, one we refer to as the "jam technique." If the head is thrown in front of the

rusher and the hips remain to the outside, the rusher will often run through the blocker's head. We want to be in a position and on our feet so that we can jam him onto the blocker next to us. We have a rule that goes like this: Any time you leave your feet to execute a block, you must have your opponent on the ground or be able to recover and block him before he gets to the play. The jam technique is very difficult and requires a great deal of work to master. Of course, this seems to be the case in all of our blocks—we haven't found an easy one yet.

The next rush we will take up is the outside rush. If the defensive rusher aligns himself to the outside, we ask our blocker to set on the LOS, making his first step a short one forward with the inside foot. This is done to close off the inside and force the rusher to take an outside lane. From this position, we key the legs of the defensive rusher. When his inside leg is forward and he has penetrated the LOS, we call this line "point of no return." After he has crossed the scrimmage line and his inside leg is forward, it is almost impossible for him to change directions and rush to our inside. With this in mind, we tell our players that when the defensive man gets to a point of no return, we want to close on him, that is, make contact with our inside shoulder and drive the rusher out and around the QB. We definitely put the pressure on the rusher and use a driving shoulder block.

The next rush, and the one we see most often, is the head-on. If our blocker can stay on his feet and keep his body between the defensive man and the passer, he has accomplished his assignment versus the head-on rush. Incidentally, in all of our protection we always want our

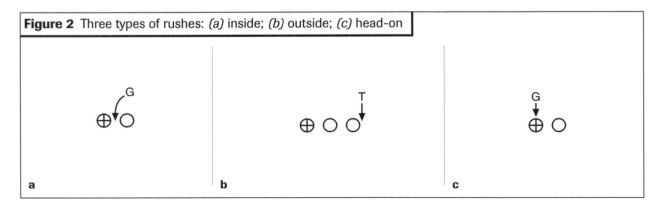

Figure 2 Three types of rushes: *(a)* inside; *(b)* outside; *(c)* head-on

a

b

c

blocker's body between the rusher and our passer, with his tail pointing toward the passer. Quite often, a head-on rush ends up in an inside or outside rush. Generally, after the initial head-on contact is made, the rusher will slide either inside or outside. Our technique against the head-on rush is one in which we must be ready to protect ourselves. We must set quickly and be ready to absorb the blow. If we hit out, we lose the leverage in our legs and end up missing the block. We try to keep our eyes on the rusher and meet him square and with the head up. Turning the head to the right or left has also gotten us in trouble. With all of these things in mind, we tell our players to break the charge with a six-inch blow but do not make it a hit-out technique. If we hit out, the defensive man will pull us to one side and continue on for the passer.

This covers the three basic rushes and brings us to an adjustment that we must make in blocking a linebacker who will rush straight or work with one of the defensive linemen in a stunt designed to foul our blocking assignments.

Our rule for blocking any defensive man who has aligned himself a yard or more from the LOS is to set approximately one yard deep and to the inside. This allows us to pick up most any kind of stunt and puts us in a position to help our teammates should the LB choose not to rush.

Now, let's take up the method by which we arrive at our blocking assignments. The first thing we want to be able to do is protect the blind side of the passer. By this, we mean that if we have called a pass to our right, we know that our first-choice receiver will be on our right side. If the passer will be looking in that direction when the ball is thrown, he will be able to see a free rusher and deliver the ball quickly. But an extra rusher from our left would hit him from the blind side. With this in mind, we want to have our maximum protection to the back side. We call all of our passes with an odd or even number. Even-number passes indicate that the ball is to be thrown to the right; odd-number passes will be thrown to the left. With this information, we assume our assignments, which are basically man-on-man (figure 3).

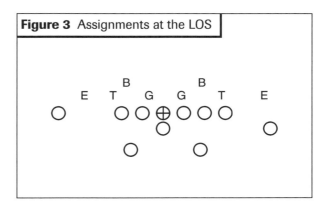

Figure 3 Assignments at the LOS

In order to get the maximum protection to the back side, we tell our center to block opposite the pass call if there is not a man lined up on him (on or off the LOS). Blocking the 6-2 would put our center to his left if we called an even-number pass. Since we are working together as a unit, each of our players knows who the center is blocking. The rest of our assignments are what are called individual blocking (figure 4). If the center blocks the first man to the left, the guard blocks the next man, and the tackle the next.

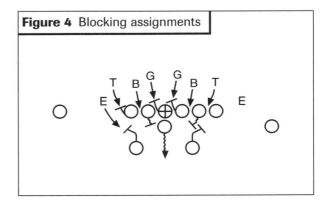

Figure 4 Blocking assignments

At this point, we bring in the back's block, which, as far as fundamentals are concerned, is identical to that of our lineman. However, his job is to take one step forward and set quickly, approximately one yard from the tackle. He blocks the first free man that shows. Blocking against the 6-2, if the defensive right end does not rush and the LB drops off (figure 5), we have a possibility of having two blockers with no one to block. If this is true, we ask them to be ready to help their teammates. We do not want two men blocking on one. We have found that

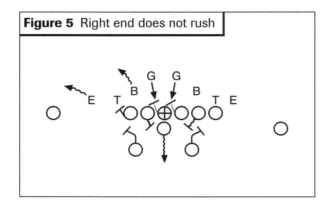

Figure 5 Right end does not rush

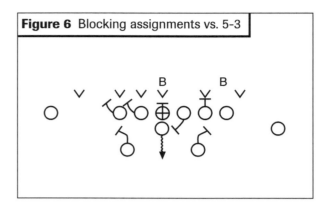

Figure 6 Blocking assignments vs. 5-3

one blocker will depend on the other and vice versa. In order to eliminate this, we want the defensive man to have to whip us one at time.

Let's go back to the LOS. If the center blocks to his left, the right guard then blocks the guard in front of him. Our right tackle is assigned to the LB. As you will recall, our rule when we block a man off the LOS is to set approximately one yard deep and to the inside. This allows our tackle to be in a position to block the tackle if the LB does not rush.

The right halfback steps up and is in position to block the first free man to show. If the LB does not rush and the tackle blocks the tackle, the halfback blocks the end if he rushes. If the LB rushes, the tackle must take him. This leaves the halfback on the tackle with the end free. But as I mentioned previously, we prefer to have the free man on the right side if we are throwing an even-number pass. We feel that this is the simplest way to teach pass blocking, and it holds up against 99 percent of the defenses. If we are blocking a 5-2 defensive alignment, our center has a man on him, which automatically tells our guards and tackles that regardless of an odd or even call, they have individual assignments.

Someone would probably ask, how do you block the 5-3 and stacked defense? Let's take up the 5-3 alignment (figure 6), and I will show you how we teach blocking assignments.

Keep in mind our basic assignments and our theory of protecting the back side to the maximum. Our center has a man over him whom he is assigned to block. We tell the right guard the middle LB belongs to him on even passes because in this defense, the opponent has a possibility of a four-man rush to our back side with-

out using the middle LB. Using his LB rule, the right guard sets to the inside approximately one yard deep. If the middle LB does not rush, our guard is in a position to help. The rest of the assignments are individual assignments.

If the defense shows us some kind of a stack arrangement, we assign the two men on either side of the stack the responsibility of blocking any type of penetration or stunt by the two stacked defensive men (figure 7).

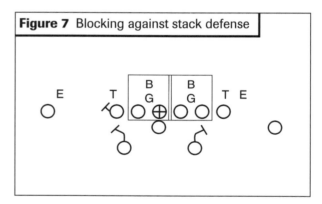

Figure 7 Blocking against stack defense

This takes care of just about all possible defensive alignments.

Now let's talk for a few minutes about defensive stunts and how we adjust to pick them up. We will start off with the 6-2 defense and a stunt or two from it. We are always on the alert for some type of game or stunt by the defense. If one of our linemen takes his position without mentally being ready for a stunt, we are likely to get in trouble.

Figure 8 shows a very basic stunt that we see quite often. Let's assume we have an even-number pass called. Since our center does not have a man over him, his job is to block to his

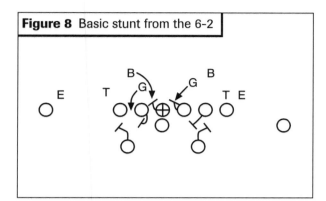

Figure 8 Basic stunt from the 6-2

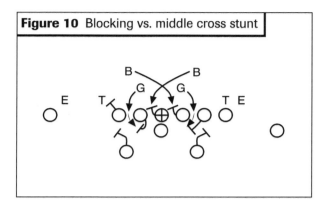

Figure 10 Blocking vs. middle cross stunt

left, away from the call. The left guard is assigned to the LB. Since most stunts start with LB movement, we have the man who is blocking the LB ready to switch assignments with the blocker next to him. As the ball is snapped and the stunt develops, we go about blocking it. As the LB starts toward the LOS, our left guard calls to our center to switch assignments.

If we get a double stunt, our right tackle and right guard work together, with our right tackle doing the switching (figure 9).

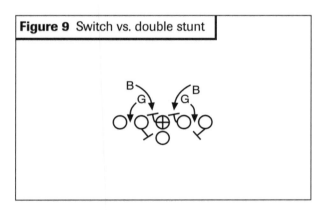

Figure 9 Switch vs. double stunt

In other words, the man assigned to the LB is responsible for calling the switch. Figure 10 shows another stunt we sometimes see from this alignment and how we block it if the defense gives us a cross stunt in the middle. Our tackle stays with the defensive tackle and tries to block him out and around the throwing lane. Our back steps up and slides to the inside to pick up the defensive end. The left guard and right tackle make a switch call, and the center and right guard block the area.

Here are some of the stunts we see from the 5-2. Figure 11 shows a very common stunt involving the middle guard and one or both LBs.

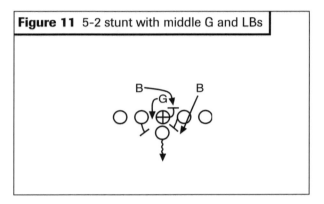

Figure 11 5-2 stunt with middle G and LBs

Remember that when we have a man head-on to the center, we are not concerned if it's an even or odd pass since we have man-on-man assignments. The blocker who is assigned to the LB must call the switch. As the LB starts to his left, our left guard switches assignments with the center. Our center must be ready to work with either guard.

If they use a tackle slanting to the inside with the LB rushing outside (figure 12), our guard switches assignments with the tackle. As you can see, we key the LB to pick up the stunt.

One more stunt before we go on to the drills. The stunt off a 4-3 alignment can give you trouble if the defense can execute it accurately. Figure 13 shows the lineup with a middle LB.

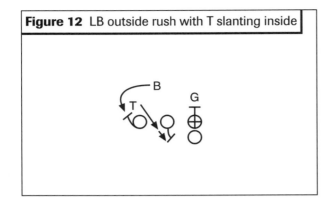

Figure 12 LB outside rush with T slanting inside

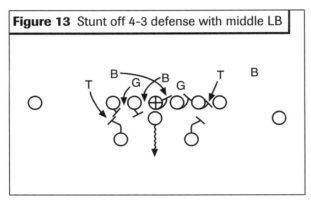

Figure 13 Stunt off 4-3 defense with middle LB

If the defense can time this stunt so that the LB who is moving from the outside toward the middle does not have to stop, it can be very effective. But this is very hard to do. We use an arrhythmic count, making it almost impossible for the defense to catch us off balance on something of this type as long as our QB does a good job of holding for a long count.

The defense's goal is to confuse the offensive assignments and cause a breakdown so as to allow them to get on our passer. Let's apply our basic rules in order to pick up this stunt.

We have told our center that anytime he has a man head-up on him, on or off the LOS, he is responsible for him. The LB rule applies here since the defensive man is head-up but off the LOS. After the center snaps the ball, he sets approximately one yard off the LOS, keying the LB. Since the middle LB crosses in front of the outside LB, our center switches with our left guard. But before this happens, the outside man has started to move down the line toward our center. Keep in mind that the ball has not been snapped. As the LB moves from outside his own defensive tackle to the inside, he be-

comes the left tackle's assignment. The left tackle now switches with our left guard. Our guard can see the LB moving toward the middle and must be ready to pick him up, turning the defensive guard over to our left tackle. This is where we have a double switch. In other words, our left guard is involved in a switch with his tackle and also with the center. As the middle LB comes in, the guard takes him. The center will then pick up the outside LB coming around.

Our left tackle sets to the inside and jams the defensive guard. This may look complicated and it sometimes can be, but we have had very good luck in picking up all of these stunts. Our halfback steps up here and blocks the defensive tackle.

We work on these various stunts each week. Some of the basic ones we will spend five minutes on every day. We brush up on the unusual stunts on Thursdays and feel we can do an effective job using this type of organization.

The main thing we have found about our type of protection is it is important to spend a little time each day and not wait until we are having trouble, then try to play catch-up. We have a drill we refer to as the "set drill." Our offensive linemen and a QB line up without a defense in front of them. On the snap signal, we practice setting as quickly as possible.

We want our blockers to set as quickly as possible and in good fundamental position. If they are slow in setting, we cannot have good protection. We have each blocker go through this drill two or three times. We feel that we must get maximum concentration from each player in order to have an effective, worthwhile drill.

The next drill we use is the shuffling drill. In this drill, we put a defensive man on each blocker and have him use fakes and deceptive moves to get to the passer. This is where we get some overanxiousness by the blockers. They must maintain balance and not lunge out if they expect to be effective. This drill helps us improve our agility and foot movement.

We also have a one-on-one pass protection drill where the coach calls different charges by the rusher. These are the calls:

1. Charge nose on
2. Charge outside

3. Charge inside

4. Fake to inside, charge to outside

5. Fake to outside, charge to inside

We generally end our individual practice time by working against stunting and blitzing LBs. Our blockers set and pick up stunts from all defensive variations. We want to develop pride in our protection. Regardless of what the defense does, we want to be able to block it.

Another drill that we use is the cover drill. Every time we throw the ball, we want our linemen and backs to be in a position to prevent a touchdown should the defense intercept. We also want to be in a position to help out if we possibly can when we complete the pass. After the quarterback has thrown the ball, the first blocker to see it yells "cover." The two guards and the center go directly to the ball. The tack-les release outside and go toward the sideline, so as to keep leverage on the ball if it is intercepted. The halfbacks also move toward the sideline and keep outside leverage on the football (figure 14).

We stress all of our fundamentals every day and feel that this is a must if we are going to have good pass protection.

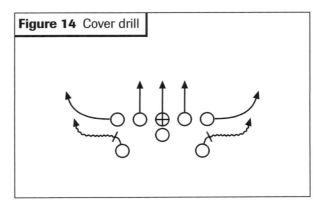

Figure 14 Cover drill

1964 Summer Manual. Jack Little was offensive line coach at Baylor University.

Building Effective Pass Protection

Jack Bicknell, Mike Maser, and Vince Martino

At Boston College, we believe in the forward pass. We come out of the tunnel throwing the ball, and then we look for run balance.

The key to a successful passing game is protecting the passer. We emphasize this phase of our offensive scheme with time in practice and with the assignment of our coaching staff.

We have two full-time offensive line coaches. Without saying a word to our team, this tells them how critical I feel this area is.

Offensive linemen are unique individuals. I have always said if I were to start a business tomorrow I would hire all offensive linemen. They would work for low wages, wouldn't care who got the credit, and would work harder than any QB, running back, or WR I could hire.

We have good-sized kids up front. We are not all hung up on height, but we do happen to have big kids. In recruiting, we take kids with good size potential. We investigate their work habits and try to find out how important football is to them. We do not overevaluate their performance on film. Most big kids are like St. Bernard puppies. They are awkward, slow, and just aren't great on film.

I believe that if you take 10 big kids, you can probably get six of them to develop into great players. If you take fewer than that, there is a chance you will be caught with not enough physical kids, and at this level you must have them.

I am not concerned with what they bench when we recruit them. I am very concerned that they have an appreciation for weight lifting. We have the ability to develop strength, but only if the kid sincerely wants to become strong. Linemen have to be highly motivated and dedicated to a year-round lifting program.

Although we believe in throwing the football, you wouldn't know it by watching our linemen in their individual drill periods. We work run techniques 50 percent of the time and pass protection drills 50 percent. I don't want us to be one of those teams that can't run the ball when needed. I also believe the intensity needed to run block is the same intensity needed to pass block.

When we sit down as a staff to talk protection schemes, the first thing we talk about is blitz pickup. We have never had a practice, either spring or fall, without a 10-minute blitz pickup period. The key to success against the blitz is simplicity. I would rather do one thing well than do five things OK.

The key to success in pass protection is assignment communication, which is why we settle on our starters as soon as possible and don't change very much. By working together, your linemen learn to communicate with one another. If we have an inexperienced lineman, we try to have experienced players on either side of him.

Pass Protection Schemes

We have two basic maximum pass protection schemes at B.C.: play action and straight dropback. As in all maximum pass protection schemes, we want to solidify the back side of the formation at all times, which means trying to get at least four men concentrating on the side away from the pattern concentration. This is built into the scheme itself from day one. We believe in teaching the protection thoroughly and modifying it slightly and only when necessary.

Play-Action Pass

Our play-action pass protection (figures 1 and 2) is derived from our sprint-draw action. It is based on a man scheme with zone principles built in. Both protections are called to the right.

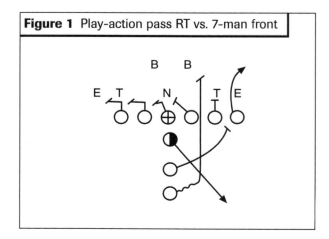

Figure 1 Play-action pass RT vs. 7-man front

These are the blocking rules for protecting the play-action pass RT versus a seven-man front:

FSE: pattern

FST: man on

FSG: down on nose to FS "G-C" gap

C: nose to BS "G-C" gap

BSG: BS "G-T" gap

FST: BS "T-E" gap

FB: FS end of line

TB: first LB FS

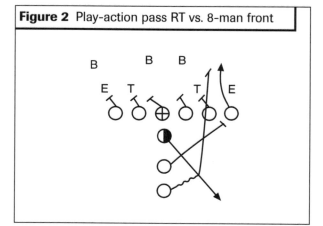

Figure 2 Play-action pass RT vs. 8-man front

These are the blocking rules for protecting the play-action pass RT versus an eight-man front:

FSE: pattern

FST: down to DT

FSG: FS "G-C" gap

C: BS "G-C" gap

BSG: BS "G-T" gap

BST: BS "T-E" gap

FB: FS end of line

TB: first LB FS

The man part of the protection scheme involves the front side tackle, FB, and TB. The other people have man-attack points, but zone principles take over if the defense changes its gap responsibilities. The back side principle is emphasized from the front side guard. If the assigned gap is not filled, a 45-degree drop to the back side is taken. The key is control and the drop angle. We want to take on the defender as far away from the QB as possible, so he doesn't feel pressure.

It is the back's responsibility to recognize secondary stunts and send an alert call to the QB, either before or after the snap, to let him know that a secondary stunt is coming and the fake will be disregarded. The alert call does not change the protection up front in any way.

Maximum Dropback Pass

Our dropback pass protection is a man scheme (figures 3 and 4). It is directed by a call in the huddle and incorporates the same three front side and four back side principles that our play-action pass employs.

Figure 3 Dropback pass vs. 7-man front

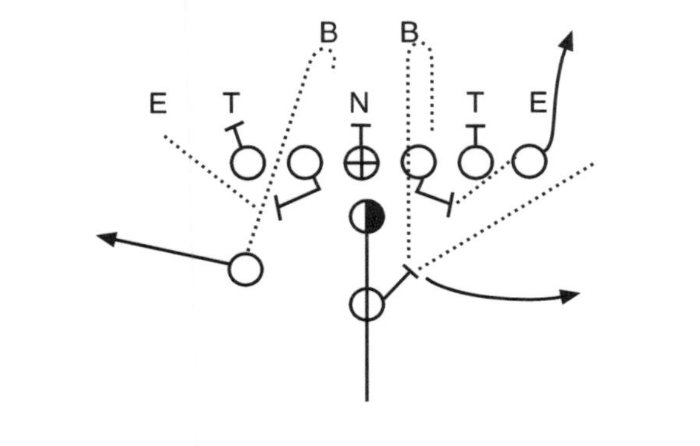

These are the blocking rules for protecting a dropback pass versus a seven-man front:

FSE: pattern

FST: number two on line

FSG: double-check one to three

C: zero

BSG: double-check one to three

BST: number two on line

FB: FSLB, to widest, to release

TB: BSLB to widest, to release

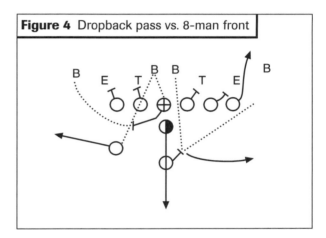

Figure 4 Dropback pass vs. 8-man front

These are the blocking rules for protecting a dropback pass versus an eight-man front:

FSE: pattern

FST: number two on line

FSG: number one on line

C: BSLB to out BS

BSG: number one on line

BST: number two on line

FB: double-check FSLB, to widest

TB: BSLB to widest, to release

Versus both the seven-man and eight-man fronts, we try to incorporate the check-release principle for our backs. Versus the seven-man front, they are tied up with the guard on checking LBs to ends. Versus the eight-man look, the tailback is tied up to the center in the same relationship, while the FB has a true double-check sequence to the front side of the play. We don't double-team the nose because we don't want our tailback or FB blocking an end-of-line rusher in a normal situation when they could get out and be a safety valve receiver. We help out the center with either guard after his double check gives him no one to block.

The big similarity between these two protections is the idea that it takes both backs and the line to protect in a maximum scheme. The backs must be aware that when we use these protections, they are blockers first and pass receivers only when their rules and checks are fully covered. Mike Godbolt, our running back coach, does a great job with these rules and principles with his kids, and more than once they've covered for us.

Hot Protections

Our philosophy is to formationally spread them out on defense and not to squeeze in and maximum protect. Also, we do not want the defense to dictate to us where we need to audible.

I would like to give you two of our most-used hot protections. The first is a directional hot read to the open end called Lucy/Ricky. The QB must read the defenders to the front side for hot.

For example, if our TE is to the left, we would use Ricky protection (figure 5). We would use Lucy if the TE is to the right (figure 6). Two TEs would give us the ability to go either direction.

Figure 5 Ricky vs. 40

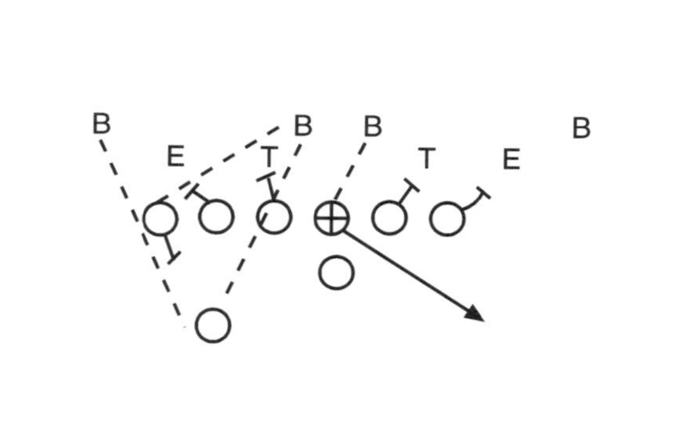

These are the blocking rules for this protection versus the 40 defense:

FST: double-check defender over the outside

FSG: block man on

C: check front side LB to front side (help twists)

BSG: block man on

BST: block number two lineman (possible ax)

BSE: check inside LB, block number four if "go," release

Back: block inside LB "go," to outside LB, release

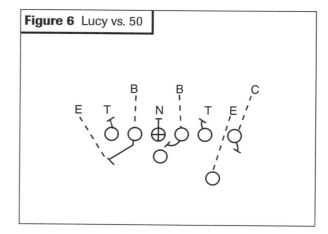

Figure 6 Lucy vs. 50

These are the blocking rules for this protection versus the 50 defense:

FST: block man on

FSG: double-check LB to DE, help OT

C: block man on (help from BSG)

BSG: single check LB to MG

BST: block man on

BSE: check secondary stunt, release

Back: block DE, release

One lineman is double-checking. If both defenders rush, it is hot. We also need to have some line calls in case the inside LB's alignment causes the back a problem (figure 7).

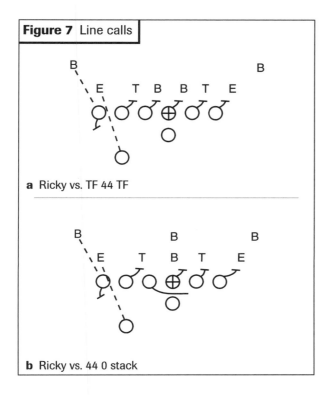

Figure 7 Line calls

a Ricky vs. TF 44 TF

b Ricky vs. 44 0 stack

Shifting the back closer to the LOS or shifting to the shotgun are other options for the tough LB alignment. This is an excellent way to protect the QB, and it allows us to run our offense without a lot of audibles.

The second directional hot protection is Lee/Ray. It is called to the TE, who is the hot receiver. We would use Ray if the TE is right (figure 8) and Lee with the TE left (figure 9).

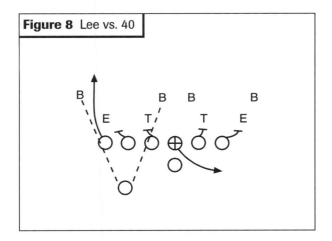

Figure 8 Lee vs. 40

In the protection, the back blocks front side with the double check. We only have six available blockers, so a secondary stunt is the QB's responsibility. The hot is the same read as in Lucy/Ricky.

These are the blocking rules for Lee protection against the 40 defense:

FST: block number two lineman

FSG: block man on

C: check back side LB to back side

BSG: block man on

BST: block number two lineman

Back: check front side LB to outside LB, release

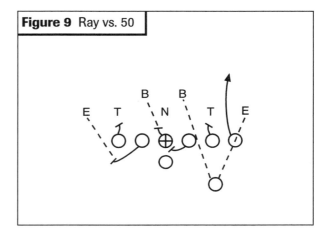

Figure 9 Ray vs. 50

These are the blocking rules for Ray protection against the 50 defense:

FST: block man on

FSG: slide to take FS "A" gap (MG)

C: slide to back side "A" gap (LB)

BSG: out for DE

BST: block man on

Back: check LB to DE, release

Again, if the LBs are in an alignment that gives our back a problem, we make a line call (figure 10).

This is an excellent protection for a zero-based defense. The QB must handle secondary stunts.

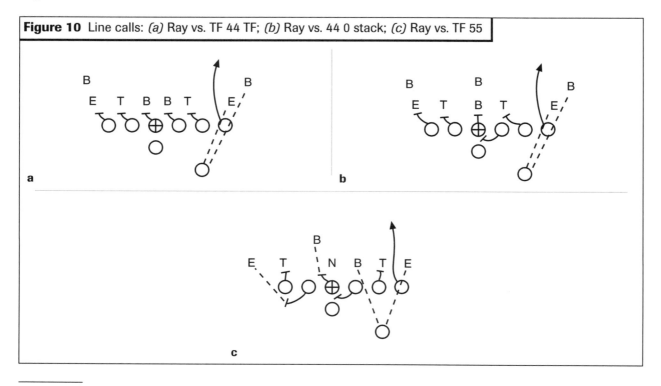

Figure 10 Line calls: *(a)* Ray vs. TF 44 TF; *(b)* Ray vs. 44 0 stack; *(c)* Ray vs. TF 55

1987 Proceedings. Jack Bicknell was head coach and Mike Maser and Vince Martino were assistant coaches at Boston College. Bicknell is head coach of the Barcelona Dragons.

Training for Multiple-Pass Protection

Kent Stephenson

Our offensive philosophy is based on a balanced attack in that we intend to be a 50 percent run and 50 percent pass team. Naturally, the course of the game may dictate a change in our philosophy. We are deeply committed to throwing the ball from dropback action. However, we have found that we also must throw the ball from play action and sprint in order to keep the outstanding defenses we play off balance. Keeping in mind that our people up front must protect the passer and block for the run with equal effectiveness, it is important that our linemen meet certain standards. We use these standards in our selection process in recruiting as well as in determining where current personnel will play on the offensive line.

Personnel Evaluation

Our center is the quarterback of our offensive line, and, therefore, football intelligence is required. We need a young man capable of making quick decisions in determining the defensive front as well as the proper blocking calls corresponding to that front. We are concerned about quickness, as well, in order to neutralize the great noseguards we play against in this league.

Our guards do a great deal of pulling. Therefore, a guard must be a fluid runner with the ability to change directions on the run. Since we face so many overshift defenses and even fronts, our guards must also have the physical stature to pass and run block versus defensive tackles. Our best athletes play guard.

We are not looking for any great speed from our tackles. However, quickness and 260-plus pounds are almost a must. Our tackles' toughest assignment is dropback pass blocking of quick defensive ends from the outside position.

There are other qualities that we feel are imperative in the development of superior offensive linemen. We work very hard to develop these qualities to the highest possible level.

We want our linemen to be the leaders of our weight room in attendance and rate of strength gain. We will be on the field a little longer than the rest of the team and take pride in doing this. We have numerous individual meetings to encourage a burning desire to become the best our God-given talents will allow.

We work very hard during individual meetings to develop a completely unselfish attitude. We have a motto that must typify an offensive lineman's role: "It's amazing how much a person can accomplish when he doesn't care who gets the credit."

Pass Protection Technique

Since our linemen come in all shapes and sizes, we treat them individually in determining the best stance. However, we adhere to the following principles, no matter how tall they are:

1. Feet: Heels are slightly broken from the ground and no more staggered than toe to heel.

2. Weight: We want little weight on our hands; we form our weight base with our fingers but will allow the thumb on the ground. This allows movement laterally, forward, or retreat with equal effectiveness.

3. Back: We want the eyes up and the back as level as possible, with the hand- and foot-stagger principles having priority. A few of our taller athletes have their tails a little higher in order to move easily from this stance.

We believe the ability of a lineman to assume a proper pass-blocking position from his stance will determine his success. We use a short set step with the staggered foot and drive back off that set step to the desired depth.

We use the following as a set drill. From a three-point stance on the snap count, linemen will set in a pass-protection stance. Coaches check for quickness of set and to insure that players are not overextending on the set step. Players will also set step with an inside move, to simulate response to a defensive man in head-up or inside eye technique.

The next logical progression is to move the players right, left, forward, and back on the coach's commands. Coaching points are to keep the feet wide at all times. Never cross over and don't bring the feet together. Players should shuffle, keeping feet low to the ground in what is practically a quivering movement. Knees should remain slightly bent. Linemen should feel a tightness in their thighs if they're shuffling properly. This drill always ends with a cover call, to simulate the pass being thrown and players sprinting past the coach.

The push-pull drill is used in a manner that becomes progressively tougher for the player.

1. First, players pair off into offensive and defensive groups. The offensive player assumes a basic pass protection stance with the exception that his hands are behind his back. The defensive man places his hands on the

offensive man's shoulders and attempts to push or pull him off balance. The offensive man must keep a wide base, shuffle feet, and not fight the defensive man's pressure too severely or he will lose his balance.

2. In the second part of the drill, allow the offensive man to extend his hands forward and allow the defensive man to move to the right and left as well as forward and backward.

3. In the final part of this drill, allow the defensive man to use different pass-rush techniques, such as swim technique, as well as pushing and pulling. Note: This is an excellent drill to use in preseason before pads are allowed.

For the eye opener drill, players line up facing each other. The offensive man assumes a pass-protection stance, shuffling his feet. On the coach's command, the defensive man steps forward and the offensive man punches with open hands to neutralize the charge of the defensive man. He then shuffles to the next defender, repeating with a punch, and so on.

Four Pass Schemes

The four basic Kansas protections are the fire series, flood series weak, flood series strong, and sprint-draw pass.

Fire Series

We use regular cup protection and rules; however, the line is aggressive to keep defenders' hands down. Backs block first man outside the tackle box, keeping hands down (figure 1).

Flood Series Weak

The weak back releases immediately, and the center, weak guard, weak tackle, and strong guard slide weak. The FB checks the strong backer and the TE blocks (figure 2). If we want the TE in the pattern, he is hot to route, and the FB has double read from the LB to the strong end (figure 3).

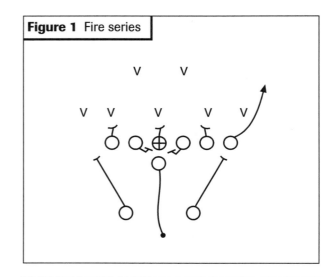

Figure 1 Fire series

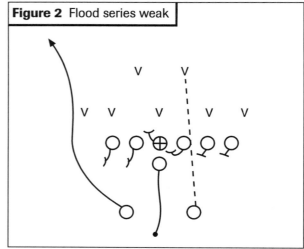

Figure 2 Flood series weak

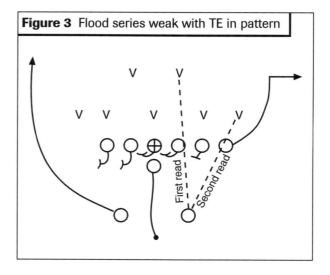

Figure 3 Flood series weak with TE in pattern

Flood Series Strong

The strong back will release immediately and run a designated combination route with the TE and flanker. The line will slide strong with the weak back staying (figure 4).

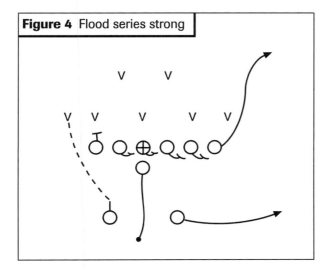

Figure 4 Flood series strong

Sprint-Draw Pass

The FB blocks the first man outside of the tackle. The tailback has a fake, the strong LB, and blitz responsibility. Onside linemen will mirror any man on them, no man, block inside. Our center and offside linemen will make 45-degree turns and block their back side (figure 5).

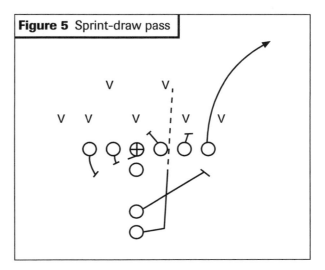

Figure 5 Sprint-draw pass

1982 Summer Manual. Kent Stephenson was assistant coach at the University of Kansas.

PART IV

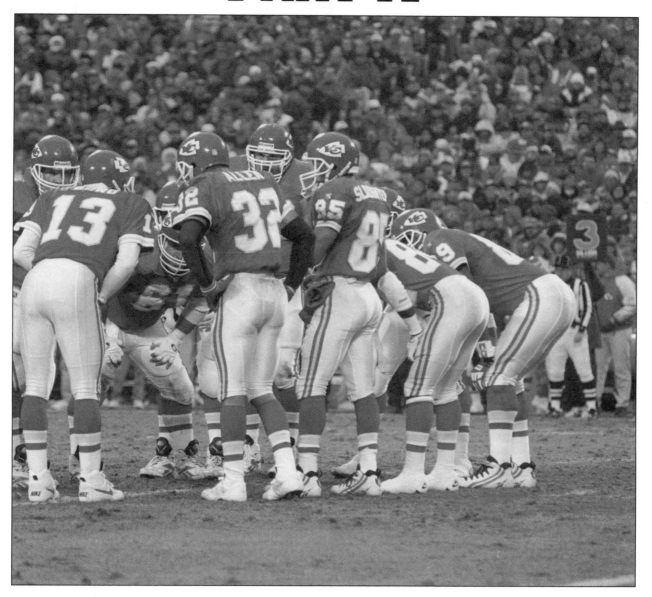

Down-and-Distance Decisions

Part IV—Down-and-Distance Decisions

Play-Calling on Third Down

Pokey Allen

We have devised a ready sheet that deals with every situation we will confront during a football game. After extensive research, careful thought, and an exchange of ideas, we put our heads together and came up with what we believe to be the best approach.

It is our belief that decisions about play calling are made more rationally during the week than on game day under what are often emotional circumstances. Therefore, Monday night, when we begin to consider our preliminary game plan, we give a good deal of thought to what plays we are going to run in each situation, and out of what formations we are going to run each play. We are a multiple formation team, so this plays a big part in our preparation.

Wednesday night, when we finalize our game plan, we sit down and put these plays into the order in which they will be called. This helps eliminate the spur-of-the-moment decisions that often can be inconsistent with our game plan. It also enhances our ability to get the play in quickly, avoiding delay-of-game penalties and allowing the QB time to audible if necessary.

We title each situation as follows:

Openers: first 20 plays; first and second downs only

Running game: all game-plan runs

Control passes: hooks, outs, quick passes, option screens, delays

Play action: bootleg, fire passes

Second and long: eight or more yards; used only after the first 20 plays are completed (runs and passes)

Third and short: one to two yards (passes)

Third and long: 5 to 10 yards (runs and passes)

Red zone + 35 to + 10: passes

Red zone + 10 to + 5: passes

Goal line, short-yardage, two yards or less: runs and passes (three tight-end group)

Home runs: deep balls, gadgets

Two-minute: plays run only when clock is stopped

Two-point plays

The subject of discussion today is third down situations. We will be speaking purely from a passing standpoint, but it is important to note that we do not just pass or just run in these or any other situations.

Third and Short

This is a 70 to 80 percent running situation for us, so it is natural that when we decide to throw the ball, it should be off some form of play action. As a general rule, defenses are more pressure-oriented in this situation, so in many cases we are looking to move our QB from his conventional dropback point. The bootleg off counter action (figure 1) is one of our favorites.

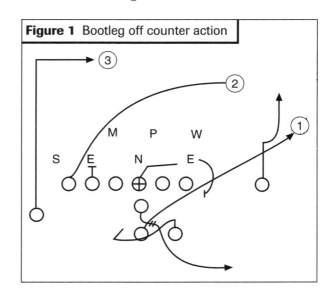

Figure 1 Bootleg off counter action

We have several variations of this play from a multitude of formations and situations, but the bottom line is our objective to get the Willie LB to freeze or chase the pulling tackle. This, we hope, allows clearance for the FB's path to the flat and allows the QB an opportunity to break containment.

The crossing guard action can often distort LB reads and impede the LB's ability to efficiently retreat from his responsibility. This, coupled with the crossing action of the backs, is very difficult for LBs to deal with in man-to-man situations.

Third and Medium

This situation can also be a pressure down for many defenses. If we are going to dropback pass, our mentality is to protect and throw quickly. Our hot receiver package is a large part of our passing game, and we believe it can be implemented in this situation if necessary. We have had success with the TE choice route (figure 2).

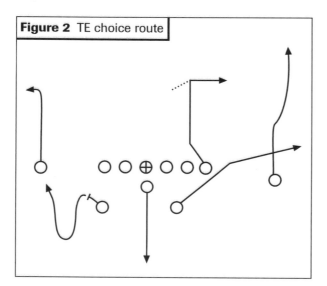

Figure 2 TE choice route

The TE has an inside hot release and will option the drop to the first LB inside. The FB has a free release into the flat. The split end runs a 10-yard speed out and will run a fade versus any roll coverage. The QB will take a five-step drop and will sight adjust with the TE.

If the QB feels the lane is squeezed by any two defenders, he will dump the ball to the FB. If, on the presnap read, the QB sees the FS cheating toward the TE, he knows there is a strong possibility that he has single coverage on the split end and can go to him on the out.

Third and Long

We have a multitude of things to do in this situation, but the personality of the defense will generally dictate which plays we prioritize. Against pressure teams or teams that do not like to roll or press with their cornerbacks, we will run the double square out. Double means both the split end and flanker run mirrored routes. The speed out is a 10-yard out breaking cut designed to be thrown on time.

It is critical that the receiver does not lose speed coming out of his break. We use what we call a "speed cut." We want to eliminate the receiver planting the inside foot and, thus, slowing down. A good speed cut will help the QB time the throw and give the defender virtually no time to close on the throw.

The QB will take five quick steps and throw on time to the target area of the receiver's hip. We do not want to lead the receiver because if the ball is thrown on time, he will not have gathered enough speed to run and get it. Figure 3 is an example of how we run the double square out.

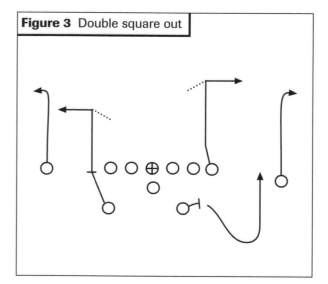

Figure 3 Double square out

Both wide receivers run 10-yard square outs. The TE runs a choice route at eight to 10 yards. The halfback checks and runs an option route opposite the drop off the first LB inside. The FB checks and runs a medium route.

On a presnap read, the QB reads the best-located safety. By this, we mean the safety in the worst position to help on the square out. As he drops, he reads the side he has chosen. If he chooses the X side, he will read the throwing lane through the Willie LB. If the

Willie LB is in the throwing lane, he should look to the halfback.

It is the halfback's responsibility to beat the inside LB, preferably on an outside cut. If the QB chooses the Z side, he should read the throwing lane through the flat defender (i.e., SS or Sam LB). If this defender is in the throwing lane, the QB should look to the TE.

It is the TE's responsibility to beat the first inside LB, again preferably on the outside cut. If both lanes are squeezed, the ball should be dumped to the FB.

1988 Summer Manual. Pokey Allen was head coach at Portland State University.

Beating the Clock

Marv Levy

Many of the so-called "little things" in football are neglected or paid such cursory attention that when the time comes to use them, a team is destined to fail. One area to which such superficial treatment is often given is that which involves a team's "beat-the-clock" offense.

The occasion may arise only rarely when a team must call upon its plan for beating the clock. When that situation does occur, however, the whole difference between winning and losing hangs in the balance.

There are three components that comprise our approach to beating the clock, and we feel that if we are negligent in any one of these areas, we are not being sound. These components are

1. how we present our philosophy of beating the clock to our squad,
2. exactly what our basic plan is in the game for beating the clock, and
3. how we practice this plan.

Let me develop each of these points in more depth.

Developing Clock Awareness

One of our evening team meetings during the preseason (usually around the fifth or sixth evening) is devoted entirely to the discussion of what we are going to do when a beat-the-clock situation arises during the season.

One page in our players' notebook deals with our plan for beating the clock, and they open their notebooks to this page throughout the discussion. We read through this page with them during the meeting and stop to elaborate on the points that merit stressing.

We cover thoroughly the ways in which the clock can be stopped, and the next day the players are given a written test that covers, among other things, these points:

- A called time-out.
- Going out of bounds.
- An incomplete forward pass.
- A penalty.

During this meeting, we stress the importance of being well prepared for the beat-the-clock situation when it arises. We make the point that this moment of truth is an inherent part of the game and that it is a circumstance they should expect to face at some time. They need not think of it as a moment of desperation, but rather as a likely occurrence in a football game.

Teams that win the thrillers and the championships must expect that they will be called upon to put their plans into effect and, therefore, we have a plan. For illustrative purposes, we use examples from games (college and professional) of the previous season in which beat-the-clock situations determined the outcome. Good examples come from games that received national attention, although the best example is one that has occurred in a game involving our own team.

Next, we let the players know that we will devote the following morning's practice entirely to working on our beat-the-clock offense. From there, we progress to detailing our specific plan on the blackboard.

We conclude this presentation by showing an actual film of a beat-the-clock sequence from one of our own games or from a film we have procured specifically for that purpose.

We consistently make the point that successful implementation of beat-the-clock offense involves an attitude of poise, not one of desperation. It is not a matter of hurrying; it is a matter of discipline.

Planing to Beat the Clock

Since we do not employ the dropback pass as part of our basic offense, we construct our beat-the-clock plan in such a way that we need not call on dropbacks in this situation, either. We feel that if we incorporate dropbacks only for the purpose of our beat-the-clock approach, we will be very poor in executing this part of the game. Also, such an alteration would create a sense of panic or desperation among our players, thereby diminishing our chances to succeed.

Since we are basically a sprint-out team, we will continue to use an approach based on the sprint-out. We will go into our beat-the-clock

offense only when less than two minutes remain on the clock. If we are in our opponent's territory, we prefer to wait until 1+ minutes or less remain before calling upon our beat-the-clock tactics.

When the necessity for time conservation finally comes during the game and we no longer feel that we have time to huddle, our QB will yell, "Mayday!" We will line up immediately in the formation shown in figure 1.

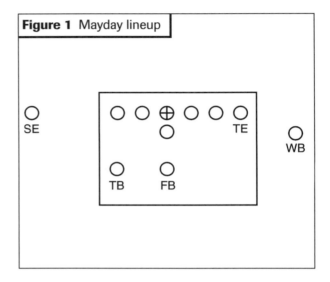

Figure 1 Mayday lineup

The nine players shown in the boxed area always will line up exactly as indicated. If the wingback and split end are on the other side of the formation, we do not want them wasting the time it would take to run across the field in order to line up as shown in figure 1. In such an instance, our wingback lines up one yard off the LOS to the left and our split end lines up on the LOS to the right as shown in figure 2.

Since we never do release our TE on a play from Mayday, it does not matter that he is ineligible in the example depicted by figure 2.

As soon as our team is lined up, our QB yells either "51" (our basic sprint-out pass to the right) or "59" (our basic sprint-out pass to the left). On the next sound from the QB, the ball is snapped. The WR toward whom we are sprinting on these plays has a three-way option he can run according to the reaction of the secondary defender playing him.

After starting to bend out at five yards, the receiver drives upfield. If the receiver is able to

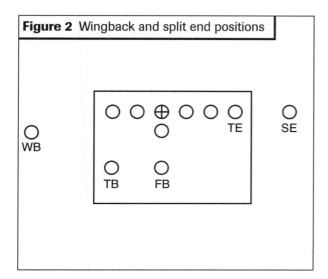

Figure 2 Wingback and split end positions

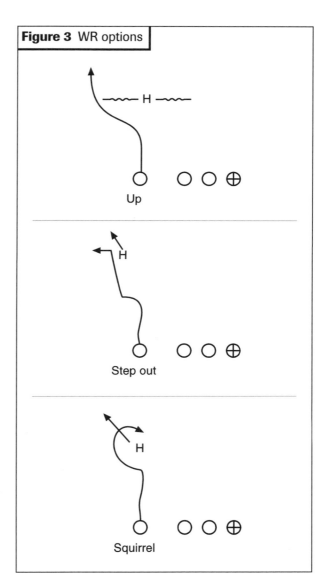

Figure 3 WR options

drive by the defender, he does so, and, in effect, runs our up pattern. If the defender has laid off deep, our receiver breaks out again at approximately 12 yards' depth and effects our step out pattern. If the defender has laid off deep and to the outside, anticipating the step out, our receiver turns to the inside at approximately 12 to 15 yards' depth and effects our squirrel pattern. These options are shown in figure 3.

We prefer incorporating this three-way option (which is a part of our basic passing attack) into our beat-the-clock approach in order to afford us an opportunity to call on a play that has yardage-gaining potential. This is particularly true in a third down situation, and it is an absolute necessity in a fourth down situation where we cannot afford to merely kill the clock.

We want four-man protection on the side toward which we are sprinting. Figure 4 shows our 51 play from the Mayday. The total pattern for all receivers is shown, and I will not describe the cuts in detail.

If the quarterback had called 59, we run the play shown in figure 5. Note that the TE does not release. This helps protect us against having an illegal receiver downfield in the event that our split end lined up on the right.

From this point, any time the clock is stopped, our team huddles and the QB calls any of our plays that might be appropriate to the situation. If the clock continues to run, we automatically line up in our Mayday, and the QB again calls either the 51 or 59 from the LOS.

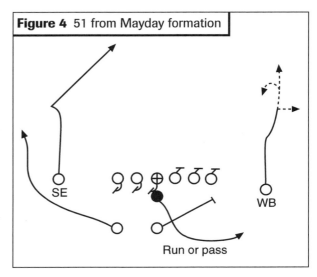

Figure 4 51 from Mayday formation

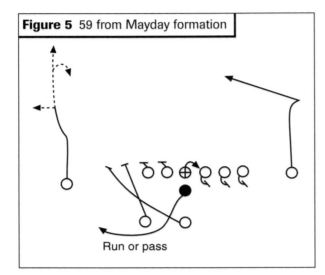

Figure 5 59 from Mayday formation

Run or pass

There are situations when our total concern involves stopping. In any situation where stopping the clock is the all-important factor and when no time-outs remain, the QB will yell for his Mayday formation and then make a call of either "51 kill" or "59 kill."

On these plays, the receiver merely runs a quick out pattern and the QB delivers the ball almost immediately in such a manner that, if the receiver isn't obviously wide open, the ball will be thrown over his head out of bounds. The 51 kill is shown in figure 6. This call, of course, must never be made on fourth down.

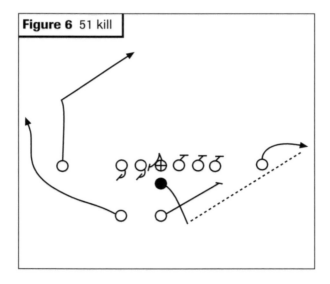

Figure 6 51 kill

The only other eventuality for which we feel it is essential to prepare as a part of our beat-the-clock offense comes up when we are in a Mayday and a vital short-yardage situation

prevails. This could come with inches to go for a first down, with enough time remaining on the clock to allow us additional plays after picking up the first down. It could also come on a very short goal line situation as the clock is running out with no time left for us to huddle. In situations such as these, our QB will have available a call of "44," and we will run a wedge with the fullback hitting at the right leg of the center (figure 7).

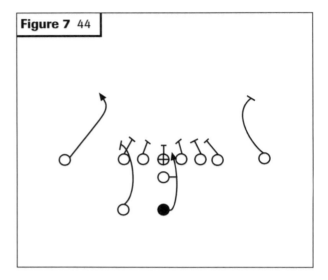

Figure 7 44

In review, the QB has the following calls available to him from the Mayday: 51 or 59; 51 kill or 59 kill; and 44.

Any time we huddle, of course, the QB can select any appropriate call from our offensive repertoire. We stress to him that it is not necessary to go all the way in one play.

We feel that the approach he takes should involve moving in chunks of yardage and feel also that along the way, so far as his huddle calls are concerned, he can call on some running plays to pick up sizeable yardage against prevent-type defenses. This is particularly true when more than one minute remains and we have done a good job of preserving our time-outs.

Practicing Our Plan

To our way of thinking, this is by far the most important element involved in preparation for beating the clock. Everyone has a relatively simple plan available, and we feel that ours is by no means one that encompasses great ingenuity. The success of any plan depends upon practicing it diligently, and although even that does not assure success, it at least allows us to enter the game with peace of mind. Also, it ingrains in the players the confidence that comes from feeling prepared.

The morning practice following the evening meeting where we introduced our beat-the-clock offense is devoted entirely to practicing the plan as we outlined it the evening before. To practice, we go into the stadium and turn on the game clock. We feel this is essential to practicing beat-the-clock offense correctly.

We feel that the first practices must be under full scrimmage conditions. Once the season begins, we can afford little scrimmage, and there is no way we can make up what might have been missed earlier. After a brief dummy review on the field, we go to live scrimmaging of our beat-the-clock offense.

Players not engaged in the on-the-field practice sit as a group in the stands with coaches who comment as the situation develops on the field. The QBs will sit to one side of this group with their coach in order to discuss the specific quarterbacking considerations as they happen.

We construct artificial time, score, and field position situations, all of which fall into the scope of our beat-the-clock offense. We feel it is very important at first to create the situation in such a way that the likelihood of success is with the offensive team. For that reason, we go against our weakest defensive team and construct the situation so that the QB has three time-outs remaining.

This session should be filmed, making certain that the scoreboard is shown between all downs. Only the head coach is on the field during the attempted drive, and absolutely no coaching takes place at this time. Notes will be kept during the drive, and when it is over the team assembles.

Corrections and reflections are made immediately, but briefly. Then another situation is constructed and the procedure is repeated.

As the morning practice progresses, the situations are varied. In some, for instance, a field goal might be the winning margin. In some instances, we limit the time remaining even more. In still other instances, fewer or no time-outs are allowed.

It is important to employ a cool, poised, analytical approach. Plenty of excitement is inherent in the situation, and the players get a great deal of enjoyment out of this practice session, especially when they succeed. In those instances when the drive is not successful, we feel the coaching staff must not exhibit concern or act upset, as this shakes the players' confidence. It is vital that confidence be built at this time.

When a drive doesn't succeed, we try to use it as an object lesson and analyze the reason why it did not succeed, making certain we phrase our remarks so that blame is not indicated.

At the team meeting that evening, we briefly discuss the practice and the events that occurred. We also administer a short written test that relates to considerations involved in our beat-the-clock offense.

On at least two additional occasions prior to our opening game, we practice a variety of beat-the-clock situations. In these sessions, we again go into the stadium and turn on the game clock.

Although we will not devote an entire practice session to working on this phase of the game (except for the introductory session I have already discussed), we allow enough time to give thorough, unhurried attention to it.

All of our preseason, beat-the-clock practices are carried out under full, live-scrimmage conditions, in the stadium, with the game clock running.

On the Saturday prior to our opening game, we have a regular scrimmage session, as most teams tend to do. At the conclusion of this scrimmage, we devote 30 minutes to working specifically on our beat-the-clock tactics. We feel that this helps to prepare our team to meet such a problem while they are somewhat tired from the prior work they have done.

When they are called upon in the game to move the ball a long distance in a short period of time, it will come at the end of the game, when they are likely to be tired and when discipline and poise are most essential. It is necessary, therefore, that they be exposed to practicing under just such a condition.

Once our regular season games begin, we rarely practice beat-the-clock situations live. We do, however, have a controlled type of beat-the-clock practice on the field every Thursday as part of our "special situations" period. There is no week in which we neglect to practice these tactics. On occasion, we construct the situation so that it begins on fourth down. The purpose of this, of course, is to actually expose our QB to the fourth down consideration. If he makes a mistake, we can then correct it on the basis of his experiences. Also, at our team meeting on Friday prior to each game, we review verbally and by quiz (usually oral) our beat-the-clock plan.

If a beat-the-clock situation occurs in our game or if the televised professional game on Sunday involves a beat-the-clock situation, we make certain to review and discuss what occurred when our squad meets on Monday. The best teaching examples, by far, are those in which our squad members are actually involved or those with which they at least had some vicarious association.

In discussing our approach to beating the clock, I detailed the three components involved in preparing our squad as a whole. Although all of the material discussed pertains to the QB also, we feel that additional instruction is required if the QB is to function effectively.

The QB meeting (on the day our squad meets to discuss beating the clock) also is used to discuss these tactics in even greater detail. One point stressed heavily with the QB is his awareness of the down and yardage situation, with the thought in mind again of avoiding a 51 kill or 59 kill call on fourth down. The importance of conserving time-outs is also a topic we review thoroughly with the QB.

We feel that the least important aspect of beat-the-clock offense is the set of plays the coaches decide to use. There are several sound approaches as far as play selection is concerned.

However, you must present your plan to the squad in a manner that helps the players to understand thoroughly what you are trying to accomplish, and in a manner that helps them

believe they are going to succeed in accomplishing their objectives.

Most important, they must be fully exposed to the execution of this plan by actual on-the-field practice. They must learn not only what to do by virtue of this practice, but they must gain the poise and discipline necessary for success, and they must profit from the practice mistakes that are likely to occur.

In summarizing, realization of the following points helps highlight the approach we want in our beat-the-clock offense:

1. Players must understand that, as an inherent part of the game, they will face situations requiring them to snatch victory from the jaws of defeat.

2. Players must understand that poise and discipline, not hurry and desperation, form the foundation for succeeding.

3. You must have a specific plan, and it must be simple.

4. When first practicing the plan, the situation should be constructed so that success is likely.

5. Coaches should not coach while the plan is being practiced.

6. Review each beat-the-clock drive attempt immediately after it is completed in practice.

7. Team members not participating in a specific beat-the-clock drive attempt in practice should observe it and learn from it.

8. The plan must be practiced in the stadium with the game clock running.

9. Any plan is worthless unless it is practiced considerably and correctly.

A team may do all of these things and still fail to succeed when the time comes in a game to use the beat-the-clock offense. Nevertheless, coaches and players have the assurance of knowing that failure comes not as a result of negligence or laziness. At the same time, the percentage for success is greatly increased in favor of the team that has made a wholehearted preparation.

1967 Summer Manual. Marv Levy was head coach at the College of William and Mary.

Executing in the Four Critical Zones

Paul "Bear" Bryant

In order to discuss offense in the critical zones, we must first have an understanding of what are critical zones. Offensively, we think in terms of four critical zones: from the 20-yard line to the goal line going in to score; from the goal line to the 25-yard line coming out; late in the second quarter; and late in the fourth quarter when we must maintain control of the football to win. We also feel that anytime we have the ball on third or fourth down with short yardage and we are going for a first down, that's critical. We will not give the zones a priority because at certain times any of the four could be more important than the others. We will discuss them as critical zones one, two, three, and four in the order they are listed.

Critical Zone One

Of the many factors that go into selecting a play, probably the most important single factor is field position. To aid our QB in his play selection, we divide the field into different areas and zones as illustrated in figure 1. Each zone is given a name, and there are some important objectives concerning each area.

We divide the field into the following areas and zones, with the most important objectives listed. The gut zone extends from the 20-yard line to where the defense goes into its goal line defense, usually around the eight-yard line. These are our objectives in the gut zone:

1. We must out-gut them.
2. We try to get six yards or more in the first two downs.
3. We make first down on third down.

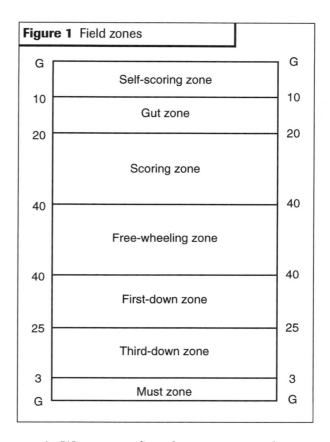

Figure 1 Field zones

4. We pass on first down or waste down.
5. We select plays that won't lose ground or take us out of the scoring zone.

When we get inside the 20-yard line, we like to think in terms of six points. By this we mean we do not consider settling for a field goal until after the third down play is over.

When we are inside the opponent's 20-yard line, we think of two plays that have been good to us: our option 29 and pass 55 X-circle. Figure 2 shows option 29 against the Oklahoma defense. In option 29, our line blocks regular one,

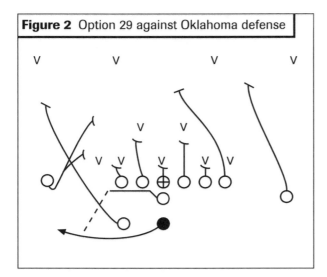

Figure 2 Option 29 against Oklahoma defense

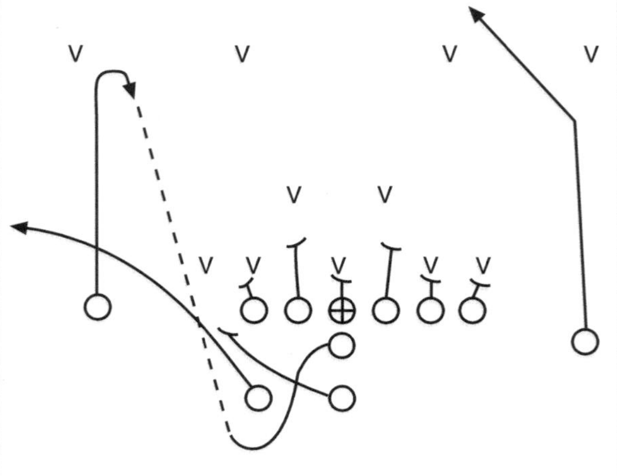

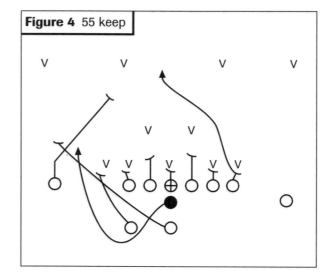

Figure 3 Pass 55 X-circle

two, three. The weak back junction blocks on 1/3. The QB options the end (he does not pitch too quickly). The FB positions the QB for the pitch.

The option 29 against the Oklahoma defense in the gut zone gives us a good play according to our objectives. It is capable of breaking for a good gain. If our QB does what he has been taught, we should not lose ground. It puts pressure on the defense both inside and outside.

One thing we try to emphasize to our QB is that the quicker he attacks the end, the better chance he has for a good play. We also face the 43 defense quite often, but with option 29, there is no rule change in our blocking. The weak tackle's block will vary according to alignment of the defensive end and LB. This will be determined by which is playing inside or outside.

Pass 55 X-circle should give us a good play in the gut zone, as shown in figure 3.

This is a sprint-out pass to our weak side. The weak end fires off the line to about eight yards and hooks to the inside. The weak tackle blocks over or outside. The weak guard and center block outside gap over. The strong guard and strong tackle block inside gap over. The strong end blocks inside gap over. The weak back releases into the quick flat, looking for the football on the third step. The strong back releases down and through the safety. The FB blocks the first man outside the weak tackle. The QB springs out behind the weak tackle, squares his shoulders with the LOS, and challenges the defense to a run or pass. If he throws,

he should throw quickly. Again we have a play that agrees with our objectives. The 55 X-circle pass gives us an option to throw or run. As the QB sprints out, if the defense challenges the run, he throws; if not, he runs the ball. This is a good play to run on any down in the gut zone.

We have certain plays in which we have prepared for the gut zone of the opponent. If our opponent stays with its regular defense in the gut zone, there are many good, sound plays that are suitable, as we have four plays to get the first down.

A play that has really helped us in the gut zone is 55 keep, which we run mostly on second and third downs (figure 4).

This plays looks very much like 55 X-circle. The blocking for the offensive line is the same as on 55 X-circle except that the line blocking is

Figure 4 55 keep

aggressive, which will include LBs. The strong end releases downfield on 55 keep.

We feel if we have done a good job of coaching and selling our players on what we are trying to do in the gut zone, we should reach a field position where our opponent will go into his goal line defense. We call this point the "self-scoring" zone. This zone is a continuation of the gut zone, but we have to make an offensive adjustment now to match the goal line defense.

The first thing to do is bring our strong back in. Figure 5 shows the offensive adjustment with the strong back in.

We have established the goal line defense. We have other objectives for the self-scoring zone that are very important.

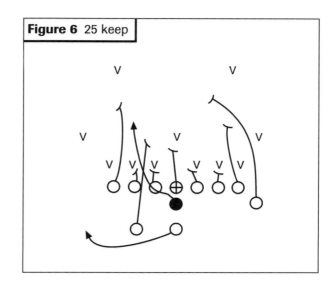

Figure 6 25 keep

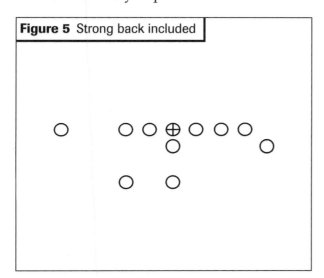

Figure 5 Strong back included

1. The QB keeps the ball as much as possible.
2. We run quick-hitting plays.
3. We run behind the best blocker.
4. This is not a "fool 'em" zone, but we have to take it to them.
5. We must score.

Many of our opponents use the 6-5 goal line defense, and the plays that have been good to us against the 6-5 are the 25 keep (figure 6), the counter 21 help (figure 7), the 64 power (figure 8), and the QB wedge (figure 9).

Much of the time, we will tighten up the weak end in the self-scoring zone. We will also bring the weak end in tight on counter 21 help

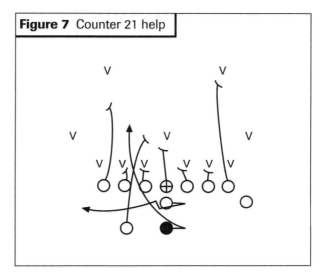

Figure 7 Counter 21 help

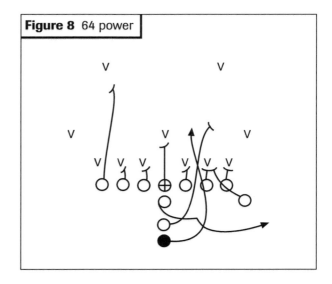

Figure 8 64 power

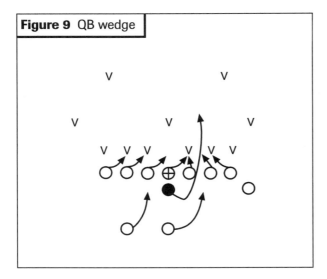

Figure 9 QB wedge

and block him on the end man. We think this is an ideal play because the counter fake by the QB and FB helps the block on the middle LB, and the halfback blocks the over LB. The linemen up front are blocking regular. Our strong back in motion gives the threat of an option.

Our line blocks regular one, two, and three. The strong back drives to the outside leg of the tackle. He blocks the first color that shows, which is usually the LB. The FB drives through the outside leg of the guard. He blocks the first color to show, which is usually the middle LB.

All linemen wedge to the apex over the strong guard. It is very important for our linemen to stay on their feet and keep moving. We have to get penetration. This play is used on short-yardage downs or scoring from within the one-yard line.

To conclude this discussion of the gut and self-scoring zones, we have three "musts" that have to be accomplished for us to reach our objectives:

1. We must not get a penalty.
2. We must not break an offensive signal.
3. We must each block our man.

Critical Zone Two

The "must zone" extends from the goal line to the 25-yard line coming out. Our offensive thinking coming out is basically the same as going in. We must get the ball out to the three-yard line. We like to kick from a spread punt formation, and our kicker lines up 13 yards deep. From the goal line to the 12-yard line, especially inside the three, we run QB wedge, FB wedge (figure 10), and 64 power.

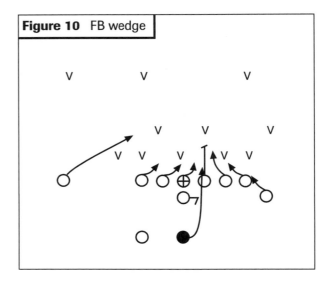

Figure 10 FB wedge

We must run a quick-hitting play with power at the point of attack. Down close to the goal line, we expect the defense to charge hard and low. According to the situation, we kick most of the time on third down. After reaching the 12-yard line, we go with our game plans. Occasionally, we may run a sweep trap or a delayed pass play, but basically we run 66 lead (figure 11), 25 (figure 12), option 29, pass 55 X-circle, and pass 66 deep regular (figure 13).

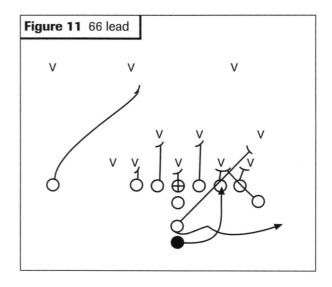

Figure 11 66 lead

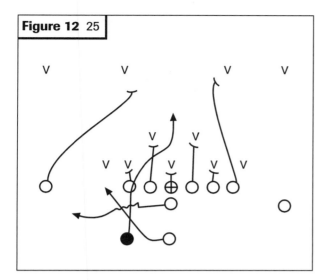

Figure 12 25

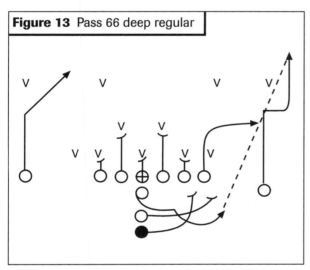

Figure 13 Pass 66 deep regular

From the 3-yard line to the 25-yard line could be called the three-down zone. If we do not make a first down on third down, we are forced to kick the ball. We must reach our objective to get the ball past the 25-yard line; then if we are forced to punt, our opponent will receive the ball in its three-down zone. Again, we have reached our objectives in the three-down, or must, zone.

1. We must make a first down with three plays.
2. Normally, we will kick on third down with five yards or more to go.
3. We do not like to punt while in this zone. If we can hold the football until we get

past the 25-yard line, we can put the opposition in its three-down zone with a 40-yard kick.

4. We think trap, sweep, or delayed passes are good in this zone.
5. We also look for pressure defenses here. We will play cautiously from the three-yard line to the 12-yard line, but once we reach the 12-yard line, we will go with our basic offense.

Critical Zone Three

As we approach critical zone three, we are being pressured by the clock late in the second or fourth quarter, and we are behind. We have to move the ball to win. This is not a critical zone in the first quarter, but in the fourth quarter with time running, it becomes a critical zone.

When in this situation, we are reminded of our Ole Miss game in 1965. We had the ball late in the second quarter, trailing 9-0. We received the ball on our 44-yard line. In eight plays, we scored, and at intermission we were trailing only 9-7. Ole Miss came back and scored in the second half to put us down 16-7. We managed a field goal to trail by only six. With 7:33 left in the fourth quarter, we took over the ball on our 11-yard line and, 18 plays later, with two crucial fourth-down plays, we went ahead 17-16 with 1:19 remaining in the game.

It is always an important point in any critical zone to run your best back behind your best blocker. In the last drive against Ole Miss, the two fourth-down situations were fourth and one yard on our own 20-yard line and fourth and two yards on our own 29-yard line. Both times we gave the ball to Les Kelly running behind Cecil Dowdy and Wayne Cook. Play selection by our QB, Steve Sloan, was excellent.

Our personnel made very few mistakes during these two drives. Plays selected in these drives were based on our scouting report and what had been going for us throughout the game. However, the most important thing we did was to sell our players on the importance of winning in the fourth quarter. We work our boys hard, and they are conditioned and trained to win in the fourth quarter. If this aspect fails, then we have done a poor coaching job.

During this drive, we let our QB make some calls, but this is the time when the coaches in the press box can do the most good. We rely on them very much when we find ourselves in critical zone three. This zone puts a lot of pressure on the offensive teams, since one mistake could cost us the ball. We prepare each week for the plays that will be run in critical zone three. We will decide what plays to discuss each week according to our scouting report. Of course, play selection is determined by the score, whether we are behind or ahead, the time remaining, and also whether it is the second or fourth quarter.

During the second quarter, it is important not to press our offense in critical zone three to the point that if we make a mistake, it would give the opponent a score that would put us out of the game. Even though we may be seven points behind, we will not try to score unless the field position is right. It may be to our advantage to run out the clock. Then we go to the half seven points behind and make our second half plans to win. We could do something in desperation and go in at halftime 10 to 14 points behind, making our task harder. We must remember, in this zone we are not only playing the opposition, we are racing against the clock.

In the fourth quarter we will go with our game plans or whatever it takes to win the ball game.

1967 Summer Manual. Paul "Bear" Bryant was head coach at the University of Alabama.

Critical Zone Four

Many games are won or lost on big plays. We never know when one big play will win the game. Many of these opportunities occur in short-yardage situations. Whether we maintain control of the ball on third or fourth down may decide the outcome. This critical area has no specific zone, as it may occur any place on the field.

There is little we can say concerning this zone, as the plays used are determined according to field position, the defense we are facing, condition of the field, what our best attack for the situation would be according to our personnel, and time remaining in the game.

We feel that in our overall planning of our offensive attack, if we can accomplish the following things our offense will be successful:

1. Get the ball past the 25-yard line before kicking.

2. Get a score when we get the ball inside the 20-yard line.

3. Don't get a penalty to stop a drive.

4. Never give the opposition the ball outside the 40-yard line.

5. Score enough to win.

Excellent and thorough preparation during the week for executing in these critical zones will pay dividends on Saturday.

Moving the Chains

Grant Teaff

Before I delve into our short-yardage offensive philosophy, let me paint the broader picture of our total offense. Our offensive philosophy has always adhered to three basic principles:

1. Use the available personnel to the maximum.

2. Always have a balanced offense, preferably 60 percent run, 40 percent pass.

3. Keep it simple!

Last year, we were not nearly as productive from the I, and we failed to recognize that we no longer had the big, strong, durable back who could run the formation. Also we dropped below 50 percent on pass completions. So, in the spring, we evaluated our personnel and set out to develop an offense that could take advantage of the plus factors we possessed.

One plus factor was two outstanding, experienced QBs who had the ability to throw the ball. Second, we had a bevy of good running backs, but none you would consider great. Third, we had outstanding receivers, again none that would be recognized as truly great, but all very good. We wanted to incorporate a running game that would average 180 to 220 yards a game and a passing attack with 50 to 55 percent completion. For years, we ran the veer offense and were very successful. We decided to take our knowledge of the veer, incorporate it into the dropback passing game we had already established through many years of coaching, and then come up with a concept for the short passing game that would give us ball control.

In observing our offense, you might think that the third point of our philosophy, that of keeping it simple, had not been taken into consideration. We run from the Power I formation, Split Backfield, One-Back, No-Back, and all forms of motion. But the key for us, though

it might seem complicated to the defense, is very simple for our players and does fit our philosophy.

Twenty-three years as a head football coach on the college level gives you a lot of experience doing a lot of different things offensively. As I have indicated, we vary that offense based on the personnel we have. But one portion of our offense does not vary and has remained consistent, and, I might add, very successful over the many, many years: our short-yardage offense.

I have used the same basic short-yardage offense almost from the time I started coaching. The success of the short-yardage offense is measured in terms of the number of first downs made or converted when looking at third and short or fourth and short.

Now here is a look at what has been accomplished through part of our season. The statistics in the table (see next page) show our conversion percentage up through the time when this article was written. Since that time, our conversion percentage has remained about the same.

First of all, I want to give you the basic philosophy and diagram of our offensive set. I have always believed in giving the defense the maximum number of holes to defend in a short-yardage situation; thus, the two tight ends. We believe that an 18-inch to two-foot split gives us the greatest advantage versus any defense. We also believe that by keeping our formation set to the offense's right, we are at an advantage.

The advantage is in teaching. We teach the right side of our offensive line strong-side attack with the extra blocker set at halfback. We teach the weak side of the line, or the left-hand side, the attack to that side, which includes the option play. I found this to be helpful in teaching our offense, and I also think it adds to our QB's recognition of what the defensive alignment is.

Third-and-Short Yardstick

Opponent	Yards needed	Yards gained	Result	Ball-carrier
Georgia*	2	0	Over on downs	TB
USC	1	2	First down	TB
USC	1	5	First down	TB
USC	1	2	First down	TB
USC	1	3	First down	TB
USC	2	4	First down	TB
USC*	1	10	First down	TB
Texas Tech	1	4	First down	TB
Texas Tech	2	2	First down	TB
Texas Tech*	1	3	First down	TB
Texas Tech*	1	40	Touchdown	TB
Houston	1	0	Fourth down	TB
Houston*	1	0	Over on downs	Inc.
SMU	3	5	First down	QB
SMU	1	3	First down	TB
SMU	1	3	First down	TB
SMU	1	2	Touchdown	QB
A&M	2	1	Fourth down	TB
A&M	1	2	First down	TB
A&M	1	3	First down	TB
A&M	1	1	First down	TB
A&M	1	2	First down	TB
A&M	3	7	First down	QB
A&M	1	3	First down	TB
A&M*	1	0	Over on downs	TB
A&M*	1	1	Touchdown	TB

*Fourth-down plays

We practice our short-yardage offense each day. We like to work against a variety of defenses so that no matter what the defense might be, we have looked at it and blocked it on numerous occasions. An advantage I have not mentioned is that we treat our short-yardage offense as a specialty team. For instance, in terms of personnel on this year's short-yardage offense, we had four TEs playing the normal two TE positions, a FB, and the tailback. We had a flanker playing the wingback position, and this year we had a regular QB playing the QB.

In most previous years, we had players from other positions playing the QB. For instance, due to his ability to run the option and his overall running ability, our fullback played the short-yardage QB for us. We have always run the option out of the short-yardage offense, even when we did not run it from the regular formation.

Now, let me show you the basic alignment of our short-yardage offense (figure 1).

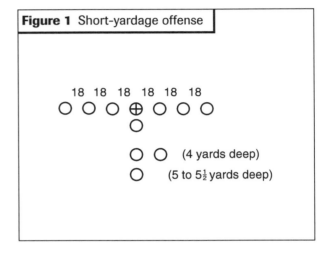

Figure 1 Short-yardage offense

You will notice that our set halfback or wingback lines up with his feet four yards from the LOS, splitting the inside leg of the offensive tackle. The FB, feet four yards from the LOS, lines up directly behind the QB. The tailback, in a two-point stance, lines up no deeper than 6 yards, preferably 5 to 5-1/2 yards deep.

This is a quick-hitting offense, so we have backs closer to the LOS. Our numbering system is the same as our regular offensive numbering system: small numbers inside working out; even numbers to the right, odd numbers to the left.

We will run the QB sneak, plus we have two basic plays to the right and two basic plays to the left. Those are running plays. Then we will throw a play-action fake off each running play.

The power play to the right side of the formation is the basis for the existence of the formation. If people stay in a balanced defense, you have a one-man advantage. Subsequently, we always run to the power side against a balanced defense. If they unbalance the defense toward the power side, we like to run to our left, or the weak side, away from formation.

I am not going to cover the power play or weak side option. I would like to concentrate on a pass, plus two plays that are critical for making short-yardage conversions. Most of your short-yardage attempts will be a yard or less. The ability to make that yard is what keeps the chains moving.

If there is one thing, overall, that explains our success over the many years, it has been our ability to move the chains. Possession of the football and ball control translates to the best defense that you can have. The percentage of conversions that you get on third and short or fourth and short actually determines your possession time and your ability to score.

Figure 2 shows our numbering system. Our tailback series is the 40 series; thus if we run 46, it is power at the six hole; 42 is the isolation lead at the two hole; 43 is isolated at the three hole; 49 is the option attacking the wide side of the field, away from the power.

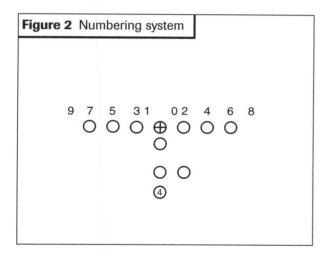

Figure 2 Numbering system

Now let's talk about the isolation and look at one pass that can be extremely effective off the isolation fake. Let's begin with 43, the tailback series to the three hole (figure 3). It is a read all the way. Once the play is called, the offensive guard, tackle, and end to the side of the call read the defensive alignment.

The blocking rule is simple: The guard blocks the first down lineman, the tackle blocks the second down lineman, and the end blocks the third down lineman. The FB's responsibility is to block the LB to the side of the call. The tailback's responsibility is to take the football and read the block of the FB.

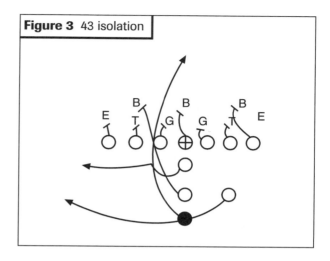

Figure 3 43 isolation

On his initial step, the FB looks directly at the guard. On the snap, he is able to either preread or fast-read the movement of the guard. He cuts opposite to the movement of the guard. For instance, if the guard blocks the two technique or the defensive guard in, the FB automatically will go the guard's outside hip and meet the LB in the hole.

The fullback has unique responsibility in that he not only must read the guard but that his second read is the offensive tackle and his third read is the offensive end. For instance, on an even man front, if you were to get both the guard and a tackle on an inside slant, the FB would carry his block to the outside hip of the offensive tackle, reading on the move. Therefore, the tailback would follow to the outside hip of the offensive tackle. Normally, the end will be able to turn out on the defensive end because either the tackle or the LB will have the "C" gap.

The QB rotates and gets the ball to the tailback at the deepest possible point, pushes off his back foot, belly rides the tailback, then steps behind him, faking the option play. The set halfback trails as the pitch man. You can see what this does to the outside corner and to the defensive end. When there is a threat of the option, it keeps them from closing inside on the isolation.

Now, let's look at an odd man alignment (figure 4). The guard doubles on the nose, and the FB automatically reads the tackle's block. If the tackle is in a five technique and stays out on contact, then the FB knows that the LB will be

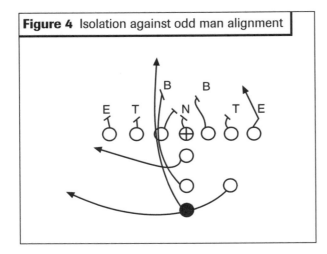

Figure 4 Isolation against odd man alignment

coming through the "A" and "B" gap, basically the "B" gap. All other action by the other players is identical to an even man front.

If you run 43 into a gap defense, this usually occurs with less than one yard to go, as the defense is trying to get penetration. The rules are the same: first down lineman, second down lineman, third down lineman. The FB's responsibility is to seek the LB as he reads the block of the offensive lineman. He still must block the LB. We have made more big plays and long runs against a gap defense than against almost any other defense we have ever played against.

Now let's go to the strong side of the formation and look at the isolation 42 (figure 5). Everything is the same against an even man and odd man front, with your guard tackling in your fullback and tailback. The only difference is that you have an extra blocker running to the formation side.

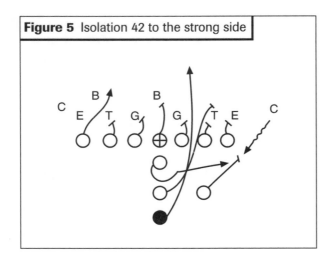

Figure 5 Isolation 42 to the strong side

If we get into a situation where the defense lines its cornerbacks up outside the defensive ends and brings them in a ripper action on the snap of the ball, we will go to the formation with the isolation series. That allows the set halfback a block on the ripper, keeping the cornerback from picking off the tailback from behind.

If we do not show a ripper to the side of the call, we double-lead the set halfback and FB. This is a devastating block against a 6-2 defense because you end up shoulder to shoulder on the LB.

I talked about the option play to the weak side to keep the cornerback and even the safety from caving in on the isolation play. Though we do not run the option to the strong side, we do throw a neat little pass that is devastating to a secondary wanting to react too quickly to the isolation.

Here is a look at the play that is simply referred to as pass 422 (figure 6). Again, we block one, two, three on the LOS. The FB's responsibility is a LB; the tailback's responsibility is to go up and over on a fake. The set halfback's responsibility is to run right at the cornerback, avert a collision, then go straight up the field, looking over the inside shoulder. The QB fakes to the TB with a good ride, then steps back and throws the ball, complete, we hope, for six points.

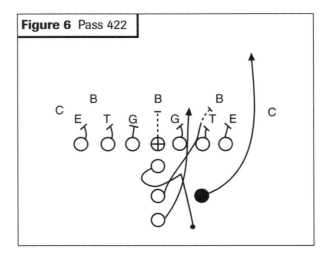

Figure 6 Pass 422

We have been notorious through the years for our flying tailbacks on short yardage. This does not come as an accident. It is prearranged, planned, taught, and executed. One of the first things we do with all of our incoming freshmen backs is to teach them to fly. I do this personally, because I want to make sure that the young man has the proper techniques for a safe landing.

We have a simple drill we use to teach players to fly on 42 or 43. To fly means to leave the ground, angle upward and over the offensive and defensive lines, and fall safely to the ground, across that mass of humanity for a big first down. I stack square blocking dummies to the height of no less than three feet. We align the QB two yards up from the landing area.

We teach our tailbacks the proper steps to the point of launching, then teach them to rotate their shoulders slightly once they launch, always keeping their heads up so that their bodies end up in a flat plane over the LOS. It is important to teach that when the head goes down, the body goes down. Over the years, many dramatic shots of our tailbacks have been taken, flying for four to six yards for big touchdowns that win football games for us.

Short yardage should be an integral part of your offensive philosophy. Use your personnel, have a definite plan, and keep it simple. Work your plan so that there are no surprises in any ball game. You can determine the philosophy of a defense as you watch film, and you can evaluate what it is going to do in short-yardage situations. Then you plan your attack. Then you teach your players that there is absolutely no way a team can stop you from making a yard. If they go to the LOS believing they are going to make it, a high percentage of the time they will make it, if they are correct in their attack and know whom to block, and how.

1986 Proceedings. Grant Teaff was head coach at Baylor University. Teaff is the AFCA's Executive Director.

Gaining the Most Important Yard

Bruce Snyder

Two of the most important situations in offensive football are short yardage and goal line. Our philosophy, as illustrated in figure 1, is that the more difficult the task, the more time commitment is required.

Understanding means appreciating the head coach's responsibilities and authority.

- Head coach has full responsibility to develop this part of the offense.
- Head coach conducts all meetings.
- Head coach conducts all drills and assignment issues.
- Head coach selects all personnel.
- Head coach rewards behavior and conduct necessary for success.

- Head coach determines amount of practice time allotted.

The message sent to the players and the staff is that the head coach considers this to be a very important factor in the success of the program. This point does not take much time to get across. The players recognize immediately that this is important.

Knowledge takes a little more time and practice. There are four basic principles in executing any play in short-yardage and goal line offense:

- On the LOS, we want to be up on the ball to crowd the LOS.
- It is important that we cut down the splits between linemen.

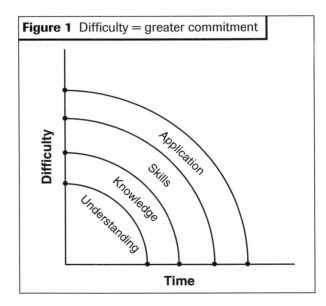

Figure 1 Difficulty = greater commitment

- Everybody needs to understand and be able to execute his first step properly.
- We need exact knowledge of assignments, including the snap count.

We have broken up the development of *skills* into three time periods: spring practice, fall camp, and during the season.

In spring practice, meetings are conducted by the head coach. Verbal description and videotapes are used to begin the understanding and development of skills. Drill work and group work are conducted on the practice field by the head coach versus the scout team or offensive personnel holding bags. We conclude most of our spring practices with a goal line scrimmage versus our defense to emphasize various skills.

Fall camp begins with meetings conducted by the head coach. We use videotape widely, particularly teaching reels from spring practice. The drills and group work are conducted by the head coach versus the scout team. In many of our practices, we scrimmage using short-yardage and goal line situations.

During the season, our game-week schedule allowed a Tuesday prepractice meeting of 10 minutes, with the head coach introducing both short-yardage and goal line game plans, as well as a brief scouting report of the opponent. We began each practice with a teaching period, half of which (approximately five minutes)

was a walk-through of our short-yardage offense versus our opponents. Later in practice, there was a group period (Tuesdays), and we spent 10 minutes on a goal line offense versus our scouts. On Thursdays, the next time the material was addressed, we spent five minutes on short yardage and 10 minutes on goal line during the group period, all versus the opponent scout team.

Application has three stages: spring, fall camp, and season. Spring scrimmages were versus our defense, approximately 70-75 total snaps during the entire spring practice. Over 10 days in fall camp, we scrimmaged versus our defense. The total number of snaps of actual scrimmage was 45-50. Once the football season began, we decided that there would be no scrimmaging of short yardage and goal line. Our application of all the work that we had put in would be done during the games. As it ended up, we had 66 total snaps of goal line and short yardage during our 11-game season. In 8 of the 11 games, we graded at 100 percent in both short yardage and goal line. In two of the other three games, we were 100 percent in either short yardage or goal line.

Our short yardage measurement for success was whether the snap resulted in a conversion to a first down (e.g., on third and one, if we attempted a conversion and did not achieve it, then converted it on fourth down, that would be 50 percent success because the third down did not convert but the fourth down did).

Our standard of success on goal line was concluding the drive with a touchdown. Giving up a turnover, being stopped on downs, or attempting a field goal was considered unsuccessful (even if the field goal was successful). In 11 games in the 1990 season, we had 66 attempts for a total of 169 yards, approximately 2.6 yards per attempt. We were successful in 8 of 11 games (100 percent in both categories of short yardage). There were only two attempts all year in which we did not successfully convert. In goal line, there were only two offensive drives that did not result in touchdowns once we were in a goal line situation.

In game planning, we had a separate short-yardage game plan and a goal line game plan, for the most part. In each of these categories, we tried to limit the number of runs in our game plan to three. We would carry one pass per situation. The other noteworthy thing we attempted to do was that we did not repeat a formation or play that we had run within three weeks. We felt that opponents scouting our film would pay attention to our most recent films. Therefore, we decided that we would have a three-week period before we repeated a play or formation.

These are just a few of our thoughts regarding short-yardage and goal line offense. This is a critical part of virtually every game played. We have had success in this area this year because of the commitment of each and every person concerned, from the head coach to each member of the coaching staff to each player on the team. The most difficult thing to ask players for is the appropriate amount of time and effort commitment in order to be successful.

1991 Proceedings. Bruce Snyder was head coach at the University of California, Berkeley. Snyder is head coach at Arizona State University.

Passing at the Goal Line

Denny Stolz

One of the most difficult phases of football is passing the ball successfully in the goal line area. No component of college or pro football is more difficult to execute successfully than the goal line pass game.

We feel our offense must master two aspects of our goal line package to be successful in the scoring area: control the blitz inside the 20, and our jet game and adjustments.

Before we start, let's define the goal line area as the 15-yard line and in. Also, we are not a sprint-out team, so I will limit my discussion to the dropback phase of goal line pass.

Controlling the Blitz

Our first priority in passing the football is to protect our QB. We know that the possibility of a blitz in the goal line area is very high, so we must defeat the defense in order to be successful with our passing game in this area of the field.

Figure 1 shows a weak corner or Will blitz. I'll first explain how our QB and split end team up to control this blitz. Obviously, we have a protection here where the weak corner will get home free, so we must go to our hot or quick principles.

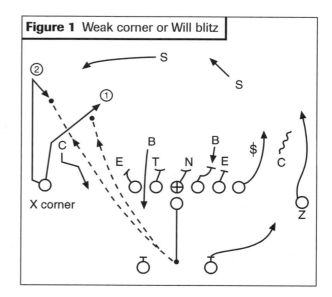

Figure 1 Weak corner or Will blitz

First, the X yells "corner-corner-corner" to alert the QB to the blitz as soon as he reads it. He may yell prior to the snap or as the ball is snapped and adjust his route accordingly. The X in figure 1 has two choices. If the corner and inside LBs blitz together and the safety is soft, he can come under inside and receive a quick pass from the QB. If only the corner blitzes and the safety is soft, he will just hitch at four to five yards, take the quick pass, and go one-on-one with the safety. If in doubt, he will always run the hitch.

In figure 2, the weak corner blitz is worked with bump man coverage. Our split end and QB now team up with an automatic burn route and, we hope, we can get the big play here.

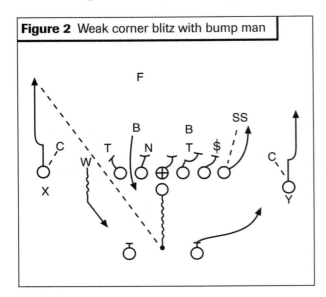

Figure 2 Weak corner blitz with bump man

In both of these cases, if the inside LB does not blitz, then the tailback is free to block the blitz in our scheme, and we would have a little more time.

We control the strong safety blitz on the TE side the same way. However, in our base protection, we pick up the strong safety with our TE, but we still play the hot, quick game with our flanker. Figure 3 shows the strong safety blitz in the goal line area and soft man cover.

The Z, or flanker, now has the same options as the X did on weak secondary blitz. He calls "corner-corner" and he may hitch at four or five yards, or come under if the LB blitzes with the strong safety. We like to have the Z hitch more often than come under, because the free safety can be a problem on his under route. Again, if we get bump coverage, we run a burn route and the QB lays the ball up and over to the flanker.

One more point: if we are in Spread, the TE calls "corner-corner" versus a SS blitz, and we control this strong side blitz exactly the same as we do the weak corner blitz (figure 4).

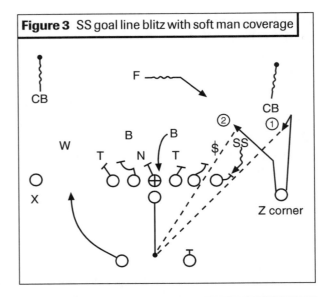

Figure 3 SS goal line blitz with soft man coverage

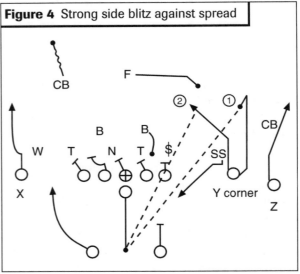

Figure 4 Strong side blitz against spread

Our QB uses the backpedal when he hears a "corner" call, and he will probably throw on the second or third step. If the QB does not throw to the quick receiver because he knows the protection will pick up the blitz, he knows our other receivers will stay on the routes called in the huddle and most likely will use their man getaway techniques to get open.

We spend hours on these read routes and adjustments, and we have been able to control the blitz in the scoring zone, the most important aspect of goal line play pass. Even though an action pass has been called in the huddle, our QB will forsake the play action and execute as described.

The Goal Line Jet Game

Our jet game on the goal line, which has been really successful and helped us to score a lot of points with our passing package, is exclusively a signal system between the WR and the QB. As in the blitz control, our jet game requires a lot of practice, and we work on it every day.

The QB simply goes into the huddle and calls "strong right-jet pass." Our two WRs take their splits and signal back to the QB one of three signals indicating the route they think they can run: hitch, slant, or fade (figure 5). The QB decides where to go with the ball. We have different signals on different sides. The quarterback's judgment and film study will tell him where to put the ball, and he uses only a two-step drop.

Let's say the defensive back gets cute with us and changes his alignment drastically after we signal. For example, X signals a hitch because he reads loose coverage, but during the cadence, the corner takes a quick bump alignment. The QB and X automatically turn this into a fade or burn. Conversely, if the corner

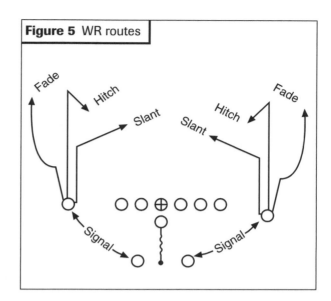

Figure 5 WR routes

goes from tight coverage to loose, the pattern changes to a hitch.

This fairly simple scheme allows us to get the right thing on at the right time. With proper coaching and practice, the offense makes it difficult for the defense to be correct with its coverage regarding this phase of our goal line package.

1986 Proceedings. Denny Stolz was head coach at San Diego State University.

Putting It in the End Zone

Jim Tressel and Jim Bollman

The largest single factor involved in our goal line success was the quality and character of the young men on the field. We try to remind ourselves that we are not better than what our players can execute. It is not what our players know and understand on the board, but what they know and understand from repetition on the practice field that enables them to execute in the heat of battle.

Keeping that train of thought, we helped ourselves by not creating an entirely separate goal line scheme. In most situations, our weekly goal line package was simply a limited version of our base offense, allowing us to minimize

our goal line practice time and concentrate on potential problem situations.

Our team period each Wednesday began with 10 minutes of goal line emphasis. On Thursdays, we reviewed potential problems. If we were going to see an unusual defensive front, we might include a 5 to 10 minute period on Tuesday, but usually the two days allowed us to be efficient.

Using one basic formation is another factor that enables us to get a sufficient number of repetitions in a short amount of time. Many times, we will not huddle and simply call the play at the LOS, so we get as many reps as possible.

In goal line situations, as well as anywhere else on the field, we want to have the threat of attacking from sideline to sideline. More important, we want to start with a base play and have just enough complementary offense to take advantage of possible defensive adjustments.

Whenever we can present a simple play progression that continually gets repetition, it really helps our players understand the offense and greatly enhances communication during a game.

Our goal line running attack involves six running plays, all of which I'm sure you have seen before and probably run yourself. We use two simple FB plays, an inside dive and a cutback belly. The old-fashioned TB isolation ended up as our most frequently called play, and our TB power off tackle is the starting point of our progression. We also use two types of options to complement these inside runs.

The base formation we use is an I backfield with two TEs and a flanker. Using two TEs helps our back side blocking and allows our runs to be mirrored. Giving the defense width with our flanker forces the opponent to remove at least one inside man and become more predictable in perimeter responsibility. In a few instances, we have used a single TE and two WRs, or two TEs and a power I, but the vast majority of the time, we are in two TEs and a flanker.

In our base goal line formation, we tighten our splits: guards in a six-inch to one-foot split, tackles in a one- to two-foot split, and TEs in a one- to two-and-a-half foot split. The exact width of the split will vary with down and distance and the type of play we are running.

We do move our alignment closer to the LOS in goal line situations. Our FB aligns his heels at five yards, and our TB aligns with his heels at eight yards deep. Our flanker takes a normal split. With the ball on the hash, he aligns two yards outside the opposite hash; ball in the middle, he aligns on the numbers.

Most of the time, we get some form of 6-2 defensive alignment in goal line situations. I will use this basic defensive front to diagram our plays and present our progression versus common adjustments we see each week.

As we mentioned earlier, the TB power off tackle is our starting point (figure 1). This play

employs a basic gap scheme, so our splits are closed down to prevent any penetration. The front side TE combo blocks with the front side tackle. The TE closes his inside seam, keeping his shoulders parallel to the LOS, and drives for the outside number of the front side DT. If the DT makes an inside move, the TE works upfield to the back side LB.

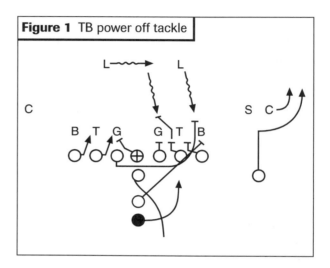

Figure 1 TB power off tackle

In all other situations, the TE drives the DT unless forced off late by his front side tackle to pick up the back side LB flowing over the top. The front side tackle must also keep his shoulders parallel to the LOS and hit the inside number of the DT, ready to handle any of four defensive reactions:

1. The DT makes an inside move: the front side tackle drives him to the inside and does not let the DT come back across his face.

2. The front side LB attacks or blitzes the G-T gap: the front side tackle comes off the DT and seals the LB to the inside.

3. The back side inside LB flows and then attacks the G-T gap: the front side tackle stays on the DT until he sees the back side inside LB stepping up into the gap, then comes off the DT and seals the LB to the inside.

4. The back side inside LB flows over the top of his block: the front side tackle stays on the DT, working for more midline to outside position while maintaining pressure.

The front side tackle gets movement on the DT. He doesn't sacrifice pressure for position. The front side guard drives the outside number of the front side defensive guard. This block is more under control since there is no help involved. The C blocks back on the back side defensive guard, stopping penetration first, then seals to the back side. The back side guard pulls to block the front side LB.

The G must get into the hole with his shoulders parallel to the LOS, right off the butt of the TE, and anticipate meeting the front side inside LB in the hole. The back side tackle and back side TE both zone cutoff to the inside. The FB lead-steps for the outside foot of the OT and traps the hips of the TE. The QB reverses out past six o'clock, delivers the ball to the TB, then sets to fake a sprint-draw pass.

The TB lead-steps, receives the ball, runs the lane inside the FB following the front side guard into the hole. The flanker blocks the defender covering him or, more often, runs him off, since we usually see some sort of inside man technique.

One of the adjustments we will see to stop our off-tackle play is a definite outside control DT with a very low, hard charge to prevent movement on the combo block. This makes the defense a little softer inside and is when we like to run our isolation play (figure 2).

The iso ended up as our most frequently called goal line play, due partly, in fact, to the DT technique described previously. Another reason was that whenever we were very close to the

goal line, we closed down to virtually no splits, called the iso and jumped for the goal line.

Normally, if outside the three- or four-yard line, we will tend to be on the wider side of our goal line splits to create a little more room. However, we are still primarily concerned with getting our TB to the LOS cleanly, letting him run or jump for some tough yards. The front side TE drives the inside number of the front side outside LB; he can't get beat inside. The front side tackle drives the inside number of the front side defensive tackle; he can't get beat inside.

The FB lead-steps for the inside leg of the front side tackle and blocks the front side LB opposite the front side tackle's block. The QB reverses out past six o'clock, delivers the ball to the TB as deep as possible, then sets to fake a play-action pass.

The TB drop-steps with his back side foot to gain separation, receives the ball, and runs opposite the block of the front side tackle. The flanker again blocks the defender on him or runs him off in man coverage.

Another common adjustment versus our off-tackle play is for our opponents to play their outside LB extremely heavily on our TE. The outside LB jams the TE and then comes off of his butt and attacks the inside shoulder of our FB. This makes upfield movement on the combo block more difficult and usually causes the ball to bounce to an unblocked DB and scraping inside LB. Our G option comes into play when we see this technique (figure 3).

This option helps us seal the corner of the defense and get outside with speed. The front

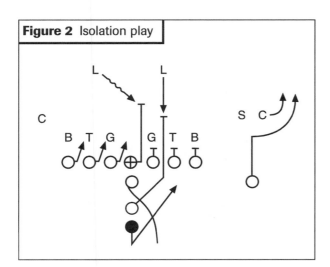

Figure 2 Isolation play

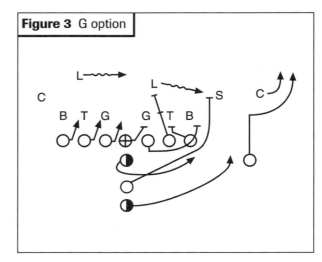

Figure 3 G option

side TE blocks down on the DT, primarily concerned with stopping penetration and sealing the DT inside. The front side tackle blocks down inside, securing the C's reach on the front side defensive guard and, in some instances, he can get upfield enough to affect the back side inside LB's pursuit.

The front side guard pulls to log the outside LB and is ready to cut the outside LB if he is coming upfield hard off the TE's block. If he is soft and trying to react back outside, the front side guard stays on his feet and runs for upfield outside number pressure. The C reaches the front side defensive guard and stops his penetration. The back side guard, back side tackle, and back side TE all zone cutoff to their inside. The FB lead-steps, aims for the outside foot of the TE, and blocks the front side inside LB opposite the front side guard's block.

The QB reverses past six o'clock and sprints to attack the inside shoulder of the primary force for the pitch read. The TB lead-steps downhill and sprints for pitch relationship. The flanker, as usual, blocks or runs off the man defending him.

Yet another way people try to stop our off tackle or isolation is to bring a DB off the corner to tackle our TB. If extremely close to the goal line, we will bring our flanker in and motion him across to protect the corner at the front side of the isolation. However, if we are a little farther from the goal line, we would rather not bring another DB into the picture.

In this situation, we like to run our load option (figure 4). This allows our QB to front out versus the crashing DB and holds the rest of the defense inside with our dive action.

In our load option scheme, our front side TE drive blocks the outside LB. The front side tackle drive blocks the DT. The front side guard drives through the outside number of the front side defensive guard and works upfield for the back side LB in pursuit. The C reaches the front side defensive guard. The back side guard, back side tackle, and back side TE all zone cutoff inside. The FB lead-steps for the butt of the front side guard, fakes the dive, and takes the best available course to block the front side inside LB. The QB opens to five o'clock, rides the FB hip to hip, and attacks the inside shoulder of the primary force for pitch read.

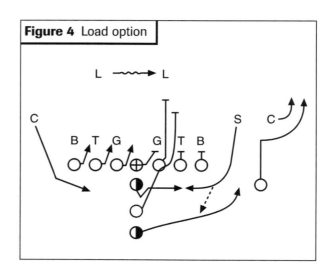

Figure 4 Load option

If the DT or outside LB flow and do not allow the quarterback to reach the primary force, the QB must keep the ball up inside. The TB lead-steps downhill and sprints for pitch relationship. Keep in mind that the QB and TB are aware that we are calling the play in anticipation of a crashing DB and are ready to execute the pitch immediately, if necessary. The flanker makes sure his man is blocked or run out of the play.

We use the two FB plays mentioned earlier primarily between the five- and one-yard lines before a defense gets into a 6-2 front. We have used the belly (figure 5) in situations versus the 6-2 when we felt we could get exceptional back side movement for a cutback.

We have used the dive (figure 6) versus the 6-2 as a change for a quick-hitter or jumping play when we feel the LBs are overly occupied with our TB.

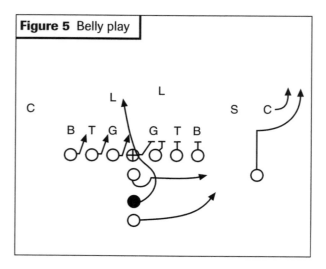

Figure 5 Belly play

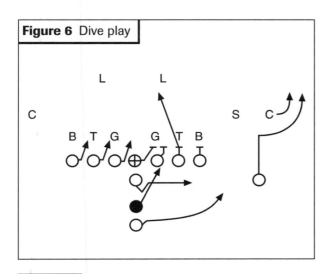

Figure 6 Dive play

In summary, let me review the two major ideas behind our present goal line package without regard to any specific plays. First, when we can keep this portion of our game plan within the confines of our overall base offense, we really help ourselves with regard to practice time and repetition, as well as adding to the confidence that should already exist in our base offense.

Second, we will always try to have a sequential play progression that our players can comprehend. This helps our players anticipate a defensive adjustment and, as a result, enhances their execution in this critical aspect of each game.

1990 Summer Manual. Jim Tressel is head coach and Jim Bollman was an assistant coach at Youngstown State University. Bollman is an assistant coach at Michigan State.

Executing in the Red Zone

Gary Pinkel and Mike Dunbar

It is vital for an offense to develop a sound philosophy for attacking the defense once you enter the part of the field referred to as the red zone. This critical area extends from the 25-yard line to the opponent's 6-yard line. We consider a specific goal line package from the 5-yard line.

Philosophy

Our offensive philosophy in the red zone can be summed up in one thought: "Score!" We have developed run and pass components that are selected elements of our offensive package. The selection of all-purpose plays, those that we execute to a high degree of proficiency regardless of the defense, has proven successful. Since these are common elements of our base offense, we do not deviate from our overall offensive philosophy.

We strongly believe in a multiple, balanced, attack-oriented offense. We want to mix our calls and keep the pressure on the defense. We strive to remain consistent in our approach and unpredictable to our opponents.

These are some considerations for the red zone:

- Our emphasis on the field or in the classroom is important to the way our team views the urgency of the situation.
- Most defenses have a philosophy in the red zone. An opponent's breakdown will tell us if the defensive structure is pressure-based or zone-oriented.
- If we incorporate motion and movement to a greater degree, we can create indecision—and advantages for the offense.
- Do we have three or four downs to accomplish our goal?
- We work to protect field position and ensure a high scoring percentage by avoiding potential negative plays.
- Practice time allows our offense the opportunity to develop a sense of poise and purpose and to refine execution of the task at hand.
- We avoid obvious passing situations; the defense will have numerous types of zones and bracket coverages to defend favorite routes.

Preparation

We try to remind ourselves continually that we are no better than what our players can execute. It is a matter of what our players know and understand from repetitions on the practice field. Our approach is that we will execute because of our detailed preparation and practice time commitment.

Preparation includes

- staff identification of our run and pass components;
- consistent evaluation of red zone tendencies—both self-scout and defensive trends;
- scouting reports of fronts/coverages-blitz/ zone tendencies, down and distance tendencies, and personnel mismatches;
- plays practiced repeatedly to develop proficiency and confidence, and a practice plan that includes spring practice, preseason camp, and game week priming;
- skill development, including use of a variety of teaching methods—classroom meetings and video sessions, walk-throughs, and practice implementation in the spring and fall; and
- game plan development that includes limiting number of calls, selecting from a previously designed and practiced bank of plays, repetition versus all situations (incorporate a red zone period in every practice), and overtime, a new situation for the 1996 season.

Execution

Do not allow yourself to fall victim to failure due to a lack of execution. In practice we constantly work on situations within the red zone that we anticipate we will experience during the course of a season. Our players develop confidence in their ability to react to the various situations that affect our chances of winning.

Without a doubt, one of the most worked situations by our squad is the red zone situation. All great teams have the same characteristic: They convert when in the red zone. We want our players to understand the key coaching points for being successful in the red zone. Red zone alerts include the following:

- Quarterbacks: make the percentage plays, don't force the football, allow no sacks.
- Protect the football—no turnovers, ball leverage.
- Draw no penalties—make no mental errors.
- Anticipate defensive tendency.

In pressure situations, watch for the dog and blitz percentage to increase (stunting and stemming fronts, blitzing LBs, safety and corner blitzes). One change that we have seen in defensive schemes in this situation has been the use of more zone coverages so watch for them. Therefore, expect C-2 for disguise purposes and coverage rotations, combination coverages (be more alert for bracket and robber techniques), and zone blitzes. Look for personnel changes.

Innovative planning and bold play-calling are essential when preparing a red zone attack. Each week, the application of our red zone run and pass components will establish our game plan. With practice time commitment, we believe we can accomplish our goal: Score!

Pass Components

From a philosophical perspective, four types of passes are needed: dropback (three- and five-step), play action, sprint-out, and screen. Use a protection-first philosophy. Maximum protection considerations should be game-planned. Attack the defense on first down with vertical stretch routes: corner routes, go routes, and post routes.

Increase the use of motion to create an advantage for the offense. Create one-on-one situations. Identify coverage before the snap. Create personnel mismatches. Stress the defense by use of multiple sets. Incorporate break, loop, and drag routes with the bunch concept.

In the +10 area, an offense will lose some of the vertical stretch. Use of the fade route offers maximum gain with little risk—a touchdown or an incompletion. The slant route should be considered as a complement to the fade.

The QB will take a five-step drop for this vertical stretch route. The line will maximum protect from a one-back set with the back and TE check releasing. In the pattern, the Z will run a post with a breaking point of 8-12 yards, determined by the coverage. Our H-back runs a corner route with a breaking point of 10-12 yards, pushing high into the corner toward the back flag. The X runs a smash route at eight yards, gaining width and depth. He will throttle versus zone and work inside against man coverage. The QB will look to the post versus man coverage, especially with the FS locked on coverage. He may stay with the corner route if there is a mismatch. If the QB has any doubt about his coverage read, he should stay with the two-receiver side. Against zone he will stay to the two-receiver side, reading the deep third flat defender and throwing off him.

Run Components

Once inside the red zone, we consider four basic components:

- Get outside with our surest and quickest method.
- Get inside with quick hitters.
- Run counter versus fast flowing defense.

- Be physical to the point of attack with isolation.

Our top priority is to protect the point of attack and allow the tailback to run to daylight.

The defensive rush is generally more intense or upfield in the red zone; traps and draws are good change-ups.

Do not increase the chance of tackles for loss. Plan to control penetration. It may be necessary to account for the safeties as LBs in the blocking scheme because of the defensive trend to force with the safeties.

Stress the defense by using multiple sets and incorporating the use of two- and three-TE sets to create an unbalanced advantage through movement, and wing sets to attack the mindset of an aggressive upfield defense.

A summary of the University of Toledo's red zone production in 1995 will demonstrate the importance of preparing to execute in the red zone: we converted 54 of 84 red zone chances for 84 percent efficiency, scoring 43 touchdowns and eight field goals and running out the clock three times.

Our staff and players at the University of Toledo have enjoyed the many challenges that the red zone has presented. As is always the case, if you have something that you really believe in, sell it to your players and practice it diligently; it will usually work for you.

1996 Summer Manual. Gary Pinkel is head football coach and Mike Dunbar was the offensive coordinator at the University of Toledo. Dunbar is head coach at Northern Iowa.

Scoring Inside the 20

Dal Shealy

Thanks to our coaches and players, we have had measured success in reaching our goal of putting points on the board when in scoring territory (the opponent's 25-yard line). We also strive to avoid S.T.P. (sacks, turnovers, and penalties).

We have situation scrimmages in the spring and in August camp. One of the situations is

an overtime period. We place the ball on the +25 yard line with first down and 10 yards to go, as in the overtime play-off rule. We feel that this helped bring success this past fall, as we had four overtime periods versus the University of Massachusetts before winning 52-51.

We were able to score in all four of the overtime periods. Our players were there in practice and knew our philosophy and how to thrive under pressure. We lost several close games in 1986, so, as we entered the 1987 season, we worked hard to sell winning in the overtime and scoring when we crossed the opponent's 25-yard line.

Our philosophy is to maintain our basic wide line splits (figure 1). We also want to use a variety of formation alignments and some motion as we attack the defensive scheme. Against reading technique defense, we want to attack north and south. Against the gap-type defenses, we block down and run outside, or pass the football.

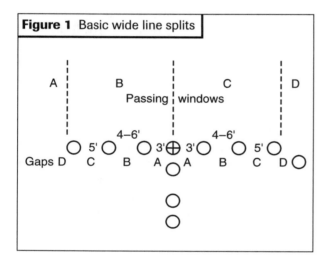

Figure 1 Basic wide line splits

In our offensive scheme, each running play has a play-action pass or a bootleg, and our passing attack consists of the three-step, five-step, and seven-step packages off the sprint-draw action. When we state our offensive attack plan for each week, we plan to major in three to five formations and several types of motions.

As we enter the practice week, we strive to help our players better understand the game plan. We concentrate Tuesday's practice on first- and third-down plays and number one goal line package. Wednesday is third-down conversion day as we concentrate on third and long (seven yards or more), third and medium (three to seven yards), and third and short (two yards or less). We seek a 50 percent third-down conversion rate. Wednesdays, we also work on goal line package number two.

Thursday's practice combines down and distance situations with field position plans. This is run basically like a dress rehearsal with our team working the field positions from left hash mark, left goal post, middle of the field, right goal post, right hash mark, and the coming-out offense beginning at the minus-one yard line, the free-wheeling zone between the 35-yard lines, and then scoring territory as we cross our opponent's 25-yard line. We concentrate on goal line packages one and two, as well as our minuteman offense, the two-minute drills.

In teaching from the basic I formation, we can run plays in a series establishing the run, complementing each run with a play-action or misdirection pass, and the show passing attack complemented with draws and screens. The offensive linemen use blocking schemes that enable them to use wide line splits and adjust to stemming defenses, defensive stunts, and blitz pickups.

If our offensive linemen can learn the five basic blocking schemes and make the proper adjustments to the defenses we face, we can run our entire offensive package and avoid sacks, turnovers, and penalties.

Our passing game is set to attack the zone, man-to-man lock-on, man with a free safety and some pressure, or the full house blitz.

When we face balanced defenses, we run north and south. Against unbalanced defenses, we attack the three-man side of the defense, or use the Tight formation (figure 2) or Twin formation (figure 3) with our Z-back in motion (figure 4).

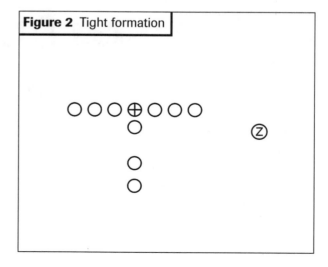

Figure 2 Tight formation

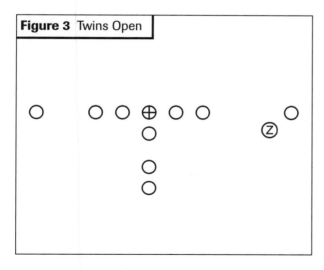

Figure 3 Twins Open

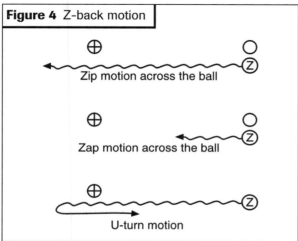

Figure 4 Z-back motion

Zip motion across the ball

Zap motion across the ball

U-turn motion

Basic Running Plays

We will concentrate primarily on our four basic running plays from the I formation, a few play-action and bootleg passes off of the running plays, and touch on a pass to take care of the passing down and blitz that may be coming. We will try to be brief, yet thorough, in covering these plays to give some basic understanding of how the blocking schemes and series system works, and would invite you to come visit us if you are interested more details about the system.

The four basic running plays we will cover are pitch to the A-back, belly to the B-back, isolation to the A-back, and the counter trap. We use play-action passes and bootlegs off these runs.

Also, we will discuss a three-step pass that we use in attacking defenses in scoring territory. We found that by utilizing the I formation and establishing a full-flow attack, we anchor the defense with our FB, spread the defense with formations and motions, attack the outside with the A-back, and when the defense is running with the flow, the counter and bootleg action hits the long gainer. Dropback pass action tones down secondary pressure.

The first basic play is the pitch sweep to the A-back (figure 5). Our offensive line takes basic splits. The TE to the call side blocks the end man on the LOS inside, straight back, or to the outside so that the A-back can read his block to take the play off tackle or slide it to the outside. Our play-side tackle blocks the tackle area; the play-side guard pulls and runs off the TE's block to be responsible for the defensive man in the contain position.

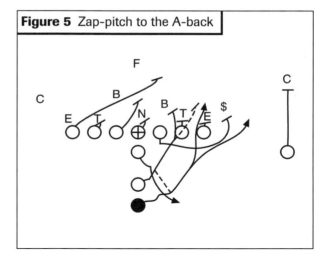

Figure 5 Zap-pitch to the A-back

The center blocks zero, no zero, first man inside, the back side guard, and tackle, and the TE reach blocks the "A," "B," and "C" gaps before sprinting downfield for a second blocking effort. The Z back is responsible for blocking the defensive man in the outside one-third of the field, while the B-back (FB) blocks the play-side LB by reading the tackle's block and going through the "B" or "C" gap to make contact and cut off the LB.

We believe that with wide line splits, the A-back can gain the first down or make five yards off tackle. We want him to take the most direct route, but if the TE has logged his man inside, he slides outside on the pulling guard's hip and looks for the larger gain.

Figure 6 shows the same play execution with the ball on the hash and the formation into the boundary. Zap motion is used in order to let the Z-back double-team a wide nine technique on the TE, causing problems in getting the ball outside.

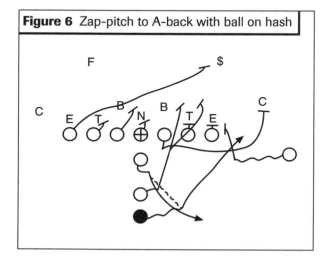

Figure 6 Zap-pitch to A-back with ball on hash

Figure 7 illustrates a change in the blocking scheme from the base pitch scheme with the guard pulling to the guard blocking the number one man on the LOS, the tackle blocking number two on the LOS, the TE blocking number three on the LOS, and the FB reading and running off the tackle's block to lead on the play-side LB.

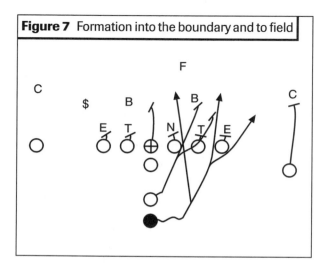

Figure 7 Formation into the boundary and to field

The A-back is able to take the pitch and cut downhill through the "A," "B," "C," or "D" gaps. This provides us the opportunity to cut back the pitch sweep should the defense try to fast flow on the pitching action by the QB. This is also an excellent scheme on the goal line against the 60 or 6-2 type defenses.

In order to anchor down a defense that is fast flowing and keying the A-back for the pitch, we run the belly to the B-back (figure 8). If the B back is covered, the QB runs off of the guard's block.

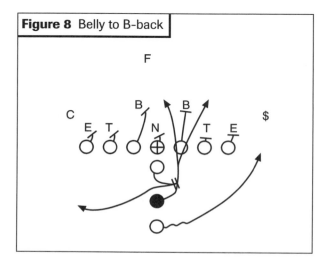

Figure 8 Belly to B-back

Our offensive line scheme is base blocking with the center blocking zero, the guards blocking number one, the tackles driving number two, and the ends driving number three. As the QB reverse pivots with good action to indicate that he is going to make the pitch and slides the ball with two hands into the FB's stomach, the FB takes a lead step to the play-side tackle's rear, so that on the third step he can read the center's block on the noseguard and run the play side "A" or "B" gap.

If the noseguard is sliding to the action, the B-back cuts behind the center's block to the back side "A" gap and runs to daylight. The A-back takes his first three steps as though he's running the pitch and turns downhill off the TE's block, running to get tackled or block the force man in the defense. The flanker would still be responsible for the defensive person in the outside one-third.

If the defense slides its noseguard to cover the offensive guard, the B-back reads the guard's block on the first down lineman and runs to daylight. We have found this to be a great play to counter the fast flow defense, and it has provided some outstanding opportunities for our B-back.

Figure 9a and b cover the isolation to the A-back.

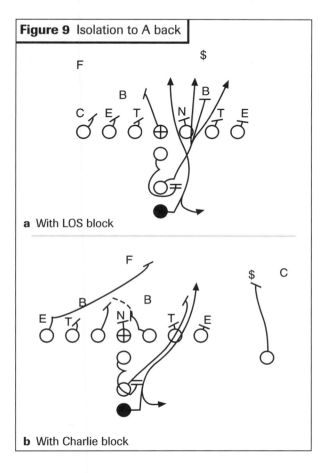

Figure 9 Isolation to A back

a With LOS block

b With Charlie block

Our first blocking scheme would be one, two, three LOS by our guard, tackle, and TE. The offensive center is responsible for zero, which in figure 9a is the back side LB. The FB steps to the play side tackle's rear and runs an attack block angle off the covered guard's block for the play-side LB.

The QB reverse pivots to six o'clock, steps to six o'clock with his second step, and transfers his weight to two o'clock to make the handoff to the A-back, who has paralleled on his initial action and started downhill, deliberately reading the FB's block on the play side LB, running to daylight.

We have found that this play might hit from the back side "A" gap to the front side "C" gap against varying defenses. If the defense continues to play in an odd man front, we use a Charlie block with our play-side guard (figure 9b). The play-side guard executes an over-and-up step to reduce his split and double-team the noseguard.

If the noseguard slants away, the on guard runs a railroad track to the back side LB. The play-side tackle blocks number two, and the play-side TE number three. The back side guard, tackle, and end are responsible for cutting off one, two, three, then continuing downfield for a second block. The FB again steps to the play side tackle's rear, reads his block on number two, and continues off that block to attack the play side LB.

The QB reverse pivots to six o'clock for two steps and transfers his weight to two o'clock, to make the handoff to the A-back as he runs to daylight off the FB's block on the play-side LB. The QB continues to fake a pass or presses the corner to set up the pass option. By running with his eyes and following the FB's block on the play-side LB, the A-back could actually run this play anywhere from the play side "A", "B", or "C" gap, making it a nice outside off-tackle play.

We've had occasions close to the opponent's goal line when the defensive tackle and end both pinch hard to the inside gap. The FB then has run off the right end's hip and blocked the play-side backer scraping to the outside, enabling our A-back to turn the isolation play into a hand sweep.

Play Action Passes

A pass play off of this full-flow action by our QB reversing out and the A-back and B-back stepping to play side is the isolation press pass. The tackle locks onto the defensive tackle; the play-side guard, center, back side guard, and tackle are responsible for the gaps away from the call. The B-back makes the initial step to the tackle's rear and attacks his outside hip to block the first defensive person in the "C" gap, while the A-back fakes the isolation and is responsible for blocking the play side LB if he fires or plays the run.

If the LB drops into pass defense, our A-back turns to the outside and replaces the LB's aligned position as a safety valve. The QB reverse pivots, taking two steps to six o'clock, and transfers his weight to two o'clock on the run fake. He kicks out of the fake and presses the corner with the run, pass-option reading the outside window of the field and the defensive man responsible for flat coverage (figure 10).

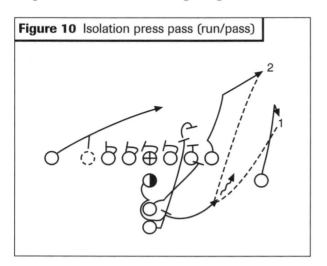

Figure 10 Isolation press pass (run/pass)

We employ the same action near the goal line when we expect man-to-man coverage, executing the same blocking scheme and backfield action except that the QB pulls up two steps out of the fake as we run the isolation cross pass (figure 11).

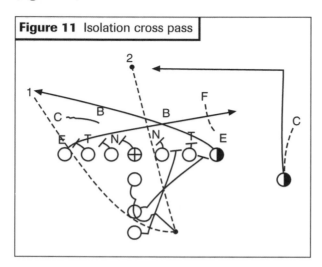

Figure 11 Isolation cross pass

The Z-back runs a square in route and is the secondary receiver. The back side TE releases to the inside and sprints hard to get to the play side flat five or seven yards deep. The play-side TE executes an over-and-up inside release as though he were double-teaming the defensive tackle, sliding off the hip of the crossing back side TE to pop clean to the back side flat.

The throwback to the play-side TE is the first read off the weak corner. If he is covered in window "A," the QB snaps his head to window "C" and passes to Z on the crossing route. This has proven to be a very effective goal line play for us over the past eight years, and it has been one of our most consistent scoring passes.

The bootleg action off of the pitch, belly, and isolation action is illustrated in figure 12.

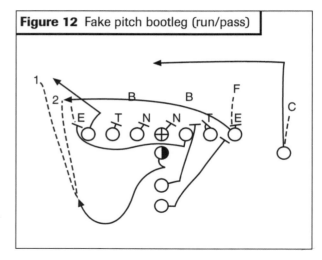

Figure 12 Fake pitch bootleg (run/pass)

We will run this out of each of the formations that we have mentioned. For simplicity, we will diagram it out of the Tight formation. The linemen to the side of the bootleg block down their inside gap, with the TE to the side of the call making an inside release and running to the flag. The TE away from the call makes an inside release and runs a drag. The offside guard pulls and will be a personal protector for the QB, while the Z-back tries to stick the defensive back in his area and cross the field to get into the QB's vision.

The QB makes a quick reverse pivot and good fake action to the B-back with a dead-hand ride. He then pushes off his left foot to gain the depth of five or six yards and twists his trunk and shoulders parallel to the LOS, resulting in a run-pass option attacking the weak-side corner.

The QB can run for the first down or touch-down, or has a choice of passing to number one flag or number two drag as they appear in his vision. This is an outstanding play against fast-flow reacting defenses.

Counter Runs and Passes

After we've established a full-flow run, a great performance play for our tailbacks—and a real fun play for our pulling guard and tackle—has been the counter trap (figure 13).

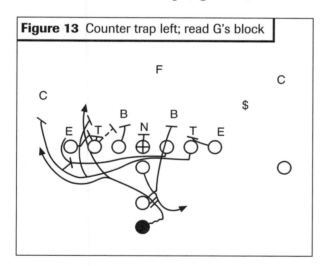

Figure 13 Counter trap left; read G's block

The QB reverse pivots and fakes to the FB, then idles his motor, securing a handoff to the A-back, who shows pitch action and then comes across the QB's face to receive an inside handoff. The A-back runs to daylight off the pulling tackle's block.

After making the handoff, the QB presses the back side corner to set up the bootleg. The play-side TE executes the over-and-up double-team on the five technique as the play-side tackle drives into the number two man and eyes the

play side LB. They are responsible for securing the "C" gap.

If the defensive tackle pinches to the inside, the tackle logs him through the "B" gap as the TE runs a railroad track to the play-side LB. The play-side guard drive blocks number one, the center drive blocks zero, while the back side guard and tackle pull to lead the play. The FB fills tight off the pulling tackle's hip to secure the back side "B" gap. The back side TE secures the "C" gap. The pulling guard reads the end man on the LOS, and if he comes upfield, traps him to the outside.

If the defensive tackle closes to the inside with the TE's over-and-up step, the guard blocks him inside as the pulling tackle reads his numbers for either turning up the off-tackle hole and looking downfield for the first wrong-colored jersey to block, or proceeding to the outside and leading the A-back downfield on the first opposing player. Over the past four years, this has proven to be one of our most explosive plays, and it sets up an outstanding bootleg (figure 14).

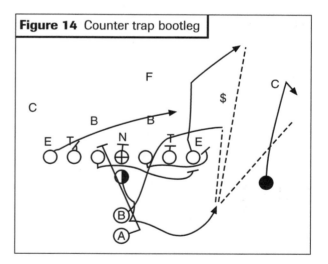

Figure 14 Counter trap bootleg

On our bootleg play, if both guards are uncovered, they pull and leave the QB, with the play-side guard securing the end men on the LOS and the back side guard acting as personal protector. Tackles block tackles, and the center blocks zero, play side. Our WR to the side of the call runs a 12-yard out; the first inside receiver runs a flag; and our back side receiver runs a drag.

The QB reverses out, making a dead-hand fake to the FB and a counter action fake to the A-back, who will secure the area of the back side pulling guard's hip. The QB then kicks to a depth of six yards and proceeds to attack downhill with a run-pass option. If our B-back is able to break through the LOS, he proceeds to the play side flat at a depth of five yards. The QB reads the flat coverage with a run-pass option, and most of the time he ends up with four receivers in his vision in the outside window of the field.

Since the counter trap bootleg has been such an outstanding play over a long period of time, I want to illustrate two pattern changes out of the Twin Open formation that have proven very successful, especially in scoring territory. Figure 15 shows the Twin Open counter trap bootleg with X running the post pattern. The inside receiver still runs the flag, the back side receiver drags. After making his fake to the play side, our B-back continues to the play side flat five yards deep as the QB pressures the corner with the run/pass option.

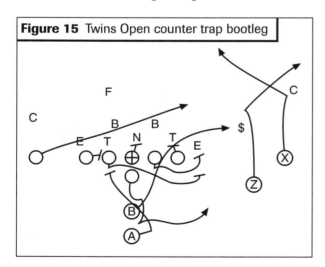

Figure 15 Twins Open counter trap bootleg

One note of interest: Our post pattern is run with a stem of seven yards as the X-receiver makes his cut to the post. If the defense has a center fielder, the X-receiver carries the post route down the play-side hash mark. If the

defense is playing a twin safety with the center field open, our X-receiver continues running the post route through the center of the field.

This has given us a great advantage with our post route and has certainly opened up the flag to the inside receiver and the flat or drag to our FB and back side receiver. To add a problem area to the defense and cut down some of the pressure, we may run Twins Open, zip motion, counter boot takeoff (figure 16).

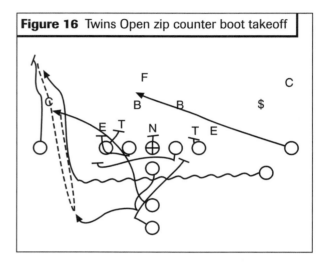

Figure 16 Twins Open zip counter boot takeoff

The Z-back is put into zip motion across the ball by the QB moving his heel. The play-side guard and tackle may cross block on the reduced down defensive tackle and end. The center continues to block zero; the back side guard pulls as the QB's personal protector. The back side tackle locks onto the tackle, and the A-back (making the counter fake) secures the "B" gap area on the back side.

After making his fake into the line, the FB continues to the play side flat five yards deep, while the takeoff call puts the WR on the deep takeoff pattern. The inside receiver coming across the formation in motion is still running the flag route underneath the takeoff. The back side receiver will stay with his rule of a drag route.

The QB again has the run/pass option, reading the play-side corner. He has a one, two, three, deep, middle distance, and shallow receiver in the outside window on the left side of the field for an outstanding play. This is one of our most consistent routes using out bootleg action.

There comes a time when you expect pressure from the defense, or you are in a must-pass situation. One of our most successful pass plays in scoring territory when we expect hard pressure or man-to-man coverage is our three-step pass (figure 17).

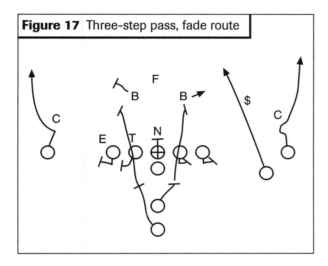

Figure 17 Three-step pass, fade route

1988 Summer Manual. Dal Shealy was head coach at the University of Richmond. He is president/CEO of the Fellowship of Christian Athletes.

The QB takes a three-step drop while reading the play-side LB on his first step for the hot pass to the inside receiver running the seam route. The two wideouts try to stick the defensive backs over them and fade to the back corner of the end zone.

The QB drops the ball on top of the wideout's outside shoulder. Our A- and B-backs step up and block LBs to their sides if the LBs come. If the LBs drop in the pass coverage, the A- and B-backs pop across the LOS and replace the LBs' alignments as safety valves.

Our linemen block man protection with the center responsible for zero, the guards for number one on the LOS, and the tackles for number two on the LOS. They perform low-firing drive blocks in order to get the defensive linemen to put down their hands to ward off the blockers, making them unable to deflect the quick pass.

Coaching for Goal Line Success

Lee J. Tressel

Seldom does a football coaches' gab session end before the inevitable question is asked, "What do you use for a goal line defense?" Articles are written, clinic speeches made, and much discussion and thought are given to those final five yards when you are on defense. I believe those final five yards are just as important to the team in possession of the ball.

Sportswriters give glowing reports of great goal line stands by the defensive team, but little is said about the fine play of the offensive team in those final few yards of a successful 50-yard drive. People assume that a team that can march 45 yards will not find it difficult to move the last five. Yet how many times does the offensive team fail?

We emphasize the importance of goal line offense. We have lost two of our last 20 games, and both of these losses can be directly attributed to the failure of our goal line offense. Newspaper accounts pointed out the success of our opponents' defenses. Our men knew each defensive success was related to an offensive failure.

How many times have you heard coaches say that they moved the ball all over the field except across the goal line? Or they say, "We just didn't get the breaks; we were inside their 10-yard line six times and gained over 300 yards but got beat 6-0. The breaks just weren't going our way." This is hogwash! An offensive team is evaluated by how many times it scores, not how many yards it gains or how many times it threatens to score.

Inches often separate winning and losing. These are the all-important plays of the games. All coaches spend a great deal of time perfecting a goal line defense, but many of us spend too little time on the offensive plays that decide the game.

Outstanding coaches such as Bear Bryant and Paul Dietzel have done an excellent job selling their defensive teams, "They will not score!" Their players believe this. It is a great selling job. This same job can be accomplished on offense: "We can't be stopped!"

Use similar tactics. Confidence must ooze from the coach. He must be sold himself before he can sell his players. The best way to build confidence is to have success. Make certain your team has success in practice. We never practice our number one offense against our number one defense on the goal line.

Emphasize your successful drives in games. Applaud and publicize them. On the locker room wall, post the date of the last time you were stopped on a goal line attack (if it has been a long time). Play up the importance of extending this record. Emphasize how many consecutive times you have scored with your goal line offense. We consider ourselves in goal line offense territory any time we can average two yards or less per down and score. For example, first and goal on the seven-yard line.

Defensive coaches talk about the morale factor. A goal line stand picks up a team's morale and is often the turning point of the game. This is true, but it is also true for the offense. Success helps morale and breaks down the defensive team's morale. Success also puts six points on the board.

We tell our players that many boys can play football between the 10-yard stripes. Inside the 10, it calls for men. This is the time we learn if you have received the values from football we claim are possible, such as the will to win, belief in yourself, poise, confidence, and raw courage. Will you accept the challenge and rise to the occasion? It is a great American game!

Success is not inevitable by talking. You must provide time in practice to work on your goal line offense, both as a unit and in drills. This cannot be done half-speed. You are taking a chance of injuries, but I feel it is an essential risk. If you are fortunate enough to have spring practice, emphasize goal line offense at that time.

Set up drills for your backs so it is necessary for them to struggle or dive for the final few inches. Nothing brings a smile to my face quicker than finding a back who "smells" the end zone, a man who won't be stopped regardless of the odds.

One of the most serious problems posed by a goal line defense is penetration. Have line drills so your linemen get ample opportunity to practice the techniques used to stop defenders from penetrating. We use the cross-shoulder, cutoff, and wedge blocks.

Many coaches believe aggressive scrimmages should be held when players are fresh, to minimize injuries. Our philosophy is just the opposite. Our goal line work is done near the end of practice. We want to know who our blue-chip players are when they are tired. Real players will rise to the occasion. We believe in the overload principle of conditioning. If a man puts out 110 percent when tired, a better-conditioned player results. A superbly conditioned young man is usually confident. It is no coincidence that the best-conditioned team is most often the winning team.

Our experience has been that the first few plays installed in practice are usually our best plays all season. Because of this, we make certain our first plays are ones we will use inside the 10-yard line, as well as other places on the field.

Another selling point to the offense is that the players know pretty much what the defense is going to do. At the most, your opponents will have only two goal line defenses. You have many more offensive maneuvers they must be prepared to stop.

From scouting games and films, your team should know your opponent's goal line defense inside and out. Well-coached teams will not change their goal line defense weekly. Know when and where they will go into their goal line defense. This is no time to be feeling out your opponent. Know what he is doing and what you must do to operate successfully. It is often necessary to deviate some from game plans during the game, but seldom in the scoring zone. Know how their ends play, who can be trapped, whom to stay away from, how they adjust to various formations, how quick each lineman is, which men in the line are normally linebackers, etc. Your game plans for your goal line offense must be well conceived. Leave nothing to chance in this important area. Know if their safety is normally a linebacker, if they use man-to-man or zone pass defense. If possible, learn their exact keys.

Strategy and play calling are never more important than near the goal line. We believe the decision should never be made by the QB. The coaching staff calls all the plays, and this is one time our QB is not permitted to change the play on the LOS.

These are a few rules that we follow the majority of the time:

1. Think in terms of your own offensive power and personnel.
2. Give the ball to your best back behind your best blockers a high percentage of the time.
3. Never allow a man who has fumbling tendencies to carry the ball in this territory.
4. Handle the ball as little as possible when in very close to the goal.
5. Attack a weak or groggy player.
6. Never run at their outstanding player (unless he can be trapped).
7. Never run a play where you might be thrown for a loss if you are in close (e.g., third and goal on the 1+-yard line).
8. Play percentages; this is no time to gamble.

We think of our goal line offense in three categories: high percentage (very short yardage, sneaks, wedges, etc.), normal goal line offense, and loosen-up offense. We feel that if we are playing strictly according to percentage, we follow this pattern:

First and goal from the four-yard line and closer: high percentage

First and goal from the eight- to the four-yard line: normal

Second and goal from the zero- to three-yard line: high percentage

Second and goal from the six- to the three-yard line: normal

Second and goal from farther than the six-yard line: loosen-up offense

Third and goal from the zero- to the two-yard line: high percentage

Third and goal from the 4+- to the two-yard line: normal

Third and goal from farther than the 4+-yard line: loosen-up offense

Fourth and goal from the zero- to three-quarter-yard line: high percentage

Fourth and goal from the three- to the three-quarter-yard line: normal

Fourth and goal from farther than the three-yard line: loosen-up or field goal

This might vary with your opponent, but in general, it is based on an opponent whose strength is similar to yours.

In the high-percentage zone, we use straight football. Our first choice is a QB sneak if possible. Our next choice is a QB wedge. The QB must learn to lean and get power in his running. Practice this play! We like to wedge with any of our running backs in this zone. Our wedge philosophy is to wedge on a man with the back nearest the hole. We number our plays on the offensive man, but we must adjust to a gap against the majority of goal line defenses we face. If a five-wedge (figure 1) is called, it must be clear to the entire offense whether to wedge the G-T gap man or the E-T gap man. We wedge on the inside gap man unless called outside in the huddle. Most goal line defenses penetrate, so we believe we must form our apex on a man to stop his penetration. Occasionally, we ask the QB to call a wedge on the LOS. He

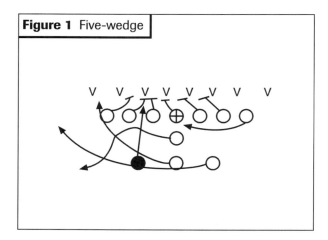

Figure 1 Five-wedge

calls a wedge in the huddle and calls the point by a key word on the line. This is seldom necessary if a team is well-scouted.

We seldom isolate in the high-percentage area because of the fear of penetration. When we do, it is outside our tackle, and we have our ballcarriers hit inside the isolation with reckless abandon, hoping to gain at least a yard or two by hitting the hole hard and bowling into any defending backs. The back side end pulls for position in case of a fumble (figure 2).

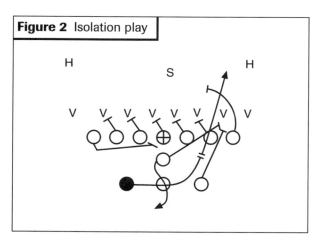

Figure 2 Isolation play

We like to run our double power off-tackle play against a strong team playing us man-on-man (9-2). This gives a double-team on both sides of the hole. The right halfback (wing) influences the man on our end and blocks the near defensive back (figure 3).

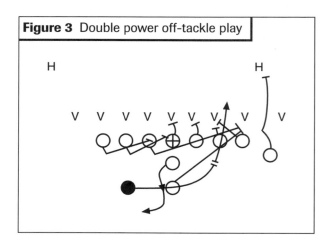

Figure 3 Double power off-tackle play

The importance of the block of the back side tackle must be emphasized. If we consider our offensive line effective in stopping penetration, we will run the QB, letting him turn upfield at the first opportunity he has to pick up a yard or two (figure 4).

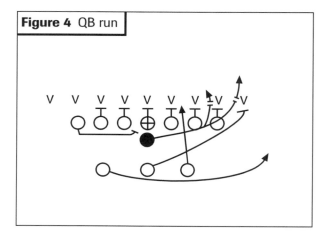

Figure 4 QB run

In the normal goal line area or zone, we will run any part of our offense we consider safe. This would include power sweeps, options, traps, inside belly, and power off-tackle. We believe most goal line defenses are susceptible to a trap (figure 5). We place emphasis on the quickness of this play in reaching the hole.

In the loosen-up area, we will run any part of our offense. We seldom pass from the pocket because of the possibility of losing ground or having a pass intercepted. We especially like the pass or run option in this area. The onside

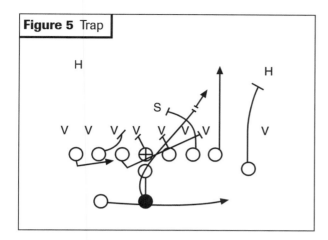

Figure 5 Trap

end lugs the defensive tackle, then releases to the flat. The left HB has the choice of sweeping or passing to the right end as the right HB keeps the defender occupied deep in the end zone. The QB seals off the defensive tackle (figure 6).

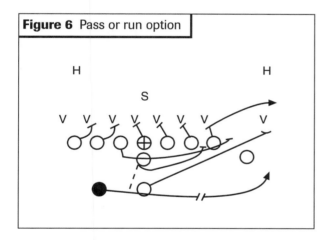

Figure 6 Pass or run option

Two components of our goal line offense are invaluable to us: the use of formations to cause defensive problems and the element of surprise.

Our biggest problem with our goal line defense is to have sound adjustments against varied offensive formations. This can be done with work if we know the offensive formations our opponents will use. If we must prepare for 20 to 30 offensive formations, our men become confused and do a lot of thinking but very little hitting. Because of this, we have included varied formations in our goal line philosophy. We scout

ourselves thoroughly in the scoring area and make a concentrated effort to vary our formations from game to game. In the past three years, we have operated from 28 various formations, all from the T-formation. A defensive team soon realizes it is almost impossible to make the correct adjustments against all these offensive formations. They rationalize by saying it is window dressing and do not meet strength with strength. The offensive team must recognize this and take advantage of the weaknesses.

If a team does try to adjust to our varied formations, we like to run on a quick count. The defense does not have enough time to recognize and adjust before the ball is snapped. A quick count also enables us to cheat our backs to give us added strength. An occasional long count is also disconcerting to the defense. A half-the-distance penalty on the one-foot line doesn't help us much, so we instruct our center to snap the ball immediately, regardless of the count, if our opponent jumps offsides. The QB will attempt to sneak across. We feel a silent count is always effective on sneaks and wedges by the QB.

In addition to split ends, slots, wings, flankers, double flankers, unbalanced line, and lonesome ends, one formation that has been a real asset to us is an eight- or nine-man offensive line. This creates considerable confusion in the defense. We can run much of our normal offense from this formation, with emphasis on quick openers and wedges (figure 7).

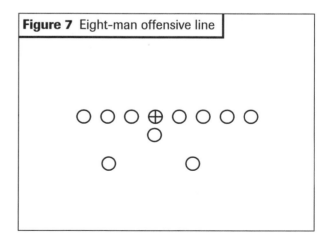

Figure 7 Eight-man offensive line

Figure 8 shows an end-over eight-man line. Think in terms of your offense and the many plays you could run from this formation with little adjustment.

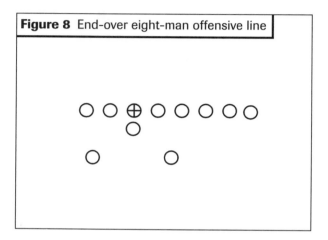

Figure 8 End-over eight-man offensive line

We also have had success by inserting a guard as a slot (blocking) back, giving the defense a different picture. It gives us a better blocker and usually results in better blocking angles. Figure 9 is a form of isolation, and figure 10 is a simple belly off-tackle play, but with a guard in better position to handle the key block on the defensive end. This diagram shows onside cutoff blocking, useful against certain teams with the help of a good-faking FB. This releases the tackle on the defensive HB or allows him to help our end with the double-team if we think it necessary.

Long and short motion also present problems to a goal line defense. The possibilities are unlimited, but we give heed to the thought,

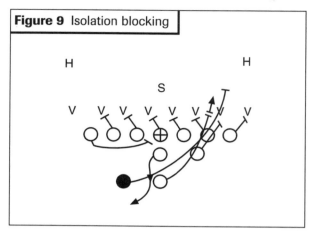

Figure 9 Isolation blocking

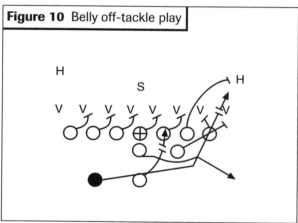

Figure 10 Belly off-tackle play

"Never beat yourself in the scoring area." We actually add very little to our basic offense. The new plays we run in order to take advantage of poor adjustments are run repeatedly in practice before they are ever used in a game. We believe variations are fine, but they take work. Above all, don't confuse your own team!

1963 Summer Manual. Lee J. Tressel was head football coach at Baldwin-Wallace College.

American Football Coaches Association Code of Ethics—A Summary

Ever since the AFCA adopted its first formal Code of Ethics in 1952, the organization has had a keen awareness of its importance and has done all in its power to keep the public aware of the AFCA's concern with morality and integrity. Vital tenets include:

■ The distinguishing characteristic of a profession is its dedication to the service of humanity.

■ Those who select football coaching must understand that the justification for football lies in its spiritual and physical values and that the game belongs, essentially, to the players.

■ The welfare of the game depends on how the coaches live up to the spirit and letter of ethical conduct and how the coaches remain ever mindful of the high trust and confidence placed in them by their players and the public.

■ The Code should be studied regularly by all coaches, and its principles should always be followed. Violations of the Code should be reported to the Ethics Committee.

This Code of Ethics has been developed to protect and promote the best interests of the game and the coaching profession. Its primary purpose is to clarify and distinguish ethical and approved professional practices from those considered detrimental. Its secondary purpose is to emphasize the purpose and value of football and to stress the proper functions of coaches in relation to schools, players, and the public.

The AFCA Code of Ethics consists of nine articles that provide guidelines for conduct concerning the following subject areas:

1. Responsibilities to players
2. Responsibilities to the institution
3. Rules of the game
4. Officials
5. Public relations
6. Scouting
7. Recruiting
8. Game day and other responsibilities
9. Acceptance of all-star assignments and other all-star coaching honors

The ultimate success of the principles and standards of this Code depends on those for whom it has been established—football coaches. Be a responsible member of the coaching profession. Coach with character and integrity.

About the AFCA

Since its establishment in 1922, the American Football Coaches Association has striven to provide a forum for the discussion and study of all matters pertaining to football and coaching and to maintain the highest possible standards in football and the coaching profession. These objectives, first declared by founders Alonzo Stagg, John Heisman, and others, have been instrumental in the AFCA's becoming the effective and highly respected organization it is today.

The AFCA now has more than 8,000 members, including coaches from Canada, Europe, Australia, Japan, and Russia. Through annual publications and several newsletters, the Association keeps members informed of the most current rules changes and proposals, proper coaching methods, innovations in techniques, insights in coaching philosophy, and business conducted by the board of trustees and AFCA committees. A convention is held each January to give members a special opportunity to exchange ideas and recognize outstanding achievement.

The Association promotes safety in the sport and establishes strong ethical and moral codes that govern all aspects of football coaching. In addition, the AFCA is involved in numerous programs that ensure the integrity of the coaching profession and enhance the development of the game. It works closely with the National Collegiate Athletic Association, the National Association of Collegiate Directors of Athletics, the National Association of Interscholastic Athletics, the National Football League, the National Football Foundation and Hall of Fame, Pop Warner, and other organizations involved in the game of football. Indeed, one of the goals of the Association is to build a strong coalition—TEAM AFCA—of football coaches who will speak out with a unified voice on issues that affect the sport and profession.

The AFCA is the team of the football coaching profession. All current and former football coaches or administrators involved with football are encouraged to join. For more information about becoming a member of the American Football Coaches Association, please log on to the AFCA Web site (www.afca.com) or contact them at

American Football Coaches Association
5900 Old McGregor Road
Waco, TX 76712
254-776-5900

More from the AFCA library

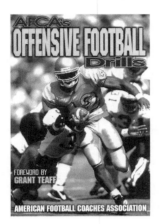

Whether teams prefer the running game, passing game, or balanced attack, *AFCA's Offensive Football Drills* will help improve individual and team performance. The book features the best drills used by many of the top college and high school offensive teams. Each of the 75 drills come with key points and are carefully diagrammed. There is also a special Drill Finder section that helps locate drills for specific needs.

AFCA's Offensive Football Drills will help players improve performance at their positions and as a team. It's the perfect practice tool for putting more points on the scoreboard.

1998 • Paperback • 184 pages • Item PAFC0526
ISBN 0-88011-526-2 • $15.95 ($23.95 Canadian)

In this day of explosive scoring and rules changes that favor the offense, fielding a competitive defense is more difficult than ever. *AFCA's Defensive Football Drills* levels the playing field by providing the defense with practice activities that teach the skills players need to excel. The book contains 70 innovative drills that develop the fundamentals every defender needs to compete in today's game—an aggressive style of play and an understanding of complex defensive strategies.

Featuring drills and insights from some of the country's finest college and high school defensive coaches, *AFCA's Defensive Football Drills* is the best defensive read a coach or player can make!

1996 • Paperback • 168 pages • Item PAFC0476
ISBN 0-88011-476-2 • $15.95 ($23.95 Canadian)

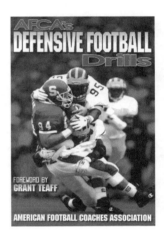

Football Coaching Strategies is an invaluable source of football wisdom. Inside there are 67 informative articles contributed during the last 25 years by many of the greatest football coaches the game has ever known. The book features 349 detailed diagrams and covers every crucial aspect of the gam.

Edited by the American Football Coaches Association, this collection of gridiron strategies taps into the creative genius and enduring principles that have shaped the game. It's the one book that every serious football coach, player, and fan will treasure.

1995 • Paperback • 216 pages • Item PAFC0869
ISBN 0-87322-869-3 • $18.95 ($28.95 Canadian)

Human Kinetics
The Premier Publisher for Sports & Fitness

To request more information or to place your order, U.S. customers call
TOLL FREE 1-800-747-4457.
Customers outside the U.S. use the appropriate telephone number/address shown in the front of this book or visit our website at:
http://www.humankinetics.com

Build champions, season after season

The West Coast Offense has been winning football championships for two decades—from the 1982 San Francisco 49ers to the 1997 Green Bay Packers. Find out how to use this high-production, low-risk passing attack in *Football's West Coast Offense*. The book is loaded with 244 diagrams, including a mini-playbook for attacking all types of defensive coverages. Keep possession of the ball and score big with the offense that's a proven winner.

1997 • Paperback • 192 pages • 6 x 9 • Item PHEN0662
ISBN 0-88011-662-5 • $16.95 ($24.95 Canadian)

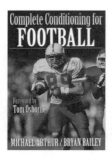

For the past three decades the University of Nebraska has set the standard of excellence for football conditioning. *Complete Conditioning for Football* presents the program the Cornhuskers use to power their way to national championships. Fully illustrated, this book takes the latest in strength and conditioning research and turns it into a detailed, practical approach that will help players develop their full physical potential and gain a performance edge.

1998 • Paperback • 296 pages • Item PART0521
ISBN 0-88011-521-1 • $16.95 ($24.95 Canadian)

In *Coaching Football Successfully*, Bob Reade shows how to build and maintain a successful football program. Learn techniques, tactics, and drills for coaching offense, defense, and special teams from the four-time national champion coach. Also emphasized are the other important aspects of coaching, including philosophy, communication, motivation, planning, and program evaluation.

1994 • Paperback • 192 pages • Item PREA0518
ISBN 0-87322-518-X • $19.95 ($29.95 Canadian)

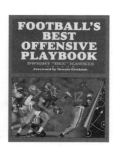

Every offensive playbook has Xs and Os that look good on paper. *Football's Best Offensive Playbook* goes the extra yard, providing precisely illustrated plays that are proven point-producers in games. Each of the 100 running, passing, and special plays comes with a diagram and coaching pointers that highlight key player positions and responsibilities. And since the book features contributions from coaches at the high school, college, and pro ranks, you'll find plays that work at all levels.

1995 • Paperback • 144 pages • Item PHAW0574
ISBN 0-87322-574-0 • $15.95 ($22.95 Canadian)

Increase your speed, power, and agility! *52-Week Football Training* takes the guesswork out of workouts and ensures players are in peak condition each season and game. Daily workouts are presented for each week of the year and include resistance training, total conditioning exercises, and position specific activities.

1999 • Paperback • 256 pages • Item PCOO0085
ISBN 0-7360-0085-2 • $17.95 ($26.95 Canadian)

Human Kinetics
The Premier Publisher for Sports & Fitness

To request more information or to place your order, U.S. customers call
TOLL FREE 1-800-747-4457.
Customers outside the U.S. use the appropriate telephone number/address shown in the front of this book or visit our website at:
http://www.humankinetics.com